ENGLISH SOCIETY AND THE CRUSADE

1216–1307

ENGLISH SOCIETY AND THE CRUSADE
1216–1307

SIMON LLOYD

CLARENDON PRESS · OXFORD
1988

Oxford University Press, Walton Street, Oxford OX2 6DP
Oxford New York Toronto
Delhi Bombay Calcutta Madras Karachi
Petaling Jaya Singapore Hong Kong Tokyo
Nairobi Dar es Salaam Cape Town
Melbourne Auckland
and associated companies in
Berlin Ibadan

Oxford is a trade mark of Oxford University Press

Published in the United States
by Oxford University Press, New York

British Library Cataloguing in Publication Data
Lloyd, Simon
English society and the crusade, 1216–1307.
—(Oxford historical monographs).
1. England. Effects of crusades, 1216–1307
I. Title
909.07
ISBN 0-19-822949-6

Library of Congress Cataloging in Publication Data
Lloyd, S. D. (Simon D.)
English society and the crusade, 1216–1307 / Simon Lloyd.
Revision of thesis (Ph. D.)—Oxford University, 1983.
Bibliography: p. Includes index.
1. Great Britain—History—13th century. 2. Great Britain—History—Edward I. 1272–1307. 3. Crusades—Later, 13th, 14th, and 15th centuries. 4. England—Social conditions—Medieval period, 1066–1485. I. Title.
DA225.L56 1988 940.1'84—dc19 88-1088
ISBN 0-19-822949-6

Processed by The Oxford Text System

Printed and bound in Great Britain by
Biddles Ltd, Guildford and King's Lynn

For my father
In memory of my mother

PREFACE

THIS book began life as a dissertation which was accepted for the degree of D.Phil. in Oxford in 1983. Much of it has been subjected to major surgery since then, following additional research and further reflection, but the book still shares more than a title with its prototype. If I were to tackle the subject five, ten, or more years hence, it would doubtless be a different work again. The process of revision and re-evaluation never entirely ceases, but there comes a time when a halt must be called, and when the ink must be allowed to flow undisturbed. Certain of my conclusions and interpretations will undoubtedly prove to be provisional, but this is how, in the pages that follow, I see my subject at present.

I have incurred a great number of obligations in writing this book. It is a pleasure to record them. I owe much to Janice Cummin and Julie Savage for their cheerful heroism at the typewriter over many months. Numerous librarians and archivists have given assistance and eased my way in the University Libraries of Newcastle upon Tyne and Durham, the Bodleian Library, Balliol College Library, the British Library, the Institute of Historical Research, the Public Record Office, and the Hereford and Worcester County Record Office, Worcester. To the University of Newcastle upon Tyne I am grateful for the funds made available to me over a number of years to allow my research in those places to continue. I acknowledge with gratitude a grant from the British Academy which helped to subsidize a six-month sabbatical in 1984.

There are innumerable debts to individual scholars. In particular, I must thank Dr P. A. Brand, Dr D. A. Carpenter, Dr P. R. Coss, Dr P. W. Edbury, Dr B. Hamilton, Miss B. F. Harvey, Dr M. H. Keen, Professor M. C. Prestwich, and Professor J. A. Watt, amongst others, for their helpful advice and suggestions on certain points and topics. Dr Coss has kindly read several chapters and offered many comments from which I have greatly profited. His encouragement over the years has been a great help. My greatest debts are to my supervisor in Oxford, Mr J. O. Prestwich, and to my wife. To J.O.P. I owe far more than can be adequately expressed here. His knowledge and judgement have saved me from many an error and led me time and again profitably to consider things anew, whilst his unstinting kindness and generosity in all things continue to be a source of wonder. My wife has tolerated the instrusions of the Plantagenets and their crusading subjects for many years. It is with very real gratitude that I thank her not only for her resilience and moral support, but also for the many helpful criticisms of a fellow medievalist.

S. D. L.

Newcastle upon Tyne
April 1987

CONTENTS

ABBREVIATIONS

Anc. Corr.	*List of the Ancient Correspondence of the Chancery and Exchequer preserved in the Public Record Office* (PRO, Lists and Indexes, 15; repr. London, 1968).
BIHR	*Bulletin of the Institute of Historical Research*
BL	British Library
'Burton'	'Annales monasterii de Burton', in *Annales monastici*, ed. H. R. Luard (RS; 1864–9), i. 181–510.
Cart. Gen. Hosp.	*Cartulaire général de l'Ordre des Hospitaliers de S. Jean de Jérusalem, 1100–1310*, ed. J. M. A. Delaville Le Roulx, 4 vols. (Paris, 1894–1906).
CCh.R	*Calendar of the Charter Rolls Preserved in the Public Record Office, 1226–1516*, 6 vols. (London, 1903–27).
CCR	*Calendar of the Close Rolls Preserved in the Public Record Office, 1272–1307*, 5 vols. (London, 1900–8).
CFR	*Calendar of the Fine Rolls Preserved in the Public Record Office, 1272–1307* (London, 1911).
CIMisc.	*Calendar of Inquisitions Miscellaneous (Chancery) Preserved in the PRO, 1219–1349*, 2 vols. (London, 1916).
CIPM	*Calendar of Inquisitions Post Mortem in the Public Record Office (Henry III-Edward II)*, 6 vols. (London, 1904–10).
CLI	*The Letters of Pope Innocent III (1198–1216) Concerning England and Wales: A Calendar*, ed. C. R. and M. G. Cheney (Oxford, 1976).
CLR	*Calendar of Liberate Rolls Preserved in the Public Record Office, 1226–72*, 6 vols. (London, 1917–64).
Councils, II	*Councils and Synods with Other Documents Relating to the English Church*, II: *1205–1313*, ed. F. M. Powicke and C. R. Cheney, 2 parts. (Oxford, 1964).
CPR	*Calendar of the Patent Rolls Preserved in the Public Record Office, 1232–1307*, 8 vols. (London, 1898–1908).
CR	*Close Rolls of the Reign of Henry III Preserved in the Public Record Office, 1227–72*, 14 vols. (London, 1902–38).
CRR	*Curia Regis Rolls Preserved in the Public Record Office, Richard I–1242*, 16 vols. (London, 1922–).
De ant. leg.	Arnold fitzThedmar, *De antiquis legibus liber: Cronica majorum et vicecomitum Londoniarum*, ed. T. Stapleton (Camden Soc., OS 34; 1846).
Dipl. Docs. i	*Diplomatic Documents (Chancery and Exchequer) I (1101–1272)*, ed. P. Chaplais (London, 1964).
DNB	*Dictionary of National Biography*, ed. L. Stephen and S. Lee, 63 vols., with supplements (London, 1885–1900); repr. 24 vols. (London, 1921–7).

'Dunstable'	'Annales prioratus de Dunstaplia', in *Annales monastici*, ed. H. R. Luard (RS; 1864-9), iii. 1-420.
EHR	*English Historical Review*
Fees	*Liber Feudorum: The Book of Fees Commonly Called Testa de Nevill, 1198-1293*, 2 vols. in 3 (London, 1920-31).
Foedera	*Foedera, conventiones, litterae, et cuiuscunque generis acta publica inter reges Angliae et alios quosvis imperatores, reges, pontifices, principes vel communitates, 1101-1654*, ed. T. Rymer; new edn., ed. A. Clarke *et al.* 4 vols. in 7 parts. (London, 1816-69).
HMC	Historical Manuscripts Commission
Journ.	*Journal*
'Margam'	'Annales de Margan (*recte* Margam) sive chronica abbreviata', in *Annales monastici*, ed. H. R. Luard (RS; 1864-9) i. 1-40.
MGH SS	*Monumenta Germaniae Historica, Scriptores*, ed. G. H. Pertz *et al.* 32 vols. (Hanover, Weimar, Stuttgart, Cologne, 1826-1934).
NS	New Series
OS	Old Series
'Osney'	'Annales monasterii de Osneia', in *Annales monastici*, ed. H. R. Luard (RS; 1864-9), iv. 1-352.
Paris, *CM*	Matthew Paris, *Chronica majora*, ed. H. R. Luard, 7 vols. (RS; 1872-83).
PR	*Patent Rolls of the Reign of Henry III Preserved in the Public Record Office, 1216-32*, 2 vols. (London, 1901-3).
PRO	Public Record Office
Proc.	*Proceedings*
Rec. Ser.	Record Series
Rec. Soc.	Record Society
Reg. Alexander IV	*Les Registres d'Alexandre IV*, ed. C. Bourel de la Roncière *et al.* 3 vols. (Bibliothèque des Écoles françaises d'Athènes et de Rome, 1895-1953).
Reg. Benedict XI	*Les Registres de Benoît XI*, ed. C. Grandjean (Bibliothèque des Écoles françaises d'Athènes et de Rome, 1883-1905).
Reg. Boniface VIII	*Les Registres de Boniface VIII*, ed. G. Digard *et al.* 4 vols. (Bibliothèque des Écoles françaises d'Athènes et de Rome, 1884-1935).
Reg. Clement IV	*Les Registres de Clément IV*, ed. E. Jordan (Bibliothèque des Écoles françaises d'Athènes et de Rome, 1893-1945).
Reg. Gregory IX	*Les Registres de Grégoire IX*, ed. L. Auvray, 3 vols. (Bibliothèque des Écoles françaises d'Athènes et de Rome, 1899-1955).
Reg. Gregory X	*Les Registres de Grégoire X*, ed. J. Guiraud (Bibliothèque des Écoles françaises d'Athènes et de Rome, 1892-1906).

Reg. Honorius III	*Regesta Honorii Papae III*, ed. P. Pressutti, 2 vols. (Rome, 1888–95).
Reg. Honorius IV	*Les Registres d'Honorius IV*, ed. M. Prou (Bibliothèque des Écoles françaises d'Athènes et de Rome, 1886–8).
Reg. Innocent IV	*Les Registres d'Innocent IV*, ed. E. Berger, 3 vols. (Bibliothèque des Écoles françaises d'Athènes et de Rome, 1884–1921).
Reg. Martin IV	*Les Registres de Martin IV*, ed. F. Olivier-Martin *et al.* (Bibliothèque des Écoles françaises d'Athènes et de Rome, 1901–35).
Reg. Nicholas III	*Les Registres de Nicholas III*, ed. J. Gay (Bibliothèque des Écoles françaises d'Athènes et de Rome, 1898–1938).
Reg. Nicholas IV	*Les Registres de Nicholas IV*, ed. E. Langlois, 2 vols. (Bibliothèque des Écoles françaises d'Athènes et de Rome, 1886–93).
Reg. Urban IV	*Les Registres d'Urbain IV*, ed. L. Dorez and J. Guiraud, 4 vols. (Bibliothèque des Écoles françaises d'Athènes et de Rome, 1899–1958).
RF	*Excerpta e Rotulis Finium in Turri Londinensi asservatis, 1216–72*, ed. C. Roberts, 2 vols. (London, 1835–6).
RHC Occ.	*Recueil des historiens des croisades: Historiens occidentaux*, ed. Académie des Inscriptions et Belles-Lettres, 5 vols. (Paris, 1844–95).
RHGF	*Recueil des historiens des Gaules et de France*, ed. M. Bouquet *et al.* 24 vols. (Paris, 1737–1904).
RLC	*Rotuli Litterarum Clausarum in Turri Londinensi asservati, 1204–27*, ed. T. D. Hardy, 2 vols. (London, 1833–44).
RLP	*Rotuli Litterarum Patentium in Turri Londinensi asservati, 1201–16*, ed. T. D. Hardy, (London, 1835).
RS	(Rolls Series) *Rerum Brittanicarum Medii Aevi Scriptores*, 251 vols. (London, 1858–96).
'Tewkesbury'	'Annales monasterii de Theokesberia', in *Annales monastici*, ed. H. R. Luard (RS; 1864–9), i. 41–180.
TRHS	*Transactions of the Royal Historical Society*
VCH	*Victoria History of the Counties of England*, ed. H. A. Doubleday *et al.* (London, 1900–).
'Waverley'	'Annales monasterii de Waverleia', in *Annales monastici*, ed. H. R. Luard (RS; 1864–9), ii. 127–411.
'Winchester'	'Annales monasterii de Wintonia', in *Annales monastici*, ed. H. R. Luard (RS; 1864–9), ii. 1–125.
'Worcester'	'Annales prioratus de Wigornia', in *Annales monastici*, ed. H. R. Luard (RS; 1864–9), iv. 353–564.
Wykes, *Chron.*	Thomas Wykes, 'Chronicon vulgo dictum Chronicon Thomae Wykes', in *Annales monastici*, ed. H. R. Luard (RS; 1864–9), iv. 6–319.

NOTE ON MONEY

Except where otherwise stated, references to money are given in £ *s*. *d*. sterling. Other moneys of account referred to are the English mark, worth 13*s*. 4*d*. (hereafter abbreviated as *m*.), and the *livre tournois*, worth 5*s*. throughout most of the period covered in this book before the wild fluctuations in the exchange rate in the early fourteenth century.

INTRODUCTION

THE general subject-matter of this book, the relationship between the crusading movement and England in the thirteenth century, scarcely requires justification, considering the important place occupied by the crusade in medieval Western societies during the period under consideration. Yet, curiously enough, the relationship between the crusading movement and the societies in which it was sponsored remains a relatively unexplored topic. Despite the considerable interest among modern historians in the history of the crusading movement, the emphasis remains either upon the crusades in their Eastern context (although here a shift has occurred towards crusades declared to places other than the Holy Land) or upon the history of the crusader states in the East, or upon the conceptual framework of the crusade and its development as an institution after its inception at the Council of Clermont in 1095. A comprehensive study of the promotion and preaching of crusades, for example, is still wanting, whilst such fundamental matters as the nature of the relationship between canon law and common law concerning the crusader, or the means whereby crusaders prepared, organized, and financed their expeditions remain imperfectly known. This is remarkable. First, conditions in the West were crucial to the success of the crusading movement from its very beginning. This has been recognized by historians, particularly since the appearance in 1935 of Carl Erdmann's *Die Entstehung des Kreuzzugsgedankens*, the seminal work upon crusading origins. Yet the effort spent upon investigation of the Western background to the First Crusade has not been matched by a similar effort in relation to later phases of the crusading movement. Second, the crusade, a complex phenomenon at the meeting-point of so many currents, necessarily influenced most areas of contemporary experience in the West, but again few attempts have been made to study the impact which it had upon the societies in which it was sponsored.

This book seeks to explore one corner of what is plainly a vast canvas. Thirteenth-century England has been selected as the area of study largely because the evidence is generally sufficient, in both quantity and quality, to allow certain themes and topics to be treated satisfactorily and to a depth which is not always possible for other contemporary societies so far as the crusade is concerned. In particular, the great series of Crown records beginning in the early thirteenth century provide a wealth of data, embedded in more or less complete sequences of record. This is supplemented or complemented by a mass of material found in estate records, registers, charters, deeds, ecclesiastical documents, both papal and English, and a variety of literary sources. Naturally there are lacunae and limitations. The medievalist rarely possesses an entirely satisfactory body of material with which to work on his selected subject, and I have sought to indicate the limitations, and the major problems attached to the utilization of sources, in the chapters which follow. Nevertheless, in relation to the topics embraced in this book, the sources are generally more than adequate. In this sense the thirteenth century sees a happy coincidence, for crusading remained an important part of contemporary English experience, whilst there exists a range and type of source material with which to explore the subject. So far as participation is concerned, the period stretching from the Third Crusade, when Englishmen first participated in large numbers under the banner of Richard I, until the crusade of 1270–2, the last large-scale expedition to leave these shores, was certainly the heyday of English crusading activity. There were later crusades, in the fourteenth century and beyond, and England continued to be regarded as an important source of aid for the crusading movement, but it is doubtful if the crusade impinged upon contemporary experience in quite the way or to the same extent as it did in the thirteenth century. This fortunate coincidence allows many themes and topics to be explored more thoroughly and more effectively than is possible for the period either before or after.

Limitations of space dictated by the series in which this work appears, combined with the need for coherence, have required that this book be a study of only selected aspects of my subject. My primary concern is to examine the impact of the call to the crusade upon contemporaries, and to assess the factors and influences which conditioned their response. Essentially, then, this book is a study in recruitment to the crusade, for that is the central issue around which others have been grouped.

My starting-point, thematically, was partly suggested by the words of Sir Maurice Powicke, who wrote in a justly famous passage that

> It is not too much to say that the recovery of the Holy Land, whether as an idea, a symbol, or an immediate duty, pervaded the minds of men in the thirteenth century. It was inseparable from the air they breathed. However indifferent or sceptical they might be, they could not escape its influence.[1]

He went on to notice that 'The preaching of a crusade was the temporary culmination of an ever-present appeal, a high tide in the perpetual flow of the spiritual life.'[2] In his view only a determined

[1] F. M. Powicke, *The Thirteenth Century, 1216–1307* (2nd edn. Oxford, 1962), 80.
[2] Ibid. 81.

preaching campaign was necessary to trigger the conversion of this all-pervasive sentiment, perennially present yet latent in society, into the recruitment and departure of a crusading force. It was, for example, exactly this which the preachers achieved between 1267 and 1270 before the sailing of the English crusade of 1270–2.[3] Their task then, in the aftermath of traumatic civil war, was eased because of 'a general desire to forget the past, to release the energies of body and spirit in unexceptionable ways, to devote treasure which could still be spared to an object higher than the domestic needs of the moment. Civil strife was expiated by an attack upon the enemy of Christendom.'[4]

For Powicke, then, the crusade was overwhelmingly a spiritual matter, shot through with not a little catharsis, and the obligation to respond to it was deeply moral, conditioning the thought of contemporaries in such a way that few could deny their duty to it. It would be churlish to belittle Powicke's perception if not grossly unfair, considering that the crusade was scarcely central to his overall theme in the works quoted above. Yet to consider the crusade as being a matter of moral obligation, and to express it thus, however poignantly, without further investigation, raises more questions and issues than it answers concerning the place occupied by the crusade in thirteenth-century English society, and the way in which the response to the crusading call was influenced by it. It is with some of these questions that this book is largely concerned.

I am not treading upon entirely virgin soil, for many hands have already tilled some parts of the field. As far as possible I have sought to avoid duplication of effort where previous studies are concerned, unless there are grounds for substantial differences of approach or interpretation, but a measure of overlap on certain issues is unavoidable. My debt to earlier works will be apparent from references as they occur, and to some extent I have been anticipated by Siedschlag, Mumford, and Beebe, each of whom has been explicitly concerned to explore aspects of the impact of the crusade upon English society in the twelfth and thirteenth centuries.[5] Sufficient scope for the present work remains nevertheless.

[3] Ibid. 219.

[4] Ibid. 223–4. See also Powicke, *King Henry III and the Lord Edward: The Community of the Realm in the Thirteenth Century*, 2 vols. (Oxford, 1947), esp. ii. 554–5, 569. He regarded English recruitment to the Fifth Crusade, again after a period of civil war, in much the same light. Participation was an act and symbol of self-purification and collective social redemption: ibid. i. 23.

[5] B. Siedschlag, *English Participation in the Crusades, 1150–1220* (Bryn Mawr, 1939); W. F. Mumford, 'England and the Crusades During the Reign of Henry III', MA thesis (Manchester, 1924); B. Beebe, 'Edward I and the Crusades', Ph.D. thesis (St Andrews, 1970); id., 'The English Baronage and the Crusade of 1270', *BIHR* xlviii (1975), 127–48.

The first chapters of the book consider the complex matter of promotion of the crusade. The precise division of material and theme is designed largely to elucidate the roles played by the different agents engaged in the business, and to clarify the various components of which promotional activity consisted, whilst revealing the degree of exposure of contemporaries to the crusading call, the manner in which that call was delivered, and the nature of the support which was sought, and from whom. Certain aspects are treated in summary or cursory fashion if they have already received extensive treatment at the hands of other scholars. In particular, the important developments in papal crusading policy and its instruments, applicable to England as elsewhere, have been exhaustively studied in a more general context by scholars such as Purcell, thus obviating the need for detailed discussion here. I am chiefly concerned to locate the English material within the broader framework, and to highlight the characteristic features of that policy in so far as it touched the raising of English crusading resources. Similarly, the materials relating to the raising of moneys for the crusade in England specifically have been subject to detailed study by Lunt in a series of monumental works. Extensive discussion of this matter is therefore omitted. On the other hand, since it is plain that England, in the papal strategy, was regarded overwhelmingly as a source of aid for the crusade to the Holy Land, rather than to other crusading theatres, the attempts of the inhabitants of the crusader states and their Eastern allies to procure aid receive more detailed treatment than they have hitherto.

The second part of the book mainly considers the nature of the response to the crusading call. That response was in some measure conditioned by contemporary attitudes and opinions concerning the crusade, but limitations of space preclude extensive coverage here. Only by the addition of a lengthy chapter could the matter be sufficiently analysed and discussed. Accordingly I do not directly engage in the current debate surrounding attitudes at the time towards developments in crusading policy and the unleashing of the crusade against others than Moslems in the Holy Land. It is, however, my central contention that discussion of recruitment to the crusade in the past has placed too much emphasis upon the free will of individuals, and that recruitment can only be satisfactorily understood if it is approached by close reference to the workings of social and political structure, and to the preferences of papal policy regarding crusading personnel. The social realities of medieval societies, in

The contributions of Siedschlag and Mumford have been rendered somewhat obsolete by more recent research and the availability of many more primary sources in print. It will become apparent that I differ from Beebe on many points and issues.

which lordship, kinship, and other ties of association were of profound importance, have tended to be overlooked with reference to this matter, partly, perhaps, because of the emphasis which has been placed upon the decisions of individuals alone. Insufficient attention has been paid to the bearing of papal crusading policy in practice, and how this combined with social and political realities, and the preferences of crusade leaders to determine much of the recruitment and composition of crusading forces.

Such an approach has important implications for our understanding of promotion of the crusade. Most obviously, it leads to questions concerning the aims of preaching to the general populace and whether such preaching was intended as a means to the recruitment of men who were expected to participate personally in crusading expeditions, or whether it was primarily concerned to raise money to subsidize those judged fit to prosecute the crusade in person, the knightly body and their retainers. Moreover, consideration of recruitment by reference to social structure automatically implies that the composition of crusading forces was largely a function of pre-existing ties, and the hierarchical ordering of society further suggests that the leadership of the great lords was most decisive precisely because of the influence which they could bring to bear upon those of their connection. By the same token, the negative response of the great men exerted a restraining influence upon the recruitment of those tied to them. It follows, then, that the major problem lies in elucidating and explaining the decision of individual great men to respond favourably, or not, to the crusading call.

The reactions of the king, in a comparatively centralized state such as thirteenth-century England, were crucial by virtue of the unique powers of royal lordship. Partly for this reason one chapter is devoted to the study of the responses of Henry III and Edward I to the crusade, and to the history of their crusading vows. Their reactions were to be critical to the overall level of English participation in the crusades during their reigns. It is not, then, simply for convenience that the regnal dates 1216–1307 have been taken as the limits to this study. Indeed, one of the central themes of this book is that the kings exerted immense influence over the entire matter of the crusade as it affected their dominions, by virtue of their influence, authority, and powers of lordship.

Once recruited, a crusading force had then to be organized if it was not to become incoherent. Crusading forces, as others, were grouped around the great lords who dominated them, but there was always the danger that they would disintegrate into a number of loosely cohesive units. I have therefore been concerned to investigate the ways in which crusade leaders sought to prevent or remedy this, a matter which has attracted limited attention in the past. Fortunately, the materials available for study of English crusading forces of the period allow the issue to be pursued with some confidence. It appears that the systematic use of formal written contracts for service on crusade came to provide much of the answer to this difficult problem, these instruments tending to reinforce those ties which bound men together through kinship, lordship, or other association. The logical consequence of this development in contract usage was that crusade leaders were responsible for much of the transport and victualling of the forces sailing beneath their banners, and for certain other practical arrangements. But here, regrettably, there are significant gaps in our knowledge, for the private archives of the leaders of thirteenth-century English forces have largely disappeared, leaving only fragmentary indications of the measures which they took. Nevertheless, I have sought to provide a picture of crusading in practice as far as the evidence allows. To help with costs, the papacy came in the thirteenth century to grant leaders the moneys raised for the crusade from various sources. The rationale behind these grants was that their beneficiaries would subsidize those crusaders dependent upon them. This aspect of financing may, then, be usefully discussed apart from the private arrangements of individuals to raise the cash required for their expeditions.

It was in this quest for funds that crusaders exerted perhaps their greatest influence upon local society and economy. I have sought to give some impression of the nature and scale of this consequence in the course of elucidating and examining the expedients to which crusaders resorted, and the social, economic, and juridical context of their actions. Crusaders' preparations, however, extended beyond fund raising to measures designed to settle their affairs and to provide for the safety of their souls. The question of security was naturally critical to the successful raising and dispatch of crusading forces, for few would have duly departed had they not been reasonably confident that their personal and family interests would remain in the state they proposed to leave them. No less important in a crusader's perception was his spiritual and moral state, for he was a penitent and a pilgrim as well as a holy warrior, participating in an enterprise from which he might not return alive. Some attempt is made to consider the steps taken by individual crusaders to prepare themselves in this vital matter.

This book consists, then, of studies of certain related aspects of the impact of the crusading movement upon English society in the reigns of Henry III and Edward I. It is hoped that these studies, whilst discrete in themselves, will provide some measure of coherence when considered together, but I remain only too conscious of the gaps and the fact that I provide coverage of only part of a very large subject: a great deal of research remains to be done upon it. This book can only be considered as a beginning.

I

PROMOTION OF THE CRUSADE (1)

Promotion of the crusade became an increasingly elaborate and complex affair in the course of the twelfth and thirteenth centuries. Its core, as always, consisted of papal crusading bulls, for popes alone possessed the authority to declare crusades and to offer the range of spiritual and material privileges enjoyed by participants and others aiding the cause. But their measures came to extend far beyond proclamation alone. Popes commonly endorsed appeals from the Holy Land and other crusading theatres, and played an important role in the transmission of news, appreciating that awareness of events helped to stir contemporaries to action. To secure divine aid, and raise consciousness further, they ordered a variety of liturgical activities on behalf of crusaders in the field and those whom they went to assist. They expended considerable effort seeking to establish international and domestic peace and stability, in their view vital for successful recruitment. They further imposed mandatory taxes upon the clerical body for the crusade, and sought additional funding from laity and clergy alike by various means. To implement and enforce such measures, the papacy had necessarily to rely largely on local agents. Hence most sections of the Church in England, as elsewhere, came to be extensively involved in promotional activities.

Promotion cannot easily be dissociated from other components of 'the business of the Cross', for it was a means towards the realization of resources to be applied as the papacy saw fit, and as the crusade became institutionalized and its organizational forms developed, so greater control came to be exercised over both moneys and men. A formidable set of instruments was elaborated to channel crusading activity and regulate resources. This had two main aspects. First, the papacy came increasingly to use the crusade for causes other than the Holy Land or the Latin East more generally. It was already being applied against, at least, Moslems in Spain and pagan Slavs in Northern Europe in the twelfth century, and its application elsewhere was seriously entertained in some quarters. In the thirteenth century it duly came to be unleashed against heretics, schismatics, and all kinds of political opponents of the papacy. In short, the Holy Land can no longer be considered the automatic goal of crusade in the thirteenth century, nor Moslems the object.[1] Secondly, the notion of crusade underwent fundamental change as a result of developments in doctrine regarding the crusader's indulgence and the papacy's more precise control over the fulfilment of vows. The crusading vow emerged increasingly in the thirteenth century as fundamentally a means of raising cash for the crusade from the general populace. Men and women were encouraged to take the Cross but without the necessary intention of fulfilling their vows in person. The moneys raised from the redemption of those vows went to swell the crusading subsidy, intended to support effective warriors in the field.[2]

Promotion, then, is an intricate subject both in its own right and in its relation to the wider 'business of the Cross', from which it cannot ultimately be divorced, since measures with an overt promotional function and those concerned more with regulation and control formed, in reality, one systematic entity. To appreciate the individual components, however, some separate discussion is necessary. This chapter considers the broad thrust of papal policy towards England, and, since England was overwhelmingly regarded as a source of aid for the Holy Land in the papal strategy, it is appropriate in this context to explore the efforts taken by Easterners to stimulate the dispatch of aid from England. The promotional measures taken locally in response to papal mandate are considered in detail in the following chapter.

Papal Crusading Policy and England

It looks as if England was neglected as a source of support for the crusade by Urban II and the popes of the early twelfth century, the papacy preferring to concentrate its efforts elsewhere. Neither the First nor the Second Crusade was promoted with any vigour in

[1] See esp. M. Purcell, *Papal Crusading Policy: The Chief Instruments of Papal Crusading Policy and Crusade to the Holy Land from the Final Loss of Jerusalem to the Fall of Acre, 1244–1291* (Leiden, 1975), esp. pp. 3–22. On the early applications of crusade to places other than the Holy Land and against opponents other than Moslems, and the difficulties in determining what was and was not a crusade, see now N. Housley, 'Crusades against Christians: Their Origins and Early Development, *c.*1000–1216', in P. W. Edbury (ed.), *Crusade and Settlement: Papers Read at the First Conference of the Society for the Study of the Crusades and the Latin East and Presented to R. C. Smail* (Cardiff, 1985), 17–36.

[2] See generally Purcell, *Papal Crusading Policy*, section B.

England.[3] Some activity may have been stimulated by Hadrian IV's encyclical of 1157, but it is not even certain that the English were included in this hazy appeal.[4] In brief, the evidence suggests that the turning-point occurred only in the course of Alexander III's pontificate. In 1165 he reissued, with certain amendments, Eugenius III's classic crusading bull, *Quantum praedecessores*, at least one copy of which reached England;[5] a further appeal was sent in 1169;[6] in 1181 he dispatched two bulls to England as part of his final promotional campaign in the West.[7] The shift was doubtless in part a response to the rapidly deteriorating position in the Latin East, following the failure of the Second Crusade, which required the recruitment net to be cast wider. It also coincides closely with the first appeals known to have been made to King Henry II by his kinsmen, the Angevin kings of Jerusalem.[8] Thereafter, Alexander's successors continued to regard England as a major potential source of aid throughout the period under consideration; and the particular link established between England and the crusade to the Holy Land, notably reinforced by the English recruitment to the Third Crusade, became especially pronounced in the thirteenth century. It emerged, indeed, as one of the hallmarks of papal policy towards England, for English support was sought for every new crusade to the Holy Land declared in the period. In 1213, 1234, 1245, 1263, 1274, and 1291 intensive promotional drives, though of variable duration, were initiated locally.[9]

[3] The comparatively limited English participation in these crusades points in the same direction. There is no indication that Abbot Gerento of St-Benigne, Dijon, sent as Urban II's legate to the royal court in 1096, promoted the crusade in England as he did in Normandy. See H. E. J. Cowdrey, 'Pope Urban II's Preaching of the First Crusade', *History*, lv (1970), 184. St Bernard of Clairvaux recommended the Second Crusade to the English in a famous letter, and Eugenius III probably included them in his plans, but the thrust of the papal effort lay elsewhere. See G. Constable, 'The Second Crusade as Seen by Contemporaries', *Traditio*, ix (1953), esp. pp. 260–1.

[4] See R. C. Smail, 'Latin Syria and the West, 1149–1187', *TRHS* 5th ser. xix (1969), 7–8.

[5] *Foedera*, I. i. 21.

[6] *Patrologiae cursus completus: Series Latina*, comp. J. P. Migne, 221 vols. (Paris, 1844–64), cc, cols. 599–601.

[7] Roger of Howden, *Chronica Rogeri de Houedene*, ed. W. Stubbs, 4 vols. (RS; 1868–71), ii. 255–9; id. (attrib. Benedict of Peterborough), *Gesta Regis Henrici Secundi Benedicti Abbatis*, ed. W. Stubbs, 2 vols. (RS; 1867), i. 272–4; *Patrologiae Latina*, cc, cols. 1294–7.

[8] See below, p. 24.

[9] For the bulls declaring these crusades specifically in England and initiating promotion, see (for 1213) *CLI*, Nos. 917–18; *Selected Letters of Pope Innocent III Concerning England (1198–1216)*, ed. C. R. Cheney, trans. W. H. Semple (London, 1953), No. 51; (for 1234) *Reg. Gregory IX*, Nos. 2200–2; Paris, *CM* iii. 280–7, 309–12; Roger of Wendover, *Flores historiarum*, ed. H. O. Coxe, 4 vols. (English Historical Soc.; 1841–4), iv. 327–30;

The emphasis upon the Holy Land is thrown into sharper relief by the very sparse promotion of other crusades in the period. Gregory IX seems to have been alone in sponsoring the crusade on behalf of the Latin Empire of Constantinople in 1237.[10] Although Urban IV initiated preaching in France in 1262 to secure aid for a crusade to oust Michael VIII Palaeologus from Constantinople, which he had seized in 1261, there is no evidence that this campaign was extended to England.[11] Again, although Benedict XI, in 1304, declared Charles II of Sicily's projected expedition to Constantinople a crusade, the circular purportedly sent to all the faithful is not known to have reached England.[12]

The crusade against the Hohenstaufen, so vigorously promoted in Germany and Italy, impinged upon England only in 1255, when Alexander IV diverted promotional activity away from the Holy Land to the infamous 'Sicilian business'. Amongst other things, this led to preaching of the Cross against Manfred in all lands subject to Henry III,[13] probably continuing until the baronial movement of 1258 in England brought about an abrupt halt. There is no evidence to suggest that the crusade against Frederick II or any of his sons was promoted at any other time in England.[14] Nor does it appear that the later Italian crusades against the Ghibellines, the Aragonese Crusade, or the other crusades against papal political opponents in thirteenth-century Europe were sponsored in England. Twice, however, the crusade was declared and applied in England against

(for 1245) *Foedera*, I. i. 254–5; Paris, *CM* iv. 456–62; 'Bulle d'Innocent IV pour la Croisade (6 février 1245)', ed. F. M. Delorme, *Archivium Franciscanum Historium*, vi (1913), 368–9; (for 1263) *Reg. Urban IV*, No. 466, also Nos. 467, 469, 2951, 397; (for 1274) *Reg. Gregory X*, No. 569; (for 1291) *Reg. Nicholas IV*, Nos. 6800–5, 6684–92, 7625; *Foedera*, I. ii. 748–50; Bartholomew Cotton, *Historia Anglicana*, ed. H. R. Luard (RS; 1859), 199–203; *Registrum Johannis de Pontissara, Episcopi Wyntoniensis, 1282–1304*, ed. C. Deedes (Canterbury and York Soc. 19, 30; 1915, 1924), i. 474–6; Walter of Guisborough, *The Chronicle of Walter of Guisborough*, ed. H. Rothwell (Camden Soc., 3rd ser. 89; 1957), 231–2.

[10] *Reg. Gregory IX*, No. 3944. An aid for the Empire was decreed in 1245, and in 1246 preachers were authorized to promise indulgences to those affording aid. Some attempt was made to collect the tax, but there is little evidence that the preachers' efforts were diverted away from the simultaneous campaign on behalf of the Holy Land: Paris, *CM* iv. 565; 'Burton', p. 278; W. E. Lunt, *Financial Relations of the Papacy with England to 1327* (Cambridge, Mass., 1939), 250–2, 435–7.

[11] A subsidy was requested from the English clergy in 1263, however: *Reg. Urban IV*, Nos. 131–2; Lunt, *Financial Relations*, pp. 228–9.

[12] *Reg. Benedict XI*, No. 1007.

[13] 'Burton', pp. 350–3.

[14] Subsidies were requested and mandatory taxes levied, however, in 1228–9 and 1239–40: Lunt, *Financial Relations*, pp. 191–3, 197–205, 247–9. We can be reasonably sure that Matthew Paris would have commented in characteristically caustic style had the crusade against the Hohenstaufen been preached in England before 1255.

political opponents of the Plantagenet king and his papal ally, in the years 1215–17 and 1263–5.[15]

Judging from the silence of the sources, England was not regarded as a major source of aid for crusades against the Slavs in Prussia and Livonia and against the Moslems of Spain. Nor yet did the threat of doctrinal heretics lead the papacy to look to England. Roger of Wendover reports that Innocent III sent preachers throughout the West in 1213 to grant full crusader privileges to all who assumed the Cross to fight the Albigensians, but this uncorroborated report is scarcely compelling evidence for active promotion of that crusade in England.[16] No other crusades against heretics were apparently declared in thirteenth-century England.

This concentration upon the Holy Land marks England out quite sharply from France, Germany, Italy, and the Spanish kingdoms, at least.[17] There, the pattern of promotion was quite different and altogether more variegated. Until a systematic study has been made of promotion of individual crusades on a regional basis only provisional explanations can be put forward, but at least it seems clear that the papacy attempted to delimit the precise areas in which a particular crusade was to be promoted, especially when two or more were projected simultaneously. One example will suffice. In May 1265 Clement IV specified exactly where his legate, Ottobuono, was to cause preaching of the crusade against the Montfortian party in England should it prove necessary: England, Wales, Ireland, Gascony, the dioceses of Poitiers and Saintes, Brittany, Normandy, Flanders, Picardy, Denmark, Norway, the kingdom of Germany, and, more vaguely, 'other parts of the empire'. Ottobuono might commute vows for the Holy Land to this crusade, but he was forbidden to commute those for Sicily, and the lands of Alphonse of Poitiers and Charles of Anjou were expressly excluded from his preaching commission.[18] Alphonse, with papal blessing, was already committed to participation in the next crusade to the Holy Land, whilst Charles

[15] The evidence is briefly presented in my '"Political Crusades" in England, *c.*1215–17 and *c.*1263–5', in Edbury, *Crusade and Settlement*, pp. 113–20.

[16] Wendover, *Flores*, iii. 266–8. *Quia maior* of Apr. 1213 anyway withdrew indulgences from those engaged against the Albigensians.

[17] This impression, based primarily upon the papal registers, would be open to doubt considering the lacunae in those sources, were it not for the confirmation supplied by the sources for local promotion in England. Moreover, the distinction commonly made elsewhere between *crux transmarina* and *crux cismarina* appears very rarely in English sources, important evidence for the limited promotion of, and recruitment to, crusades other than those to the Holy Land.

[18] *Reg. Clement IV*, No. 56; *Diplomatarium Norvegicum*, ed. C. R. Unger and C. C. A. Lange (Christiania, 1849–60), vii, No. 23.

was actively preparing for his expedition to Sicily; their interests had to be upheld.[19]

It looks further as if the precise area earmarked for the promotion of a particular campaign was dictated largely by political circumstances and interests, the papacy tailoring its appeals to the interests of those called upon to enlist.[20] Ottobuono's commission of May 1265 is again suggestive: England, Wales, Ireland, and Gascony were Henry III's dominions; Normandy and Brittany were former Plantagenet fiefs, and Henry's daughter Beatrice was married to John II of Brittany; by the Treaty of Paris, 1259, much of the diocese of Saintes was to revert to the Plantagenets, whilst both bishoprics of Poitiers and Saintes were formerly parts of the Plantagenet dominions; Flanders, Picardy, Denmark, Norway, and Germany enjoyed close economic relations with England; and since 1257 Earl Richard of Cornwall was king of Germany, at least in name. Clement had surely designated Ottobuono's area of jurisdiction with some care: herein he might meet with success in promoting the projected crusade in aid of Henry III.

If this approach to promotion of crusades is accepted then the concentration upon the crusade to the Holy Land in thirteenth-century England is largely explained: England was scarcely touched by heresy in the period; Henry III and Edward I were never declared political opponents of the papacy; within the realm, only the political crises of 1215–17 and 1263–5 were so serious that the crusade was applied in support of the Crown. The Welsh and the Scots might on occasion be compared to Saracens, but even at the height of Edward I's wars it would have been difficult to present them as vicious doctrinal heretics or implacable papal foes against whom the crusade should be unleashed. Nor was there any English pope eager to advance 'national' interests within the British Isles, in the way that the Frenchman Martin IV ardently supported the Aragonese

[19] In 1263 Urban IV consented to Charles's request that the Sicilian crusade be preached in France, Provence, the imperial dioceses lying between the eastern border of France and the kingdom of Germany, Lombardy, Tuscany, and the papal state. The march of Ancona and the patriarchate of Grado were added in 1265. See N. Housley, *The Italian Crusades: The Papal–Angevin Alliance and the Crusades against Christian Lay Powers, 1254–1343* (Oxford, 1982), 18; E. Boutaric, *Saint Louis et Alphonse de Poitiers* (Paris, 1870), 314, for Alphonse.

[20] See e.g. Housley, *Italian Crusades*, pp. 111–12. The papacy's perception, of course, was frequently influenced by those spearheading the crusade in question. See E. Kennan, 'Innocent III, Gregory IX, and Political Crusades: A Study in the Disintegration of Papal Power', in G. F. Lytle (ed.), *Reform and Authority in the Medieval and Renaissance Church* (Washington, 1981), esp. pp. 15–16, 23–6. In England, such might have been the case with regard to the crusades against Plantagenet opponents, 1215–17 and 1263–5, and the promotion of the crusade against Manfred in 1255.

Crusade to the advantage of Charles of Valois and his Capetian king, Philip III. Again, for logistic reasons, England's insularity rendered it unpromising territory for the fruitful promotion of crusades against heretics and papal opponents on the Continent, and there were minimal interests to play upon. In this connection it is significant that some of John's Gascon and Poitevin subjects were involved in the early phases of the Albigensian Crusade. In 1209 the archbishop of Bordeaux led a contingent, followed in 1211 by the archbishop of Auch, parts of whose province—notably Quercy and the Agenais—were touched by the heresy. The crusade impinged upon the Plantagenets' southern subjects in a way in which it could not have done in England, and it cannot be just coincidence that the only Anglo-Norman crusader of any note, Hugh de Lacy, earl of Ulster, was a political refugee when he departed for the Languedoc sometime after John's punitive expedition to Ireland in 1210.[21] Moreover, neither John nor Henry III can have been exactly keen to countenance the promotion of the Albigensian Crusade in their lands. Raymond VI, count of Toulouse, was John's brother-in-law and close, if ineffectual, political ally; their respective sons remained close in their common struggle against Capetian expansion in the Languedoc.

The attitude of the Plantagenet kings is important in other ways. Leaving aside the crusades declared against rebels in England, in 1215–17 and 1263–5, there was only one occasion when royal and papal political interests coincided to allow the active promotion of a 'political' crusade in England. The declaration of the crusade against Manfred in 1255 was the direct consequence of Henry III's acceptance of the throne of Sicily for his son the Lord Edmund in 1254, whereby the Hohenstaufen emerged as the common enemy of king and pope.[22] This dovetailing of interests contrasts sharply with Henry's previous stance in the papal–Hohenstaufen struggle. In 1235 the marriage of his sister Isabella to Frederick II ushered in a period of close relations between the Plantagenet and imperial courts, and Henry hoped to use the alliance to put pressure upon the Capetian king in their struggle over the Plantagenet inheritance in France. These circumstances inevitably militated against the promotion of the anti-Hohenstaufen crusade in England before Frederick's death in 1250. Even then Henry's sensibilities remained engaged because he was uncle to Isabella's son, the young Henry, who, according to Frederick's will, was to succeed his half-brother Conrad in the

[21] See *DNB* xi. 378. If Innocent III thought of promoting the Albigensian Crusade in England, the interdict and breakdown in relations with John must have ruled it out.

[22] See below, pp. 221–2.

Empire and Sicily.[23] When Richard of Cornwall was offered the throne of Sicily in 1252 he is said to have regarded it as dishonest to supplant his nephew Henry, and part of Henry III's non-acceptance of Innocent IV's offer in 1253—that his crusading vow be commuted to Sicily at that time—lay in his evident distaste at the prospect that he would become the instrument of destruction of the two half-brothers, Conrad and Henry. The removal of this restraint, with the death of both Hohenstaufen princes in 1254, was emphasized by Alexander IV in 1255.[24] The crusade could now proceed; Henry's conscience was clear, for Manfred was illegitimate, no Plantagenet kinsman by blood or through marriage.

Edward I, who was returning from the Holy Land when his father died in 1272, was marked out in the Latin East and at the papal Curia as the potential leader of a new crusade to the Holy Land from the very beginning of his reign. He seems to have considered a return as early as January 1275; he certainly declared before November of that year that he would take the Cross again.[25] The news set the scene for the rest of Edward's reign, for every pope who lived long enough to make a mark between 1275 and 1307 looked to him to make good that promise. There is not a shred of evidence to suggest that Edward ever considered fulfilling his intention other than in the East. His protracted negotiations with a succession of popes all rested on the assumption that it was the Holy Land to which he would sail. This common outlook militated against promotion of other crusades in England during those years.

Two further points may usefully be made concerning the emphasis upon the Holy Land in papal policy towards England. First, when the crusade came to be applied more widely in the twelfth century and the first decades of the thirteenth, the English never made one of these other ventures peculiarly their own, as the North French came to dominate the Albigensian Crusade and the crusades in support of the Latin Empire of Constantinople, or the Germans the Prussian and Livonian crusades, or the Spanish the crusades against Moslems in Spain. The only crusading tradition which existed in England was the crusade to the Holy Land, and, like all traditions, it tended to harden

[23] See T. C. Van Cleve, *The Emperor Frederick II of Hohenstaufen, Immutator Mundi* (Oxford, 1972), 529–30. Frederick's will was known to Matthew Paris and doubtless Henry III and Richard of Cornwall as well: Paris, *CM* v. 216–17. Henry had acted for Frederick in Sicily since 1247: ibid. iv. 613; and see E. Kantorowicz, *Frederick the Second, 1194–1250*, trans. E. O. Lorimer (London, 1931), 640.

[24] Paris, *CM* v. 347; 'Burton', pp. 339–40. Louis IX opposed Charles of Anjou's acceptance of the offer of Sicily on similar grounds in 1252. See E. L. Cox, *The Eagles of Savoy: The House of Savoy in Thirteenth-Century Europe* (Princeton, 1974), 242.

[25] *Foedera*, I. ii. 520; *CPR 1272–81*, p. 116; *Reg. Gregory X*, Nos. 945, 960.

with time. Second, the papacy very probably came to adapt its policy following its lack of success when it did seek to promote other species of crusade. For example, the attempt to prosecute the crusade in support of the Latin Empire of Constantinople in 1237–8 fell so flat that Gregory IX's successors may have come to accept that its further promotion was unlikely to pay dividends.[26] Again, the resistance to the 'Sicilian business' in the 1250s was so fierce and the opposition so publicly vociferous that later thirteenth-century popes were loath perhaps even to broach the subject of crusades against their political enemies in Italy and elsewhere. For a variety of reasons, only the crusade to the Holy Land could be expected to command widespread support in thirteenth-century England.

Crusading Resources

The papacy was not concerned simply to recruit men. Increasingly from the later twelfth century popes were concerned as much with the raising of funds through direct taxation of the clerical body, the securing of bequests and legacies for the Holy Land, the imposition of pecuniary penance, and the redemption of crusading vows. Other sources of revenue were also applied on occasion to the crusading subsidy, as we shall see.

The imposition of mandatory taxes has been exhaustively studied by Lunt, but it will be useful to set out briefly the main outlines.[27] In common with their fellows elsewhere, the English clergy were mandated to pay five taxes for the crusade to the Holy Land in our period: a twentieth of their ecclesiastical revenues for three years in 1215; a triennial twentieth in 1245, with half their revenues for three years demanded from non-resident clerics; a quinquennial hundredth in 1263; a sexennial tenth in 1274; and a further sexennial tenth in 1291. In addition, the English clergy were ordered in 1250 to pay a triennial tenth in support of Henry III's projected crusade, a burden increased to a quinquennial tenth, along with moneys derived from vacant benefices and annates, when Henry's attentions were diverted to Sicily. Subsidies were also requested. In 1222 Honorius III urged grants on behalf of King John of Jerusalem, then visiting the West to

[26] Thereafter aids and subsidies alone were sought. See Lunt, *Financial Relations*, esp. pp. 194–6, 228–9, 250–2, 434–7. The primacy of the Holy Land crusade is emphasized by C. J. Tyerman, 'Some English Evidence of Attitudes to Crusading in the Thirteenth Century', in P. R. Coss and S. D. Lloyd (eds.), *Thirteenth Century England I: Proc. of the Newcastle upon Tyne Conference 1985* (Woodbridge, 1986), 168–74.

[27] Lunt, *Financial Relations*, chs. 4–6.

raise support. In 1237–8 the English clergy were asked for a subsidy on behalf of the Latin Empire of Constantinople; a further request to the same end was made in 1263.

More revealing of the evolution in papal thinking are the attempts to solicit gifts and legacies for the crusade in return for full or partial indulgence. Gregory VIII was apparently the first pope, with regard to England at least, to attempt to raise funds in this way. In 1187 he granted partial indulgence to all contributing to the expenses of the crusade, a policy sustained by his successor Clement III in 1188. The urgent need to support the Third Crusade plainly lay behind this development.[28] The early application of the policy is glimpsed in Gerald of Wales's account of Archbishop Baldwin of Canterbury's preaching campaign in Wales in 1188. One Welshman, Cador, too old to participate in the crusade himself, craftily secured full remission of his sins by contributing two-tenths of his wealth: at first Baldwin fixed one-tenth as the sum necessary for Cador to gain remission of half his sins, but the Welshman decided to draw upon mathematical logic and offered twice the amount.[29] This means of raising funds rapidly became an established part of papal policy. After *Ad liberandam* of 1215 had set its seal to the matter, the promise of indulgence in return for financial aid was generally repeated in crusading bulls and reaffirmed at the Councils of Lyons I and II in 1245 and 1274.[30]

Innocent IV's pontificate saw a new departure for canon 15 of the Council of Lyons I instructed prelates to urge their flocks to make bequests in aid of the Holy Land or the Latin Empire of Constantinople in return for indulgences.[31] Legacies for the Holy Land already had a long history, but now the attempt was made positively to stimulate more revenue from this particular source. The precedent was frequently followed in the later thirteenth century, the decree affirmed in *Zelus fidei* of the Council of Lyons II. The development may be regarded as part of a more general attempt by Innocent IV to expand the revenue base of the crusading subsidy. Thus, in 1252 he

[28] See ibid. 419 ff.; Gerald of Wales, *Opera*, ed. J. S. Brewer *et al.* (RS; 1861–91), viii. 236–9.

[29] Gerald, *Opera*, vi. 73–4.

[30] Lunt, *Financial Relations*, p. 424; Purcell, *Papal Crusading Policy*, appendix A, where the decrees of 1215, 1245, and 1274 are conveniently printed together. In 1235 Gregory IX promised two years' remitted penance to all giving 1*d.* each week in aid of the Holy Land, with additional indulgence for those contributing more: *Reg. Gregory IX*, Nos. 2664–5. In 1234 prelates and clergy, towns, vills, and cities were urged, in proportion to their resources, to send armed men with their expenses to the Holy Land, an extension of what had been laid down in *Ad liberandam*: Paris, *CM* iii. 283–7.

[31] Paris, *CM* iv. 456–62; 'Burton', p. 278. See also Paris, *CM* iv. 565.

instructed that indistinct legacies and the restorations of usury and other illicit gains be applied to the subsidy, a policy foreshadowed in 1246 in his measures to aid the Latin Empire.[32]

Much of the preaching effort was geared to the soliciting of funds throughout the thirteenth century. In 1199 Innocent III instructed that in each church a chest was to be set up in which the faithful were to be encouraged to deposit their alms in remission of their sins.[33] Further decrees on its use followed in 1213 and 1274, with Gregory X laying down that there were to be weekly services in all churches to stimulate men to give alms for the crusade.[34]

Penitentially related to the securing of gifts, legacies, and alms was the redemption of vows, the essence of which was the raising of moneys in return for indulgence. The system never operated indiscriminately. It was tied closely to papal policy concerning personnel, and this, in its essentials, rested upon two things: the anticipated practical value of an individual's personal participation in a crusade, and the perceived obligations within society arising from that individual's birth, position, or vocation. From the very inception of the crusading movement the papacy expressed a positive preference for forces composed primarily of effective warriors and others who would be useful on campaign. It is well known that Urban II was at pains to dissuade clerics, monks, the elderly and infirm, and unaccompanied women from departing on the First Crusade.[35] His stance was followed throughout the twelfth century by successive popes, their resolution strengthened by the experience of the first crusades which taught that indiscriminate recruitment could be decidedly counter-productive. At the same time, the papacy maintained a generally inflexible attitude towards the fulfilment of vows, allowing redemption, deferment, or commutation only in special cases such as the illness, infirmity, or poverty of the *vovens*, and using ecclesiastical censures to enforce the departure of the able-bodied. As late as 1196 we find Celestine III toeing the traditional line in a bull sent to Archbishop Hubert Walter.[36]

Under Innocent III earlier practice was for the first time abandoned. In *Quia maior* of April 1213 Innocent ruled that crusading vows might now be taken by all manner of men (excepting only monks) because, he explained, aid for the Holy Land was hindered or

[32] *Foedera*, I. i. 286–7; Paris, *CM* iv. 565; 'Burton', p. 278.

[33] For England see *CLI*, Nos. 171–2; Howden, *Chron.* iv. 107–12.

[34] *CLI*, No. 917; Purcell, *Papal Crusading Policy*, p. 197. Gregory also decreed that Christians be urged to contribute 1*d.* sterling or *tournois* annually in aid of the Holy Land.

[35] See now E. Siberry, *Criticism of Crusading 1095–1274* (Oxford, 1985), ch. 1. See further below, ch. 3.

[36] Howden, *Chron.* iii. 317–18.

delayed if the suitability of each was first examined, but 'when dire necessity or plain utility may require' such vows might be redeemed, commuted, or deferred by apostolic mandate.[37] The precedent was vital for *Quia maior* became the canonical basis of later practice concerning redemption. The fundamental change consisted, of course, in a movement towards a policy which now allowed all manner of men to take crusading vows, irrespective of their fighting capability, the majority of whom were urged to redeem their vows whilst retaining the indulgence tied thereto. The cash accruing then went to subsidize those judged fit to prosecute the crusade in person, that knightly body which the papacy had always preferred.[38]

It was not until 1234, in England at any rate, that the policy was first implemented systematically. During the pontificate of Honorius III and in the first years of Gregory IX's it appears that redemption was generally allowed only in cases where *crucesignati* were unsuited to personal participation.[39] Then Gregory, in his crusading bull *Rachel videns* of September 1234, returned to *Quia maior* and repeated verbatim the declaration that all but monks might take the Cross, their vows being regulated as necessity and utility required.[40] The promotional campaign that this bull initiated also saw the most radical departure in the way in which the Cross was preached in thirteenth-century England. For the first time the Dominicans and Franciscans were systematically employed as local preachers and agents, and it is tempting to think that the two developments were directly connected. To implement the policy of general redemption of vows the papacy had to devise appropriate means at local level, above all the deployment of a sufficiently large number of agents delegated both to give and then redeem vows in the context of preaching to the populace at large. The monastic order in England may have been capable of fulfilling this role, but their vocation militated against regular and extensive popular preaching.[41] The mendicants, however, were admirably well-attuned to the demands of popular preaching by virtue of their principles, organization, and training; and, between them, the Dominicans and Franciscans had already settled most of the principal towns of southern and central England, and were pushing well

[37] *Patrologiae Latina*, ccxvi, cols. 819–20; *CLI*, No. 917; and see J. A. Brundage, *Medieval Canon Law and the Crusader* (Madison, Milwaukee, London, 1969), 69–70.

[38] See also below, p. 72ff.

[39] See e.g. *Reg. Honorius III*, No. 3041. The standard form letters of the papal chancery, and the English narrative sources, suggest no new departure at this time; nor do the *Constitutions* ascribed to Bishop Hugh Foliot of Hereford, *c.*1225–30: *Councils*, II. i. 196.

[40] *Reg. Gregory IX*, Nos. 2200–2; Paris, *CM* iii. 283–7.

[41] Cistercians, e.g., preached on the 1188 recruitment tour of Wales. See below, p. 65.

beyond the Humber, when Gregory drafted them into preaching of the crusade.[42] Their rapid rate of expansion, moreover, indicates the strength of their early popularity and standing in the eyes of most. Gregory IX may with reason have expected them to stimulate a good response to the call to the crusade and the new policy of redemption of vows, if the aim was indeed to secure a much wider assumption of the Cross than hitherto. The mendicants' role in the regulation of vows certainly struck contemporaries as noteworthy. Matthew Paris's account of the preaching campaign of 1234–5 suggests that the securing of cash through redemption was the chief aim; the friars, he says, signed men with the Cross one day and then redeemed them for cash on the next, while in 1236 Thomas, a Templar and papal *familiaris*, was sent to England to redeem vows as he saw fit.[43] There is no reason to doubt that a radical policy shift had occurred, and Thomson has effectively demonstrated that the scandalmonger of St Albans was by no means a lone and unrepresentative voice of criticism. Significantly enough, the mendicants' role as preachers of the crusade and agents in the administering and regulation of vows had a major part to play in the contemporary reappraisal of their initial image from the 1230s onwards.[44]

The promotional campaign initiated in 1234 proved to be a definitive breakthrough. Thereafter systematic redemption of the vows of the populace, virtually automatic, became a central plank of papal policy in England.[45] Wykes, for example, makes it plain that redemption money rather than personal service was to be the appropriate contribution of the 'plebeia multitudo' to the crusade of 1270.[46] Only Gregory X sought to check the inexorable development by insisting

[42] The Dominicans, arriving in England in 1221, had settled nine urban centres by 1234; the Franciscans, arriving in 1224, had settled twenty-one. See D. Knowles and R. N. Hadcock, *Medieval Religious Houses: England and Wales* (2nd edn., London, 1971), 213–20, 222–9. Only Durham, Rochester, and Winchester dioceses as yet lacked a house of one of the two orders in 1234.

[43] Paris, *CM* iii. 279–80, 287, 373–4. Thomas was probably deputed to the overall administration of redemption of vows and the proceeds.

[44] W. R. Thomson, 'The Image of the Mendicants in the Chronicles of Matthew Paris', *Archivium Franciscanum Historium*, lxx (1977), esp. pp. 16–20, 23–34. Considering Paris's sharp eye, it is unlikely that the mendicants were engaged in a systematic policy of redemption of vows before 1234, or that such a policy had been applied at all before then.

[45] Innocent IV seemingly returned to the former policy in 1247, instructing that English *crucesignati* be protected from compulsory redemption of their vows: *Reg. Innocent IV*, No. 2960. Restraint was soon thrown to the winds with the campaign in support of Henry III's projected crusade in the 1250s, redemption proceeding apace.

[46] Wykes, *Chron.*, p. 217. See also 'Continuation' of William of Newburgh, 'Historia rerum Anglicarum', in *Chronicles of the Reigns of Stephen, Henry II, and Richard I*, ed. R. Howlett, 2 vols. (RS; 1884, 1885), ii. 552.

upon the personal fulfilment of vows, except those of *crucesignati* legitimately unable to serve, in his instructions of September 1274 for the preaching of the new crusade.[47] The general trend is amply evidenced by the emergence of standard form letters of receipt for payments in redemption of vows.[48]

Two further forms of vow remain to be discussed. The first, the conditional vow, became common under Innocent IV though also known in Gregory IX's time.[49] Henry III's projected crusade was apparently the occasion for its emergence in England. In January 1251 the king promised that he would not compel any *crucesignatus* to pay a greater sum for the redemption of his vow than he had promised, or would promise, on taking the Cross.[50] In January 1252 agreements were drawn up with individual *crucesignati* that either they would go in person with the king or give in aid of his crusade the amount they would have spent if delayed in going. In July and November the promise was repeated.[51] This species of obligation became unexceptional in England thereafter, the subject of articles of inquiry under Alexander IV in 1255–6, Urban IV in 1263, and in the pontificates of Gregory X and his successors.[52]

The crusading vow had been imposed as penance only exceptionally in earlier times, but under Innocent IV, again, the device emerged as an integral feature of crusading policy.[53] In 1250 he instructed those preaching the crusade in England to absolve, by imposition of the Cross as penance, those guilty of a wide range of crimes.[54] These crimes were extended in 1263 by Urban IV, who significantly eased the process of redemption by decreeing that those signed with the Cross as penance might either go in person, send substitutes at their expense, or give part of their goods in aid of the Holy Land.[55] Gregory X continued the practice and added

[47] *Reg. Gregory X*, No. 569; and see Lunt, *Financial Relations*, pp. 448–9. Gregory was plainly aware of the dangers posed by abuse of the system.

[48] See e.g. W. E. Lunt, *Papal Revenues in the Middle Ages* (New York, 1934), ii. 517; *Letter Book of William of Hoo, Sacrist of Bury St. Edmunds*, ed. A. Gransden (Suffolk Rec. Soc. 5; 1963), 57.

[49] See Purcell, *Papal Crusading Policy*, p. 129. The first suggestion of such vows in England appears to be in *Reg. Innocent IV*, No. 2959.

[50] *Foedera*, I. i. 276; *CPR 1247–58*, p. 84.

[51] *CR 1251–3*, pp. 231, 436; *CPR 1247–58*, p. 164.

[52] Articles of inquiry reveal how common they had become. See e.g. art. 16 of the 1291–3 inquiry, in *The Rolls and Registers of Bishop Oliver Sutton*, ed. R. M. T. Hill, 8 vols. (Lincoln Rec. Soc.; 1948–86), iii. 157–9.

[53] Purcell, *Papal Crusading Policy*, pp. 114–18. For early cases in England see Lunt, *Financial Relations*, pp. 420–1.

[54] *Foedera*, I. i. 272–3, where the crimes are listed.

[55] *Reg. Urban IV*, No. 468.

blasphemy to the list of crimes in *Zelus fidei* of 1274.[56] Thereafter, as the surviving English episcopal registers reveal, pecuniary penance became entirely common.[57]

The changing thrust in policy outlined above necessitated an appropriate means of monitoring and enforcement if potential resources were to be realized in full. The first papal inquisition into unfulfilled vows in England was apparently that initiated by Celestine III in 1196.[58] Another inquiry was laid by Hubert Walter upon his suffragans in 1201 in accordance with Innocent III's mandate.[59] Thereafter inquisitions were a common occurrence, implied, although we do not always know of them in practice, in the frequent papal demands that prelates and preachers of the crusade should compel men to fulfil their vows. Their scope was initially quite rudimentary: to identify who had taken the Cross, and who had failed to fulfil their vows. As the system of redemption of vows developed, however, and as the papacy extended the range of sources from which moneys for the crusade were to be raised, so the need arose for more extensive and detailed inquiry periodically.

One of the earliest of this type occurred in 1247. In response to papal mandate the papal collectors in England, John Sarracenus and Berard de Nimpha, took measures to ensure the full collection and delivery of the crusading moneys promised to Earl Richard of Cornwall. They instructed all bishops to cite their archdeacons, and their officials, to attend them personally in London to treat concerning the matter on 19 August 1247. Robert Grosseteste was one bishop who ordered a comprehensive inquiry regarding crusading vows and moneys in his diocese preparatory to the assembly. In every parish within the diocese of Lincoln the archdeacons were to appoint trustworthy *crucesignati* to compile together with the priest a list of *crucesignati* who were dying or already dead, and to note how much each had promised or left in aid of the Holy Land. They were also to take the names of their executors and inform them to be ready to pay over the moneys on demand. The duly attested list from each parish was then to be deposited with the dean who was to collate it with other

56 Purcell, *Papal Crusading Policy*, p. 197. Gregory IX had apparently introduced this measure, but there is no sign of its implementation in England. See also ibid. 144.

57 See e.g. *The Register of Walter Giffard, Lord Archbishop of York, 1266–79*, ed. W. Brown (Surtees Soc. 109; 1904), 277–86; *Historical Papers and Letters from the Northern Registers*, ed. J. Raine (RS; 1873), 46–58; *Reg. Sutton*, iii. 12, 20, 22, 160; iv. 13, 86; v. 10, 19–20; *Register of Bishop Godfrey Giffard, 1268–1301*, ed. J. W. Willis-Bund, 2 vols. (Worcestershire Hist. Soc.; 1898–1902), 3, 32, 81, 110–13, 329.

58 The articles of the 1194 eyre, however, required investigation of *crucesignati* dying before they set out, the whereabouts, quantity, and type of their chattels: Howden, *Chron.* iii. 263–4, 317–19.

59 Ibid. iv. 73.

parochial returns, himself attest and seal the compilation, and then deliver it to the house of the Dominicans or Franciscans who had initially preached the Cross in the archdeaconry in question. The moneys now known to be due were to be collected through the view of the original preacher, or his deputy, and deposited under his seal 'in aede sacra' until the executors of the Cross, or their assigns, should demand it. Of the goods of intestate *crucesignati*, dead or dying, a certain proportion was to be applied to the fund through the counsel of the man's friends and the friars, so he could enjoy the plenary indulgence. Additional instructions dealt with legacies.[60]

Another far-ranging inquiry took place in 1255–6, clearly prompted by the need to locate and raise funds for the Sicilian business.[61] Similar inquisitions were ordered by the papacy in 1273, 1282–3, and 1291.[62] All were rigorous; each underlined the importance attached to moneys. They reveal the extent to which the crusade had evolved as a financial institution in the course of the thirteenth century, the emphasis now laid upon monetary contribution from the bulk of the population to support the personal crusading service of the few, the *bellatores peritissimi* who were to fight on behalf of all.

Appeals From the Latin East and its Allies

An important component of the promotion of the crusade to the Holy Land consisted of the newsletters and appeals for aid, often combined, from the crusader states themselves. Their dispatch arose independently of papal crusading initiatives for the most part, but popes commonly endorsed the appeals and took steps to transmit the news around the West, whilst papal reaction to them lay behind the declaration of almost every crusade to the Holy Land. The considerable effort taken by the secular and religious leaders of the Latin East, and their Eastern allies, to stimulate aid for their salvation may, then, be considered an adjunct of promotional policy.

The early rulers of the crusader states do not seem to have been very active in seeking aid from the West, but as the position of Latin Syria became progressively more precarious following the failure of the Second Crusade and the resurgence of Moslem power under Nur

[60] Paris, *CM* vi. No. 71. See also Lunt, *Financial Relations*, pp. 432–3, 436–7.

[61] Paris, *CM* vi. No. 153; 'Burton', pp. 354–60.

[62] 'Winchester', p. 113; 'Waverley', pp. 379–81 (1273); *Letter Book of William of Hoo*, No. 41; *Registrum Ricardi de Swinfield, Episcopi Herefordensis*, ed. W. W. Capes (Canterbury and York Soc. 6; 1909), 78–9 (1282–3); *Reg. Sutton*, iii. 57–9; *The Register of John le Romeyn, Lord Archbishop of York, 1288–96*, ed. W. Brown, 2 vols. (Surtees Soc. 123, 128; 1913, 1916), ii. 73 (1291–3).

ed-Din of Damascus, so more effort was put into the attempt. Initially, attention focused upon the Capetian house of France, but in the 1160s the net was cast more widely to include other leading Western princes.[63] Henry II, king of England and lord of half of France, was a highly desirable catch. He was beginning to reach the height of his power and his potential for support was unrivalled. Moreover, Henry, the grandson of King Fulk of Jerusalem, was cousin to both Baldwin III and Amalric I of Jerusalem: there were ties of blood upon which to play.[64] The first embassies imploring his aid were sent in 1168 and 1169,[65] followed by a series of requests in the 1170s and 1180s, establishing a tradition of looking for help to the royal house of England that stretched through the thirteenth century and beyond. As we shall presently see, the effort to solicit the support of Henry III and especially Edward I far outweighed that applied to their subjects.

Aid was sought by means of letters and, less frequently, diplomatic missions. A considerable volume of correspondence entered England from the East in this period.The bulk of it comprised news reports, ranging from terse summaries of events to detailed dispatches, sometimes so full that the writer felt constrained to apologize for his wordiness.[66] In some cases it is likely that the writer wished simply to report his news, but news had a significant promotional value, especially when it was dismal, and most newsletters were plainly sent with an ulterior purpose, the *narratio* serving to preface and justify an *exhortatio*. By dwelling upon a military reversal in the East, for example, the writer implied that support was needed. He may also have intended to shock his readers into a sense of outrage, or to prick their consciences by reminding them of the solidarity in Christian fraternity which bound them to the inhabitants of Outremer.[67] Sometimes the promotional intention was made quite explicit. The patriarch of Jerusalem, for example, wrote to inform the prelates of France and England of the fall of Jerusalem to the Khwarizmian Turks in August 1244, and the crushing defeat inflicted upon the Franks at the battle of La Forbie in October, precisely 'that your piety may excite your charity in compassion for the ruin of the Holy

[63] See esp. Smail, 'Latin Syria', esp. pp. 8–9.

[64] See appendix 6 below.

[65] See Smail, 'Latin Syria', p. 13 and refs. Requests for his aid may have been made earlier, in 1165–6, e.g., when taxation was voted on behalf of the Latin kingdom.

[66] See e.g. Joseph de Chauncy's apology to Edward I for the length of his account of the battle of Homs and assessment of future prospects penned in Mar. 1282: *Cart. Gen. Hosp.* iii. No. 3782.

[67] For an example of the impact of news upon recipients, see the report of the consternation of Edward I and the master of the Temple in England in 1299: William Rishanger, *Chronica et annales, regnantibus Henrico tertio et Edwardo primo*, ed. H. T. Riley (RS; 1865), 400.

Land'. He beseeched them to implore divine mercy, before stressing that further disasters would befall the Latin kingdom, so depleted now were the ranks of its defenders, unless effective aid was sent in the next passage.[68] Good news, not very common in the thirteenth century, could be used to the same purpose. The master of the Hospital judged that since Qalawun's forces had been so seriously weakened by the battle of Homs, 1281, now would be an excellent time to launch a new crusade, especially as Mongol support might be expected. This course he urged upon Edward I.[69]

These examples show that it is neither easy nor desirable to dissociate letters sent with an overt promotional purpose from the wider body of correspondence reporting news. Appendix 1 consists of a calendar of the letters known to have been sent to English correspondents from the Latin East and its allies in the period 1216–1307. It cannot be considered complete for others will doubtless come to light, particularly from manuscript sources, but it provides a basis for discussion.[70] Fifty-one of the sixty-two letters it contains were written by inhabitants of the crusader states, six were sent by the Mongol khans, and a further five came from the kings of Armenia. All contained news of recent events, many attempting an evaluation of immediate or future prospects. Appeals for aid were openly expressed in thirty-three of them, either for the crusader states themselves or for the specific institution or principal in question.

One of the most striking features of the series is the role of the Temple and Hospital. Of the fifty-one letters sent from the crusader states, thirty-six (nineteen Templar, seventeen Hospitaller) were composed by members of the two orders, apart from those letters in which their officials combined to write jointly with other leaders of the Latin kingdom.[71] Both possessed a large number of English houses and they clearly sought to keep them closely informed of their fortunes in Outremer through regular dispatches, as we might expect of

[68] Paris, *CM* iv. 337–44; BL Additional MS 46352, fos. 50b–52b (Register of St Augustine's, Canterbury).

[69] 'Lettres inédites concernants les croisades (1275–1307)', ed. C. Kohler and C. V. Langlois, *Bibliothèque de l'École des Chartes*, lii (1891), No. 5.

[70] It includes a small number of letters which were not primarily news reports but concerned rather with the narrow interests of the correspondents, e.g. Master Guérin of the Hospital's letter to Bishop Ralph Neville of Chichester, *c.*1231–6: *Dipl. Docs.* i. No. 248; *Anc. Corr.* 6. 63; *Cart. Gen. Hosp.* iv. No. 1982.

[71] Only the Order of St Thomas of Acre is otherwise represented. The omission of others probably reflects their limited English interests, but senior officials of the Teutonic knights wrote jointly with others on occasion. See the letters of 1244, 1254, and 1263 in *Chronica de Mailros*, ed. J. Stevenson (Bannatyne Club, 50; 1835), 156–62 (1244); *Foedera*, I. i. 308; 'Burton', pp. 368–9 (1254); *Foedera*, I. i. 395 (misdated); *Anc. Corr.* 55. 2; *Dipl. Docs.* i. No. 385 (1263).

such large international corporations. Nor is it surprising that they were also concerned to implore aid from their brethren in the West, especially in times of adversity.[72] In addition, both orders frequently sought the aid of the English king. As part of a general campaign seeking funds and men in the West in 1261, for example, the master of the Temple wrote to Amadeus, the English preceptor, detailing the perils facing the Latin East before the Mongol onslaught. He requested Amadeus to send speedy aid from the English Temple and urged him to make representations to Henry III on the order's behalf. The master sought the loan of the huge sum of 10,000*m*. from Henry, and Amadeus was to seek to influence Queen Eleanor to bring additional pressure upon the king.[73]

This letter further underlines the tendency of both orders to exploit the news of setbacks in the East for their own narrow interests. Their interests were by no means identical with those of the Latin East more generally, and their inclination to pursue independent and jealous policies was something for which they were frequently criticized. Nevertheless, they realized that their own interests in Outremer depended to a considerable degree upon the continued safety of the crusader states within which they were located. Occasionally, then, members of both orders sent pleas for aid on behalf of the Holy Land as well as themselves, and combined with others to make joint appeals as in 1244,[74] 1254,[75] 1260, and 1263.[76]

It would be dangerous to draw hard and fast conclusions from a body of correspondence which in part represents chance survival, but it does seem that the efforts of the Temple and Hospital far outshone those of others. Only four letters written by the patriarch of Jerusalem, or in his name, appear, along with one in which he wrote jointly with others. Only one or two bishops can be observed participating in the process, although on occasion they too were involved in joint appeals. Of the lay leaders, no letters appear from the kings of Cyprus, and only one is known from the Latin emperors of Constantinople.[77] Frederick II was altogether more active, sending

[72] Typical is the letter sent by the master of the Temple in 1220 to Alan Martel, *locum tenens* of the English preceptor. The need for subsidy from the order's houses in the West is painfully apparent: Wendover, *Flores*, iv. 77–9 (misdated).

[73] 'Burton', pp. 491–5. The request betrays ignorance of Henry's difficulties in England at the time.

[74] Paris. *CM* iv. 337–44; BL Additional MS 46352, fos. 50b–52b.

[75] *Foedera*, I. i. 308; 'Burton', pp. 368–9.

[76] *Regestă Regni Hierosolymitani, 1097–1291*, ed. R. Röhricht (Innsbruck, 1893), No. 1288 (1260); *Foedera*, I. i. 395 (misdated); *Dipl. Docs*. i. No. 385; *Anc. Corr*. 55. 2 (1263). In 1244 the masters of the Temple, Hospital, and Teutonic knights combined with Queen Alice of Cyprus *et al*. in an appeal to Innocent IV: *Chron. Mailros*, pp. 156–62.

[77] Queen Alice of Cyprus wrote jointly with others in 1244. See n. 76. This is probably explained by her regency of the Latin kingdom at the time.

reports of his crusade in 1228 and 1229,[78] and continuing, as king of Jerusalem, by forwarding news he had himself received from the East, informing Henry III and Richard of Cornwall of his crusading plans, and bewailing the threat posed to the Latin world by the Mongols. The absence of other kings of Jerusalem is not perhaps surprising considering the sequence of absentee rulers and *bailliages*, yet the regents are represented only by John d'Ibelin, count of Jaffa, writing jointly with others in 1254, Geoffrey de Sargines in 1260, and by Queen Alice of Cyprus in 1244.[79] The only feudatory writing in his own name is Bohemund VI of Antioch, and there are reasons for thinking that he had particular motives in appealing to Henry III in that year (1255).[80] Much more important than any of these in the latter part of our period were the allies of the Latin East. The kings of Armenia sent five letters to Edward I between 1291 and 1307, as well as dispatching embassies. The Mongol khans, it is well known, eagerly sought the participation of Edward and other princes in a new crusade; six letters and at least five embassies were sent to Edward in the course of his reign.[81]

There are strong reasons for thinking that the letters which survive represent but a small part of an originally much greater volume of correspondence. This conjecture is supported, first, by the interesting case of Walter de St Martin, a Dominican. He received two letters from the master of the Hospital in 1251, and a third from Joseph de Chauncy, then treasurer of the Hospital at Acre, in 1252.[82] Yet there is no certain explanation for Walter's receipt of letters beyond the fact that he had once according to Matthew Paris been in the Holy Land, and apparently maintained a personal interest in the affairs of the Hospital and wished to be informed of their news.[83] The letters

[78] *CR 1227–31*, p. 93; *Foedera*, I. i. 187; and Wendover, *Flores*, iv. 189–93. Best treated as letters dispatched by crusaders on campaign, these are included in appendix 3 below. Although king of Jerusalem, Frederick did not return to the East. His letters of the 1240s, more properly letters sent to English correspondents from other parts of the West incorporating news from the East, are included in appendix 3.

[79] See nn. 71, 76.

[80] See below, pp. 229–30.

[81] See appendices 1 and 2 below for refs.

[82] Paris, *CM* vi. Nos. 100–2.

[83] Ibid. v. 306. In the second letter he is described as a dear and special friend of the Hospital. Walter, one of Paris's informants, was confessor to Cecilia de Sandford: R. Vaughan, *Matthew Paris* (Cambridge, 1958), 13–17. Was he the Master Walter, an English Dominican, appointed preacher by the pope, who accompanied Frederick II's crusade? Paris, *CM* iii. 177. He is probably to be identified with that Walter de St Martin, 'minister Crucis Christi', to whom Hubert de Burgh left properties for the redemption of his crusading vow, *c.*1240: *The Register or Rolls of Walter Gray, Archbishop of York*, ed. J. Raine (Surtees Soc. 56; 1872), 199. If so, and if he was engaged in the business of the Cross in England, the dispatch of these letters to him is more easily explained.

survive, in transcribed form, only because he was known to Matthew Paris who chose to include them in his *Chronica majora*. But Walter cannot have been unique; many others must have received letters from the Latin East which no longer survive. The dispatch of letters no longer extant may also be postulated with some certainty from the actions of individuals. An example is Henry III's grant of 500*m*. to the master of the Temple in 1238 towards the ransom of Templars captured in battle 'in the land of Antioch between the castles of Gastum and Tripeslak'.[84] This, almost certainly, is a reference to the engagement at Darbsaq, in 1237, when a force of Templars was routed. Since it is known that the Hospital and Temple subsequently sent letters to inform the West and seek aid, Henry III may, then, be supposed to have received such a letter and to have responded accordingly.[85]

There are many references to correspondence now lost. In March 1282, for example, Joseph de Chauncy reminded Edward I of letters which he had sent 'au passage de Sainte Cruz' the previous year, but they do not apparently survive.[86] Furthermore, the military orders appear to have dispatched letters in a routine manner. In 1244 the master of the Hospital casually observed that he had been forwarding letters to one correspondent, M. de Merlai, 'in every passage', presumably every spring and autumn sailing from the Holy Land.[87] There is no reason to think that he was especially favoured. Writing to the English preceptor in 1243–4, the master of the Temple observed that 'we are bound to inform your fraternity of the state of the Holy Land by letters or nuncios as often as opportunity presents itself . . .'.[88]

It is also certain that the practice of some chroniclers has masked a number of letters from our eyes. Most with access to letters from the East used them either by reproducing them verbatim or abstracting their contents. Matthew Paris, in particular, often based his account of events in the East upon letters which he either reproduced in his main narrative, in whole or in part, or abstracted, supplying the full

[84] *CPR 1232–47*, p. 207. See *CPR 1258–66*, p. 99, for another possible case concerning the Temple.

[85] S. Runciman, *A History of the Crusades*, 3 vols. (Cambridge, 1951–4), iii. 208. Paris, *CM* iii. 404–6 gives a full account of events, suggesting access to a letter or letters now lost.

[86] *Cart. Gen. Hosp*. iii. No. 3782. In 1263 it was observed that the aid of Henry III and other princes had been frequently sought in the past, 'litteris continuatis et nunciis': *Dipl. Docs*. i. No. 385; *Anc. Corr*. 55. 2; *Foedera*, I. i. 395 (misdated).

[87] See the letter reproduced in Paris, *CM* iv. 307–11, and in considerably altered form in 'Waverley', pp. 334–5.

[88] Paris, *CM* iv. 288–91. For further indications of regular dispatches, see Wendover, *Flores*, iv. 77–9; 'Burton', p. 491.

or abbreviated text in the collection supplementary to his works, the *Liber Additamentorum*.[89] But not all writers were as punctilious as Paris generally appears to have been. For example, Paris reproduces the letter of the master of the Hospital to M. de Merlai in 1244, but comparison between the Waverley annalist and Paris on the events of 1244 in the Holy Land reveals that the annalist worked large sections of the text of the letter into his own narrative, much of it verbatim but without due acknowledgement.[90] Many more letters doubtless remain buried and unacknowledged in the chronicles and only painstaking research would reveal their presence, providing, of course, that the original letter survives, in some form, to allow identification. Nevertheless, the detailed knowledge and depth of treatment of certain events in the East argues in many cases for the writer's utilization of letters no longer extant. The conclusion is inescapable that the sixty-two letters which can be identified for certain represent only the survivals of what was originally a much greater volume of correspondence.

The sequence of letters sent from the East was occasionally punctuated, or alternatively afforced, by the dispatch of embassies, generally employed when the business in question was considered to be urgent indeed. In this sense the embassies represent the most intense lobbying of the cause of the Latin East in the West. The twenty-six embassies known to have been sent to England in the period 1216–1307 are tabulated in Appendix 2. Three were fund-raising tours of the West by the head of state concerned: those of John de Brienne, titular king of Jerusalem, in 1223; and of Baldwin II, Latin emperor of Constantinople, in 1238 and 1247. Of the rest, many can be linked to notable reversals of fortune or when prospects in the East appeared especially bleak. The best-documented is the mission of Bishop Waleran of Beirut and the Dominican, Arnulph, in 1244–5, part of a single diplomatic initiative taken by the leaders of the Holy Land in the wake of the disastrous events of 1244. A series of letters was sent to the West reporting the terrible news and appealing for aid.[91] That addressed to the prelates of France and England was entrusted to the

89 See e.g. his treatment of the letter to Walter de St Martin in 1252: Paris, *CM* v. 305; vi. No. 102. Sometimes he refers to a letter, and presumably gives a summary of it, but it does not appear in the *Liber Additamentorum*; e.g. the letter to Richard of Cornwall in 1253 concerning Moslem attacks in the Holy Land, mentioned in v. 411.

90 Ibid. iv. 307–11; 'Waverley', pp. 334–5. For another likely case, compare 'Waverley', pp. 305–7 with 'Tewkesbury', p. 72, on the truce negotiated in the Holy Land in 1229.

91 Two at least were sent to English recipients; others came via the papacy or from elsewhere in the West: see Paris, *CM* iv. 300–5, 307–11, 337–44; 'Waverley', pp. 334–5; *Chron. Mailros*, p. 163; BL Additional MS 46352, fos. 50b–52b; Röhricht, *Regesta Regni Hieros.*, No. 1124.

two envoys.[92] So desperate was the situation that the two set sail out of season, in late November 1244, on a perilous voyage across the Mediterranean. They did not reach Venice until around Ascension 1245; thence they travelled to the Council of Lyons. Arnulph read out the alarming contents of the letters to the assembled dignitaries, after which the two set out to the courts of Louis IX and Henry III hoping to secure their particular support.[93]

Other embassies seem generally to have been sent because of prior knowledge in Outremer that the English king had taken the Cross and was preparing a crusade or intended to send aid to the East. In such circumstances embassies, alone or combined with letters, served as timely reminders of the situation in the crusader states and as further stimuli towards the dispatch of aid. The news, long-awaited, that Edward I had taken the Cross in 1287 must largely account for the spate of missions and letters sent to him in the following years. The missions and letters sent to Henry III in the early 1250s were certainly inspired by the news that Henry had taken the Cross in 1250 and then, later, by the concern of the Eastern powers to see that vow fulfilled in the Latin East, rather than in North Africa or Sicily.[94]

If the series of embassies and letters are considered together some interesting points emerge. First, there was an evident change in the course of the later thirteenth century with regard to the principals. The allies of the Latin East, the Mongol khans and the kings of Armenia, came to take up the running in the course of the 1270s and thereafter. Although the Temple and Hospital continued to send news and appeals up to the fall of Acre and beyond, few others in Outremer appear to have taken action. The explanation of this rather surprising termination of appeals from these circles may lie in a sense of growing disillusionment regarding their value since so many had failed to draw an effective response in the past. There is some evidence for this surmise in the rueful observations made occasionally in letters of the mid-thirteenth century that, despite previous appeals,

92 Paris, *CM* iv. 337–44; BL Additional MS 46352, fos. 50b–52b. The same letter, but in the patriarch's name alone is in 'Burton', pp. 257–63, but it is addressed to Innocent IV and was entrusted to two Franciscans. This points to the dispatch of an earlier version of the letter. Innocent had certainly heard of the fall of Jerusalem when he summoned the Council of Lyons I and issued the crusading bulls of Jan. 1245. The letter in 'Burton' is probably a copy of the letter initially reporting the news to Innocent. Paris almost certainly copied from the letter entrusted to Waleran and Arnulph, or a copy made from it. How else did he know that twelve seals were appended to the original, as he observes? Elsewhere he reveals he had met or communicated with Waleran himself: Paris, *CM* iv. 345, 388.

93 Paris, *CM* iv. 345, 388, 431. See further appendix 2.

94 See below, pp. 219, 229.

no aid had been forthcoming. A few, indeed, came close to open reproach of the recipient, none more so than the shrill appeal sent to Henry III in 1263, the last joint letter of prelates and nobles. It was pointedly observed that news of the Holy Land had frequently been sent to the princes of the West in the past that it might lead them to rise up to aid the Holy Land. 'Ut qui igitur, rex inclite, regia potencia non consurgit et regalis dextre brachium non exurgit? Usque quo exaltabitur contra nos christiani nominis inimicus? Quamdiu terra Christi sanguine rubricata cunculari tam enormiter a bestiis enormiter . . .?'[95] It was to be the last time, as far as we know, that Henry III was made the target of so urgent an appeal, perhaps because the drift into civil war in England made him an unlikely provider of aid thereafter, but perhaps too because he had come to be regarded as a lost cause in the view of the Latin East's inhabitants.

The evident concentration of letters and embassies, from whatever source, to Henry III and, above all, Edward I is unlikely to reflect simply the better survival-rate of appeals addressed to them than those directed to their subjects.[96] Like all great princes they must have attracted the focus of attention by reason of their material strength and their position in the social and political hierarchy, and where they were seen to lead their subjects might be the more easily induced to follow. In relation to the crusade the general point is nowhere expressed more cogently than in the overtures made by Louis IX to Charles of Anjou in 1267, when the great Capetian was preparing his last crusade. He requested Charles to take the Cross 'to give example and encouragement to other men, and to dismay the more the enemies of the faith by the renown of your name'.[97] There can be little doubt that the secular and religious leaders of the Latin East fully appreciated the workings of Western social structures and knew that in seeking aid for themselves the commitment of the very highest was critical, both as *crucesignati* and as providers of money and men.[98]

There were also strong dynastic reasons why Henry III and Edward I might have been expected to lend their support to the Latin East. It has already been noted that Henry II was the grandson of

[95] *Dipl. Docs.* i. No. 385; *Anc. Corr.* 55. 2; *Foedera*, I. i. 395.

[96] The majority of the letters were sent to them: eight to Henry, and thirty-five or thirty-seven to Edward, the discrepancy arising from the letters sent to the king of Armenia by Sultan al-Ashraf Khalil on the fall of Tripoli and Acre, appearing in Cotton, *Hist.*, pp. 215–17, 217–19; *Reg. Pontissara*, pp. 481–2. Probably, but not certainly, King Hethoum dispatched copies to Edward I. They are included in appendix 1.

[97] *Layettes du Trésor des Chartes: Inventaire et documents publiés par la Direction des Archives*, ed. A. Teulet *et al.* 5 vols. (Paris, 1863–1909), iv. No. 5286.

[98] Popes certainly did. See e.g. Nicholas IV's bull to Edward I of Mar. 1291. *Foedera*, I. ii. 748; *Reg. Nicholas IV*, No. 6667.

King Fulk of Jerusalem.[99] Although the strength of this particular bond was weakened by the death of Baldwin IV and the end of the direct line of Angevin kings of Jerusalem, a close tie to the ruling house was maintained since Baldwin's sister, Sibyl, married Guy de Lusignan, king of Jerusalem (1186–92) and lord of Cyprus (1192–4). Guy's elder brother, Amalric, succeeded in both states and from him and from the offspring of his wife Isabella's previous marriages descended the lines which ruled in Cyprus and Jerusalem in the thirteenth century. Unquestionably this tie was diluted over time, but the link was reinforced when in 1220 Henry III's mother, Isabella of Angoulême, herself of a crusading family, married as her second husband Hugh X de Lusignan. He was the head of the Western branch of the family and nephew of both King Guy and King Amalric II. Hugh's sons, the notorious Lusignans in England, were very close to their uterine brother, Henry III, and may well have influenced him in the matter of the crusade. There were, synchronically, other connections as well. In particular, John de Brienne, titular king of Jerusalem, married as his third wife a great-granddaughter of Henry II, Berengaria of Castile. Their daughter Maria married Emperor Baldwin II of Constantinople, thereby establishing a remote tie with Henry III. In the next generation Edward I married Eleanor, Berengaria's niece.[100] It is, of course, one thing to show that kinship existed but quite another to demonstrate that such links could act as a positive motivation towards action on behalf of the Latin East, not least because the noble houses of the Latin world were so closely linked by an intimate web of marriage alliances. For this reason the more remote ties are of particular interest, and it is revealing that, in relation to one of the more tenuous, Henry III should refer to Maria, Baldwin II's empress, explicitly as his kinswoman when he granted 200*l.* to her in 1260.[101] Such ties clearly could count for something.

These connections gained sharper point from the fact that Henry III and Edward I were heirs to houses with traditions of pilgrimage and crusade to Jerusalem. The Plantagenet house, narrowly perceived as the counts of Anjou, included that Fulk who became king of Jerusalem in 1131 following an earlier pilgrimage in 1119. His notorious predecessor, Fulk Nerra, went on pilgrimage to Jerusalem at least

[99] That the relationship meant something to Henry is suggested by Howden, *Gesta*, i. 116, who reports that Henry proposed in 1176 to go to the East or send aid to Baldwin IV, 'his kinsman'.

[100] See appendix 6.

[101] *CLR 1251–60*, p. 505. Significantly, Paris, *CM* iv. 626, reports that when Baldwin II came to England in 1247 he declared himself Henry's kinsman, so as to find greater favour.

twice before 1040 in expiation of his exceptionally anti-social sins.[102] There was also an inherited Norman tradition. Duke Richard III sent money to Jerusalem; his brother and successor Robert I died on pilgrimage to the Holy Land in 1035; Robert's grandson, Robert II, was of course the leader of the Norman contingent on the First Crusade.[103] These ancestral precedents were somewhat remote by the thirteenth century but the examples of Henry II, Young Henry, Richard I, and John were close to hand. All had taken the Cross at some point in their reigns. Only Richard set out for the East in person, but his performance on the Third Crusade was an inspiring precedent for Henry III and Edward I to follow.

It is not surprising that the papacy and the rulers of the Latin East sought occasionally to give these ties explicit recruitment value. In 1185 Lucius III penned the first papal appeal along these lines, stressing the deeds of Henry II's ancestors in the East, whose inhabitants, he wrote, had come to regard the Plantagenet house as a patron, especially in times of adversity.[104] The theme of dynastic obligation was to be repeated occasionally in the thirteenth century.[105] By then, of course, additional pressure could be brought to bear with timely reminders of the illustrious crusading deeds of Richard I which it was hoped his successors would seek to emulate. In 1223, for example, in the course of an appeal to Henry III, Honorius III stressed the memory of Richard and the belief that his name still struck terror in the minds of the Saracens. The Holy Land awaited the advent of his nephew; the Saracens feared the coming of his successor.[106] Bohemund VI of Antioch sent perhaps the most forceful appeal of this type in 1255, combining flattery with the observation

[102] Henry II's aunt, Sibyl of Anjou, provided another link. She accompanied her husband, Count Thierry of Flanders, on the Second Crusade and again in 1157. She remained in the Holy Land, entering the convent of Bethany. See Runciman, *History*, ii. 178 n., 262, 367.

[103] From Eleanor of Aquitaine came a further tradition. Both Henry III and Edward I married into houses with crusading forbears.

[104] Howden, *Gesta*, i. 332–3; id., *Chron.* ii. 299–300. Lucius issued the bull following deliberations in Nov. 1184 with Patriarch Eraclius of Jerusalem, who brought the bull to Henry. It may reflect the arguments of Eraclius and other Easterners, rather than Lucius's independent thinking. Manuel Comnenus sent the first known appeal of this type in 1176, following the disastrous battle of Myriocephalon. He stressed the connections between his house and Henry's dynasty. See Howden, *Gesta*, i. 128–30; id., *Chron.* ii. 102–4; Ralph de Diceto, *Opera historica*, ed. W. Stubbs, 2 vols. (RS; 1876), i. 416–18.

[105] See e.g. *Dipl. Docs.* i. No. 268; *Reg. Innocent IV*, No. 6072. The theme is also found in petitions on behalf of specific institutions in the East; e.g. the bishop of Acre's letter to Henry III in 1261 concerning the Order of St Thomas of Acre: *Dipl. Docs.* i. No. 343; *Anc. Corr.* 47. 27.

[106] *Foedera*, I. i. 172–3; *Reg. Honorius III*, No. 4262.

that it was only appropriate that Henry should emulate Richard, having succeeded him in virtue as well as by hereditary right.[107]

With Edward I on the throne the emphasis appears to have shifted, the stress upon ancestral deeds and dynastic memory giving way to hope projected upon the individual in his own right—the former crusader who would yet return to the Holy Land. As Martin IV for one reminded him in 1283, he had seen for himself the lamentable condition of Outremer; he also owed a personal debt of gratitude to God for his survival of the famous attempt to assassinate him at Acre in 1272.[108] The hope projected upon him was encouraged by his own expressed desire to return to the East as early as 1275. The master of the Hospital could with reason claim in a letter to Edward in 1282 that 'vos estes le prince de crestienté qui plus avés à cuer le fait de la Terre Seinte et qui l'avés plus demostré par euvre . . .'[109] That Edward received such attention from the East in the course of his reign is no surprise then, especially as he continued to inflate hopes that he would duly depart once again on crusade.[110] And Edward was evidently eager to keep in touch with events in the East,[111] even requesting certain agencies to keep him regularly informed of developments. In 1282 Joseph de Chauncy, his friend and erstwhile treasurer, prefaced his account of the battle of Homs by recalling that Edward had instructed him to continue to send news from the Holy Land as events occurred.[112] Henry III may have been the passive recipient of news; this does not appear to have been the case with his crusading son.

The Wider Flow of News

The determination of the inhabitants of the Latin East and their allies to elucidate their plight and procure aid is, then, quite apparent, but their efforts need to be placed in a wider context, for news concerning the crusade and developments in the East entered England along

[107] 'Burton', pp. 369–71; *Foedera*, I. i. 321.

[108] *Reg. Martin IV*, No. 286; *CCR 1279–88*, pp. 235–6; *Foedera*, I. ii. 624. In ?1275 the master of the Temple made the same point: 'Lettres inédites', ed. Kohler and Langlois, No. 2. Edward apparently presented his second crusading vow of 1287 partly in terms of gratitude to God for his narrow escape at Acre: *Reg. Nicholas IV*, No. 6800; *Foedera*, I. ii. 749–50.

[109] *Cart. Gen. Hosp.* iii. No. 3781; *Anc. Corr.* 18. 139.

[110] See below, pp. 232–6.

[111] In 1304, e.g., he specifically requested the master of the Temple to send him a report: *CCR 1302–7*, p. 208.

[112] *Cart. Gen. Hosp.* iii. No. 3782. Other examples of Edward's desire to hear news include *Anc. Corr.* 18. 136, 137.

many other channels too. Letters are certainly the easiest to trace. Appendix 3 calendars those letters containing information relating to events, categorized according to principals, known to have been sent to English correspondents during the period of this study: from crusaders on campaign, the papacy, diplomatic contacts, and other Western correspondents with access to news.

Twenty-one letters sent directly to English correspondents by crusaders on campaign have been identified, but this figure can only represent chance survival.[113] All but five survive in narrative sources, suggesting that the writers who preserve them, abstracted or *in extenso*, regarded them as ready-made narratives of the expedition in question. Scores of letters of this type must have been lost simply because there was no one concerned to record them.[114]

An extensive international exchange of news is suggested by the reports forwarded to English correspondents by other Westerners. The picture, again, is distorted by our dependence upon the narrative sources, especially Matthew Paris, but there is every reason to suppose that the transmission of news, especially between courts, was both frequent and close. From survivals it appears that the Capetian and Hohenstaufen courts played a major part in forwarding news to the Plantagenets. Frederick II, for example, was plainly anxious to keep the Plantagenets informed of developments.[115] Less exalted persons were also involved in this exchange. Of particular interest is the letter of 1244–5 copied in the Melrose chronicle.[116] The recipients, John and Andrew, were probably somewhere in Scotland or England, perhaps Melrose itself, and the archdeacon either in Rome or elsewhere in the West.[117] He refers them to a letter being carried to Louis IX by the prior of the Hospital, written not in ink but in blood, he says, so terrible is the news. Although he had not seen the letter himself, he knew others who had, and he proceeded to give a

[113] Some conclude with the promise of further news, e.g. the letter of Earl William de Ferrers to Bishop Peter des Roches in 1219: *Royal and Other Historical Letters Illustrative of the Reign of Henry III*, ed. W. W. Shirley, 2 vols. (RS; 1862, 1866), i. 24; *Dipl. Docs.* i. No. 30. Others refer to letters now lost, e.g. Richard of Cornwall's letter of 1241: Paris, *CM* iv. 138–44.

[114] None concerns 'lesser' expeditions, such as Otto de Grandson's in the 1290s, suggesting perhaps that these did not command chroniclers' attention in the way that an international *passagium generale* could. No further letters appear after 1271, perhaps an indication of waning chronicler interest in the crusade.

[115] Wendover, *Flores*, iv. 187–93; Paris, *CM* iii. 173–6, 300–5; and letters mentioned in *CR 1227–31*, p. 93; *Foedera*, I. i. 187. He also informed Henry of his own initiatives in the East and his further plans to go on crusade. See e.g. Paris, *CM* iv. 26–9; and further above, n. 78.

[116] *Chron. Mailros*, p. 163.

[117] Proven by the writer's reference 'de rumoribus ultra marinis'.

summary of its calamitous contents: the military disaster of La Forbie at the hands of the Khwarizmian Turks and Baibars—'Ecce luctus et lamentatio!' The letter indicates how news received in Europe could be passed on informally before, or parallel to, the arrival of 'official' dispatches from the East.[118] Proctors and agents maintained at foreign courts also contributed to the flow of information, but only occasionally can this be glimpsed.[119] Nevertheless, the volume of news travelling along these channels was probably considerable. The papal Curia, in particular, must have acted as a major clearing-house. From Eastern nuncios arriving there English agents doubtless picked up a great deal of information which they then transmitted back home.

News spread by word of mouth completed the complex of communications linking England to the Latin East. Anyone, of course, could act as an informal bearer of news: returning crusaders and merchants, envoys, members of the military orders, and so forth. Among the inhabitants of the Latin states themselves were the alms collectors sent to England by their establishments in Outremer. They undoubtedly exploited the promotional value of news as an integral part of their craft. The evidence suggests that they were a familiar part of the English scene.[120] Mercantile connections also functioned as channels of news, although English involvement in Eastern commerce was probably limited.[121] Nevertheless, we hear of various English merchants operating out of Acre and elsewhere, and from English material comes evidence of visits by merchants of Outremer.[122] More exalted members of Eastern society visited England in various capacities. Archbishop Simon of Tyre came in 1217 and the lord of Haifa, John de Valenciennes, in 1263–4. Both

[118] For another example, see Paris, *CM* v. 165–9. In 1240 Amaury de Montfort's wife passed on to Richard of Cornwall the news received from Amaury in the Holy Land: ibid. iv. 25.

[119] See appendix 3. Apart from the principals there given, others of course maintained proctors abroad. For Richard of Cornwall's, see N. Denholm-Young, *Richard of Cornwall* (Oxford, 1947), 39–40. The letter from his chancellor in 1250 concerning the battle of Mansourah is suggestive: Paris, *CM* v. 165–9.

[120] Their presence is often known only through papal letters or episcopal licences on their behalf. See e.g. *Reg. Innocent IV*, No. 480, for collectors for the church of Bethlehem, 1245; *The Registers of Walter Bronescombe and Peter Quivil, Bishops of Exeter*, ed. F. C. Hingeston-Randolph (London, 1889), 20, 192, for collectors for the Order of St Thomas, and for the brethren of St Lazarus, 1258. For the Crown's role, see below, Ch. 6, n. 184.

[121] W. Heyd, *Histoire du Commerce du Levant*, trans. F. Reynaud, 2 vols. (Leipzig, 1936), i. 725–7.

[122] Ibid. 319, 422. Merchants of Acre are mentioned, e.g. in *CPR 1247–58*, p. 664; *CPR 1258–66*, p. 80; *CPR 1272–81*, pp. 20, 50. For one James of Antioch, merchant, see *PR 1216–25*, p. 501.

were employed in unsuccessful negotiations between the warring parties in England at those times.[123] Following the fall of Acre, Bishop Bernard of Tripoli was sent to England by Nicholas IV in 1291 on the business of the Holy Land.[124] Others visited in a private capacity. The English bishop of Tortosa, reports Paris, returned home to visit his parents in 1249.[125] At least three prelates, driven from their sees, were granted asylum in England: Bishop Augustine of Latakia, Archbishop William of Edessa, and Bishop Hugh of Gibelet.[126] That such individuals were bearers of news and information has generally to be assumed, but in some cases their role can be demonstrated. The Lanercost chronicler specifically states that much of his information concerning the fall of Tripoli in 1289 was obtained from Bishop Hugh of Gibelet.[127] According to Paris, the bishop of Tortosa reported on events in Syria and Egypt at the Council of Reading, 1249.[128]

Westerners in general and Englishmen in particular must also have been important in this oral transmission. Apart from returning crusaders specific mention may be made of the clergy whom business took abroad.[129] A considerable number of Englishmen attended the Lateran Council, 1215, and the Councils of Lyons I and II, either in their own right or as proctors, and as the business of the crusade was central to the agenda of each, these men would have returned with some substantial knowledge of events in the East.[130] General councils were rare; a more regular dispatch of news resulted from the system of assemblies held by individual religious orders. The general chapters of the Cistercians may be singled out as their role in transmitting news can be effectively demonstrated. Ralph of Coggeshall provides by far the most detailed English narrative of the Fourth Crusade, chiefly because of letters which two of the leaders, Baldwin of

123 *RHGF* xix. 636–7, for Simon; see below, ch. 4, n. 51, for John.

124 *Reg. Nicholas IV*, No. 7632; Cotton, *Hist.*, pp. 223–6.

125 Paris, *CM* v. 72.

126 See below, p. 241 and n. 191.

127 *Chronicon de Lanercost, 1201–1346*, ed. J. Stevenson (Bannatyne Club; 1839), 130.

128 Paris, *CM* v. 72; and ibid. iii. 161, 164, for information supplied by visiting Armenians in 1228 and 1252, on whom, further, ibid. v. 116.

129 For random examples of news received by chroniclers from returning crusaders, see *Chron. Lanercost*, p. 89; *Chron. Mailros*, p. 241; 'Margam', p. 36. Amongst other cases, Paris, *CM* v. 81, reports that Archbishop Boniface of Canterbury first brought news to England of the fall of Damietta to Louis IX on Boniface's return to England in Sept. 1249.

130 For those attending see *Councils*, II. i. 48, 402; II. ii. 810. Some dispatched progress reports to English correspondents. The frequent journeys on business to Rome also provided a means of transmission of news. Archbishop Boniface, hearing of the 1261 Mongol offensive, dispatched Walter de Reigate home to summon a council to discuss the matter: *Flores Historiarum*, ed. H. R. Luard, 3 vols. (RS; 1890), ii. 465.

Flanders and Hugh of St-Pol, sent to Cîteaux.[131] Ralph must have seen copies or abstracts of these letters, perhaps forwarded to his own house from Cîteaux or brought back from the general chapter by one of his conventual fellows. Paris, too, underlines the role of the Cistercians as bearers of news, observing that those returning from both the 1251 and 1252 chapters spread reports of events in Egypt and Syria.[132] English brethren of other orders, too, were doubtless apprised of news by their colleagues elsewhere.[133]

There can be little doubt, then, that communications between England and Outremer were close and frequent, and that the volume of news reaching England through these various channels was considerable. It remains to consider how far this news was then disseminated and to what overt promotional purposes it may have been put. First, certain types of news cannot have been widely publicized; for example, the confidential reports supplied by diplomatic agents to their principals at home probably remained confined to very limited circles. Second, many reports were probably not intended anyway for distribution by those who sent them. The letters sent by the military orders, for example, to their English houses or to the Plantagenet court were essentially private correspondence, as were the dispatches sent back by crusaders on campaign to their kinsmen or those appointed to safeguard their interests. Yet material clearly could spread far and wide, either informally or by design. In some cases the recipient may have taken it upon himself to publicize or pass on the news which he received. The correspondence of Adam Marsh, for example, illustrates well the way in which news could pass around members of a particular circle. Adam was himself kept well-informed of the progress of Louis IX's first crusade, the Pastoureaux movement in France which sprang up in response to his defeat, and events in the East in general. He received transcripts of letters sent to the West by Louis and Odo de Châteauroux, the crusading legate, and copies of letters sent by the papacy to the archbishop of Canterbury. These he passed to acquaintances such as Earl Simon de Montfort, Bishop Robert Grosseteste, and William of Nottingham, provincial minister of the Franciscans in England. They, in turn, can be observed forwarding transcripts of letters which they had received from various sources.[134] Further evidence of this informal distribution of news is to

131 Ralph of Coggeshall, *Chronicon Anglicanum*, ed. J. Stevenson (RS; 1875), 151.

132 Paris, *CM* v. 257, 306.

133 The regular journeys of members of the military orders to and from the East must also have provided a major channel of news. Some idea of the scale of their movements can be gained from the frequent royal grants of protections and safe conducts enrolled in Chancery.

134 *Monumenta Franciscana*, ed. J. S. Brewer and R. Howlett, 2 vols. (RS; 1858,

be found in the chronicles. Matthew Paris, for example, includes the text of a letter sent by the Templar Nicholas de la Hyde to the abbot of St Albans in 1249, in which Nicholas forwarded news of the capture of Damietta and the report, false as it turned out, that Cairo and Alexandria had also fallen to Louis IX.[135]

The appearance of so many letters in English chronicles of the period prompts the question as to how far news was intentionally distributed by certain agencies to a wider audience, because very few of these letters were directed specifically to the house in question.[136] Since some chroniclers clearly made it their business to gain access to news, and in so doing naturally exploited those of their contacts in receipt of letters, the appearance of many letters can be explained quite simply in terms of personal connections.[137] The presence of others in these sources, however, argues for a process of active dissemination within England, as in the West generally, at the behest of the papacy. For popes were no less aware than the inhabitants of the Latin East and their allies of the promotional value of news, and study of crusading bulls reveals that they generally prefaced their appeals, in *narratio–exhortatio* form, by setting out the current news and underlining the need for aid. However, it is unlikely that these bulls were commonly intended as primary sources of news, for most refer only briefly to recent events and appear to assume prior knowledge on the part of their recipients.[138] Rather, they reminded men of particulars to be learned primarily from other sources, and in this process of transmission the papacy itself played an important distributive role. In

1882), i. Nos. 17, 22–4, 26, 143–5, 181. It is suggestive of the dissemination of news that in No. 143, to Earl Simon, Marsh states that he is sending transcripts of papal letters lest 'aut famae relatio aut signatio litterae nondum ad vos usque detulerit'. For another telling observation concerning dissemination, see *Dipl. Docs.* i. No. 248; *Anc. Corr.* 6. 63; *Cart. Gen. Hosp.* iv. No. 1982.

135 Paris, *CM* vi. No. 86. For another case see Edmund of Verdun's letter to Prior Richard of Christ Church, Canterbury, regarding the assault upon Acre, 1291, in HMC, *Reports: Various Collections I* (London, 1901), 261.

136 The importance of the chroniclers in preserving letters is evident from appendices 1 and 3.

137 Paris, e.g., secured many of his materials from contacts in the royal administration, and from men such as Richard of Cornwall, Walter de St Martin, and the preceptor of the Temple, in receipt of letters concerning the crusade and the East. See Vaughan, *Matthew Paris*, esp. pp. 13–18 on his sources. Some chroniclers may have been passive recipients of materials. Diceto, for one, was known by William Longchamp to be composing a chronicle; accordingly William sent him, in 1196, a copy of a letter concerning the death of Conrad de Montferrat in the East for Diceto's use: Diceto, *Opera*, ii. 127–8.

138 Some chroniclers, however, regarded the more informative bulls as ready-made narratives of events. Thus Guisborough, *Chron.*, pp. 231–2, copied the first part of Nicholas IV's crusading bull of 1291 on the fall of Acre, leaving off precisely where *narratio* gives way to *exhortatio*.

1227, for example, Gregory IX dispatched a circular to all the faithful in which he announced that he had received letters from Outremer. These were apparently transcribed in their entirety in the bull: open letters from the Patriarch Gerold and other dignitaries, containing an account of recent events in the East, the failure of Frederick II to meet his crusading obligations, and an appeal for further aid.[139] Similarly, in 1237 the Dominican priors in France and England were forwarded a letter sent to Gregory IX from Prior Philip of the Order of Preachers in the Holy Land. Therein Philip joyfully announced his successes in converting certain Nestorians to the Latin faith.[140] With this certain evidence of distribution it is possible to account for the presence of a number of other letters found in narrative sources. Matthew Paris, for example, preserves the text of a letter sent by the bishop of Marseilles to Innocent IV in 1249 reporting the supposed fall of Cairo to Louis IX's forces. It is revealing that it should have been noted at the end of the letter that 'These letters the lord pope received on the Sunday after the Feast of Holy Trinity.'[141] How was this known unless the pope had forwarded the letter under a covering note with a statement to this effect?[142]

If wide distribution was intended the papal chancery made transcripts and distributed them to metropolitans or other prelates in the first instance. It was then for them to set in motion the machinery for more local distribution which was used to disseminate crusading bulls and other materials, as we shall see.[143] That machinery can sometimes be glimpsed in operation. Adam Marsh, for example, once informed Simon de Montfort that the transcript of news he was sending had been received from the archbishop of Canterbury who, Adam reported, had sent copies to all the English prelates. The news in question was contained in a papal letter concerning the ravaging of Antioch and the Holy Land.[144] The same administrative machinery was seemingly employed to distribute copies of the letter of the patriarch of Jerusalem and others, sent to the prelates of France and

[139] Wendover, *Flores*, iv. 145–8.

[140] Paris, *CM* iii. 396–9. See also 'Dunstable', pp. 62, 69–74; *Chron. Lanercost*, p. 27; Walter of Coventry, *Memoriale fratris Walteri de Coventria: The Historical Collections of Walter of Coventry*, ed. W. Stubbs, 2 vols. (RS; 1872, 1873), ii. 240–3, for certain evidence of transmission to England via the papacy of news and prophecies from Damietta, 1219–21.

[141] Paris, *CM* vi. No. 87; compare v. 87, 118. The same letter, with the same note, appears in a Tewkesbury abbey register: BL Cotton Cleopatra A. vii, fos. 103v–104.

[142] Sometimes popes were urged to act. Thus in 1244 the patriarch of Jerusalem requested Innocent IV to send his own letters to Henry III and Louis IX regarding the disasters of that year: 'Burton', p. 262. See Paris, *CM* v. 306 for Cardinal John Tolet sending letters concerning events in the East to the Cistercian general chapter, 1252.

[143] See below, ch. 2.

[144] *Mon. Franciscana*, i. No. 143.

England reporting the calamitous events of 1244, which was brought to England by Bishop Waleran of Beirut and Friar Arnulph in 1245. One copy is in the Register of St Augustine's, Canterbury; another text is preserved by Matthew Paris.[145] Paris observes at the end of his text that 'Duodecim sigilla appensa fuerunt huic scripto originali; quod erat hujus exemplum.' From this helpful note it may be deduced that Paris copied from a transcript, perhaps that addressed to his own superior, the abbot of St Albans.

Finally, local preachers were expected to utilize news reports as they promoted the crusade. Sometimes the responsibility was made quite plain. In October 1266, for example, Clement IV instructed his legate in England, Ottobuono, and those employed with him, to preach upon the recent loss of Caesarea, Ashdod, and Safed to Baibars, and the decimation of Templar and Hospitaller ranks, precisely to excite all the faithful to vindicate these injuries.[146] If, then, news was widely disseminated as an integral part of promotional activity, and if reports, literary or oral, spread from contact to contact throughout society, it may be postulated that most Englishmen would have been exposed to a considerable amount of news and information. This can only have eased the overall task facing preachers of the crusade for successful promotion depended in part upon contemporary awareness of the plight of Outremer, its prospects, and the need for aid.

145 BL Additional MS 46352, fos. 50b–52b; Paris, *CM* iv. 337–44. The bishop of Marseilles's letter to the pope in 1249, concerning events of Louis IX's crusade, was probably handled in the same way. Copies are found in Paris, *CM* vi. No. 87; BL Cotton Cleopatra A. vii, fos. 103v–104.

146 *Reg. Clement IV*, No. 1146; *Thesaurus novus anecdotorum*, ed. E. Martène and U. Durand, 5 vols. (Paris, 1717), ii, cols. 422–3, No. 402.

2

PROMOTION OF THE CRUSADE (2)

In *Cor nostrum* of 1181 Alexander III called upon the faithful, especially *viri bellicosi*, to take the Cross or send aid to the Holy Land. A concurrent bull, *Cum orientalis terra*, instructed prelates to cause publication of *Cor nostrum* in all churches, to announce crusader privileges to all the faithful, and to expand upon them so that the faithful be moved to send aid.[1] Whether, or in what manner, the prelates acted upon these instructions does not appear, but this was seemingly the first crusading appeal to envisage energetic and systematic promotion locally in England. The twin devices of disseminating crusading bulls and related materials and of preaching locally became the chief components of promotional activity thereafter.

Dissemination of Crusading Bulls and Other Materials

To secure the wide publication of *Cor nostrum* Alexander III evidently envisaged the production and distribution of transcripts of the bull in England.[2] The task almost certainly fell to individual episcopal chanceries. This, at any rate, was the routine procedure in the thirteenth century. It is most effectively illustrated by the measures taken consequent to Nicholas IV's crusading call of 1291. The papal initiative began in March 1291, when Nicholas declared a new crusade and commissioned the archbishops of Canterbury and York, their suffragan bishops, and the provincial heads of the Dominicans and Franciscans to preach the Cross in England.[3] In August, on hearing of the assault upon Acre, Nicholas forwarded reissues of these bulls and shortly afterwards he wrote to the archbishop of Canterbury and all prelates of the province instructing that a provincial council be

[1] Roger of Howden (attrib. Benedict of Peterborough), *Gesta Regis Henrici Secundi Benedicti Abbatis*, ed. W. Stubbs, 2 vols. (RS; 1867), i. 272–5; id., *Chronica Rogeri de Houedene*, ed. W. Stubbs, 4 vols. (RS; 1868–71), ii. 255–9. For the shift in policy towards England under Alexander, see above, pp. 9–10.

[2] Howden, *Gesta*, i. 272–5; id., *Chron.* ii. 255–9.

[3] *Reg. Nicholas IV*, Nos. 6684–92; *Foedera*, I. ii. 748–50.

summoned to consider the means where by the Holy Land might best be aided. A concurrent bull contained proposals for the union of the Temple and Hospital, a matter to be discussed at the projected council.[4] The dissemination of these various materials can be observed, though only imperfectly, in practice.[5] Particularly instructive is the manner in which the bulls of August, those concerning the union of the orders and the holding of a provincial council, were disseminated. Upon their receipt on 21 December 1291, Archbishop Pecham forwarded them the very next day to Richard Gravesend, bishop of London, who was given the general responsibility of summoning a provincial council at the New Temple, London, on 13 February 1292. In accordance with this mandate, which he received on Christmas Day, Bishop Richard then instructed the bishops of the province to cite all prelates of churches within their dioceses to appear at the council on the appointed day. He enclosed transcripts of the papal bulls along with the covering instructions of Archbishop Pecham and himself.[6]

Richard's chancery acted as the central clearing house for the province of Canterbury in this matter. His clerks must have been very busy over Christmas and the days that followed, transcribing and dispatching these lengthy bulls and consequent instructions. Two of Richard's mandates have survived, those addressed to Ralph Walpole, bishop of Norwich, dated 26 December 1291, and to John de Pontoise, bishop of Winchester, dated 20 January 1292. In the case of the diocese of Norwich the process of dissemination can be pursued one stage further with the help of the chronicler and monk of Norwich, Bartholomew Cotton. On 31 December Bishop Ralph wrote to his own official, enclosing the instructions of Archbishop Pecham and Bishop Richard along with copies of the papal bulls. The official was to execute the business in the diocese and certify Bishop Ralph of subsequent developments by 2 February 1292. Whether the official then wrote to the prior of Norwich, from whom Bartholomew Cotton

[4] *Reg. Nicholas IV*, Nos. 6800–5, 7625; Bartholomew Cotton, *Historia Anglicana, necnon ejusdem Liber de archiepiscopis et episcopis Angliae*, ed. H. R. Luard (RS; 1859), 199–204; *Registrum Johannis de Pontissara, Episcopi Wyntoniensis, 1282–1304*, ed. C. Deedes, 2 vols. (Canterbury and York Soc. 19, 30; 1915, 1924) 474–6, 477–9; Walter of Guisborough, *The Chronicle of Walter of Guisborough, Previously Edited as the Chronicle of Walter of Hemingford or Hemingburgh*, ed. H. Rothwell (Camden Soc., 3rd ser. 89; 1957), 231–2. In accordance with papal mandate, Archbishop Romeyn of York also arranged for a provincial council in Dec. 1291: *The Register of John le Romeyn, Lord Archbishop of York, 1288–96*, ed. W. Brown, 2 vols. (Surtees Soc. 123, 128; 1913, 1916), ii. 13; *Historical Papers and Letters from the Northern Registers*, ed. J. Raine (RS; 1873), 96.

[5] For one bishop's authentication of the proclamation of Mar. 1291, and the preaching commission of the archbishop of York and suffragans, see *Records of Antony Bek, Bishop and Patriarch, 1283–1311*, ed. C. M. Fraser (Surtees Soc. 162; 1953), 26–7.

[6] Cotton, *Hist.*, pp. 199–205; *Councils*, II. ii. 1100–3; *Reg. Pontissara*, pp. 477–9.

derived the materials which he inserted in his text, or whether the chronicler himself utilized the bishop's archive—which he certainly did on occasion—is unclear.[7] Nevertheless, it is quite apparent that it was for the official to arrange the production and distribution of copies of the bulls within the diocese of Norwich. A similar procedure must have been instituted in the other dioceses.

The system that we can glimpse in operation in 1291–2 illuminates the clear chain of communication and administrative measures leading downward from the papal Curia. The efficiency and speed with which the materials were disseminated within England at the time is certainly striking, but the procedures were not in any way novel or exceptional in 1291–2. It just happens that in this particular case we can, for once, trace the workings of the system in some detail through its various stages. This means of systematic dissemination of crusading bulls and other materials was complemented by the activities of preachers in the field, for one of their chief duties lay in reciting and expanding upon crusading bulls, a responsibility occasionally made explicit in papal mandates.[8] It is further apparent from the instructions of individual prelates to those whom they delegated to preach in their dioceses.[9]

The evident importance of this sort of publicity to the success of recruitment drives is underlined by the Crown's active role in the process of disseminating materials on two occasions, in the early 1250s and in 1291–2. Since the king, on each occasion, had taken the Cross and was making preparations to depart for the East, he doubtless considered that by lending his support in this way a greater response in men, but above all in money, would be stimulated. Perhaps the clearest evidence of the Crown's role lies in the instructions sent to the executors of the Cross in England in December 1252. Henry III forwarded the tenor of papal letters 'de negotio Crucis Christi', and requested that they transmit them to the archbishops and bishops of England and Wales, and to other prelates as they saw fit, enjoining them to cause the letters to be solemnly published and expounded throughout their dioceses. In this case it was for the prelates to produce copies in their own chanceries for local distribution, but the initial royal stimulus is plain.[10] Shortly before, in November 1252,

[7] Cotton, *Hist.*, pp. 199–205; *Councils*, II. ii. 1100–3.

[8] See e.g. Innocent IV's instructions in Apr. 1250 for preaching: *Foedera*, I. i. 272–3. The local diocesan clergy also had a part to play. See below, pp. 51–2.

[9] See e.g. *Records A. Bek*, pp. 27–8, for the duties laid upon the prior of Durham and the dean of Chester-le-Street in promoting the crusade in Durham diocese, 1291. See also Godfrey Giffard's observations concerning the friars' duties in 1275: Hereford and Worcester County Record Office, Register of Godfrey Giffard, BA 2648/1 (i), fo. 61d.

[10] *CR 1251–3*, pp. 437–8. The enrolment is specified 'De litteris domini Pape promulgandis'. In June 1250 Henry laid down instructions for the publication of the

Henry had instructed the prior of the Hospital in England to deliver without delay to the executors 'instruments touching the business of the Cross in England . . . through which they might be more fully certified of the state of the Holy Land'.[11] It looks as if Henry was seeking to press into promotional service the newsletters which the prior may be presumed to have received recently concerning the East.

Henry also sought to ensure wide publication of his own pronouncements concerning recruitment to his projected crusade. In July 1252, for example, proclamation was made that all *crucesignati* setting out with the king would have a moratorium on any debts owing to the Jews, that all would enjoy speedy justice in the royal courts, and that no *crucesignatus* should be compelled to pay more in redemption of his vow than he had promised on its assumption. The archbishop of York was to communicate this grant to his suffragans and to publish it throughout his province by the friars and others deputed to the business of the Cross. The bishop of Chichester received similar instructions, and since he was one of the executors of the Cross at the time, it would seem that he was intended to cause publication throughout the realm.[12]

Development and Organization of Preaching

Bare recitation of crusader privileges and other pronouncements were not enough. In addition, energetic and effective preaching to whip up enthusiasm was required if men were to be moved to commit themselves to the crusade. Alexander III made the point succinctly in *Cum orientalis terra* for all prelates of churches, apart from announcing crusader privileges, were to admonish the faithful to set out on crusade 'that through your solicitude and exhortation that land may experience the aid and assistance of the faithful . . .'[13]

Cum orientalis terra may be regarded as inaugurating a process of evolution in the preaching of the crusade that extended through the later twelfth century and into the thirteenth. It consisted both of the

tenor of papal bulls, conferring crusader privileges upon him, throughout the lordship of Ireland. In this case, the royal chancery had been busy producing transcripts: *CR 1247–51*, p. 358; *Foedera*, I. i. 274.

[11] *CR 1251–3*, p. 281.

[12] Ibid. 231. In Nov. 1252 these concessions, expressed in greater detail, were authorized for extensive publication by the friars. They were renewed in 1254: *CPR 1247–58*, p. 164. For Edward I's involvement in the promotion of his projected crusade in 1291, see esp. *Issues of the Exchequer* (*Extracts, Hen. III–39 Hen. VI*), trans. F. Devon (London, 1837), 105–6.

[13] Howden, *Gesta*, i. 272–5; id., *Chron.* ii. 255–9.

progressive harnessing of the personnel and organization of the Church in England to preaching, and of the growth of an appropriate central administration in England to supervise and control the local preaching effort. It is not, however, easy to reconstruct this development in its entirety, for the evidence is fragmentary and often inconclusive. This patchiness makes analysis difficult and certain conclusions tentative, but the broad outlines of development and organization are clear enough.

The basic foundations of the entire system were first laid down in a period of experimentation in the years 1195–1213, and the system which prevailed after 1213 probably grew largely out of the lessons learned from this previous experience. Up until 1195 responsibility for promotion appears to have rested solely upon individual prelates, mandated in a general way to impress the cause of the crusade upon their flocks. There is no sign of a central co-ordinating authority in England iself, and in the bulls associated with the call to the Third Crusade there is no indication of a clear chain of command. Much depended in the circumstances upon individual commitment and initiative, and preaching must have been patchy and often incoherent. It is suggestive of the situation that Gerald of Wales observes that when Archbishop Baldwin of Canterbury's preaching tour of Wales in 1188 reached Oswestry they found little to do because Bishop Reiner of St Asaph had already been active in the area.[14] Other prelates doubtless shirked the task.[15] The need for greater efficiency and the advantages of instituting some form of centralized control combined to bring about a change, but change was rendered more pressing by other considerations. The demoralizing effect of the failure of the Third Crusade served to increase scepticism and criticism of the crusade, in some quarters at least.[16] The papacy probably sought to counter its effects by stepping up the promotional effort. Moreover, it was at this time that indulgences for pecuniary contributions to the crusade first became established, and to apply those indulgences and to collect the proceeds an appropriate form of

[14] Gerald of Wales, *Opera*, ed. J. S. Brewer *et al.* 8 vols. (RS; 1861–91), vi. 142.

[15] Peter of Blois, shortly before this, had urged preaching of the crusade, denouncing those who failed in their duty: *Patrologiae cursus completus: Series Latina*, comp. J. P. Migne, 221 vols. (Paris, 1844–64), ccvii, cols. 529–34; and see R. W. Southern, 'Peter of Blois and the Third Crusade', in H. Mayr-Harting and R. I. Moore (eds.), *Studies in Medieval History Presented to R. H. C. Davis* (London, 1985), esp. pp. 213–14.

[16] For some English opinion, see in particular 'Itinerarium Peregrinorum et Gesta Regis Ricardi', in *Chronicles and Memorials of the Reign of Richard I*, ed. W. Stubbs, 2 vols. (RS; 1864, 1865), i. 439–40; and the uneasy reflections of William of Newburgh, 'Historia rerum Anglicarum', in *Chronicles of the Reigns of Stephen, Henry II, and Richard I*, ed. R. Howlett, 2 vols. (RS; 1884, 1885), i. 374–5, 379–80.

administration was required. The 1190s also saw the first systematic inquiries regarding the fulfilment of vows. This again necessitated more effective control at the centre.[17]

In 1195 Celestine III took the first step towards the creation of a general executive office for the business of the Cross in England. He instructed Archbishop Hubert Walter of Canterbury, and all prelates within the province, to preach the Cross, and in addition Hubert was required to urge the crusade upon Richard I and to undertake a preaching tour of the *provincia Anglicana*. Prelates were to receive him honourably and obey his mandates concerning this business.[18] From his terms of reference it is clear that Hubert was given overall executive charge, but although he acted as the first general executor of the business of the Cross in England he was not, apparently, accorded the title *eo nomine*. Presumably it was subsumed in his more general legatine powers in England at the time. Innocent III's legacy in this matter, as in so many others, was ultimately to prove decisive. At first, for the campaign initiated in 1198, he split the provinces of Canterbury and York and appointed two separate executors for each.[19] In April 1213, however, he returned to the model of 1195, combining again the two provinces and setting three executors over the whole.[20] In common with their colleagues appointed elsewhere in the West they were given general responsibility for executing current promotional policy.[21] They were themselves to preach and cause preaching of the Cross, set up chests to receive alms from the laity and clergy in aid of the Holy Land and deposit the proceeds, ensure that liturgical activities on behalf of the Holy Land were implemented, and in every way to promote the cause to the full. They were to inform the pope of their progress through annual reports.[22] The magnitude of the task clearly lay beyond the capacities of the executors alone. As we have seen, Hubert Walter in 1195 was to enjoy the obedience of prelates to his commands concerning promotion of the crusade, and for the 1198 campaign the executors were authorized to associate a Templar and an Hospitaller with them in their work. In 1213,

[17] See above, pp. 17, 22.

[18] Ralph of Diceto, *Opera historica*, ed. W. Stubbs, 2 vols. (RS; 1876), ii. 132–5.

[19] *CLI*, Nos. 38–9; Howden, *Chron.* iv. 70–5.

[20] *CLI*, Nos. 917–18; *Patrologiae Latina*, ccxvi, cols. 817–22, 822–3; C. R. Cheney, *Innocent III and England* (Stuttgart, 1976), 263.

[21] Innocent describes them as holding legatine office, but like their German counterparts they were probably delegates only for the business of the Cross. See P. B. Pixton, 'Die Anwerbung des Heeres Christi: Prediger des Fünften Kreuzzuges in Deutschland', *Deutsches Archiv*, xxxiv (1978), 172–3.

[22] *Patrologiae Latina*, ccxvi, cols. 817–22, 822–3, 906–7. For the first time, apparently, guidelines were laid down for the performance of their duties. In essence, they were to act and comport themselves in such ways as would not prejudice their success.

however, the executors were for the first time accorded the unambiguous power to co-opt and appoint their own delegates from amongst the English clergy as they saw fit. This was probably in response to difficulties which had arisen in this connection in previous campaigns.

The evidence for the 1213 campaign further suggests that for the first time the realm was systematically subdivided for promotional purposes according to individual dioceses and archdeaconries.[23] Delegates were then appointed, under the control of one of the executors, to each distinct unit of administration, and charged with the due implementation of decreed measures. Only one of these delegates is known: Richard de Morins, prior of Dunstable, who acted, we are told, in Huntingdonshire, Bedfordshire, and Hertfordshire.[24] The compactness of Richard's area of jurisdiction invites discussion because at first sight it would appear, if his delegation was typical, that England was divided up according to units of secular administration into blocks of contiguous shires, a delegate appointed to each block. It is extremely unlikely, however, that ecclesiastical units were ignored as the basis of organization, and the reference in the annals of Dunstable probably refers in reality to archdeaconries and rural deaneries. The county of Bedford was conterminous with the archdeaconry of Bedford, the archdeaconry of Huntingdon comprised Huntingdonshire and the greater part of Hertfordshire, whilst the remainder of Hertfordshire lay within the jurisdiction of the archdeacon of Middlesex.[25] If this surmise is correct, and if the realm was divided into three groups of dioceses and thence into archdeaconries—one executor supervising each group—then it may be concluded that Prior Richard was deputed to the two archdeaconries of Bedford and Huntingdon (both dioc. Lincoln), under the control of the executor concerned with the diocese of Lincoln. It follows that by Hertfordshire the annalist meant that part of the county falling within the archdeaconry of Huntingdon.

The procedures instituted in 1213 set the pattern for successive promotional campaigns in the thirteenth century. The available evidence indicates that henceforth Canterbury and York were treated together as one unit to be subdivided according to convenience. In

23 See esp. Ralph of Coggeshall, *Chronicon Anglicanum*, ed. J. Stevenson (RS; 1875), 168: 'three preachers were assigned to the three parts of England to collect arms, money and ships, and to sign men with the Cross to aid Jerusalem'. Also, 'Waverley', p. 281. Innocent apparently left the division to the executors to determine, but the precise demarcation eludes us.

24 'Dunstable', p. 40.

25 See A. H. Thompson, 'Diocesan Organization in the Middle Ages: Archdeacons and Rural Deans', *Proc. of the British Academy*, xxix (1943), 165.

one sense, however, the 1213 arrangement stands out because thereafter it was customary for one executor, or more commonly two, to be appointed with powers over the whole English Church to oversee the business of the Cross.[26] Only once again (May 1254–May 1255) were three executors appointed, when the bishops of Norwich and Chichester and the abbot of Westminster held office. For this term, happily, there survives the only detailed information regarding the way in which the realm was precisely administered for promotional purposes. On the Patent Roll for 1254 a memorandum records that in the London parliament, held three weeks after Easter, the three executors

> divided the provinces of Canterbury and York between them as follows, to wit, the bishop of Norwich to take the diocese of London except the archdeaconry of Middlesex, Ely, Norwich, Lincoln, Coventry and Lichfield, cities and dioceses, and the whole province of York in England: the bishop of Chichester to take Canterbury, Rochester, Chichester and Winchester, cities and dioceses: the abbot of Westminster to take Salisbury, Bath and Wells, Worcester, Exeter, Hereford, St. David's, Llandaff, Bangor and St. Asaph, cities and dioceses, and the archdeaconry of Middlesex.[27]

This precise territorial assignation may only have been *ad hoc*; it need not represent an older division going back to the campaign of 1213. Nevertheless, practicalities dictated some form of division, according to dioceses and archdeaconries, for every campaign in the thirteenth century, regardless of the size of the central executive board. The system, not surprisingly, was broadly similar to that utilized in the assessment of crusading tenths and other taxes in the thirteenth century, reflecting that close institutional relationship between promotion and the raising of moneys which became so marked a feature of papal crusading policy.[28]

From the terms of their commissions it is apparent that executors of the Cross were themselves expected to preach the crusade. Sometimes they can be observed in action. Richard de la Wych, the saintly bishop of Chichester, became co-executor with Master Hugh of St Edmunds, archdeacon of Colchester, in October 1250.[29] Both Ralph

[26] No clear pattern emerges as far as the personnel of executors is concerned. Relatively humble men might be appointed, such as Master Hugh of St Edmunds in 1250, but generally English prelates were deputed. The dispatch of papal legates could lead to complications and jurisdictional problems. For the details, see my 'English Society and the Crusade, 1216–1307', D.Phil. thesis (Oxford, 1983), 108–31.

[27] *CPR 1247–58*, p. 370. The unequal division is reflected in the expenses which the executors were to receive annually from the proceeds of the triennial tenth: the bishop of Norwich, 500*m.*, the bishop of Chichester, 200*m.*, the abbot of Westminster, 300*m.*

[28] See W. E. Lunt, *Financial Relations of the Papacy with England to 1327* (Cambridge, Mass.; 1939), esp. chs. 5, 6, 8.

[29] *Reg. Innocent IV*, No. 4872.

Bocking and John Capgrave refer in their *Lives* to Richard's preaching activities in the period immediately preceding his death in April 1253, though with tantalizing brevity. They record that he set out on a preaching tour from Chichester to Canterbury, 'per loca maritima transiens', but only three specific locations are mentioned: Chichester, Canterbury, and Dover.[30] The no less saintly Edmund Rich, the future archbishop of Canterbury, appears from his biographers to have been given general executive responsibility for promoting the crusade in England, in connection with Gregory IX's renewed recruitment effort, in 1231 or 1232.[31] Reference is made in the *Lives* to Edmund's preaching at Worcester, Leominster, Buckland (Som.), Oxford, Gloucester, and a few other places. They are specified only because miracles associated with his preaching occurred at these places, so he may have preached over a wider area. Nevertheless, only places in the western dioceses are recorded, perhaps indicating that Edmund took responsibility for promoting the crusade in those areas, whilst others acted elsewhere.[32]

Executors of the Cross must have been busy men. Even if they were keen to preach through personal aptitude and inclination, the extensive range and scope of their various responsibilities presumably exhausted much of their time and energies. They had of necessity to rely upon the services of deputies. Their powers to co-opt and depute members of the clergy as they saw fit eased their way in organizing promotional campaigns and implementing papal decree, but they were also assisted by the fact that popes generally commissioned

[30] John Capgrave, 'Vita S. Richardi Episcopi Cicestrensis', in *Acta Sanctorum quotquot toto urbe coluntur vel a catholicis scriptoribus celebrantur* (Antwerp, Brussels, 1643–), *April* i. cap. iii. 281; Ralph Bocking, 'Vita S. Richardi Episcopi Cicestrensis', ibid., caps. iv, vii. 295, 306. See also Peter of Peckham, 'La Vie Seint Richard', ed. A. T. Barker, in 'Vie de Saint Richard évêque de Chichester', *Revue des langues romanes*, liii (1910), pp. 245–396, esp. ll. 1187–274.

[31] See esp. Bertrand of Pontigny, 'Vita B. Edmundi', in *Thesaurus novus anecdotorum*, ed. E. Martène and U. Durand, 5 vols. (Paris, 1717), iii. col. 1799. He may have been employed as a preacher in the late 1220s, but more probably only in and after 1231–2. See C. H. Lawrence, *St. Edmund of Abingdon: A Study in Hagiography and History* (London, 1960), 123, 129; *DNB* vi. 407. Nicholas Trevet, *Annales sex Regum Angliae 1135–1307*, ed. T. Hog (English Historical Soc.; 1845), 218–19, records *sub anno* 1232 that Edmund was appointed 'hiis temporibus'.

[32] Bertrand of Pontigny, 'Vita B. Edmundi', in *Thesaurus*, cols. 1799–1800. For the legate Ottobuono's preaching, after he emerged as chief executor of the Cross in 1266, see William Rishanger, *Chronica et annales, regnantibus Henrico tertio et Edwardo primo*, ed. H. T. Riley (RS; 1865), 57; Trevet, *Ann.*, p. 271; *Flores Historiarum*, ed. H. R. Luard, 3 vols. (RS; 1890), iii. 14; 'Chronicle of Barlings', in *Chronicles of the Reigns of Edward I and Edward II*, ed. W. Stubbs, 2 vols. (RS; 1882, 1883), ii. cxv–cxvi. He probably preached at the parliament of Northampton, June 1268, as well. According to the 'Continuation' of Florence of Worcester, *Chronicon ex Chronicis*, ed. B. Thorpe, 2 vols. (English Historical Soc.; 1848, 1849), ii. 201, Ottobuono there gave the Cross to Lord Edward and other nobles.

particular individuals to promote specific crusades. For example, in September 1274 Gregory X instructed the archbishops of Canterbury and York, along with their suffragan bishops, to preach the new crusade in their dioceses. Concurrent mandates to preach went out to the provincial minister of the Franciscans and the prior provincial of the Dominicans.[33] These bulls of commission, in conjunction with other materials, provide a fairly clear picture of the type of personnel drafted into preaching of the crusade in the thirteenth century.

The role of the ordinary parochial clergy seems to have been limited. From a few scattered references it looks as if their contribution consisted primarily of reciting crusader privileges and of implementing liturgical activities connected with the crusade. In 1255, for example, the executors appointed to promote the crusade against Manfred instructed deans to ensure that crusader privileges were announced frequently in all chapters and parish churches.[34] As far as liturgy is concerned, Gregory VIII, in 1187, was seemingly the first pope to issue specific instructions for the implementation of liturgical activities in England, embracing fasts during Lent for five years, special masses between Advent and Christmas, and abstinence from meat on Wednesdays and Saturdays.[35] His successor, Clement III, further ordered general prayers to be said constantly for the peace and liberation of the Holy Land and for the delivery of Christian captives.[36] Typically, it was Innocent III whose definition of measures to be taken was the basis of instructions issued thereafter. In 1213, reaffirmed by the Lateran Council of 1215, Innocent decreed that there be general processions every month, presumably in every church, to seek divine intervention for the liberation of the Holy Land. Each day, prayers were to be recited in all masses, along with Psalms 78 and 67 and a special prayer, the text of which was set out in the bull.[37] These measures soon became crystallized as a conventional part of later promotional activity, helping to explain the casual nature of the occasional references thereafter to liturgical activity in English sources.[38] Indeed, the only detailed directives sent to the English

[33] *Reg. Gregory X*, No. 569. Lunt, *Financial Relations*, p. 449, and *Councils*, II. ii. 811, suggest that only the Minors were committed to preaching, but the papal bulls of Sept. 1274 reveal that the Preachers were also appointed.

[34] 'Burton', pp. 359–60.

[35] To Gregory the loss of Jerusalem to Saladin was a divine warning; only through a general spiritual renovation would divine clemency be won: Howden, *Gesta*, ii. 15–19; id., *Chron.* ii. 326–9, 329–30.

[36] For how this was implemented in St Paul's, London, see Howden, *Gesta*, ii. 53–4; id., *Chron.* ii. 359–60.

[37] *CLI*, No. 917.

[38] See e.g. the *Statutes* of the diocese of Worcester, II (1229), in *Councils*, II. i. 175. The Norwich clergy talked in 1292 of the customary prayers, vigils, and fasts for the recovery of the Holy Land, 'more solito': Cotton, *Hist.*, p. 207.

clergy after 1215 appear to be those of Innocent IV. In 1249 he instructed that there be a mass for the liberation of the Holy Land at least once each week in all churches, and that once a month there be a general procession at which sermons were to be preached setting before the people the state of the Holy Land, the cruelty of the Tartars, and the injustices of Frederick II.[39] In 1252 all prelates in Henry III's dominions were mandated to implement a set of spiritual measures in connection with the king's projected crusade: prayers, masses, and processions, to be instituted throughout their dioceses. The clergy were also to urge their flocks to abstain from dancing, gaming, and other lascivious entertainments, and to lead more sober lives. Thereby divine aid might more surely be secured 'to snatch [the Holy Land] from the hands of the iniquitous'. The form of prayers was laid down in the bull. Every day Psalm 78 was to be recited along with the special prayer, originally stipulated by Innocent III, beseeching God's protection for the crusader, Henry III, and the delivery of the Holy Land. As these prayers were offered in church, two bells were to be rung so that those at home or at work might, on hearing them, recite the Lord's Prayer and such other prayers as God should inspire. Finally, there was to be a solemn procession of clergy and people once every month, at which the mass of the Holy Cross was to be sung and a sermon delivered that the faithful might pray for Henry, his crusading company, and the Holy Land, and that God deliver it from the hands of the pagans.[40]

These materials reveal that the parochial clergy might preach the crusade in their churches on a regular basis, but it is quite apparent from other evidence that the onus of local preaching fell upon others. Bishop Robert Grosseteste, for example, in instituting his inquiry concerning crusading vows and moneys in the diocese of Lincoln in 1247, refers specifically to the Dominicans and Franciscans who had initially preached the Cross in the individual archdeaconries: there is no suggestion that the parochial clergy had been active.[41] Again, episcopal mandates instructed archdeacons, officials, deans, rectors, and their vicars to afford aid to the friars preaching the Cross

[39] Paris, *CM* vi. No. 89.

[40] Religious, throughout Henry's dominions, were also to offer prayers for his success, along with regular processions and litanies: *Reg. Innocent IV*, Nos. 6035–6; *Foedera*, I. i. 286–7. See also 'Anglo-Norman Bidding Prayers from Ramsey Abbey', ed. K. V. Sinclair, *Medieval Studies*, xlii (1980), 454–62. Part of the orison was concerned with the Holy Land, that it be delivered from pagan hands. Sinclair's attempt to relate it to Lord Edward's crusade of 1270 is unconvincing, considering the evidence for earlier liturgical measures on behalf of the Holy Land.

[41] See above, pp. 22–3.

locally,[42] and to collect clergy and people together to hear their preaching as and when they should see fit.[43] In short, there is no indication that in practice the parochial clergy played a major role in preaching the crusade themselves.

The evidence, patchy though it is, suggests that prelates, deputed members of the diocesan clergy, and selected *magistri* were the mainstay of preaching campaigns before the introduction of the friars in 1234 wrought a radical change. But even then their services continued to be called upon. Wendover and Paris, for example, reveal that parallel to the efforts of the friars in 1235 was the preaching of prelates and 'able masters of theology'.[44] In the campaign inaugurated in the diocese of York in 1291, Archbishop John le Romeyn and three masters of theology preached along with Franciscans and Dominicans, but in this case Romeyn's intention was to launch the new promotional campaign in fine style; it does not appear that either he or the three *magistri* took any further part in the preaching effort.[45] All the available evidence points to the conclusion that the friars came to take on more and more of the preaching load as the century progressed, the role of the traditional agents of promotion tending to become limited to the initiation of campaigns and preaching on special occasions.[46]

This transference of regular preaching to the friars is partly explained by the varied duties and responsibilities ordinarily laid upon the secular clergy: their performance could only suffer if they were engaged in preaching with any frequency. Simon de Brie, cardinal legate in France, observed in December 1267 that although he had called upon archbishops and bishops to preach the Cross in France, 'we believe them to be frequently occupied in business concerning their churches'. For this reason he appointed, for one, the warden of the Franciscans of Anduze to cause preaching in

[42] e.g. Register of Godfrey Giffard, BA 2648/1(i), fo. 61d; *The Rolls and Registers of Bishop Oliver Sutton*, ed. R. M. T. Hill, 8 vols. (Lincoln Rec. Soc.; 1948–86), iii. 195.

[43] e.g. *Hist. Papers*, p. 46 (misdated).

[44] Roger of Wendover, *Flores historiarum*, ed. H. O. Coxe, 4 vols. (English Historical Soc.; 1841–4), iv. 330–1; Paris, *CM* iii. 279–80. In May 1252 Henry III requested preaching by friars and others whom the prelates knew to be suitable: *CR 1251–3*, p. 219.

[45] See below, pp. 55–6.

[46] See below, pp. 57–60. Only in 1291 can it be shown that bishops were expected to appoint members of their diocesan clergy to preach on a regular basis: *Records A. Bek*, pp. 26–7, 27–8. Prelates were frequently instructed to cause preaching by those they knew to be suitable. See e.g. Innocent IV's instructions of Apr. 1250: *Foedera*, I. i. 272–3. But it looks as if it was the service of suitable *friars* which the papacy generally had in mind.

the province of Narbonne.[47] But the friars were themselves especially well-suited to systematic local preaching: their superior training as preachers, and their apostolate and organization, fitted them admirably for the task. The Franciscans and Dominicans were first introduced to preaching of the crusade in England in 1234,[48] and they presumably discharged their new duty effectively since Gregory IX's successors consistently employed them thereafter in promoting the crusade. By 1291, moreover, the time of the last great promotional effort in our period, both orders had established houses in most of the principal towns of England.[49] Their geographical spread, though not even, provided a good network of centres from which extensive preaching in all dioceses could be instituted with comparative ease.

Individual friars were deployed in consequence of bulls mandating the prior provincial of the Dominicans and the provincial minister of the Franciscans to cause preaching of the Cross, or sometimes upon the instructions of the executors of the Cross.[50] With one exception the sources are silent with regard to the numbers involved in any one preaching campaign: in 1291 Nicholas IV instructed that fifty brethren of each order be committed to preaching.[51] In practice, it looks as if these numbers were scaled down in the campaign that followed, for Oliver Sutton, bishop of Lincoln, observed in April 1292 that thirty-five Minors had been deputed by their provincial minister to the task of preaching 'in the province of England'.[52] The specific personnel to be employed in any campaign was left, quite naturally, to the heads of the two orders to decide. They were simply required to appoint those whom they knew to be suitable,[53] or, as Henry III put it when he commanded the provincial heads in March 1252 to depute friars to attend him in London, those brethren 'qui habeant scienciam

[47] *Layettes du Trésor des Chartes: Inventaire et documents publiés par la Direction des Archives*, ed. A. Teulet *et al.* 5 vols. (Paris, 1863–1909), iv. No. 5339.

[48] See above, pp. 19–20. The only evidence for the participation of other mendicant orders in England is the report in Cotton, *Hist.*, p. 435 that the Austin friars preached alongside the Minors and Preachers in 1292. There appears to be no evidence that other mendicants were drafted in. Considering the limited numbers, resources, and future prospects of such orders as the Carmelites, Friars of the Sack, Trinitarians, and Crutched Friars, this is not surprising.

[49] The Franciscans had settled in fifty-two, the Dominicans in forty-four. For details, see D. Knowles and R. N. Hadcock, *Medieval Religious Houses: England and Wales* (2nd edn., London, 1971), 213–20, 222–9.

[50] In 1267, e.g., Ottobuono instructed the friars to preach: Wykes, *Chron.*, p. 217; 'Continuation' of William of Newburgh, ii. 552.

[51] *Reg. Nicholas IV*, Nos. 6684–92; *Foedera*, I. ii. 748–9.

[52] *Reg. Sutton*, iii. 195. To initiate the campaign in the diocese of York alone, however, Archbishop Romeyn sought the services of eighteen Minors and seventeen Preachers. See below, p. 55.

[53] See e.g. *Foedera*, I. i. 172–3.

predicandi de cruce . . .'.[54] The area entrusted to any one friar in the early years, when both orders were still thin on the ground, is unclear, but by 1247 at least the archdeaconry had emerged as the basic unit of assignation, if the evidence relating to Lincoln diocese in that year is representative.[55] We know that in 1292 the Franciscan Walter de Langele had been appointed by his provincial minister to preach in the two archdeaconries of Oxford and Buckingham.[56]

Co-operation and consultation between the individual bishop and the friars preaching in his diocese was vital to the smooth running of local preaching, but the bishop may also have applied to the provincial heads of the two orders requesting the provision of brethren.[57] Thereby he could fulfil the responsibility laid upon him by the papacy to cause preaching of the crusade in his diocese.[58] Generally, bishops seem to have been content to leave it to the friars themselves to arrange the details of their preaching in the dioceses, but the measures taken in York diocese in 1291 suggest that the launching of a new campaign might see a more purposeful episcopal role. On 4 September 1291 Archbishop Romeyn called upon the services of all houses of the Franciscans and Dominicans within his diocese.[59] The wardens together were to provide thirty-five friars (eighteen Minors, seventeen Preachers) to preach the Cross simultaneously on 14 September, aptly enough Holy Rood Day. Romeyn specified precisely where he wished individual friars to preach, their wardens dispatching them

54 *CR 1251–3*, pp. 201–2.

55 Paris, *CM* vi. No. 71.

56 *Reg. Sutton*, iii. 195.

57 This is suggested by the simultaneous commissioning of both prelates and the provincial heads to preach the Cross, but presumably only the latter could command the deputation of individual brethren. In 1275 Bishop Giffard observed that 'ministro fratrum minorum administrationis anglicane et *per eum* [my emphasis] fratribus eiusdem ordinis in favorem et utilitatem terre Jerosolimitane officium sancte predicationis a sede apostolica, est commissum': Register of Godfrey Giffard, BA 2648/1 (i), fo. 61d. See also *Reg. Sutton*, iii. 195, for the observation that the provincial minister had been authorized to 'elect' Minors to preach in 1292.

58 The *exact* personnel deployed in any diocese apparently depended largely upon the decisions of the wardens of individual houses. In 1267 Simon de Brie authorized the warden of Anduze to appoint suitable Franciscans to preach the Cross since he did not 'have notice of all brothers of your order suitable': *Layettes*, iv. No. 5339. Executors of the Cross, however, could co-opt any ecclesiastic whose services they required. They, or individual bishops, perhaps sometimes requested the services of particular named friars. Robert Grosseteste was one prelate who certainly did, though whether for preaching of the crusade is another matter. See *Epistolae Roberti Grosseteste Episcopi Lincolniensis*, ed. H. R. Luard (RS; 1861), Nos. xiv, xvi.

59 *Hist. Papers*, pp. 93–6; *Reg. Romeyn*, i. 113. The houses named are: (Franciscan) Nottingham, Doncaster, York, Beverley, Scarborough, Richmond, Preston; (Dominican) York, Beverley, Scarborough, Yarm, Lancaster, Pontefract. Nine were to provide three preachers each, four were to provide two.

to the named locations. In the majority of cases the archbishop indicated a particular town, vill, or centre of population. Thus, the Franciscans of Nottingham were to have one of their brethren preaching in Nottingham, another in Newark, and a third in Bingham. For the four areas of Kendal, Lonsdale, Copeland, and Preston (Lancs.), however, it was left to the warden of the house concerned to determine which exact location would be most appropriate. Romeyn, perhaps, was unfamiliar with the parts of his diocese lying to the west of the Pennines. Nevertheless, the clear emphasis upon preaching in centres to the east reflects the pattern of distribution of population and wealth, itself mirrored by the plantations of the friars. On the same day Romeyn also commissioned three distinguished members of the secular clergy, all trained theologians.[60] Master Thomas of Corbridge was to preach in Beverley Minster,[61] Master Thomas of Wakefield in Ripon,[62] and Master John Clarel in Southwell Minster.[63] Archbishop Romeyn would preach himself in York Minster on the appointed day, 14 September.

The aim of this carefully co-ordinated preaching initiative was plainly to obtain coverage of some of the most important centres of population within the diocese, whilst the precise selection of locations and preachers was presumably intended to avoid duplication as far as possible. Both mendicant orders possessed houses in Scarborough, for example, but while a Dominican was to preach on his home territory, and another of his colleagues at Pickering, the Franciscans were to post one of their number at Bridlington and another at Whitby. Again, although each order had colonized Beverley, neither was to preach there, assuredly because Thomas of Corbridge was given that particular task. Not all important centres of population in York diocese are included in Romeyn's list of locations, but since his instructions were designed only to launch the new preaching campaign throughout the diocese by selecting specific points in a concerted strategy, it may be presumed that the friars would have covered other centres in later stages of the campaign, about which, regrettably, no information has come to light.[64]

60 *Reg. Romeyn*, ii. 8–9.

61 For his career, see *Reg. Romeyn*, esp. i. 385–9; ii. 84; *The Register of William Wickwane, Lord Archbishop of York, 1279–85*, ed. W. Brown (Surtees Soc. 114; 1907), 4; *The Register of Thomas of Corbridge, Lord Archbishop of York, 1300–4*, ed. W. Brown (Surtees Soc. 141; 1928), II. xii; A. B. Emden, *A Biographical Register of the University of Oxford to A.D. 1500*, 3 vols. (Oxford, 1957–9), i. 485.

62 For his career, see Emden, *A Biographical Register*, iii. 1955; *Reg. Romeyn*, i. 36–7.

63 For his career, see *Reg. Romeyn*, i. 282 and n.

64 Romeyn can have done little beyond initiating the campaign. He left for Rome shortly after, receiving licence to go abroad on 20 Sept: *CPR 1281–92*, p. 443. He sent letters home from France on 10 Dec: *Hist. Papers*, p. 96; *Reg. Romeyn*, ii. 13.

It will be apparent that considerable gaps remain in our knowledge of the way in which preaching of the crusade was developed and organized in thirteenth-century England. Many central questions remain unanswered for lack of evidence, especially those concerned with the mechanics of what were clearly complicated operations. The answers to others must remain tentative, not least because the argument rests upon scraps of evidence sometimes separated by decades in time. Nevertheless, it can be confidently asserted that by the end of the century the Church had successfully elaborated the means not only to publish in all parish churches papal crusading bulls, the privileges they contained, news from the Latin East, and other materials, but also to expose all but the remotest parts of the realm to the rhetoric of preachers.

Preaching in Practice

Two broad types of preaching may be usefully identified by virtue of their somewhat distinct functions and context. The first comprised preaching of the crusade before solemn assemblies of Church or State. Extending back to the example set by the Council of Clermont in 1095, these were carefully stage-managed occasions, designed to make public the secular ruler's assumption of the Cross, or to secure the vows of important men in attendance, to launch promotional campaigns with panache, or to sustain a campaign previously instituted. The council which met at Geddington in February 1188 is an early English example. At Henry II's command, Baldwin of Ford, archbishop of Canterbury, and Gilbert Glanville, bishop of Rochester, preached before the assembly of dignitaries, and to such effect, we are told, that many of those present at once took crusading vows. Henry had already taken the Cross in January 1188, and it is quite clear that he regarded the council as the occasion to make public in England his vow, to whip up crusading fervour, to initiate a comprehensive recruitment campaign, and, above all perhaps, to secure the commitment of his greater subjects in England. Their vows would be critical to the size and power of the force which the king hoped to lead to the liberation of Jerusalem. Moreover, like its twin held earlier at Le Mans for Henry's French lands, the council was also the opportunity to institute measures for the levying of the Saladin tithe and for ordinances regulating the conduct of crusaders once the expedition should have departed. Soon afterwards, Archbishop Baldwin set out on his celebrated preaching tour around Wales.[65]

[65] Howden, *Gesta*, ii. 30–3; id., *Chron*. ii. 334–8; Newburgh, *Hist*. i. 271–5; Gerald, *Opera*, i. 73; viii. 239–41; Diceto, *Opera*, ii. 51; Gervase of Canterbury, *The Historical Works of Gervase of Canterbury*, ed. W. Stubbs, 2 vols. (RS; 1879, 1880), i. 406, 409–10, 422–3.

Preaching before such assemblies continued in the thirteenth century. Archbishop Stephen Langton, for example, reinforced the call to the Fifth Crusade by preaching the Cross at Henry III's second coronation in May 1220.[66] In June 1236 a Dominican preached before Henry III and a council of nobles at Winchester. This was the occasion for Richard of Cornwall and others to take the Cross, thereby creating the nucleus of the 1240–1 English crusading force which departed with the earl, and giving direction and invigoration to the promotional campaign initiated in 1234.[67] The king himself made use of the device when he took the Cross on 6 March 1250 at the hands of Archbishop Boniface of Canterbury. The occasion was an assembly of the citizens of London, summoned specially to the great hall at Westminster, along with certain prelates and nobles. According to Matthew Paris, the hall and the palace were filled to overflowing. Many others took the Cross along with the king, among them his *familiares* William de Valence, Ralph fitzNicholas, Paulinus Pepper, John Mansel, Philip Lovel, and Edward the clerk. Doubtless it was hoped that their eager response, along with Boniface's preaching, would induce many Londoners to take vows themselves, and it is interesting that Henry should have first attempted to win them over by tearfully craving their forgiveness for his unjust exactions, his violation of their liberties, and other past injuries. In the circumstances, as Paris points out, they had little option but to grant their pardon, but whether they then responded favourably by taking vows themselves is by no means apparent.[68]

The Londoners were certainly unimpressed when Henry summoned them to attend another publicity stunt at Westminster in 1252. Royal letters patent issued in June indicate that Henry publicly assumed the Cross a second time at the assembly which had duly convened on 14 April; he certainly used the occasion to bind himself formally by oath to depart for the East on 24 June 1256.[69] The assembly has every appearance of being intended to step up the promotional campaign inaugurated in 1250 and to proclaim in the most public manner Henry's sincere commitment to the crusade, something doubted in certain quarters. The bishops of Worcester and Chichester and the abbot of Westminster were commanded to deliver sermons, and once again it was certain royal *curiales* who eagerly

[66] Coggeshall, *Chron.*, p. 88; 'Continuation', of William of Newburgh, ii. 527; Walter of Coventry, *Memoriale fratris Walteri de Coventria: The Historical Collections of Walter of Coventry*, ed. W. Stubbs, 2 vols. (RS; 1872, 1873), ii. 244; Trevet, *Ann.*, p. 206.

[67] Paris, *CM* iii. 368–9; Trevet, *Ann.*, p. 221; 'Winchester', p. 87.

[68] Paris, *CM* v. 101; id., *Historia Anglorum sive historia minor*, ed. F. Madden, 3 vols. (RS; 1866–9), iii. 71.

[69] Paris, *CM* v. 281–2; *CPR 1247–58*, p. 158; *Foedera*, I. i. 282.

responded, doubtless by prior arrangement. The king at once embraced them, calling them his brothers. Few of the Londoners took the Cross, however, according to Paris, who may have been present, so Henry angrily denounced them as 'ignobiles mercenarios'. One wonders what success the friars enjoyed, summoned to be with Henry in London on the same day, 14 April, presumably to preach in the city.[70]

The reign of Edward I saw the tactic repeated. Archbishop Pecham, for example, preached the Cross following the marriage of Princess Margaret to John of Brabant in July 1290, in the course of the very long Easter parliament held at Westminster. Otto de Grandson, Earl Gilbert de Clare, Robert de Tatteshale, and Thomas Bek, bishop of St David's, were among those said to have taken vows at the time. Since Otto de Grandson's expedition was in active preparation—he left for Acre shortly afterwards—and since Edward I himself was *crucesignatus*, it is probable that Pecham's preaching was intended to sustain the momentum and secure additional commitment from the social élite in attendance.[71]

Preaching of this kind was *ad hoc* and exceptional, aimed at the great and other groups whose support for the crusade was especially valued. It stands in contrast to the second and normative type of preaching, that carried out at the local level in the shires and forming the backbone of promotional campaigns for the crusade in the thirteenth century. And, as we have seen, its ulterior purpose was increasingly to secure moneys rather than vows to be fulfilled in person.[72]

To achieve maximum coverage and to utilize resources to the full, some form of advance planning was clearly a prerequisite. Simon de Brie impressed the point upon the warden of the Franciscans of Anduze in 1267 when he appointed him to preach the crusade in the province of Narbonne. Together with the bishops and other religious engaged in the business, he was to take particular care to distinguish

[70] *CR 1251–3*, pp. 201–2. Henry's involvement in the preaching is symptomatic of his concern to stimulate recruitment to his projected crusade, as we have seen. He further sought to ease the labours of the executors by requesting the prelates and friars to aid them when required, and by granting them $2\frac{1}{2}$ *m.* per day in Dec. 1252 whilst preaching the Cross: *CPR 1247–58*, pp. 164, 168, 372, 377. For other grants and action on their behalf, see *CR 1251–3*, pp. 97–100, 397, 454; *CLR 1251–60*, p. 41. For grants to others involved in promotion at this time, see *CR 1251–3*, pp. 69, 210; *CR 1247–51*, pp. 447, 540; *Foedera*, I. i. 276, amongst others. The Dominicans of Haverfordwest were one body of mendicants to benefit, granted 10*m.* in 1256 for preaching the Cross: *CPR 1247–58*, p. 482.

[71] Cotton, *Hist.*, pp. 177–8; see C. L. Kingsford, 'Sir Otho de Grandison (1238–1328)', *TRHS* 3rd ser. iii (1909), 138.

[72] See above, pp. 18–21.

times and places so that the efforts of those preaching were not duplicated.[73] Archbishop Romeyn sought, of course, to do precisely that in his instructions for preaching in York diocese in 1291, but his were only opening shots of a campaign; planned itineraries were necessary for the extensive preaching to follow. The first well-documented preaching tour of this kind was that undertaken by Archbishop Baldwin of Canterbury in Wales in 1188. He was sent there after the Council of Geddington by Henry II to recruit both Welsh and English for the king's projected crusade.[74] Amongst those accompanying Baldwin was Gerald of Wales, the ebullient archdeacon of Brecon. It is to him that we owe our detailed knowledge of the preaching tour,[75] essentially a circuit around the boundaries of Wales in March and April 1188.[76] Tours as extensive as that covered by Baldwin almost certainly came to an end in the thirteenth century. Richard de la Wych's tour of the dioceses of Chichester and Canterbury in 1253 is the last known, indeed, to have taken in more than one diocese.[77] There was no English metropolitan in the mould of Simon de Beaulieu, archbishop of Bourges, who preached the Aragonese Crusade in the course of a tour of his province in 1284.[78] Nor does it appear that any English bishop preached systematically throughout his diocese. After 1213, moreover, it is apparent that the area to which individual local preachers were deputed shrank as more personnel came to be harnessed to the cause, especially with the introduction of the friars after 1234. It has been argued that as early as 1213 the prior of Dunstable was responsible for just two archdeaconries, Bedford and Huntingdon, and we know that one Franciscan preached the Cross in the archdeaconries of Oxford and Buckingham in 1292.[79] Nevertheless, itineraries and forward planning for preaching even on this scale remained necessary to ensure coverage yet avoid duplication of effort. No such itinerary appears to have survived from England, although the evidence from the *Lives* of Richard de la Wych and Edmund Rich is suggestive.[80]

[73] *Layettes*, iv. No. 5339.

[74] Henry, perhaps, was particularly eager to secure the services of Welsh archers, famed for their expertise and valued by the king. See, generally, J. Boussard, 'Les mercenaires au XIIe siècle: Henri II Plantagenêt et les origines de l'armée de métier', *Bibliothèque de l'École des Chartes*, cvi (1945–6), 189–224.

[75] His major treatment of the journey is his 'Itinerarium Kambriae', in Gerald, *Opera*, vi; but the 'De Rebus a se Gestis', in ibid. i, also incorporates sections of this material, some of it in expanded form.

[76] The route can be worked out in detail from Gerald's account, but the precise dating is uncertain since he provides only two firm dates.

[77] See above, p. 50.

[78] C. V. Langlois, *Le Règne de Philippe III le Hardi* (Paris, 1887), 152.

[79] See above, pp. 48, 55.

[80] But see the well-known account of preaching in northern France, *c.*1265: 'Compte

Gerald's account of Baldwin's tour of Wales is sufficiently detailed to allow close comparison with the evidence relating to preaching of the crusade in the field in the thirteenth century. It is at once apparent that most of the fundamental features of that preaching had already been established by the end of the twelfth century. The thirteenth century saw no startling innovations but, rather, development and elaboration upon earlier practice.

The first requirement was an audience collected at a predetermined time and place. Some prior arrangement with the clergy of the neighbourhood concerned was necessary, the preacher sending advance notice that he intended to preach on a certain day at a specific location, and requesting that the faithful be collected together accordingly. That Archbishop Baldwin sent out notice of his intentions is clear enough: in recounting the preaching at Haverfordwest, for example, Gerald states that the clergy and people of the region had been summoned to attend.[81] The attendance of certain secular leaders upon the archbishop was certainly no chance occurrence, and Arthenus, at Abergavenny, significantly enough apologized for being late.[82] Gerald also reveals that censure was used to punish non-attendance. Owain Cyfeiliog of Powys was excommunicated 'because alone among the Welsh princes he had not hastened with his people to meet the archbishop . . .'[83] These practices continued in the thirteenth century. Wendover reports that in 1235 archdeacons and deans 'collected together all the people of each diocese, men and women, under pain of anathema' to hear preaching of the crusade by the friars and masters of theology.[84] Wendover was not guilty of exaggeration. Papal mandates authorized the use of ecclesiastical censure to compel the clergy and people to attend preaching, and the local clergy were to be obliged to collect their flocks at the places which preachers deemed suitable.[85] These sanctions were reinforced by episcopal mandates.[86] For his own preaching of the crusade in 1275, Bishop Godfrey Giffard

d'une mission de prédication pour secours à la Terre Sainte (1265)', ed. Borrelli de Serres, *Mémoires de la Société de l'Histoire de Paris et de l'Ile de France*, xxx (1903), 243–51. Some detailed itineraries in advance of diocesan visitations survive for England. See e.g. *Register of Bishop Godfrey Giffard, 1268–1301*, ed. J. W. Willis-Bund, 2 vols. (Worcestershire Hist. Soc.; 1898–1902), 482.

81 Gerald, *Opera*, vi. 82–3; i. 74.

82 Ibid. vi. 14, 49.

83 Ibid. 144.

84 Wendover, *Flores*, iv. 330–1. See Paris, *CM* v. 73, for similar action in 1249.

85 See e.g. *Foedera*, I. i. 272–4; *Reg. Urban IV*, No. 466. Preachers appointed from the local diocesan clergy were also accorded the power to collect the faithful together as and when they saw fit. See *Records A. Bek*, pp. 27–8.

86 See e.g. the general instructions on behalf of the Franciscans preaching in York diocese in July 1275: *Hist. Papers*, p. 46 (misdated). For a mandate issued on behalf of a particular preacher deputed to a specific area, see *Reg. Sutton*, iii. 195.

instructed the dean of Worcester to order parish priests in the city of Worcester and for a distance of two leagues around to announce to their flocks that on 26 May the bishop would preach the Cross in Worcester Cathedral. Every priest was to attend in person.[87]

Incentives came to be used to the same end. Innocent III was the first to decree that partial indulgences should be granted to those attending sermons, and the progressive increase in the indulgence offered by his successors may provide, as Throop considered, a measure of waning enthusiasm for the crusade. From ten days under Honorius III the figure rose to 450 under Gregory X.[88] But these were maximum figures: in 1275 Godfrey Giffard offered just 100 days indulgence to those attending his own preaching.[89] Indulgence also came to be extended to attendance at processions on behalf of the crusade. In 1249 Innocent IV authorized English prelates to relax twenty or forty days of enjoined penance at their discretion. By 1263 this had risen to 100 days; it was still so in 1291.[90]

The choice of suitable locations for popular preaching of the crusade was also important. Preachers went to those places where a good turn-out could be expected, and from Gerald's account it is clear that locations were determined with some care. He observes generally that in south Wales, at least, preaching occurred 'everywhere in such places as seemed fit'; more specifically, Baldwin chose Haverfordwest as a location because it was in the centre of the province of Dyfed.[91] Gerald also reveals that precise sites within these centres of population were preferred. We hear of preaching in churches, at public meeting-places in towns and vills, at castles, and at route-centres such as the bridge over the river Teifi near Cardigan. The strategy continued in the thirteenth century. Edmund Rich, in particular, had a marked predilection for open-air sites judging by the miracles which prevented or suspended downpours from malignant clouds whilst he

[87] Register of Godfrey Giffard, BA 2648/1(i), fos. 52d–53.

[88] P. A. Throop, *Criticism of the Crusade: A Study of Public Opinion and Crusade Propaganda* (Amsterdam, 1940), 263. From the time of Martin IV and until the pontificate of John XXII, however, one year and forty days was the standard indulgence. See N. Housley, *The Italian Crusades: The Papal–Angevin Alliance and the Crusades against Christian Lay Powers, 1254–1343* (Oxford, 1982), 125.

[89] Register of Godfrey Giffard, BA 2648/1(i), fos. 52d–53.

[90] Paris, *CM* vi. No. 89; *Reg. Urban IV*, No. 466; M. Purcell, *Papal Crusading Policy: The Chief Instruments of Papal Crusading Policy and Crusade to the Holy Land from the Final Loss of Jerusalem to the Fall of Acre, 1244–1291* (Leiden, 1975), 62–4. Parallel to this extension of the indulgence were the spiritual and material rewards accorded to preachers and others involved in the business of the Cross. See ibid. 60–2, 163; Lunt, *Financial Relations*, 541 ff.

[91] Gerald, *Opera*, i. 74. Private addresses were also made to specific groups and individuals. See ibid. vi. 16, for two such cases.

was preaching the crusade.[92] In 1267 Ottobuono preached in St Paul's, London, and later at Lincoln and Barlings. In Lincoln he may have preached in the cathedral, or perhaps at the place 'where the friars preached and the citizens had their games'.[93] The locations chosen by Archbishop Romeyn in 1291 are no less revealing, for preaching, as he put it, was to be 'in singulis locis sollemnibus, burgis, et foris'.[94]

This evident concentration on urban centres made very good sense, not least because the manpower available for preaching of the crusade was not unlimited. The figure of 100 friars to be deployed for the campaign initiated in 1291, apparently reduced in practice as we have seen, indicates that resources had to be carefully husbanded.[95] It gives additional point to that Franciscan text which sought to justify the urban emphasis of the Minors' preaching partly by reference to the limited number of friars.[96] The mendicants' organization, apostolate, and their persistent urban identification predisposed them towards preaching centred upon towns. There is evidence that they went through the countryside, but only in the larger vills might they expect congregations of a size to justify the effort.[97] There is no reason to suppose that they approached preaching specifically for the crusade any differently. But if the crusading call was not taken to some rural communities that does not mean that their populations were left in the lurch. The clergy were expected to co-operate with the friars and other preachers by collecting their flocks together at the places earmarked for preaching.[98]

The efficacy of preaching depended in large part upon the stature of the preacher, his eloquence and rhetorical powers, and a suitably charged emotional atmosphere. The latter was partly achieved through liturgical activity, but Gerald of Wales has little to say about this. He mentions masses and confessions as the prelude to preaching, but of processions and other liturgy we hear nothing.[99] Extensive

92 Bertrand of Pontigny, 'Vita B. Edmundi', col. 1800. The churchyards of All Saints and of St John's, Oxford, Gloucester castle, and the courtyard of King's Hall, Oxford, are specifically mentioned in this connection.

93 *Flores*, iii. 14; Trevet, *Ann.*, p. 271; Rishanger, *Chron.*, p. 57; 'Chronicle of Barlings', pp. cxv–cxvi; *Rotuli Hundredorum temp. Hen. III et Edw. I in turr. Lond. et in curia receptae scaccarii West. asservati*, 2 vols. (Record Commission, 1812, 1818), i. 312a.

94 *Hist. Papers*, pp. 93–6. This was in accordance with papal mandate: *Foedera*, I. ii. 748–9.

95 See above, p. 54.

96 See D. L. D'Avray, *The Preaching of the Friars: Sermons Diffused from Paris before 1300* (Oxford, 1985), 30–1.

97 Ibid., esp. pp. 39–41.

98 See above, pp. 53, 61.

99 e.g. Gerald, *Opera*, vi. 73, 110, 125–6, but his silence regarding other liturgy does not necessarily mean it was not employed. See above, pp. 51–2, for its early

liturgical measures certainly played an important role in the thirteenth century. In describing the campaign initiated in 1234, for example, Matthew Paris reports that the Franciscans and Dominicans took care 'to be received at monasteries and in cities in solemn processions, with banners and flaming candles, and garbed in festive vestments . . .'[100] In 1275 Bishop Godfrey Giffard insisted that all priests of the parish churches of Worcester and for two leagues around were to attend his preaching of the crusade in the cathedral, each priest preceding his flock in cope and surplice, carrying the banner of the Cross. Measures of this sort represent local implementation of apostolic mandate.[101] Reports by preachers such as Oliver of Paderborn underline this use of liturgy.[102] As the business of the crusade was peculiarly *opus Dei* it comes as no surprise to find frequent reports of miracles attending preaching. They too served to heighten the emotional atmosphere and helped to induce a favourable response, since miracles indicated divine favour for the preacher and his cause, and betokened the eventual success of the expedition in preparation. A clear instance of their role is provided by Oliver of Paderborn's report of an aerial apparition when he preached the Cross at Bedon, Frisia, in 1214: 'Hoc signum quidam laicus de insulis videns quasi prophetia certitudine ponens preteritum pro futuro dixit: nunc sancta terra recuperata est et crucem statim accepit.' His example was followed by countless others, we are told.[103]

Gerald, in his characteristic way, would have us believe that he was the star preacher on Archbishop Baldwin's tour of Wales, though he gives others their due. Unfortunately, however, he says very little about the act of preaching itself, the content of sermons, or texts used.[104] We are left wondering whether Gerald and his colleagues

implementation in England. A distinction, of course, must be drawn between the regular liturgical activities instituted in churches and those specifically employed on occasions of preaching.

[100] Paris, *CM* iii. 287; and v. 73, for 1249. See also 'Chronicle of Barlings', pp. cxv–cxvi, for Ottobuono's preaching in 1267.

[101] Register of Godfrey Giffard, BA 2648/1 (i), fos. 52d–53. See *Reg. Urban IV*, No. 466, for an example of the powers granted in this connection to preachers, in this case Bishop Walter Cantilupe of Worcester and those whom he should appoint.

[102] 'A propos de Jacques de Vitry: Une lettre d'Olivier de Cologne', ed. D. U. Berlière, *Revue Bénédictine*, xxvii (1910), 521–4.

[103] Ibid. See also 'Une prédication de la croisade à Marseille en 1224', ed. E. Baratier, in *Économies et Sociétés au Moyen Âge: Mélanges offerts à E. Perroy* (Paris, 1973), 690–9. For English reports in the 13th c., see esp. Wendover, *Flores*, iv. 144–5, 331–2; Bertrand of Pontigny, 'Vita B. Edmundi', col. 1800.

[104] Of the structure of sermons, Gerald, *Opera*, i. 75, says only that at Haverfordwest he divided his sermon into three parts and reserved his 'strong power of persuasion for the close of each'. He tells us more about the languages used, an intriguing problem. Baldwin clearly spoke no Welsh and his sermons were given in Latin or French, then

composed their own sermons or made use of the compositions of others. Possibly they had access to the crusading *excitatoria* of Peter the Venerable, St Bernard of Clairvaux, and other luminaries. Gerald had been in the schools of Paris for some years and may well have come into contact with appropriate material. Archbishop Baldwin, a Cistercian, might have known St Bernard's contributions, and for part of the journey the company was joined by the two Cistercian abbots of Whitland and Strata Florida, both of whom preached the Cross.[105]

More is known about the sort of materials used in the thirteenth century. In the course of the later twelfth and thirteenth centuries preaching underwent a profound evolution, characterized particularly by a marked revival in popular preaching. This reorientation was attended by a remarkable growth in the production of materials designed to ease the task of the preacher confronting popular audiences on a regular basis: manuals of themes, distinctions, and authorities, collections of model sermons *ad status*, compilations of exempla, *artes praedicandi* concerned with composition, delivery, technique, *florilegia*, and so forth.[106] In common with all species, preaching of the crusade was deeply conditioned by this important development. However, few individual sermons survive, because, in part, preachers depended largely upon model sermon collections, perhaps the most important type of preaching aid in use in the thirteenth century and disseminated widely throughout Europe. They aimed to provide ready-made sermons which the individual preacher could use as the basic structure for his own compositions, although he may have modified or expanded upon the model according to inclination and need.[107] Some of these collections contain sermons specifically for use in preaching the crusade, and three *ad status* collections in particular enjoyed an international popularity in

translated by Gerald or other members of the party: ibid. vi. 14, 55, 126. Only when he preached at Haverfordwest does Gerald mention the languages he used, Latin followed by French: ibid. 83. Generally, preachers must have used the vernacular appropriate to the audience in question, but for foreign dignitaries this was plainly impossible. See 'Chronicle of Barlings', pp. cxv–cxvi, for Ottobuono's preaching at Barlings in 1267.

105 Gerald, *Opera*, vi. 119, 126.

106 See, generally, A. Lecoy de la Marche, *La Chaire française au Moyen Âge, spécialement au XIIIe siècle* (2nd edn., Paris, 1886); D'Avray, *Preaching*, ch. 2; and on preaching of the crusade, Lecoy de la Marche, 'La Prédication de la Croisade au XIIIe siècle', *Revue des questions historiques*, xlviii (1890), 5–28.

107 See esp. D. L. D'Avray, 'The Transformation of the Medieval Sermon', D.Phil. thesis (Oxford, 1976), esp. pp. 33–4, 47–8, 139, 209; id., *Preaching*, ch. 2, esp. pp. 126–31. It is doubtful if friars had either the time or energy to do more than repeat the same sermon more or less verbatim to the different audiences they encountered on tours preaching the crusade. Sermons preached to the social élite may have been different.

their time—those composed by Jacques de Vitry, Guibert of Tournai, and Humbert of Romans. Their use, in England as elsewhere, would help to explain the very limited survival of independent sermons for the crusade of the thirteenth century.[108] Exemplum collections were another preaching aid widely used. Containing an extensive range of anecdotes culled from histories, the Bible, saints' lives, and other genres, they provided a mine of appropriate material for insertion into all manner of sermons. Of those including exempla relating to crusading themes is the *Speculum Laicorum*, written in the later thirteenth century by an Englishman who was almost certainly a friar. The work contains a number of exempla admirably suited for the preacher in the field, some of them deriving from experience of preaching the crusade in England itself.[109]

A particularly interesting work, the *Ordinacio De Predicatione Sanctae Crucis in Anglia*, combines features of both exemplum collections and model sermons. It must have been one of the earliest works composed specifically as an aid for preachers of the Cross *per se*, perhaps *c.*1216 for the enlightenment of those recruiting for the Fifth Crusade. It is almost certainly English and may perhaps have been written by Master Philip 'de Oxonia', one of the three executors appointed by Innocent III in 1213.[110] Its contents and organization reveal that it was written to help preachers to construct their sermons, and to provide a source of suitable texts and illustrative matter which could be quickly and easily tapped. The first and most extensive part of the work consists of alternative opening themes for the sermon with the relevant biblical references or texts. Sin, the consequent need for redemption, and the salvatory nature of the Cross are particularly stressed. The remainder of the work is divided into three sections headed 'De circumstanciis Crucis', 'De carne et eius deliciis', and 'De vocacione hominum ad crucem', each subdivided into items consisting of homilies on various matters appropriate to preaching of the

[108] See B. Smalley, 'John Russel, O.F.M.', *Recherches de Théologie Ancienne et Médiévale*, xxiii (1956), 280–1, for fragments probably of a draft sermon which Russel composed for use in preaching the crusade, *c.*1291. In F. M. Powicke, *Stephen Langton* (Oxford, 1928), appendix ii, p. 174 is a reference to a sermon ascribed to Langton, 'Ad crucissignatos'.

[109] *Speculum Laicorum*, ed. J. Welter (Paris, 1914), iii–vii, Nos. 32, 148–9, 151, 324–5. See also *Liber Exemplorum ad Usum Praedicantium*, ed. A. G. Little (British Soc. of Franciscan Studies, 1; 1908), esp. No. 152. This was written by an English Franciscan of the province of Ireland, *c.*1270–9.

[110] Printed in *Quinti Belli Sacri Scriptores Minores*, ed. R. Röhricht (Société de l'Orient Latin, 2; 1879), 3–26. Röhricht's identification of Master Philip as author is speculative. His dating of the work on the grounds of a reference to the Albigensian Crusade is scarcely conclusive: ibid. ix–x.

crusade. The last section in particular uses mainly exempla, each leading up to a ringing call to assume the Cross.

No further English work designed specifically for the crusade, if written, appears to have survived, but one which surely was known and used in England is the *De Praedicatione Sanctae Crucis* of Humbert of Romans, *c.*1266–8, probably the most thorough and exhaustive work ever devoted to the art of preaching the crusade specifically. A comprehensive manual for the aid of preachers in the field, its perceived value is indicated by the survival of no less than eighteen MSS, although none is known from English scriptoria.[111] Humbert's main purpose was to collect in one compact and coherent work those materials and arguments which he considered most pertinent to the needs of preachers. His treatment of the subject deserves the fullest respect since he was a preacher of the crusade himself. He also wrote an important treatise on the art and practice of preaching generally, the *De Eruditione Praedicatorum*, the second book of which contains his model sermons *ad crucesignatos*, and at Gregory X's behest he compiled the *Opus Tripartitum*, an exhaustive survey of public opinion concerning the crusade, along with advice on the ways and means to succour the Holy Land. Humbert, then, was exceptionally well qualified to compose such a manual. He was intimately familiar with the attitudes of contemporaries; through personal experience he was conscious of the difficulties involved in preaching the Cross; and he knew what produced results.[112]

With materials of this kind to aid and assist them there can be no doubt that those preaching the crusade in the thirteenth century were altogether better equipped to undertake the task than the likes of Gerald of Wales in 1188. In this respect, as in others, promotion of the crusade had become a more professional business in the thirteenth century.

Co-ordination and Consultation

There was always a danger that promotion would lapse into incoherence. All manner of ecclesiastics came to be employed in the variety of tasks involved in taking the call to the crusade throughout the realm, then regulating the fulfilment of vows and monitoring the collection of the various moneys arising from promotional activity.

[111] T. Kaeppeli, *Scriptores Ordinis Praedicatorum Medii Aevi* (Rome, 1970–), ii. 288.

[112] For brief analysis of the *De Praedicatione*, see Lecoy de la Marche, 'La Prédication'; E. T. Brett, *Humbert of Romans: His Life and Views of Thirteenth-Century Society* (Toronto, 1984), ch. 10.

Additional complications arose from the conflicting jurisdictions of secular and religious clergy, the claims to immunities and exemptions, the jealous safeguarding of rights and privileges, and the rivalries between different sectors of the English Church. Such divisions posed a very real danger to the smooth running of as complex an operation as the *negotium Crucis*. The necessary co-ordination of men and measures was achieved in a number of ways and at different levels. Of central importance was the overriding authority accorded to executors of the Cross, designed partly to prevent disintegration and ensure collaboration, and partly to provide a focus of authority which all engaged in the business should heed. Perhaps the fullest extant statement of their authority, as it had evolved by the later thirteenth century, is provided by the commission of Walter Cantilupe, bishop of Worcester, in 1263. From this we can see that in all matters to do with the crusade Bishop Walter's authority was supreme, with no appeal to the pope allowed.[113] By virtue of such powers the executor could mandate any member of the different parts of the English Church to perform any task connected with the *negotium Crucis* and enforce its due implementation. But the executor was necessarily dependent upon the goodwill and co-operation of ecclesiastics at the local level; he could not possibly oversee every activity. That bishops and their deputies were responsible for implementing measures within their dioceses will already be apparent. It will suffice here merely to reiterate that it was for them to take the leading role in disseminating crusading bulls and related materials, cause preaching, institute liturgical measures, ensure that chests were set up in every church to receive alms, carry out inquisitions regarding the fulfilment of vows and the raising of moneys, and to ascertain that every aspect of current policy was implemented within their dioceses. Unfortunately, the limited survival of episcopal registers of the thirteenth century, and the somewhat idiosyncratic recording of episcopal acts in those that do survive, precludes any detailed survey of the overall manner in which an individual bishop set about fulfilling the responsibilities laid upon him, and ensuring the co-ordination of the men and measures involved in promoting the crusade. That he played a pivotal role, however, is beyond doubt.

Ecclesiastical councils and synods provided another means of co-ordinating action, the occasion for executors and others to impose duties and measures, and an opportunity for consultation and discus-

[113] *Reg. Urban IV*, Nos. 397, 466, 468, 472. His powers bear close comparison to those accorded to Simon de Brie, in July 1266, to promote the crusade in France: *Layettes*, iv. Nos. 5175–6.

sion which enabled the clergy to air their views and suggestions.[114] An early example of their use is the provincial council of Canterbury held at Westminster in August 1201, when Hubert Walter requested his suffragans to make inquiry throughout their dioceses concerning the fulfilment of crusading vows. Arrangements for the preaching of the Cross were probably discussed as well.[115] Although councils and synods were undoubtedly concerned with crusading matters throughout the century, only occasionally can their role be glimpsed through reports of conciliar proceedings and decrees. In the 1250s, for example, Henry III's assumption of the Cross and the papal grant of moneys gave rise to discussion at a series of councils. The financial aspect dominated proceedings, judging by the extant reports, but it is almost inconceivable that wider matters of promotion were not also considered:[116] that they were discussed at the Council of Bury St Edmunds in February 1267 is clear since the unfavourable response of those assembled survives.[117] The subsequent legatine councils held in London in June 1267 and April 1268 almost certainly considered matters relating to the crusade as well, although the only sure indication lies in the instructions for processions for the peace of the realm and on behalf of the Holy Land at the 1268 assembly.[118]

The views of the clergy at large regarding the crusade were occasionally sought by the papacy. In 1213 Innocent III requested information and advice as part of his preparations for the projected Fifth Crusade.[119] In response to Alexander IV's call for provincial councils to discuss measures to be taken against the Mongol threat, a council of the province of Canterbury was held at Lambeth in May 1261, although the matter was quickly swamped by more pressing domestic

[114] Executors doubtless appreciated that successful promotion was best achieved by associating the clergy with their plans and measures as far as possible. Sometimes they used assemblies to present their credentials, letters of commission, and relevant papal bulls. See e.g. the materials printed in W. E. Lunt, 'A Papal Tenth Levied in the British Isles from 1274 to 1280', *EHR* xxxii (1916), esp. pp. 66, 71–2. The 'feedback' value of such assemblies is well illustrated by the advice given the collectors concerning the safe deposit of crusading moneys in 1277: ibid. 75–6.

[115] Howden, *Chron.* iv. 173. See also Cheney, *Innocent III*, pp. 241–2, who suggests that the business of the crusade was also discussed at the Council of Westminster, Sept. 1200.

[116] *Councils*, II. i. 448–51, 474–9, 481–3, 501–3, 504–10, 524–30. However, it was at the London parliament of 1254 that decisions were taken regarding the division of the executors' responsibilities: *CPR 1247–58*, p. 370.

[117] *Councils*, II. ii. 732–4. Before the council Ottobuono expressed his intention of having the matter discussed, observing that whatever was found to be expedient at the council would be implemented: ibid. 732.

[118] Ibid. 735–8. See ibid. 816–17, 822–3, 824–5, for councils considering at least the 1274 sexennial tenth in 1275, 1277, and 1278.

[119] No resulting memoirs appear to survive.

business.[120] In 1272–3 Gregory X requested further advice from the clergy, and perhaps the Councils of Westminster and the New Temple, London, in January and October 1273, were concerned partly with the business.[121] The archbishop of Canterbury was required by Honorius IV in 1287 to summon a council of his clergy to devise means to aid the Holy Land following the pope's receipt of news describing the critical situation in Acre.[122] Finally, in this period, provincial councils of Canterbury and York met in early 1292 in response to Nicholas IV's request for advice concerning the best means to aid the Holy Land, and the proposed union of the Temple and Hospital. The surviving replies of the clergy are of interest for the light they shed on contemporary attitudes regarding the utility, practicality, and promotion of the crusade.[123]

120 *Councils*, II. i. 660–92.
121 *Councils*, II. ii. 804–7, 807–9; and see Throop, *Criticism*, pp. 19–25.
122 HMC, *Eighth Report* (London, 1881), I. ii. 345b.
123 *Councils*, II. ii. 1097–1113.

3

THE NATURE OF THE RESPONSE

It is not easy to quantify accurately the response to promotional campaigns. We know that preachers listed the names of those who took vows or otherwise bound themselves to aid the crusading cause,[1] and that further lists were subsequently compiled by those appointed to inquire minutely into the fulfilment of vows and other incurred obligations. Comparison allowed identification of those whose obligations remained outstanding.[2] Unfortunately, very few of these lists now survive,[3] so we are obliged to rely upon other types of record whose purpose was other than to provide extensive lists of *crucesignati*: these cannot provide an adequate or dependable measure of the response to the call to the crusade. Moreover, by no means every *crucesignatus* fulfilled his obligation by departing on crusade in person.

There are other difficulties. Of those who can be shown to have departed on crusade, or intended to do so, the majority are known only, or chiefly, through references to them as *crucesignati* in the records of Chancery and Exchequer.[4] Although these records are especially important in identifying individual crusaders, certain classes of crusader tend to be screened out from view since the overwhelming majority known from these sources fall into one of two categories, often overlapping. They were either members of the social élite, who had good reason to invest in royal judicial protections and other privileges and could afford to do so, or *curiales* and *familiares* to whom the king extended his patronage and support, for their crusades as for other enterprises, in the various ways available to him.[5]

This overall impression of the response tends to be reinforced by other sources. Contemporary writers frequently recorded the vows or departure on crusade of the great men in society, but they dismissed the response of lesser men with vague phrases or suspiciously

[1] See e.g. Roger of Wendover, *Flores historiarum*, ed. H. O. Coxe, 4 vols. (English Historical Soc.; 1841–4), iv. 144, referring to the roll of one Master Hubert, who preached in 1227.

[2] See the instructions of Bishop Grosseteste in 1247, discussed above, pp. 22–3.

[3] Two well-known survivals, both of the 1190s, are printed in HMC, *Reports: Various Collections I* (London, 1901), 235–6; HMC, *Fifth Report* (London, 1876), 462.

[4] Notably the Patent, Close, Fine, Charter, Liberate, and Memoranda Rolls.

[5] See below, ch. 5.

rounded numbers to imply that a great host also accompanied their social superiors or took vows. Ecclesiastical records, notably episcopal registers, help to provide a balance especially with regard to the clergy, yet their limited survival for the thirteenth century, coupled with the quirks of their compilation, render them imperfect indicators of the clerical response. The Crown's legal records reveal something of the response of lesser freemen, but only those involved in litigation before the royal courts generally come to our notice. Cartularies and land registers, while useful, commonly refer only to crusaders making dispositions concerning their property in anticipation of departure. Nevertheless, as far as personal participation is concerned, this emphasis on the role of the great men is likely to give a true reflection of realities and is not a distorted image produced by the lopsided survival of certain classes of evidence. Papal policy, the controls and restraints immanent in society, and the attitude of crusade leaders in the face of the immense difficulties presented by crusading in practice combined to determine much of the pattern of participation.

Non-Combatants

On the eve of the Third Crusade, the Anglo-Norman Ralph Niger articulated a cogent argument for restricting the participation of individuals of particular social classes.[6] He accepted that some clerics would be necessary on crusade for sacramental and liturgical purposes, and he condoned the participation of a limited number of 'other ranks', such as messenger boys and laundry women, on the grounds of functional utility, but otherwise women, clerics, monks, and lesser laity should stay at home. They should leave the prosecution of crusade to those best-qualified in the art of war. Niger was quite adamant that crusading should be primarily the preserve of knights. His argument, or one close to it, underlay the papacy's policy towards crusading personnel. It culminated, as we have seen, in a shift towards the systematic redemption of the vows of non-combatants in England after 1234.[7]

As far as the regular clergy were concerned, it is well-known that the papacy frowned upon their participation in no uncertain terms from the time of the First Crusade. In England, Urban II's stance was supported by St Anselm, who instructed Bishop Osmund of Salisbury

[6] Ralph Niger, *De re militari et triplici via peregrinationis Ierosolimitanae*, ed. L. Schmugge (Berlin, 1977). For a more wide-ranging discussion of those functionally disqualified from crusading, see now E. Siberry, *Criticism of Crusading 1095–1274* (Oxford, 1985), ch. 1.

[7] See above, pp. 18–21.

to act to prevent the departure of monks in his diocese.[8] Anselm was aghast at flagrant abuse of the monastic vow; in particular, the abbot of Cerne was not only preparing to depart on the crusade itself, but had even dispatched one of his monks to join the expedition.[9] Anselm's response is a particularly early example of the action required if monks were to remain cloistered, their crusading aspirations checked. Reinforcement was supplied by episcopal visitation, conciliar decrees, and synodal statutes.[10] Cap. 52 of the canons of the Council of Oxford, 1222, for example, stipulated that religious were not to leave their houses without their superiors' licence, that such permission be granted only for 'certain and honest cause', and that the monk or nun should return within a fixed term.[11] The monastic orders themselves also sought to restrict the wanderings of their brethren. The English Benedictines, for example, occasionally legislated against travels unless reasonable cause was adduced and prior permission obtained. In 1277 the chapter of the province of Canterbury entirely forbade 'evagaciones monachorum' and even decreed that no monk should be permitted to make a vow of pilgrimage.[12] Individual churches also laid down rules. According to the *Regula* of Hereford Cathedral, *c.* 1250, resident canons were permitted to make but one pilgrimage each year within England, and none was to make more than one pilgrimage overseas during his life.[13] Finally, although there was a change in papal policy towards the crusading vows of the regular clergy, following the relaxation of restrictions by Innocent III in 1213, the traditional view remained resilient. Commentators such as Hostiensis harked back to the age of Gratian,

[8] See H. E. J. Cowdrey, 'Pope Urban II's Preaching of the First Crusade', *History*, lv (1970), 183; also R. Somerville, 'The Council of Clermont and the First Crusade', *Studia Gratiana*, xx (1976), esp. pp. 330–1.

[9] Such reactions rapidly found an echo in the developing corpus of canon law. See J. A. Brundage, *Medieval Canon Law and the Crusader* (Madison, Milwaukee, London, 1969), esp. pp. 32, 43–4, 101–2; further, id., 'A Transformed Angel (X 3. 31. 18): The Problem of the Crusading Monk', in *Studies in Medieval Cistercian History Presented to J. F. O'Sullivan* (Spencer, Mass., 1971), 56–7.

[10] See e.g. *Register of Bishop Godfrey Giffard, 1268–1301*, ed. J. W. Willis-Bund, 2 vols. (Worcestershire Hist. Soc.; 1898, 1902), 87–8, for instructions following the bishop's visitation of Llanthony priory in 1276 concerning travels.

[11] *Councils*, II. i. 123; for later provisions, ibid. II. i. 152, 191; and the detailed regulations concerning nuns in 1268, ibid. II. ii. 789–91.

[12] *General and Provincial Chapters of the English Black Monks (1215–1540)*, ed. W. A. Pantin (Camden Soc., 3rd ser. 45; 1931), 83; also, ibid. 11, 17–18, 39–40, for earlier legislation.

[13] *Regula* (or *Consuetudines*) of Hereford Cathedral (extract), ed. J. Merewether, *Archaeologia*, xxxi (1845), 251 n. For further examples, see *Statutes and Constitutions of the Cathedral Church of Chichester (1198–1832)*, ed. F. G. Bennett *et al.* (Chichester, 1904), 9; *Statutes of Lincoln Cathedral*, ed. H. Bradshaw and C. Wordsworth, 3 vols. (Cambridge, 1892–7), i. 281.

paying little regard to the evolution in papal policy,[14] and his conservatism was shared by Matthew Paris for one, judging by his denunciation of the abbot of St Edmunds for taking the Cross in 1250. Abbot Edmund, remarks Paris, met with the derision of all, setting a pernicious example to monks and violating his monastic vow. Moreover, the abbot's action smacked of ingratiating deference to the king since he took the Cross in the presence of Henry III and upon his prompting.[15]

Greater latitude was allowed towards the secular clergy, but synodal statutes and concilar decrees stressed that they should remain at their posts. Non-residence was to be permitted only in exceptional circumstances.[16] Nevertheless, it was early accepted that a cleric might set out on crusade provided he obtain licence from his ordinary, and that no danger to the cure of souls would result from his absence.[17] The implementation of these regulations in practice may be illustrated by a large number of entries in the surviving episcopal registers of the period,[18] but perhaps the most interesting case in this context is that concerning Adam de Radeford, vicar of Hucknall Torkard (dioc. York). Adam had not only received his vicarage at the archbishop's own hand, but had sworn on oath to reside there in person. At some point before February 1292, however, he had gone without licence to the Holy Land. Archbishop Romeyn, plainly piqued, informed his official that as Adam was guilty of perjury, of visiting the Holy Land without licence, and of neglecting souls, the fruits of the vicarage from the day of Adam's departure were to be sequestered.[19] No case illustrates more clearly the degree of episcopal control exercised, or at any rate claimed, over the clergy in the matter of the crusade.

Nor were archbishops and bishops entirely free agents. They, apparently, were expected to secure papal licence to crusade, and they too were obliged to ensure that cure of souls would not be

[14] Brundage, 'A Transformed Angel', pp. 59–62.

[15] Paris, *CM* v. 101; also, v. 196.

[16] See e.g. *Councils*, II. i. 313–14, 362, 519, 610, 648; II. ii. 757–8, 1016–17.

[17] For brief discussion of the crusading cleric, see Brundage, *Medieval Canon Law*, pp. 32, 100–2, 177–9; M. Purcell, *Papal Crusading Policy: The Chief Instruments of Papal Crusading Policy and Crusade to the Holy Land from the Final Loss of Jerusalem to the Fall of Acre, 1244–1291* (Leiden, 1975), 139–40, 161–3.

[18] e.g. *The Register of Walter Giffard, Lord Archbishop of York, 1266–79*, ed. W. Brown (Surtees Soc. 109; 1904), 64. In some cases the crusader was to provide a sum for alms for the poor of his parish. See e.g. *Registrum Thome de Cantilupo, Episcopi Herefordensis, 1275–1282*, ed. R. G. Griffiths (Canterbury and York Soc. 2; 1907), 6–7. For a case in which provision of a fit substitute was made the condition of a licence to crusade, see *Reg. G. Giffard*, p. 285.

[19] *The Register of John le Romeyn, Lord Archbishop of York, 1288–96*, ed. W. Brown, 2 vols. (Surtees Soc. 123, 128; 1913, 1916), i. 306.

jeopardized.[20] But their participation might be cautiously welcomed since prelates, in their capacity as tenants of baronies, could be expected to lead useful fighting forces. In December 1289, for example, Nicholas IV granted Robert Burnell, bishop of Bath and Wells, the first year's fruits of all dignities and benefices which might become void in his diocese for up to three years, since he proposed to set out on crusade with a fitting body of warriors, but he was to ensure that cure of souls was not neglected in the meantime.[21]

These various restrictions help to explain the very modest participation of ecclesiastics in the crusades of the thirteenth century. Only two abbots are known to have made preparations to depart for the East: Abbot Robert of York in 1218, and the abbot of Netley in 1270.[22] Sylvester of Evesham, bishop of Worcester, seems to have departed for Damietta in 1218.[23] In 1219 William Cornhill, bishop of Coventry, certainly set out, appointing his seneschal to represent him at the Exchequer.[24] He was followed in 1227 by Peter des Roches, bishop of Winchester, and William Brewer, bishop of Exeter, leaders of the English contingent which joined Frederick II's crusade, and the last English bishops known to have gone on crusade in person in our period.[25] Archbishop Boniface of Canterbury, Bishop Walter Cantilupe of Worcester, and Peter Aigueblanche, bishop of Hereford, followed Henry III in taking the Cross in 1250.[26] Godfrey Giffard, bishop of Worcester, took the Cross, and perhaps in 1275 when he was active in preaching the crusade.[27] Thomas Bek, bishop of St

[20] Episcopal residence was occasionally the subject of legislation. See e.g. *Councils*, II. ii. 769–70. The possible material injury to the dioceses of *episcopi crucesignati*, should they depart, was often emphasized. See e.g. *Reg. Honorius III*, No. 3041, concerning Bishop Richard Marsh of Durham, 1221.

[21] *Reg. Nicholas IV*, No. 2025.

[22] *PR 1216–25*, p. 161; *CPR 1266–72*, p. 485.

[23] *PR 1216–25*, pp. 143–4.

[24] PRO, E 159/2, m. 2d. See also *Acta Stephani Langton Cantuariensis Archiepiscopi, 1207–1228*, ed. K. Major (Canterbury and York Soc. 50; 1950), No. 49.

[25] Peter apparently took a second vow before his death in 1238: Paris, *CM* iii. 489. Pandulf, bishop of Norwich and by then former legate, took the Cross prior to Michaelmas Term 1224: Henry de Bracton, *Bracton's Note Book*, ed. F. W. Maitland, 3 vols. (London, 1887), No. 942. Walter Mauclerc, bishop of Carlisle, commuted his vow during Gregory IX's pontificate, it seems: W. E. Lunt, *Financial Relations of the Papacy with England to 1327* (Cambridge, Mass., 1939), 430 n. 5. Either Henry of Wengham or Henry of Sandwich, successive bishops of London, apparently took the Cross *c.*1260–73: *Calendar of Entries in the Papal Registers Relating to Great Britain and Ireland: Papal Letters I (1198–1304)*, ed. W. H. Bliss (London, 1893), appendix, No. 300.

[26] Paris, *CM* v. 99; id., *Historia Anglorum sive historia minor*, ed. F. Madden, 3 vols. (RS; 1866–9), iii. 71. Cantilupe may have taken his vow in 1247: Paris, *CM* iv. 629.

[27] *Register of Bishop William Ginsborough, 1303–7*, ed. J. W. Willis-Bund (Worcestershire Hist. Soc.; 1907), 50. He left 50*l.* in his will for the fulfilment of his longstanding vow.

David's is said to have taken vows in 1290.[28] His brother, Antony Bek, bishop of Durham and titular patriarch of Jerusalem, took a second vow in 1303 or 1305; he had accompanied the Lord Edward in a more lowly position in 1270.[29] Like their royal masters, however, none of these prelates set out. Some perhaps never intended to do so; their vows may have been a device to encourage recruitment in the context of preaching campaigns. The vows of curialist bishops such as Thomas Bek, a former keeper of the king's wardrobe, however, suggest other forces at work.

Lesser clergy accompanied each of the expeditions which left England in the thirteenth century, but numerically they appear insignificant. Many can be shown to have been in the service of crusading lords, and their participation clearly owed much to those ties. Some, as Ralph Niger pointed out, would be required for sacramental and liturgical purposes, and every crusading lord's household may be presumed to have included at least one cleric competent to administer. A certain Walter, for example, chaplain to Hugh de Neville, accompanied his lord on crusade in 1266. He witnessed Hugh's will, drawn up at Acre, and received a bequest of 8*m.* per annum to chant for his lord's soul.[30] Others accompanied their lords presumably because of their administrative and bureaucratic skills. Bishop Peter des Roches was followed by Roger, archdeacon of Winchester, and Peter de Cancellis. In 1231, at the bishop's instance and for their faithful service on crusade, both men received papal dispensation for non-residence in their various benefices.[31] But the influence of such ties is best evidenced by those clergy in the service of the king or his kinsmen. A number attached to the Lord Edward accompanied him in 1270. Antony Bek, a royal clerk as early as 1266, rose to be keeper of Edward's wardrobe on crusade, and acted as one of the executors of his master's will drawn up at Acre.[32] Two former keepers, Lawrence de Lovershale and Philip de Willoughby, also set out in 1270. Philip's good service on crusade contributed to his rise as Chancellor of the Exchequer. In 1301 he was granted the notable

[28] Bartholomew Cotton, *Historia Anglicana, necnon ejusdem Liber de archiepiscopis et episcopis Angliae*, ed. H. R. Luard (RS; 1859), 177.

[29] C. M. Fraser, *A History of Antony Bek, Bishop of Durham, 1283–1311* (Oxford, 1957), 163–5.

[30] See the will printed by M. S. Giuseppi in 'On the Testament of Sir Hugh de Nevill, Written at Acre, 1267', *Archaeologia*, lvi, part 2 (1899), 352–3.

[31] *Reg. Gregory IX*, Nos. 638–9. For Peter, see further *Rotuli Hugonis de Welles, Episcopi Lincolniensis*, ed. W. P. W. Phillimore and F. N. Davis, 3 vols. (Canterbury and York Soc. 1, 3, 4; 1908–9), ii. 39.

[32] Fraser, *Antony Bek*, pp. 10–12.

privilege of returning to the Exchequer at will; as late as this his service in the Holy Land was specifically recalled by the king.[33]

The known careers of such men suggest that their freedom of action was limited. If their crusading masters desired their personal participation by reason of their particular talents, then they had little option but to oblige. Equally, they could expect preferment and reward for their services. These considerations did not extend to the general body of churchmen. Their participation was neither expected nor desired, but many plainly took vows. In their replies to the papal request for financial aid against Frederick II in 1240, the rectors of Berkshire significantly commented that all, or nearly all, had taken the Cross and were now being pressed to fulfil those vows in person or through substitutes.[34] There can be no doubt that the papacy preferred to see the rectors, and their colleagues elsewhere, redeem their vows rather than set out in person.

The crusades of women were no more welcome in papal eyes. They, too, should generally redeem their vows unless they would be accompanied by useful fighting forces.[35] Some canonists held that women might take crusading vows without the consent of their husbands or guardians, but it is altogether improbable that such freedom was commonly enjoyed in practice. In 1291, for example, Nicholas IV authorized redemption of the vow of Eva, wife of Robert Tiptoft, as she was gravely ill, observing that her vow had been taken with Robert's consent.[36] Moreover, few of the Englishwomen who are known to have departed on crusade in the thirteenth century did so independently of their husbands. Amongst other examples, Countess Eleanor of Leicester journeyed as far as Brindisi with Simon de Montfort in 1240, remaining there to await the birth of her second son.[37] Eleanor of Castile accompanied the Lord Edward thirty years later, but unlike her namesake she reached the Holy Land, and there gave birth to a daughter, Joan of Acre. Whether they pestered their

[33] *CPR 1292–1301*, p. 615. For other clergy sailing in 1270–1, see appendix 4.

[34] *Councils*, II. i. 291.

[35] In 1200 and 1201 Innocent III enunciated the principles which guided his successors. Women might accompany their husbands, but the primary intention was to relax restrictions, deriving from conjugal vows, which hampered husbands wishing to take the Cross. In this regard, Innocent's ruling did not meet with unreserved approval, but there was general agreement that women normally should be dissuaded from crusading in person. See Brundage, *Medieval Canon Law*, chs. 2, 3, *passim*; id., 'The Crusader's Wife: A Canonistic Quandary', *Studia Gratiana*, xii (1967), 425–41; id., 'The Crusader's Wife Revisited', *Studia Gratiana*, xiv (1967), 241–52; Purcell, *Papal Crusading Policy*, pp. 57–9.

[36] *Reg. Nicholas IV*, No. 4490.

[37] Paris, *CM* iv. 44; C. Bémont, *Simon de Montfort, Earl of Leicester, 1208–1265*, trans. E. F. Jacob (Oxford, 1930), 64.

husbands to allow them to go on crusade or whether they went under pressure is unknown, but it appears that no *crucesignata* of so high a social stratum fulfilled her vow independently of her consort. Lower down the social order a few women are known to have departed independently, but it looks as if a restrictive papal policy combined with social and family controls to produce only a very limited number of women crusaders in this period. The attitude of crusade leaders was probably in accordance with the strictures of Ralph Niger. Henry II, for one, laid down in 1188 that no crusader should be accompanied by any woman, except perhaps a washerwoman of good repute.[38]

One of the greatest problems which might face a crusade leader was the participation of a host of poor non-combatants. Lacking adequate military training, equipment, and financial means, they were considered to be of little practical value, if not a positive hindrance, a drain on the resources of others more useful than themselves. In large numbers they placed intolerable strains on available food supplies, and always present was the problem they posed for discipline and organization. It is scarcely surprising that they were frequently denounced as unsuitable personnel, and from an early date.[39] The experience of the First and Second Crusades led Frederick Barbarossa to take steps to prevent their participation in the German contingent on the Third Crusade. In March 1188 he decreed that no foot soldier unskilled in the use of arms and unable to finance himself for a minimum of two years should set out, since in the past the 'vulgus inbelle et debile' had impeded expeditions to Jerusalem.[40] In the same year Henry II laid down that burghers and *rustici* who took the Cross without their lords' licence were to pay the Saladin tithe in full, a measure which may be regarded in part as an attempt to restrict their participation.[41] Occasionally in the thirteenth century regulations were drawn up with the indigent low-class crusader in mind. Menko informs us in some detail of the ordinances of 1269 governing those crusaders of Frisia intending to join Louis IX's

[38] Roger of Howden (attrib. Benedict of Peterborough), *Gesta Regis Henrici Secundi Benedicti Abbatis*, ed. W. Stubbs, 2 vols. (RS; 1867), ii. 32; id., *Chronica Rogeri de Houedene*, ed. W. Stubbs, 4 vols. (RS; 1868–71), ii. 337. The moral issue should not be forgotten, of course.

[39] See, esp. Odo of Deuil, *De Profectione Ludovici VII in Orientem*, ed. and trans. V. G. Berry (New York, 1948), 94. Odo's strictures were partly intended as salutary advice for future crusaders.

[40] 'Historia Peregrinorum', *Quellen zur Geschichte des Kreuzzuges Kaiser Friedrichs I*, ed. A. Chroust, *MGH SS*, NS 5, 126. The measure was approved unreservedly by the Anglo-Norman 'Itinerarium Peregrinorum et Gesta Regis Ricardi', in *Chronicles and Memorials of the Reign of Richard I*, ed. W. Stubbs, 2 vols. (RS; 1864, 1865), i. 43.

[41] Howden, *Gesta*, ii. 32; id., *Chron.* ii. 336.

second crusade by sea. Each was to take on the voyage at least 7*m.* sterling, six jars of butter, a leg of pork, a side of beef, and half a measure of flour, along with military equipment which Menko unfortunately does not specify, mentioning only vaguely 'vestes et arma necessaria'.[42] The intention was to prevent the departure of a host of indigent crusaders.

Measures of this kind were not always or altogether successful.[43] Nevertheless, as far as the English are concerned, it appears from contemporary writers that although considerable numbers of low-class crusaders left for the East in the years 1218–22, 1227, and 1229, their numbers dwindled fast thereafter. Very little is heard of them after this date, apart from those individuals in the household service of crusading lords. Nor do we find reports in English sources of portents and aerial apparitions, commonly associated with popular crusading enthusiasm, after those mentioned by Wendover in connection with the promotional campaign of 1227.[44] The crusading enthusiasm of the 'plebeia multitudo', as Wykes describes them, appears increasingly to have become converted into cash to swell the crusading subsidy.[45]

Distinctions need to be made if the influences operating upon *rustici* in the matter of the crusade are to be appreciated. Those of servile status enjoyed as little freedom therein as they did in other things and, as the 1188 crusading ordinances suggest, seigneurial permission to take a crusading vow was required.[46] How far this restriction was effectively upheld is by no means clear, and there were always runaway serfs, but it can scarcely have favoured participation in crusades. Nevertheless, arrangements of mutual benefit to both lord and villein could be drawn up. At some point between 1190 and 1210 William de Staunton granted a charter of manumission to his villein Hugh Travers, and his family, for the express reason that Hugh would go to Jerusalem in his lord's place.[47] It is unlikely that such an arrangement was anything but exceptional, although vicarious

[42] 'Menkonis Chronicon', *MGH SS* xxiii. 554.

[43] 'Historia Peregrinorum', pp. 157, 168 gloomily reports the presence of the 'vulgus debile et inbelle' in Asia Minor, Barbarossa's edict notwithstanding.

[44] Wendover, *Flores*, iv. 144–5.

[45] Wykes, *Chron.*, p. 217, concerning the redemption of vows preceding the 1270–2 crusade.

[46] Canonists acknowledged that serfs might not freely take vows by virtue of their lords' authority over them. Hostiensis, however, held that the crusading vow was the exception to this general principle. See Brundage, *Medieval Canon Law*, esp. pp. 100–2. It is doubtful if his position met with lords' approval in practice.

[47] 'Early Manumissions at Staunton, Nottinghamshire', ed. F. M. Stenton, *EHR* xxvi (1911), 95, esp. Nos. I, II. It is by no means evident that the occasion was Richard I's crusade, as Stenton thought.

crusades were quite common. The most surprising feature is William's choice of an individual as low-born as Hugh to fulfil his obligation.

Freemen possessed somewhat greater discretionary right, but they cannot have escaped easily the consequences of ties of lordship and service. The difficulties confronting such men are well illustrated by the case of a certain carpenter of Chichester in the service of Bishop Ralph Neville. At some point *c.* 1220–*c.* 1230 Simon, dean of Chichester, informed the bishop that he had been approached by the carpenter, '*crucesignatus* and wishing to set out on his journey'. The carpenter was evidently bound by some form of contract, but he had found a substitute whom Simon considered to be competent. He therefore sent the carpenter to discuss the matter with Bishop Ralph and to bring back his reply.[48] That reply is unknown, but if Ralph had agreed to the substitution then the carpenter would presumably have been free to fulfil his vow.

Crusading aspirations were certainly thwarted on occasion. A particularly revealing example (though not English) concerns one Master Assault de Marsilia, a skilled siege engineer, whom Alphonse of Poitiers was eager to recruit for his second crusade. In May 1268 Alphonse offered him 5*s. tours* per day for his service on crusade and pressed him to accept. There was a difficulty, however, because Assault was already in the service of King Alfonso X of Castile, but Alphonse promised that if Assault wished to accept his offer then he would write to the king to secure his release. Assault's reply must have been positive because Alphonse learnt from him in December 1268 that he was unable to secure release from his royal master. Not wishing to poach, Alphonse instructed that Assault be excused from their agreement; he desired, he said, that neither of them should incur the royal indignation.[49]

These cases reveal the sort of obstacles which men in service might face if they wished to participate in a crusade. Equally, there can be little doubt that a crusading lord could induce, perhaps even compel, certain of his retainers to accompany him if he required their particular services. Hugh de Neville's retinue at Acre in 1266–7, for example, included Jakke, his page, Colin, his clerk, Lucel, the cook, Thomas, his groom, and Master Reimund, the marshal.[50] On the other hand, a crusading lord's needs could stimulate new ties of household service. In 1203 a certain William de Weston, pleading

[48] 'Letters of Ralph de Neville, Bishop of Chichester and Chancellor to Henry III', ed. W. H. Blaauw, *Sussex Archaeological Collections*, iii (1850), No. 487, p. 75.

[49] *Correspondance administrative d'Alfonse de Poitiers*, ed. A. Molinier, 3 vols. (Paris, 1894–1900), i. Nos. 783, 987.

[50] Giuseppi, 'On the Testament of Sir Hugh de Nevill'.

crusader status in a land plea before the royal justices in Northamptonshire, produced in court a 'breve . . . patens' of William de Hommet 'in which it is contained that he has retained him *de familia sua* to take him to Jerusalem . . .'[51] For men of distinctly limited means, service in a crusading lord's household made very good sense: they had someone to maintain them for the duration of the crusade. From the evidence available there can be little doubt that the majority of commoners leaving England on crusade in the thirteenth century did so in the confinement of a lord's household.[52]

Yet crusades were expensive ventures, and a lord's resources were not unlimited. He could afford to support only so many retainers and each would have to earn his keep by fulfilling one or more functions. Moreover, with the application of contracts as a means of organizing crusading forces before their departure, we can see that the number of retainers permitted to the contracted party was limited. The contracts employed by the Lord Edward in 1270 stipulated that he would provide passage and water 'for as many persons and horses as befits knights'.[53] Other contracts for the same crusade were more specific. Count Guy of St-Pol, for example, agreed to serve Robert II of Artois with twenty-nine other knights. It was specified that for each simple knight, in addition to himself, passage would be provided for one *armigerus*, one groom, and one horse; for each banneret, two *armigeri*, two grooms, and two horses; for Count Guy, ten persons, his chaplain, and four horses.[54] Louis IX himself sought to restrict the other ranks accompanying his own contracted knights, doubtless seeking to limit transport costs as Contamine has suggested.[55] Quite obviously, it was in the financial interest of the contracting parties to restrict the number of their retainers on crusade to a minimum.

Military Classes

If a policy of exclusion operated with respect to non-combatants generally, then towards members of the military classes an altogether

[51] *CRR 1201–3*, p. 294.

[52] The only notable exceptions were the marine enterprises in which, from the time of the First Crusade, Englishmen participated. The best-known is the combined Anglo-Norman and Flemish assault upon Lisbon in 1147.

[53] See below, p. 119.

[54] *Layettes du Trésor des Chartes: Inventaires et documents publiés par la Direction des Archives*, ed. A. Teulet *et al.* 5 vols. (Paris, 1863–1909), v. No. 844. Pierrot de Wailly, an esquire, was to receive maintenance for just himself, two grooms, and three horses. See 'Diplomatique des actes de Robert II, comte d'Artois (1266–1302)', ed. Comte de Loisne, *Bulletin Philologique et Historique* (1916), 205–6, No. II.

[55] P. Contamine, *War in the Middle Ages*, trans. M. Jones (Oxford, 1984), 68.

warmer welcome was extended. It was from their ranks, especially those of the degree of knighthood, that crusading personnel was primarily sought. They were best equipped to wage war by virtue of their profession and material substance, and the Church regarded the crusade as the most fitting context for the exercise of their martial abilities.[56]

The broad pattern of their response, in so far as it is crudely represented by personal participation, may be briefly outlined for our period.[57] There was some response to every crusade to the Holy Land declared in the thirteenth century.[58] The Fifth Crusade attracted considerable numbers. The nucleus of the forces which sailed in a series of passages between 1218 and 1221 consisted of Earl Ranulf of Chester, William de Ferrers, earl of Derby, William de Albini, earl of Arundel, Saher de Quenci, earl of Winchester, Henry de Bohun, earl of Hereford, Henry fitzCount, who claimed the earldom of Cornwall, and a group of powerful barons including Robert fitzWalter, John de Lacy, Brian de Insula, Geoffrey de Luci, William de Huntingfield, John and William de Harcourt, and Gerard de Furnivall. The stature of these men makes it certain that a considerable number of lesser men followed them, but the records provide only a partial listing. The main force, apparently under the leadership of Ranulf of Chester and William of Derby, left England around Whitsun 1218 and landed at Damietta in late August or September 1218.[59] In the following year, probably in the spring passage, a further force sailed, including Saher de Quenci, William de Albini, Robert fitzWalter, and Geoffrey de Luci.[60] Two lesser expeditions left in 1220, the first with Henry fitzCount, the second with Philip Daubeny.[61]

The ignominious failure of the Fifth Crusade and the declaration of a truce led, in 1222, to the deferment of the further expedition being

[56] It is a commonplace that the Church sought to influence their behaviour by instilling an ethos which depicted service of God and Church as the apogee of knightly endeavour.

[57] Space precludes detailed individual references.

[58] This is impressed more firmly when it is remembered that large numbers can be shown to have taken the Cross but not to have set out in person.

[59] *Annales Cestrienses or Chronicle of the Abbey of S. Werburg, Chester*, ed. R. C. Christie (Lancashire and Cheshire Rec. Soc. 14; 1887), 50, in a good position to know, although this is a late compilation, reports their departure in the week following Whitsun, 3–6 June.

[60] 'Dunstable', pp. 54–6; 'Waverley', pp. 289, 292, are two chroniclers who distinguish between the two expeditions. Others, such as Wendover, *Flores*, iv. 44, conflate them. Earl Saher's independent departure is confirmed by the safe conduct for the ship he was preparing for his crusade in Jan. 1219: *PR 1216–25*, p. 185.

[61] Arriving at Damietta shortly before its fall, Philip decided to sail on to Acre. See his letter to Ranulf of Chester in Wendover, *Flores*, iv. 75–7 (misdated).

prepared by Peter des Roches, bishop of Winchester, and Faulkes de Bréauté.[62] Only around June 1227 did Bishop Peter finally depart with William Brewer, his friend and episcopal colleague, to join Frederick II's forces in the Holy Land.[63] They were joined there by Philip Daubeny and William Paynel in 1228, and by Gilbert Marshal, soon to become earl of Pembroke, in 1229. Thereafter there was a trickle of crusaders to the East, swelled by the third expedition of Philip Daubeny in 1235. A few, such as Ralph de Thony, departed with the French crusade of 1239, but the next major contribution came in 1240–1.

This crusade is conventionally described as the crusade of Richard of Cornwall, but in reality three distinct expeditions set sail: those of Earl Richard and William Longespee, claimant to the earldom of Salisbury; of Simon de Montfort, earl of Leicester; and of William de Forz, count of Aumâle and lord of Holderness. The origins of the first can be traced to June 1236 when Earl Richard, Longespee, Earl Gilbert Marshal, and Earl John of Chester, amongst others, took the Cross at Winchester.[64] In June 1240, according to Paris, Earl Richard left England with Longespee and seven bannerets: Philip Basset, John de Beauchamp, Geoffrey de Luci, John de Neville, Geoffrey de Beauchamp of Bedford, Peter de Brus, and William de Furnivall.[65] Travelling through France, they embarked at Marseilles and landed at Acre in October 1240.[66] Paris also informs us that the second force, under Simon de Montfort, set out independently and sailed from Brindisi. Simon's expedition was composed of Frenchmen as much as Englishmen judging by Paris's list of his bannerets. Only five out of the ten named can be described as English or with strong English connections: Amaury de St-Amand, Thomas and Gerard de Furnivall, Hugh Wake, and Wischard Leidet. Fulk de Baugé was from Anjou, whilst Peter de Chauntenay, and the brothers Gerard, Punchard, and William de Peaumes were Burgundians, though in receipt of annual fees from Henry III. The evidence suggests that Earl Simon's crusade arose from his independent initiative and that

[62] 'Dunstable', p. 75.

[63] Wendover, *Flores*, iv. 145 suggests that Bishop William also deferred his passage in 1222.

[64] Paris, *CM* iii. 368–9. The earls of Pembroke and Chester did not sail. Earl John died in 1237, and Gilbert Marshal at the Hertford tournament, 1241. See esp. ibid. 476, 620; iv. 135–6. If Baldwin de Redvers, earl of Devon, departed with Earl Richard in 1240, he returned speedily: see Wykes, *Chron.*, pp. 86–7.

[65] Paris, *CM* iv. 43–4.

[66] Ibid. 44–7. According to 'Chronica Albrici monachi Trium Fontium', *MGH SS* xxiii. 948, Richard led *c.*800 knights.

he did not wish to integrate his force with Earl Richard's.[67] Finally, William de Forz set out after the other leaders, perhaps in 1240 but more probably in 1241. He was accompanied by Peter de Maulay, Ebelin de Rochefort, John Ansard, Alexander de Hilton, and Geoffrey de Chandelers, amongst others.[68]

In response to the crusade declared by Innocent IV, a further expedition left England in July 1249, led by William Longespee, Richard of Cornwall's erstwhile companion. His force came to form a division of Louis IX's army.[69] Many others were *crucesignati* at the time, including Humphrey de Bohun, earl of Hereford, Robert de Quenci, Simon de Montfort, Walter Cantilupe, bishop of Worcester, and Geoffrey de Luci. The prospective crusader magnates met in council at Bermondsey in April 1250, fixed their passage for June, and appointed Bishop Walter their *capitaneus*.[70] Their numbers were swollen by Henry III and those who followed his lead in the years 1250–4, but none set sail. The combined efforts of king and pope prevented their departure.[71]

Recruitment to the crusade to the Holy Land declared by Urban IV in 1263 was severely hampered by the crisis in domestic politics in the early 1260s, but two expeditions ultimately departed in 1270–1, the Lord Edward sailing in August 1270, his brother Edmund in spring 1271.[72] Theirs was the last major crusade force to leave England in our period. The only tangible result of so much recruitment activity during Edward's reign was the relatively small force which left with Otto de Grandson in July 1290.[73]

67 Paris, *CM* iv. 44–5. Simon took his vow independently of Earl Richard, at some point before Feb. 1238. See *Reg. Gregory IX*, No. 4094. He was absent for much of the time in France and Italy whilst Richard prepared his crusade: Bémont, *Simon de Montfort*, tr. Jacob, esp. pp. 55–64.

68 Paris, *CM* iv. 89, 174. There was a strong Poitevin element to this force, suggesting that those Poitevin *crucesignati* resident in England looked to William, himself a Poitevin, as their natural crusader leader. R. V. Turner, 'William de Forz, Count of Aumale: An Early Thirteenth-Century English Baron', *Proc. of the American Philosophical Soc.* cxv (1971), 248, argues that William sailed with Earl Richard, but nowhere does Paris, well-informed of events, connect the two expeditions. He apparently considered them distinct ventures.

69 Paris, *CM* v. 76, 130–1. He reports William being accompanied by *c.*200 knights. Guy and Geoffrey de Lusignan accompanied Louis and may have led some English crusaders, but theirs was primarily a French venture. They sailed with Count Hugh X of La Marche and Angoulême, and his son Hugh XI, who contracted to accompany Alphonse of Poitiers: *Cartulaire des Comtes de la Marche et d'Angoulême*, ed. G. Thomas (Angoulême, 1934), Nos. xi, xiii. Guy de Lusignan certainly served with Alphonse, and was paid for his service up to Dec. 1250: *Layettes*, iii. No. 3910.

70 Paris, *CM* v. 102; id., *Hist. Anglorum*, iii. 72.

71 See below, pp. 91–2.

72 For the 1270–2 crusade, see below, ch. 4.

73 C. L. Kingsford, 'Sir Otho de Grandison (1238–1328)', *TRHS* 3rd ser. iii (1909), 136 ff.

The size and nature of the English response invites further discussion. First, considerable controls operated to limit the freedom of action of members of the military classes as much as others'. Many were undoubtedly deterred from going on crusade as a consequence of the terms of service to their lords. A good illustration of the practical significance of such bonds is provided by the record of the action brought in 1279–80 by Robert de Joneby, of a knightly Yorkshire family, against William de Percy of Kildale to recover £110 arrears of an annual retainer of 100*s*. which William had granted to Ivo, Robert's father, in or before 1258–9. The terms of their agreement were presented to the court. The sum was to be paid until William granted Ivo lands or escheats of equivalent value, but strict conditions were attached: Ivo was to remain in household service; he was not to leave William's *mesnie* without licence; and it was specifically stipulated that he should not depart from the realm or go to the Holy Land unless William's permission was first secured.[74] Agreements of this kind cannot have been uncommon in the thirteenth century, whether or not departure for the Holy Land was specifically covered in the terms. Plainly, men in household service found it difficult to go on crusade, if they valued their fees and hoped for future prospects, should their lords refuse permission.

At the apex of the social and political hierarchy, the king exercised a degree of influence much greater than that of any other lord. For his *familiares*, dependent upon royal patronage and benevolence, the king's attitude was supremely important. If he required such a man to act at home there was little choice but to acquiesce in the royal will. For those beyond immediate household service the king's stance was no less significant. One of the most notable features of Plantagenet government was the attempt to harness the social élite to its own ends as it came to convert royal right into public obligation. Nowhere is the principle more succinctly expressed than in that famous passage in the *Dialogus de Scaccario* when the Scholar observes 'I seem to gather from what you have said that any knight or other discreet man may be appointed sheriff or bailiff by the king even if he holds nothing of him, but holds only of others.' The Master replies that it pertains to the royal prerogative 'that, if the king perceives the necessity, any man may be freely taken and deputed to the king's service regardless of whose man he is, or for whom he serves or fights'. The Scholar aptly comments that now he perceives the truth of Ovid, that the hands of the king extend far indeed.[75]

[74] *Yorkshire Inquisitions (1241–1316), II*, ed. W. Brown (Yorkshire Archaeological and Topographical Assoc., Rec. Ser. 23; 1898), 19 n.

[75] Richard fitzNeal, *De necessariis observantibus scaccarii dialogus commonly called Dialogus de Scaccario*, ed. and trans. C. Johnson (London, 1950), 84. I have adapted Johnson's translation.

Henry II and his immediate royal descendants sought with success to give substance to these opinions. Gradually the activities of all classes came to be strongly influenced by the Crown, and it has been argued recently that under Henry III the practice of public obligation was taken to its limits.[76] Those qualified for knighthood, in particular, became essential to the efficient operation of government, serving in a host of capacities in accordance with the varied responsibilities heaped upon them. Greater lords too were integrated into the scheme as ambassadors, military commanders, and administrators, thereby imposing restrictions upon their freedom of action, their crusading plans included. Simon de Montfort, for example, was employed in all these capacities by Henry III, and his appointment as seneschal of Gascony in 1248 necessitated the laying aside of his second crusading vow of 1247.[77]

Control was also exercised over the king's immediate kinsmen; they too were required for responsibilities at home, especially if they were heirs to the throne at the time. Part, at least, of Henry III's evident opposition in 1238 to the projected crusade of Richard of Cornwall probably lay in the fact that until the birth of the Lord Edward in June 1239 the earl was heir to the throne.[78] Edward's own crusading plans some thirty years later met with initial resistance from Henry, and, as Hilda Johnstone demonstrated, Edward as king was no less concerned to monitor closely the actions of his own heir, Edward of Carnarvon.[79]

The king's permission was theoretically required before any of his subjects could leave the realm; the crusade was no exceptional circumstance.[80] Generally, that licence can have been only a formality,

[76] S. L. Waugh, 'Reluctant Knights and Jurors: Respites, Exemptions, and Public Obligations in the Reign of Henry III', *Speculum*, lviii (1983), 937–86.

[77] Paris, *CM* v. 77, reports that Simon went to Gascony having commuted or deferred his vow; and see Bémont, *Simon de Montfort*, tr. Jacob, pp. 90–2.

[78] *Reg. Gregory IX*, Nos. 4095, 4267–8, 4608; and see Paris, *CM* iii, 340, for Henry's refusal, on the same grounds, of Frederick II's request in 1236 that Richard lead an expedition against Louis IX.

[79] H. Johnstone, *Edward of Carnarvon, 1284–1307* (Manchester, 1947). Henry II's opposition to the independent crusading aspirations of his sons provides perhaps the most instructive illustration of this pattern. He protested vehemently at the Young Henry's vow in 1183, pressing him to revoke his decision: Howden, *Gesta*, i. 297–8; id., *Chron.* ii. 276. John was refused permission to leave with the patriarch of Jerusalem in 1185: Gerald of Wales (Giraldus Cambrensis), *Opera*, ed. J. S. Brewer *et al.* 8 vols. (RS; 1861–91) viii. 208–9. Richard was upbraided for taking vows without prior consultation in 1187, Henry insisting that he wait until he himself was ready to depart: ibid. viii. 244; Ralph de Diceto, *Opera historica*, ed. W. Stubbs, 2 vols. (RS; 1876), ii. 50.

[80] Howden, *Chron.* ii. 299–300, e.g., reports Henry II granting general licence to all his subjects to take the Cross in 1185, when Patriarch Eraclius came to England. For

but on occasion precise conditions were attached if the services of the crusader in question were required at home. In January 1217, for example, the brothers Peter, Nicholas, and Walter de Letres were permitted to go on crusade and pledge their lands held in chief, providing they gave security that they would not leave England without royal licence and before the general passage of crusaders.[81] The regency council's desperate need for military service at this critical time was undoubtedly the vital consideration. In certain circumstances the needs of king and realm could even lead to outright refusal of permission to take the Cross, as when Henry II reacted against the aspirations of Abbot Samson of Bury St Edmunds in 1188. Shortly after taking the Cross himself, Henry came to Bury to pray at the saint's tomb. Samson had secretly made a Cross of linen cloth and, holding it together with needle and thread, asked Henry's permission to receive it. However, at the instance of Bishop John of Norwich, *crucesignatus* himself, Henry refused Samson on the grounds that 'it would not be expedient for the country [*patria*] nor safe for the counties of Norfolk and Suffolk, if both the bishop of Norwich and the abbot of St Edmund departed at the same time'.[82] Henry's response emerges as statesmanlike when it is remembered that the abbot possessed eight and a half hundreds in west Suffolk, a consolidated bloc which dominated that part of the county and one of the very largest private franchises in England. The abbot's role and influence in local government and society was immense.[83]

Even after an individual had taken the Cross he might be obliged to remain at home or return thither. Robert Burnell, for example, intended to set out with his master, the Lord Edward, in 1270,[84] but either he never sailed or else he turned back within days, because he was sent on Edward's behalf to Llywelyn ap Gruffydd on 30 August 1270.[85] Thereafter he rose to become one of Edward's attorneys during his absence. Quite possibly Edward had not given

Lord Edward's licence from Henry III to set out on crusade, see 'Winchester', p. 109; 'Worcester', p. 459.

[81] *PR 1216–25*, pp. 21, 25. The three appear in royal service from Oct. 1214, close associates of the infamous Philip Marc, sheriff of Nottingham.

[82] Jocelin of Brakelond, *Cronica Jocelini de Brakelonda de rebus gestis Samsonis abbatis monasterii Sancti Edmundi*, ed. and trans. H. E. Butler (London, 1949), 53–4.

[83] See H. M. Cam, *Liberties and Communities in Medieval England* (London, 1963), ch. 13, for the abbot's position. The bishop of Norwich also possessed private hundreds, one and a quarter in Suffolk: id., *The Hundred and the Hundred Rolls* (London, 1930), 55. Henry's refusal of Samson may be more particularly related to the continuing friction between Henry and Roger Bigod over Roger's claim to inherit the earldom of Norfolk. See W. L. Warren, *Henry II* (London, 1973), 384.

[84] He received a judicial protection and letters of attorney: *CPR 1266–72*, pp. 440, 450.

[85] Ibid. 457.

up hope of forcing through his candidature of Burnell as the new archbishop of Canterbury, and therefore ordered him to remain at home.[86]

Above all, perhaps, the king required the services of his subjects for his wars, and in this connection a close correlation between military activity at home and the departure of crusaders can be observed. It cannot be just coincidence that the Fourth Crusade elicited a negligible response from England at a time when Richard I and John urgently required military service in defence of the Plantagenet inheritance in France, whilst Edward I's series of great campaigns in the thirty years after 1277 seem to have played a major part in limiting the participation on crusade of the military classes then. Indeed, the needs of the king and realm at such times allowed the imposition of restraints upon the movements of knights and men-at-arms. In 1205, for example, John issued that famous writ whereby knights and others who failed in their duty to defend the realm, against what was perceived as imminent Capetian invasion, were left in no doubt that they and their heirs ran the risk of being disinherited forever.[87] The Montfortian regime attempted to mobilize these selfsame classes in its defence in 1264–5,[88] while Edward I was so enraged by a group of important barons and knights who deserted the Scottish campaign of 1306 without leave, apparently to tourney overseas, that he ordered the seizure of their lands and goods and instructed that they be kept in close custody in the Tower. Not until January 1307 were they reconciled to the king.[89]

If it could be demonstrated that the king's interests or the safety of the realm were at stake, then the papacy provided reinforcement. This was early made apparent in 1189 when Richard I secured from Clement III the privilege of retaining at home those *crucesignati* whose services he required to safeguard his lands.[90] Hugh du Puiset, bishop of Durham, was one such, appointed co-justiciar of the realm and created earl of Northumberland.[91] In December 1189 Clement for-

86 Wykes, *Chron.*, p. 235, records Edward's unsuccessful lobbying of the Canterbury chapter before his departure. See ibid. 238–40, for the dispatch home of Henry of Almain to provide for the government of England and Gascony, before his murder at Viterbo.

87 *RLP* p. 55.

88 See, amongst others, M. R. Powicke, *Military Obligation in Medieval England: A Study in Liberty and Duty* (Oxford, 1962), 91–4.

89 *CFR 1272–1307*, pp. 543–4; *CCR 1302–7*, pp. 481–2. Throughout the period of the Scottish wars Edward sought, though not always successfully, to regulate the movements and activities of his subjects. See esp. *CCR 1296–1302*, p. 370, for the case concerning Earl Henry de Lacy.

90 Howden, *Chron.* iii. 17; Richard of Devizes, *Chronicon Richardi Divisensis De tempore regis Richardi primi*, ed. and trans. J. T. Appleby (London, 1963), 6.

91 Howden, *Gesta*, ii. 87; id., *Chron.* iii. 13; Devizes, *Chron.*, p. 6.

bade him to depart whilst Richard was absent, recalling that Richard had deputed Hugh to the custody of the realm. It was indeed at the royal instance that Clement was urging the bishop to lay aside the Cross; besides his dignity did not fit him to prosecute the crusade.[92] Amongst other *crucesignati* kept at home by Richard were three of the associate justiciars: Hugh Bardolf, William Brewer, and Geoffrey fitzPeter. Their vows were only suspended, not redeemed, and soon after John succeeded to the throne they became the subject of stormy and protracted negotiations between the king and Innocent III. They are of some interest for the light they shed on the predicament which faced those *crucesignati* caught in a conflict between a king who desired their services as *curiales regis* and a pope who sought their services as *milites Christi*.

Faced with the critical struggle with Philip II over the Plantagenet inheritance, John was quite naturally loath to countenance the departure on crusade of such devoted, able, and important royal servants of many years' experience. It was probably in 1202 that he sought from Innocent the absolution or deferment of the vows not only of these three, but of William de Stuteville, Robert de Berkeley, and Alan and Thomas Basset besides.[93] Innocent, however, was less inclined to indulge the English king in this matter than Clement III, not least because he wished to maximize participation in the Fourth Crusade.[94] And unlike Richard, John was not about to depart on crusade himself: his needs were neither of the same order nor so pressing in the papal view. Innocent ordered an inquiry, and he was clearly suspicious of the claim that de Stuteville and de Berkeley had procured absolution beforehand.[95] John responded by sending an embassy to Rome in 1202 but Innocent refused to give way. Enraged at being balked, John prohibited his subjects from receiving any papal emissary, according to Innocent's admonitory letter of February 1203.[96] As far as Geoffrey fitzPeter, his justiciar, was concerned, John was at least partially satisfied in the long run. In November he took up the matter again, underlining the grave situation in which he found himself, the duty of his subjects to defend his interests, and the

[92] *Historiae Dunelmensis Scriptores Tres, Gaufridus de Coldingham, Robertus de Graystones, et Willelmus de Chambre*, ed. J. Raine (Surtees Soc. 9; 1839), appendix xliv. Those who had taken vows at Hugh's instance were to follow suit. The due fulfilment of Hugh's vow upon Richard's return was a matter deliberately left open, but it seems that Hugh redeemed his vow, the chroniclers suggesting before Richard's departure.

[93] *CLI*, No. 364. John wished no less to retain the services of certain Norman officials: ibid., Nos. 356–7.

[94] Ibid., Nos. 261, 350, 439.

[95] Ibid., No. 439.

[96] Ibid., No. 465; *Selected Letters of Pope Innocent III Concerning England (1198–1216)*, ed. C. R. Cheney, trans. W. H. Semple (London, 1953), No. 17.

pressing need for fitzPeter's counsels.[97] He requested that his crusade be deferred for four or five years, but in July 1205, in response to the justiciar's own plea, Innocent agreed only to a three-year postponement.[98] But fitzPeter never sailed; he commuted his vow for 2000*m*. on his deathbed in 1213.[99]

Innocent's reactions stand in marked contrast to the attitude of his successors, who were quite prepared to put the interests of king and realm before the crusade. Honorius III was the first to grant dispensations more or less automatically to those whom the king required at home. In the exceptional circumstances of 1217 it comes as no surprise to find Honorius authorizing Guala, his legate, to suspend the vows of royalist *crucesignati* until peace and stability were restored to the realm. In the meantime they should assist the young Henry III.[100] Yet even after the settling of England Honorius was ready to indulge the interests of the Crown. In January 1219 he instructed the legate Pandulf to examine and take action upon Hubert de Burgh's petition that he be dispensed from his vow because his absence on crusade would be injurious to king and realm. The apparent ease with which Hubert duly procured dispensation provides a sharp contrast to the difficulties which faced Geoffrey fitzPeter, his predecessor as justiciar.[101] Nor was Hubert alone, for in March 1219 Honorius instructed Pandulf to redeem the vows of those nobles, and their followers, whose services were useful to the king.[102] Later popes consistently maintained Honorius's stance judging from the available evidence. In 1238, for example, Gregory IX attempted to prevent the departure of Richard of Cornwall, Simon de Montfort, William Longespee, and their followers on the grounds of national security. The loss of their material support and counsel would only jeopardize the realm, Gregory explained in forbidding them to sail until they received special papal licence to proceed, and threatening to withdraw their crusaders' indulgence if they disobeyed.[103] This

97 *Foedera*, I. i. 91 98 *CLI*, No. 633.

99 C. R. Cheney, *Innocent III and England*, (Stuttgart, 1976), 260. None of the other six appears to have gone on crusade.

100 See below, pp. 208–9.

101 *Reg. Honorius III*, No. 1842. Hubert almost certainly took his second vow in 1232: *Reg. Gregory IX*, Nos. 1561–3; 'Tewkesbury', p. 86; 'Dunstable', p. 128. This was redeemed in 1240: *The Register or Rolls of Walter Gray, Archbishop of York*, ed. J. Raine (Surtees Soc. 56; 1872), 199.

102 *Reg. Honorius III*, No. 1959. His stance is emphasized by his strenuous efforts otherwise to secure departure of *crucesignati* on the Fifth Crusade: ibid., Nos. 1716, 2422; *RHGF* xix. 668.

103 *Reg. Gregory IX*, Nos. 4094–6, and further Nos. 4267–72, 4608–9. Gregory's motives were mixed. He preferred to see redemption of those vows, probably to provide cash for the struggle against Frederick II, and he seems, with reason, to have feared that Frederick would seek to deploy these forces to his own advantage. The imperial and

instance, however, reveals the limitations to papal influence in the face of great men of substance determined to go on crusade.[104]

If the king himself was *crucesignatus* and his project enjoyed papal blessing, then the combination of royal and papal pressures was so intense as to be almost irresistible: the measures taken in response to Henry III's assumption of the Cross in 1250 most clearly illustrate the point. One of Henry's initial reactions was to petition Innocent IV to prevent the prior departure of those of his subjects who were already *crucesignati*, for Henry naturally wished to be accompanied by as many of them as possible. According to Paris, however, the magnates met in council at Bermondsey in April 1250 and fixed their passage for 24 June, declaring that they would not 'defer their duty to the heavenly king for the service of any earthly king'. Henry, quite clearly, had sought to persuade them to depart in his company, and Paris further indicates that the king, learning of their intentions before the council, had sent to Rome for papal reinforcement of his position.[105] This was no baseless gossip on Paris's part for, unless we are to add forgery to his many presumed sins, he preserves the texts of two of Innocent's mandates, of June and November 1250, in appropriate response to Henry's petition.[106] Thereafter, Innocent consistently supported Henry in this matter and once the king, in April 1252, had fixed his passage for 24 June 1256, he took action at Henry's instance to compel all *crucesignati* to sail with him under pain of censure.[107] Henry threatened secular penalties as well. In October 1252 Robert de Quenci, for one, was warned that, under pain of losing his lands, he should by no means leave the realm except with special royal licence.[108]

Control over the timing of their passage gave way to control over the goal to which crusaders should address themselves, following Henry's acceptance of Sicily for the Lord Edmund in 1254.[109] In May

Plantagenet courts had drawn close together following the marriage of Frederick and Isabella Plantagenet in 1235. In Feb. 1238 Frederick invited Richard to pass through his lands *en route* to the East: Paris, *CM* iii. 471–2. Gregory's fears can only have been compounded by Henry's dispatch of a force under Henry de Trubleville to aid the imperial army in northern Italy: ibid. 491; *CPR 1232–47*, p. 221; *CLR 1226–40*, p. 364.

[104] For the Lord Edward's determination to see through his crusading plans, see below, pp. 114–15, 231–2.

[105] Paris, *CM* v. 103–4. He also says, ibid. 135, that Henry instructed the keepers of Dover and other ports to prevent their departure. See *CPR 1247–58*, p. 79.

[106] Paris, *CM* vi. Nos. 97–8; v. 104, 135; 'Tewkesbury', p. 141. From Paris, *CM* v. 103–4, it appears that Innocent's intervention was indeed heeded.

[107] See e.g. *CR 1251–3*, p. 210; *Reg. Innocent IV*, No. 5979.

[108] *CR 1251–3*, p. 434. Robert, *crucesignatus* by Nov. 1247, perhaps wished to join the crusade at this time: *Reg. Innocent IV*, No. 3475; Paris, *CM* v. 99.

[109] See below, pp. 221–5.

1255 Alexander IV authorized the commutation to Sicily of the vows of Haakon IV of Norway and those of his subjects. No appeal was allowed, and ecclesiastical censure was threatened if it proved necessary.[110] Henry's own subjects were under no less pressure. For example, those who refused to commute their vows were to lose any moneys for the crusade which they had already been granted, an immensely persuasive sanction.[111] At the papal Curia there was some intense lobbying concerning the vows of *crucesignati* of the lordship of Ireland. The archbishop of Tuam and his suffragans successfully petitioned Alexander IV to restrain John fitzGeoffrey, the justiciar, and other royal bailiffs from preventing *crucesignati* proceeding in aid of the Holy Land, but in a private audience with Alexander the king's proctors succeeded in producing something of a fudge: the letters would not extend to fitzGeoffrey and his fellows, and they were not to be prejudiced thereby.[112] Since only a handful of Henry III's subjects are known to have departed for the East in the 1250s, the claim made by the barons in January 1264 before Louis IX seems largely justified: the vows of Henry 'and of all his people' had been commuted to the Sicilian business.[113]

The crusade, then, was a complicated business. There were all sorts of restraints and controls, and the pitfalls of royal and papal policies to avoid. Yet if men were prevented from taking the Cross or fulfilling their vows, or if self-imposed restraints induced them to remain at home, they could nevertheless support the crusade in other ways: by making voluntary grants to the crusading subsidy, by making provision in their wills, by dispatching paid substitutes as vicarious crusaders, or by directly patronizing institutions in the Latin East. Plenty of examples of these devices can be found, but the case of Richard of Cornwall's support may be cited by way of general illustration. In 1238, already *crucesignatus*, he granted a large sum of money to Emperor Baldwin II of Constantinople on the occasion of Baldwin's first visit to England.[114] In 1245, on hearing of the fall of Jerusalem, he sent around 1000*l.* to the aid of the Holy Land via the Hospital, probably to hire knights or bolster the defences of Ascalon

[110] *Foedera*, I. i. 320–1.

[111] Ibid. 322. It was now that Alexander IV ordered preaching in England of the crusade against Manfred: 'Burton', pp. 350–3.

[112] *CPR 1247–58*, p. 512; *Calendar of Documents relating to Ireland Preserved in Her Majesty's Record Office, 1171–1307*, ed. H. S. Sweetman and G. F. Handcock, 5 vols. (London, 1877–86), ii. No. 480.

[113] *Documents of the Baronial Movement of Reform and Rebellion, 1258–1267*, selected R. F. Treharne, ed. I. J. Sanders (Oxford, 1973), No. 37c, p. 278. Strictly speaking, Henry's vow was not commuted. See below, p. 124.

[114] Paris, *CM* iii. 480–1.

which he had helped to fortify when on crusade a few years earlier.[115] Richard plainly kept in close touch with events in the East and may well have continued to send part of his legendary wealth to Outremer on a regular basis.[116] Matthew Paris says of him that none was more solicitous about the state of the Holy Land.[117] If Guisborough is correct, he took the Cross for a second time, his son Henry of Almain bearing his Cross vicariously in 1270.[118] That he left money to the Holy Land is certain: in September 1272 Gregory X instructed that his considerable legacy of 7,000*m.* be procured from his heir, Edmund of Cornwall.[119] Richard was exceptional by virtue of his birth, station, and wealth, and only the greatest could match his contribution to the crusade, but it was a difference of scale rather than kind. Those who wished could meet their obligations to the crusade in ways appropriate to their own standing, personal commitment, and circumstances. Some were more penny-pinching than others. Robert de Bingham, for example, left 2*s.* in aid of the Holy Land in 1304, 'providing that nothing further is to be sold of my goods in aid of that Holy Land for whatever reason'.[120] There were limits to a man's generosity.

Motivation and Recruitment

Crusader motivation is a notoriously difficult business. Some were obliged to take the Cross, both Church and Crown regarding the imposition of the Cross as condign punishment for a variety of sins, and malefactors from England and elsewhere continued to travel to the Holy Land in the thirteenth century, either as penitents or as refugees fearing retribution at home for their crimes.[121] However, as the thirteenth century progressed it became quite normal for the

[115] Ibid. iv. 415–16. For his fortifications at Ascalon, see ibid. 142–3; *Reg. Innocent IV*, No. 1784.

[116] For news reports reaching Richard, see Paris, *CM* iv. 25, 147–53, 300–5; v. 165–9, 411. Two of his messengers went to the East in 1250. See B. Z. Kedar, 'The Passenger List of a Crusader Ship, 1250: Towards the History of the Popular Element on the Seventh Crusade', *Studi medievali*, 3rd ser. xiii (1972), 270.

[117] Paris, *CM* v. 411.

[118] Walter of Guisborough, *The Chronicle of Walter of Guisborough*, ed. H. Rothwell (Camden Soc., 3rd ser., 89; 1957), p. 205.

[119] *Reg. Gregory X*, No. 830.

[120] HMC, *Middleton MSS* (London, 1911), 84.

[121] See e.g. the testimony of Burchard of Mount Sion, discussed in A. Grabois, 'Christian Pilgrims in the Thirteenth Century and the Latin Kingdom of Jerusalem: Burchard of Mount Sion', in B. Z. Kedar *et al.* (eds.), *Outremer: Studies in the History of the Crusading Kingdom of Jerusalem Presented to Joshua Prawer* (Jerusalem, 1982), 293.

penitent to redeem his vow, even in the most notorious cases.[122] For example, on 21 August 1279 Bishop Godfrey Giffard of Worcester heard the extraordinary case against Peter de la Mare, constable of Bristol castle, and certain of his accomplices, excommunicated for violating sanctuary by forcibly dragging William de Lay from the church of SS Philip and James, Bristol, detaining and then beheading him in the castle. This outrage evidently fired local opinion, for the unfortunate William emerged as something of a cult figure, and Bishop Godfrey had to take action to counter assertions that William was a martyr who performed miracles, and to proscribe songs and compositions about him in public. Popular feeling may explain the nature of the onerous penances imposed. The principal villains were to exhume the body and head and carry them to be buried in the churchyard of SS Philip and James; to go in solemn procession to the church from the Minors' convent by the most public ways on four consecutive market days, barefoot, heads uncovered, wearing only shirts and breeches; and to receive discipline at the church door. Peter himself, and those others whose hands were not directly stained with William's blood, was to perform just one of these public penances, but he was also to endow a priest to chant for William's soul in perpetuity, erect a stone cross and cause 100 poor to be fed at the cross every year, each pauper receiving 1*d*. However, Bishop Godfrey further ruled that if the excommunicates took the Cross then their punishment might be reduced to one procession and one discipline. It was a tempting offer, and two days later the bishop announced that if Peter and his henchmen should send one of their number to the Holy Land at their cost, or hire a substitute, then nothing further would be exacted so far as the crusade was concerned. Whether a sum was then paid, or a suitable warrior sent to the East, is unknown, but Peter, the instigator of the crime, certainly remained in England and in the king's service.[123]

The Crown also looked to the crusade and pilgrimage to the Holy Land as an appropriate penalty for crimes touching the king's jurisdiction.[124] Less frequently, the Crown sought to pack political dissidents off to the Holy Land. According to one chronicler, the

[122] Innocent III insisted as a general principle that such penitents should go on crusade, even if they could not fight, provided they were able-bodied. See *CLI*, No. 261, e.g. His successors were altogether more indulgent.

[123] *Reg. G. Giffard*, pp. 110–13. The excommunication was lifted on 22 Aug. Close and Patent Roll entries reveal Peter's presence in England until his death in 1296. His royal pardon for William's death reveals that William was beheaded after he broke prison: *CPR 1281–92*, p. 152.

[124] See N. D. Hurnard, *The King's Pardon for Homicide* (Oxford, 1969), *passim*, and esp. pp. 227–8, for the exceptionally well-documented case of William de Munchensi of Edwardeston.

troublesome William de Forz was banished for six years to serve in the Holy Land upon the suppression of his rebellion in 1221, but if so the sentence must have been relaxed for Count William remained in England.[125] On the surrender of Bedford castle in August 1224, three of Faulkes de Bréauté's men were sentenced to take the Templars' habit and to fight in the Holy Land.[126] In the 1280s Edward I sought to deal with two of his most dangerous opponents in the same way. In 1282 Archbishop Pecham informed David ap Gruffydd that if he took the Cross the king would provide for him in a manner commensurate with his status, on condition that he did not return until recalled by Edward. Pecham met with a stinging reply, and David remained to meet his gruesome death shortly afterwards.[127] In 1286, in Paris, Edward and Philip the Fair discussed, *inter alia*, the possibility of a new joint crusade. That inveterate troublemaker Gaston de Béarn inevitably figured high in the deliberations, and amongst other conditions for the venture it was suggested that Gaston's fortresses be dismantled, Gaston himself 'to go to the Holy Land to remain there, unless he should be recalled by the king of England'. Gaston's lands would remain in Edward's hands at his pleasure against the debt owed to him by Philip.[128] As Ellis has commented, the scheme to deal with Gaston by taking him to the Holy Land and then unceremoniously leaving him there was unscrupulous, but it is indicative of the perceived threat to stability which he posed.[129] Gaston, like David ap Gruffydd, did not set out, but Edward's attempt to remove both men from the scene is indicative of his perception of the crusade as an appropriate, if occasional, means of ridding his dominions of political dissidents.

Yet the great majority took the Cross voluntarily, but precisely because the crusade existed at the intersection of so many social and cultural currents, and since its attraction was never monolithic for this reason, the problem of motivation is rendered peculiarly intractable. It is possible to point to a series of mundane and spiritual motives but, put bluntly, the crusade could mean all things to all men, and the exact reasons which led an individual to take the Cross voluntarily cannot be positively asserted with any confidence. Nevertheless, certain influences and factors can be usefully discussed. With

125 'Worcester', p. 413.

126 'Dunstable', p. 88. Faulkes later testified that he and his men were already *crucesignati*: Walter of Coventry, *Memoriale fratris Walteri de Coventria: The Historical Collections of Walter of Coventry*, ed. W. Stubbs, 2 vols. (RS; 1872, 1873), ii. 265, 267.

127 *Registrum Epistolarum Johannis Peckham Archiepiscopi Cantuariensis (1279–92)*, ed. C. T. Martin, 3 vols. (RS; 1882–5), ii. 467, 471.

128 PRO, C 47, 29/2/2.

129 J. Ellis, 'Gaston de Béarn: A Study in Anglo-Gascon Relations (1229–90)', D.Phil. thesis (Oxford, 1952), 505–8.

particular reference to those of the degree of knighthood, it may first be stressed that the crusade had deeply penetrated their culture in the thirteenth century. Thanks to the Church's promotion of the figure of the *miles Christi*, the parallel formulations of romance and epic, and the very practice and experience of the first crusades, few could have escaped its impact. A significant proportion of the literature composed for their entertainment was concerned with the deeds of knights confronting the infidel. The struggle lay at the heart of the Charlemagne cycle and provided the crucial focus of the *chansons de croisade* and compositions which celebrated later crusading heroes such as Richard I. Arthurian romance held up the ideal in somewhat different fashion, but works such as *Perlesvaus* and the *Queste del Saint Graal* served equally to instil the notion that the knight should wield his sword in a sacred cause.[130]

The *chansons* and romances were not intended only to entertain. Mehl has pointed out that nearly all of the Middle English romances survive in collections which for the most part contain religious and didactic works, and he warns against divorcing the romances from devotional literature in general, underlining further that most of them glorify particular exemplary heroes.[131] The works concerning conflict with the infidel are no exception, and it is clear that they were regarded partly as edificatory tales, with a strong exemplary component, bearing a certain affinity to saints' lives.[132] This would seem to be the case with the Anglo-Norman and French works which preceded them and upon which most of the Middle English romances were based.[133] Some works, indeed, were explicitly composed as exempla, like William de Briane's Anglo-Norman translation of the *Pseudo-Turpin*, *c*.1214–16, which treated of the legendary deeds of

[130] Guy de Beauchamp's donation of books to Bordesley abbey in 1306 provides a rare glimpse of the exposure of a man of his class to works with a crusading flavour: *inter alia*, his collection included a volume 'qe parle des quatres principals Gestes de Charles', a *Titus and Vespasian*, a *William of Orange*, a *Sir Ferumbras*, a *Saint Graal*, and the 'Romaunce de Willame de Loungespee', which surely celebrates the hero of Mansourah, 1250, and not his father as Blaess suggests. See M. Blaess, 'L'Abbaye de Bordesley et les livres de Guy de Beauchamp', *Romania*, lxxviii (1957), 511–18.

[131] D. Mehl, *The Middle English Romances of the Thirteenth and Fourteenth Centuries* (London, 1969), esp. pp. 10–13, 17–21, 253–4.

[132] The affinity of saints' lives and *chansons* as exempla, from the Church's point of view, is well expressed by Thomas of Chobham in his *Poenitentia*, quoted in H. J. Chaytor, *The Troubadours and England* (Cambridge, 1923), 3. Paris theologians of the early 13th c. approved the recital of edifying stories, the true jongleur recounting princely deeds and the lives of saints. See J. W. Baldwin, *Masters, Princes, and Merchants: The Social Views of Peter the Chanter and His Circle*, 2 vols. (Princeton, 1970), i. 203–4.

[133] See M. D. Legge, *Anglo-Norman Literature and its Background* (Oxford, 1963), 243–4.

Charlemagne in Spain.[134] Those engaged in promoting the crusade eagerly sought to press such works into service. In particular, Humbert of Romans recommended that preachers utilize histories of the crusades and *chansons*, including the *Pseudo-Turpin*, the *Chanson d'Antioche*, Jacques de Vitry's *Historia Orientalis*, and certain apposite saints' lives.[135] He further devotes an entire chapter of his *De Praedicatione Sanctae Crucis* to the recruitment value of the crusading heroes of old, fastening specifically upon the deeds of Charlemagne in Spain, Godfrey de Bouillon and other figures of the First Crusade, and Richard I and other leaders of the Third Crusade.[136] Evidently, the works treating of the conflict with the infidel, and the attitudes they convey, helped clear the way for the favourable reception of the preacher's message, and they were appropriate because the hypothetical audience could have been expected to be well-versed in the legendary deeds of the likes of Charlemagne, and the heroics of leaders of the historical crusade.[137]

The considerable adulation accorded contemporary crusading heroes, and the proportion of works in which some crusading experience is almost obligatory for legendary heroes such as 'Gui de Warewic' or 'Sir Beues of Hamtoun' indicates that participation in crusades was widely accepted as an integral feature of that standard of knightly behaviour which, if few achieved, all should strive to attain. This is further underlined by the pertinent observations in many chivalric treatises. Ramon Lull, for example, considered that the first duty of a knight is to defend the faith against the infidel.[138] For Baudouin de Condé the crusade marks the highest grade of

134 *The Anglo-Norman 'Pseudo-Turpin Chronicle' of William de Briane*, ed. I. Short (Anglo-Norman Text Soc. 25; 1973), ll. 23–7. See also *The Old French Johannes Translation of the Pseudo-Turpin Chronicle*, ed. R. N. Walpole, 2 vols. (Berkeley, 1976), i. 106–8.

135 Humbert of Romans, *Tractatus Solemnis Fr. H. de Praedicatione Sanctae Crucis*, ed. P. Wagner (Nuremberg, *c.*1495), caps. 30–43. Humbert passes over Arthurian romance, but its didactic and exemplary qualities were apposite, at least in works such as *Perlesvaus* and *La Queste del Saint Graal*. Stephen of Bourbon was one preacher of the crusade to utilize Arthurian romance, judging by his collection of anecdotes. See Stephen of Bourbon, *Anecdotes Historiques, Légendes et Apologues d'Étienne de Bourbon*, ed. A. Lecoy de la Marche (Soc. de l'histoire de France; 1877), 86–7.

136 *De Praedicatione Sanctae Crucis*, cap. 16. The value of historical exempla had long been appreciated by the clergy as a means to urge reform of the laity. See Orderic Vitalis, *Historia Ecclesiastica*, ed. M. Chibnall (Oxford, 1969–80), vol. III, book VI, pp. 216, 226–8, for the well-known case of Gerold, chaplain to Earl Hugh of Chester, who made telling use of stories of soldier saints and the exploits of William of Aquitaine in Spain.

137 These works possessed three particular qualities which helped the preacher. They revealed divine support in the conflict with the infidel; they 'proved' the past success of Christian arms; and they recounted the deeds of exemplary heroes whose exploits should be emulated.

138 See M. H. Keen, *Chivalry* (New Haven, London, 1984), 9.

knighthood. If a bachelor wishes to be considered a perfect knight, then he must leave the tournament behind him and take the Cross: only upon fighting the infidel will he have become a true *prudhomme*.[139] Precisely because that standard of knighthood embraced all members of the peer group, and those who aspired to join their ranks, additional force was lent to those appeals which stressed knights' obligations towards the crusade. The appeal might be resisted, but that the crusade existed as an expression of ideal knightly behaviour—a theoretical imperative, incumbent on all—could not easily be denied by contemporaries who valued honour and prestige so highly and were concerned to cut a figure in their world. The crusade had become an *idée fixe*, and the call could not simply be ignored as a consequence.

Such considerations help to explain the continuing appeal of the crusade, but it is extremely difficult to ascertain their precise recruitment value. Some, as Humbert of Romans hoped, may have been fired by the tales of heroic knights, past and present.[140] To many the crusade may have represented both a Christian gesture of concern for the fate of the Holy Land and an enterprise in which the crusader was simultaneously *miles Christi* and knight errant: eager for adventures, desirous of displaying his martial prowess and other chivalric qualities, and seeking to win enviable prestige on earth whilst laying up merit in heaven. In commenting upon Earl Ranulf of Chester's deeds on the Fifth Crusade, the Barnwell annalist neatly made the point through his observation that 'Thereby he acquired for himself glory and honour before God and men.'[141]

This mingling and interpenetration of Christian and secular values in the knightly perception of the crusade has recently been explored afresh by Keen. More particularly, he has shown that tournaments, notwithstanding the fierce and consistent opposition of the Church, were closely connected in chivalric circles with the promotion and preparation of crusades.[142] The one was not opposed to the other in knightly culture; on the contrary, crusade and tournament provided an opportunity of displaying the same chivalric qualities and of winning that adulation and prestige so jealously sought, whilst in the

[139] Keen, *Chivalry*, 56, 98.

[140] It is significant that one of the first vernacular versions of the *Pseudo-Turpin* was translated for Count Hugh of St-Pol, one of Richard I's crusading companions. A related work, the *Descriptio*, was apparently translated for another of his companions, William de Cayeux. Warin fitzGerold, another crusader, probably commissioned William de Briane's Anglo-Norman version of the *Pseudo-Turpin*. See R. N. Walpole, 'Charlemagne and Roland: A Study of the Source of Two Middle English Metrical Romances, *Roland and Vernagu* and *Otuel and Roland*', *University of California Publications in Modern Philology*, xxi (1944), 399; *The Anglo-Norman Pseudo-Turpin*, pp. 2–5.

[141] Coventry, *Memoriale*, ii. 246.

[142] Keen, *Chivalry*, chs. 3, 5, *passim*.

view of some, such as Baudouin de Condé, tourneying was, or should be, a preparation for that highest of jousts—with the infidel.[143] It is, then, interesting to find that many prominent English crusaders were keen participants in tournaments. Of the thirty-eight knights specified by name as receiving equipment from Edward I for the Windsor tournament of July 1278, fifteen had been on crusade in 1270 or taken vows for that expedition.[144] To their number should certainly be added Edward himself, the Lord Edmund, Roger de Leyburn, Hamo Lestrange, Henry of Almain, and James de Audley: all were renowned for tourneying.[145] More remarkable is the fact that no less than fourteen of the seven earls and ten barons prohibited by Henry III from tourneying at Northampton and Cambridge in 1234[146] departed on crusade between 1239–41, or took vows. Here already was the nucleus of the English crusading forces, including, of the leaders, Richard of Cornwall, William de Forz, and William Longespee, and four of the bannerets named by Paris. Earl Gilbert Marshal, significantly enough, died at the Hertford tournament of 1241 on the point of departure for the East.[147] This correlation is not altogether surprising for crusade leaders primarily required the services of strenuous and effective knights. Aside from campaigns, tournaments were the chief training grounds for acquiring experience of the martial skills of knights in practice, and those keen to tourney were perhaps the more likely to respond to crusading appeals precisely because they took chivalric values sufficiently seriously to indulge in such pursuits.

It may be presumed that those who went on crusade, or took vows, more than once were genuinely devoted to the cause of the Holy

143 Henry III's commissioning of wall-paintings celebrating his crusading ancestors' deeds gains added significance as a result. See below, pp. 199–200. In the romances and epics touching on conflict with the infidel the challenge to single combat is a stock topos.

144 The earls of Cornwall, Gloucester, and Surrey, William de Valence, Roger de Clifford, Robert Tiptoft, Hugh fitzOtto, Payn and Patrick de Chaworth, Giles de Fiennes, Gerard de St-Laurent, John II of Brittany, Bartholomew de Brianso, William de Geneville, Roger de Trumpington. See 'Copy of a Roll of Purchases Made for the Tournament of Windsor Park, in the Sixth Year of Edward the First', ed. S. Lysons, *Archaeologia*, xvii (1814), 297–310.

145 See N. Denholm-Young, 'The Tournament in the Thirteenth Century', in R. W. Hunt *et al.* (eds.), *Studies in Medieval History Presented to Frederick Maurice Powicke* (Oxford, 1948), 251, 255–60, and sources cited. Many of their crusading companions participated in that débâcle of a tournament at Chalon, 1273, on their return from the East.

145 *CPR 1232–47*, p. 68.

147 Paris, *CM* iv. 135–6. The bannerets were Peter de Brus, Hugh Wake, Philip Basset, and Gerard de Furnivall, who was fined in 1235 for tourneying at Cambridge: *CR 1234–7*, p. 210. The remaining *crucesignati* were William de Vescy, Ralph de Thony, a participant of the 1239 French crusade, Robert Marmion, John and Richard de Grey, and Earl John of Lincoln.

Land, and found crusading to be compatible with their ideals and chivalric values. Philip Daubeny, for example, went to the East in 1221, 1228, and 1235. That he was considered to be a model of chivalric behaviour is suggested by his appointment as 'magister et eruditor' to the young Henry III.[148] That paragon of chivalry, William Marshal, also a crusader, had preceded him by being entrusted by Henry II with the unenviable task of tutoring the reckless and irresponsible Young Henry.[149] Like William, Philip Daubeny was a highly respected figure, a consistently loyal Plantagenet servant who combined administrative flair and military competence with a reputation for honesty.[150] In noticing his death on crusade in 1235, Matthew Paris comments fondly:

> this noble man, devoted to God and strenuous in arms . . . after he had fought for God several times in the Holy Land by reason of pilgrimage, at length, closing his last day and making a laudable end, merited burial in the Holy Land, which when living he had long desired.[151]

He was buried before the south transept entrance to the Church of the Holy Sepulchre, Jerusalem.

Others may have felt a general obligation to aid their kinsmen established in the Latin East. For example, Guy de Montfort, the earl of Leicester's uncle, married Helvis d'Ibelin in 1204, and their son became lord of Toron and later of Tyre. Simon de Montfort may have been influenced in part by these ties to assume the Cross himself.[152] The Montforts were essentially French, and it should be emphasized that if such ties possessed significant recruitment value in themselves, then the fact that very few English families enjoyed direct kinship or material ties with the Latin East may help to explain their limited response relative to that of many French families in particular. The only notable layman known to have established himself in the Latin East in the thirteenth century is Hamo Lestrange, who accompanied the Lord Edmund in 1271 and then married Isabella d'Ibelin, lady of Beirut, before dying in the East in 1273.[153]

148 Wendover, *Flores*, iv. 75.

149 S. Painter, *William Marshal, Knight-Errant, Baron, and Regent of England* (Baltimore, 1933), 31–2. Guy Ferre, who went on crusade in 1270, became *magister* to the future Edward II. See J. C. Parsons, *The Court and Household of Eleanor of Castile in 1290* (Toronto, 1977), 15–17.

150 See Wendover, *Flores*, iv. 75, for one assessment of him. He came to play a crucial role in the critical years 1214–17, his talents recognized by the regency council in his appointment to the defence of the south coast in Jan. 1217, or before: *PR 1216–25*, p. 25. Between his crusades in later years, he acted as administrator, diplomat, and field commander in England, Gascony, the Channel Islands, and elsewhere.

151 Paris, *CM* iii. 373.

152 On these connections, see J. S. C. Riley-Smith, *The Feudal Nobility and the Kingdom of Jerusalem, 1174–1277* (London, 1973), 23.

153 Ibid. 28.

Simon de Montfort may equally have been motivated by dynastic precedent. Earl Simon's father had participated in the Fourth Crusade and played, as *eminence grise*, a leading role in the earlier stages of the Albigensian Crusade. His brother, Amaury, one of the leaders of the French crusade to the Holy Land in 1239, had also been engaged against the heretics of Languedoc. So too had his uncle and his other brother, both named Guy.[154] In this sense the Montforts illustrate the tendency for certain families to make crusading a dynastic tradition.[155] Of particular interest here are the Joinvilles because of their later connections with England, where they were known as Genevilles, and because Jean de Joinville, the author of the *Vie de Saint Louis*, showed himself to be fully conscious of the deeds of his forebears.

Geoffrey III de Joinville initiated the tradition through his participation in the Second Crusade. Jean's grandfather, Geoffrey IV, died at Acre on the Third Crusade in 1190. Geoffrey V accompanied his father and later participated in the Fourth Crusade. His younger brother Robert died before he could set out. Simon, Jean's father, took part in the Albigensian Crusade and later sailed to Damietta on the Fifth Crusade. Jean's assumption of the Cross in 1248, it has been inferred, owed something to these precedents.[156] He refused to accompany Louis IX on his second crusade, but the dynastic tradition was maintained by his brothers Geoffrey and William, who followed Lord Edward in 1270.[157] They doubtless applauded their elder brother's measures to commemorate their forebears' crusading deeds. In 1253 Jean returned from the Holy Land with the shield of their uncle, Geoffrey V, who had died at Krak fifty years earlier, and hung it in the family chapel of St-Laurent, Joinville. Later, in 1311, Jean composed the text for the epitaph which he placed in the chapel to celebrate the crusading exploits of the family.[158] Crusading had become an integral

[154] When admonishing Earl Simon in 1263 for his political activities in England, Urban IV, interestingly enough, appealed specifically to his ancestors' deeds in the Church's service. Their crusading must have been in mind: *Reg. Urban IV*, No. 585.

[155] Furthermore, through his marriage to Amice, co-heiress of Earl Robert IV of Leicester, Simon II de Montfort inherited the crusading legacy of the twelfth-century Beaumont earls: Robert III visited the Holy Land in 1179 and died at Durazzo on the Third Crusade; Robert IV accompanied him in 1190. The wider Beaumont clan included Earl William of Warwick, who went East in 1184, and Waleran, count of Meulan and earl of Worcester, who sailed in 1147, amongst their crusading number.

[156] See esp. H-F. Delaborde, *Jean de Joinville et les Seigneurs de Joinville* (Paris, 1894), 35, 37, 42–5, 55. The Joinvilles were also related to the Ibelins.

[157] For Geoffrey, soon to be Edward I's justiciar of Ireland, see ibid. 223–6; Powicke, *Henry III*, ii. 498, 699–700. PRO, C 66/88, m. 15d. reveals that William *Gessevill* is printed in error for *Genevill* in *CPR 1266–72*, p. 480. For William, see Delaborde, *Jean de Joinville*, pp. 67, 326, 329–30; *Cal. Docs. Rel. Ireland, 1252–84*, No. 645.

[158] Delaborde, *Jean de Joinville*, pp. 45, 122; *Documents historiques inédits*, ed. M. Champollion-Figeac, 2 vols. (Paris, 1841–3), i. 632–6.

part of the Joinville inheritance, and tradition, once established over generations, was a powerful influence which laid a certain imperative upon members of a dynasty that could not easily be ignored, much less forgotten. On the contrary, precisely because crusading remained a prestigious activity in chivalric circles, ancestral participation was proudly cherished.[159]

The point is further underlined by the way in which the memory of participation was perpetuated in certain religious houses patronized by families with a crusading record. Contained within the coucher book of Furness abbey, for example, is a genealogy of the Mowbrays, together with a record of what was considered noteworthy of their deeds, 1066–1380.[160] Reference is made to Roger de Mowbray's participation in the Second Crusade, his crusade of 1164, and his death on crusade in the Holy Land in 1186. The expedition of Nigel de Mowbray is also mentioned: he accompanied Richard I on the Third Crusade and died at Acre in 1192. Finally, the crusade and death of John de Mowbray in 1368 is recorded.

In the light of these considerations it is no surprise to find that analysis of thirteenth-century English *crucesignati* indicates that dynastic tradition almost certainly played a part in providing recruits. Some traditions stretched back to the twelfth century and the Third Crusade in particular, when large numbers from England participated for the first time. Gerard I de Furnivall, for example, accompanied Richard I and took the Cross again in 1202.[161] His son Gerard II died on the Fifth Crusade in 1218 or 1219.[162] In the next generation, his sons Gerard and Thomas sailed as bannerets of Simon de Montfort in 1240. William de Furnivall accompanied Richard of Cornwall.[163] Other traditions developed only in the course of the thirteenth century. Henry de Bohun, earl of Hereford, set out on the Fifth Crusade.[164] His son Humphrey V took the Cross in 1250, but like most of that generation of English *crucesignati* he almost certainly never sailed.[165] Humphrey's younger son, John, took out a crusader's protection and letters of attorney in 1290, probably accompanying

[159] For the memory of Henry III and Edward I, see below, pp. 198–200.

[160] *The Coucher Book of Furness Abbey*, ed. J. C. Atkinson and J. Brownbill, 5 vols. (Chetham Soc. N.S. 9, 11, 14, 76, 78; 1886–1919), ii, part 2, 289–92. In 1444 it was still remembered at the priory of St Pancras, Lewes, that Earl William III de Warenne, a patron, had died on the Second Crusade and was buried in the Holy Land: *The Chartulary of the Priory of St. Pancras of Lewes*, ed. L. F. Salzman, 2 vols. (Sussex Rec. Soc. 38, 40; 1933, 1935), i. xvii; and ii. 15, 19.

[161] F. M. Powicke, *The Loss of Normandy, 1189–1204: Studies in the History of the Angevin Empire* (2nd edn., Manchester, 1961), 245–6.

[162] *RLC* i. 390.

[163] Paris, *CM* iv. 44.

[164] Ralph of Coggeshall, *Chronicon Anglicanum*, ed. J. Stevenson (RS; 1875), 188.

[165] Paris, *CM* v. 99.

Otto de Grandson to the East.[166] Not all traditions were as neatly patrilineal as these, and for the more remote ties of kinship it would be dangerous to assume that their significance for crusader motivation was very great; a distinction needs to be made between the direct lineage and the kin in the broadest sense of the term. Nor should dynastic tradition be overstated in the overall context of recruitment. *In toto*, twenty-one English families were represented in the direct lineage by two members, of different generations, in the thirteenth century; fourteen families by three members; and twelve by four or more.[167]

The maddening problem with crusader motivation, yet equally a key perhaps to the crusade's appeal, is that it is possible to postulate an almost limitless number of motives, most of them incapable of empirical proof or disproof, or dangerously dependent upon inference. There were doubtless some with a taste for travel, fed by the literary fare they consumed and diverse travellers' tales. Crusaders were pilgrims and tourists as well as holy warriors.[168] Yet others perhaps took the Cross hoping to escape some personal, political, or legal difficulty. Another 'old chestnut' commonly maintains that younger sons found crusading especially attractive, principally because the establishment of strict inheritance customs limited their prospects at home. Although the argument may be valid as an explanation of some of the recruitment to the early crusades, notably the First, it cannot be sustained for the thirteenth-century crusades from England.[169] This is not to say that the effects of primogeniture were insignificant in an area where it was fast established as the norm for military fiefs at least, nor that younger sons ignored the crusade, but the evidence does suggest that the crusade was no more nor less appealing to them than to their elder brothers. Part of the explanation may be that the circumstances of the Latin East in the thirteenth century scarcely promised glittering prospects for younger sons eager

166 *CPR 1281–92*, pp. 371, 373.

167 The most important crusading families by this criterion were: Ardern, Basset, Beauchamp, Bohun, Bruce, Daubeny, Furnivall, Lacy, Mandeville, Mowbray, Neville, Quenci. The Plantagenets, and the families of Béthune, Lusignan, and Montfort (whose chief interests lay outside England), are excluded. There was no family comparable to the house of Blois-Champagne, represented on virtually every major expedition to the East between the First Crusade and the 1270 crusade.

168 'Annales Herbipolenses', *MGH SS* xvi. 3 listed the 'desire to learn about strange lands' first among motives for crusading. Honorius of Autun suspected as much for some. See E. M. Sanford, 'Honorius, *presbyter* and *scholasticus*', *Speculum*, xxiii (1948), 405. Tourist souvenirs included relics from the East, of course.

169 The argument best applies where communal possession of land by members of one family operated. The classic study of G. Duby, *La Société aux XIe et XIIe siècles dans la région mâconnaise* (2nd edn., Paris, 1971) is concerned with an area where the *frérêche* dominated. Conditions in 13th c. England were entirely different.

to win lands.[170] Equally, the emergence at home of devices to provide for younger sons, such as the use, served to reduce the material attraction of the crusade to the victims of primogeniture in the thirteenth century. English society in this period was peculiarly open-ended, and Holt has recently emphasized the ease with which younger sons acquired estates and established junior lines in comparison to their continental fellows. This was a distinctive feature of English society that was appreciated by contemporaries.[171] Survey of those younger sons who took the Cross suggests that it was their ties of service to a crusading lord, implying limited freedom of will in the matter, which counted for most.[172]

Some reference should be made to political structure, for the very restrictions upon the activities of individuals resulting from the Plantagenet mode of rule could explain part of the crusading enthusiasm of some. Turbulent spirits such as Richard Siward, the epitome of the *miles strenuus*, flourished in time of war. Restless in time of peace, hankering after action, they were never happier than when in the saddle. Siward first came to prominence in the minority of Henry III, when he fought at the battle of Sandwich, an epic contest, in 1217.[173] Order being restored, he joined William de Forz in his unsuccessful rebellion in 1220–1, but he had jumped the wrong way and was exiled, before his pardon in September 1221.[174] His sword and lance were clearly valued by the king: he fought in Gascony in 1225 and accompanied Henry to Brittany in 1230; in 1231 he is found in royal service in Wales.[175] In 1233 he played a major part in the rebellion of Earl Richard Marshal, and helped Hubert de Burgh spring from his prison at Devizes.[176] He was outlawed for his pains, but was then reconciled to the king in 1234 and employed in the pursuit of Peter des

[170] It is noteworthy that Hamo Lestrange, an elder brother, remained in the East, whilst his younger brother, Robert, returned to England from the 1270 crusade.

[171] J. C. Holt, 'Feudal Society and the Family in Early Medieval England: III. Patronage and Politics', *TRHS* 5th ser. xxxiv (1984), 15–16. See also id., 'Feudal Society and the Family in Early Medieval England: IV. The Heiress and the Alien', *TRHS* 5th. ser. xxxv (1985), 9 ff., for the effects of the ruling, *c.*1130–5, regarding partition of lordships between heiresses, for the problem of younger sons.

[172] Geoffrey de Langley junior is an example. The younger son of a notable Plantagenet servant, he seems initially to have been attached to Earl Robert de Ferrers, transferring on Robert's downfall to Lord Edmund, *c.*1268. See P. R. Coss, 'The Langley Cartulary', Ph.D. thesis (Birmingham, 1971), i. 73–4. Thereafter he was closely associated with Edmund, and his participation on crusade with Edmund plainly owed much to these ties.

[173] Paris, *CM* iii. 29.

[174] *PR 1216–25*, pp. 283–4, 300–1.

[175] *PR 1225–32*, p. 401; *CR 1227–31*, p. 566.

[176] *CPR 1232–47*, pp. 25–7; *CR 1231–4*, pp. 271, 325, 545. For his various other misdemeanours, see N. Denholm-Young, *Richard of Cornwall* (Oxford, 1947), 28–9.

Rivaux.[177] Predictably he was soon back in trouble, incarcerated in Gloucester prison in 1236 for a variety of offences.[178] It was in that year that he took the Cross with Richard of Cornwall, and thereafter he slowly gained the king's confidence.[179] It is not certain that he duly went on crusade in 1240, but his intent is indicated by his attendance at the assembly of prospective crusading nobles at Northampton in November 1239.[180] He certainly accompanied the king to Gascony in 1242, before dying in 1248.[181] In the context of his energetic, martial career, Richard Siward's crusading vow of 1236 makes good sense. If he could not use his sword and lance with impunity at home, then he would have to look elsewhere.[182] The crusade was a congenial outlet.

To this cocktail of general influences and considerations, some further ingredients, the product of social structure, should be added, for close analysis of the *crucesignati* known to us suggests that ties of association were extremely important in the process of recruitment. Lordship ties were undoubtedly paramount, and the greater the lord the wider his direct influence upon recruitment. If the king took the Cross then almost inevitably many of his *familiares* and *curiales* followed his lead. The Barnwell annalist, for example, on recording John's 1215 vow, reports that several of his *familiares* took the Cross with or after him, 'ipso ad hoc . . . instigante'.[183] Not that the king's example was always followed out of genuine piety or crusading enthusiasm. Master Henry of Whiston, royal clerk, judge, and subdeacon, informed Innocent III in a moment of rare candour that he took the Cross on account of the love and favour of Henry II rather than piety.[184] Gerald of Wales, when seeking commutation of his vow in 1189, made it plain that it was the hope of financial subsidy that had

[177] *CPR 1232–47*, pp. 49, 58; *CR 1231–4*, p. 436.

[178] *CR 1234–7*, pp. 363–4, 367; Paris, *CM* iii. 368–9.

[179] *CR 1237–42*, p. 97; Paris, *CM* iii. 368–9. He bore one of the sceptres at the queen's coronation: *The Red Book of the Exchequer*, ed. H. Hall, 3 vols. (RS; 1896), ii. 756. In 1239 he had custody of the castle and county of Oxford, and from 1237 was in receipt of an annual fee from the king: *CLR 1226–40*, pp. 254, 310–11, 434, 443.

[180] Paris, *CM* iii. 620.

[181] *CPR 1232–47*, p. 296.

[182] Since Richard moderated his anti-social activities after taking the Cross, it may be that contrition had attracted him to the crusade as a fitting means of penance for a man of his particular talents. His vow apparently helped his release from prison in 1236. Robert Grosseteste lobbied Henry III on his behalf as a *crucesignatus: Epistolae Roberti Grosseteste Episcopi Lincolniensis*, ed. H. R. Luard (RS; 1861), No. xxix. 'Dunstable', p. 144, reports that Archbishop Edmund of Canterbury secured his release, Richard then 'in domesticam familiam regis assumptus'.

[183] Coventry, *Memoriale*, ii. 219. See above, pp. 58–9, for Henry III in 1250 and 1252.

[184] *CLI*, No. 737. His vow was redeemed in 1207.

induced him to accept Henry's overtures.[185] Elsewhere, perhaps with himself in mind, he describes how Henry sought to stimulate recruitment amongst not only his friends and *domestici* but also his adversaries, through a combination of threats, promises, and flattery.[186] Characteristically, Gerald ascribes murky measures and motives to Henry II, but the substance of his account may be accepted as representative of the pressure which kings might exert to swell recruitment. Thus, Louis IX is said to have distributed robes to his *familiares* with the Cross already sewn upon them at Christmas 1245; his deception succeeded because of the great dishonour and public shame which would have been incurred through laying aside the Cross in such circumstances.[187] The moral dilemma which some felt as a result of royal pressures is captured in Joinville's account of a discussion between two of Louis's knights in 1267, the day before the king took the Cross once more. One observed 'if we do not take the Cross, we shall lose the favour of the king; if we do take it, we shall lose that of God, since we shall be doing so not for His sake but through fear of the king'.[188]

Lesser lords exerted a correspondingly more limited influence, but it was a difference of scale not kind.[189] Moreover, ties of dependence affected members of the military classes as much as clerks and lesser freemen. These might envisage crusading with the lord concerned. The indenture of 1306 between Humphrey VIII, earl of Hereford and Essex, and Bartholomew de Enfield stipulated that Bartholomew would serve the earl for life, 'on this side and beyond seas, and in the Holy Land if the earl goes there'. If he failed to meet his obligations, he would lose the 40*m.* of land which, among other things, Humphrey granted to him for life.[190] In 1310 Aymer de Valence, earl of Pembroke,

[185] Gerald, *Opera*, i. 84–5. See also William of Newburgh, 'Historia rerum Anglicarum', in *Chronicles of the Reigns of Stephen, Henry II, and Richard I*, ed. R. Howlett, 2 vols. (RS; 1884, 1885), i. 275. Gerald took the Cross again in 1201, for self-interested reasons as much as piety. It was redeemed in 1203: *CLI*, No. 488.

[186] Gerald, *Opera*, viii. 251.

[187] Paris, *CM* iv. 502–3. Less subtly, Henry III peremptorily ordered all those attending the London parliament of Oct. 1268 to take vows had they not yet done so: 'Continuation' of William of Newburgh, ii. 554–5.

[188] Jean de Joinville, *Histoire de Saint Louis*, ed. J. Natalis de Wailly (Paris, 1872), 486–8, who also reveals the pressure upon himself. The translation is that of R. Hague, *The Life of St. Louis by John of Joinville* (London, 1955), 212.

[189] See e.g. the account of how Peter des Roches's assumption of the Cross stimulated the vows of several of his *familiares*, in Coventry, *Memoriale*, ii. 250.

[190] *Calendar of Documents Relating to Scotland Preserved in the Public Record Office*, ed. J. Bain, 4 vols. (Edinburgh, 1881–8), ii. No. 1899. Only injury or illness was allowed. If there was a crusade, but the earl was unable to set out, Bartholomew might nevertheless leave Humphrey's service, notwithstanding his obligations, presumably for the duration of the expedition.

received John Darcy into his service and promised to enfeoff him in tail with 20*m*. of land or rent providing John took up knighthood and served him for life in both peace and war, at home and overseas, and 'in going to the Holy Land when required'.[191] Such agreements helped to provide a lord with the nucleus of his household establishment should he go on crusade.[192]

In addition to their direct dependants, crusaders quite naturally looked to their kinsmen, friends, and acquaintances for support. The role played by kinship ties is most readily apparent from the tendency for sons to accompany their fathers, nephews to sail with uncles, or for brothers to join brothers. The English contingents of the Fifth Crusade provide some illuminating examples, including: Saher de Quenci, earl of Winchester, and his two sons, Robert and Roger;[193] John de Harcourt and his brother William;[194] Baldwin and Roger de Vere;[195] two illegitimate sons of King John, Oliver and Richard fitzRegis;[196] William de Ferrers, earl of Derby, and his nephew Robert de Ferrers.[197] The role played by more distant kinship bonds is much more difficult to assess, but the *Itinerarium Peregrinorum* is one source which specifically picks out some of the extended family units found on crusades. Amongst the arrivals at Acre in 1191 are noted 'Stutevillenses', 'milites de Praels [Préaux]', 'milites etiam agnominati Torolenses', and Roger de Tosny with 'plures fratres et consanguinei de Corneby [*recte* Torneby]', his kinsmen.[198] Kinship through marriage also seems to have played a part. It may be objected that such ties meant little in themselves since the social élite was linked by a web of marriage alliances, and such unions were,

191 *A Descriptive Catalogue of Ancient Deeds in the Public Record Office*, 6 vols. (London, 1890–1915), iv. No. A 6404 (misdated). See J. R. S. Phillips, *Aymer de Valence, Earl of Pembroke 1307–24* (Oxford, 1972), 255.

192 But some agreements expressly excluded service on crusade. See, for example, the indenture of 1297 between John de Grey and Robert de Tothale: *Yorkshire Deeds, I*, ed. W. Brown (Yorkshire Archaeological Soc., Rec. Ser. 39; 1909), 185. For similar exclusion clauses relating to the Holy Land, see the indenture of 1297 between Sir John Bluet and William Martel: BL Additional Charter 1351. Also that printed by M. Jones, 'An Indenture between Robert, Lord Mohaut, and Sir John de Bracebridge for Life Service in Peace and War, 1310', *Journ. of the Soc. of Archivists*, iv (1972), 384–94.

193 'Waverley', p. 292, amongst other sources.

194 Ibid.; 'Dunstable', p. 54; *RLC* i. 402b, 438.

195 'Dunstable', p. 56; Coggeshall, *Chron.*, p. 190. Roger was nephew of Robert de Vere, earl of Oxford, who did not, as is sometimes stated, set out on crusade himself.

196 Wendover, *Flores*, iv. 44; *CRR 1219–20*, pp. 326–7. Richard's departure in 1218 seems certain from the dating of references to him in the Chancery rolls.

197 For Robert's vow, see Deputy Keeper of the Public Records, *Third Report* (London, 1842), appendix II, p. 200. Earl William certainly sailed in 1218.

198 'Itinerarium Peregrinorum' pp. 217–18. The role played by extended kinship bonds in crusading forces needs further research.

anyway, frequently the product of prior connections. Nevertheless, amongst the leaders of the Fifth Crusade were three earls who were brothers-in-law by virtue of the marriages of Earl Ranulf of Chester's sisters. Agnes had married William of Derby, and Mabel was wife to William of Arundel; another sister, Hawise, had married Robert de Quenci, the brother of the crusading earl of Winchester.[199] Analysis of other crusading forces reveals that kinship bonds were equally to the fore.[200]

Cutting across, and interacting with, ties of both lordship and kinship were connections deriving from local and regional association. It is not easy to isolate and determine their precise significance, but a number of more or less discrete groupings of this type can be identified within each of the major expeditions of the thirteenth century. A fine example is provided by the Northerners who took the Cross for the 1270 crusade.[201] Many had substantial interests elsewhere, and a few undoubtedly considered their northern connections to be of secondary importance; some, in the course of their careers, spent a great deal of their time away from the north; others looked to Scotland as much as England. But all were identified with the north to a greater or lesser extent, and what Holt has revealed of their predecessors in John's reign is equally true of the Northerners under Henry III: a closely-knit regional society composed of men linked together through tenurial and marriage ties, and associated through common experience in administrative and other activities.[202] Analysis of their careers, the witness lists of their charters, their debt pledges and sureties, the pattern of their land holdings, shows how closely these men were bound together. It is not surprising that they tended to act collectively on occasion; it is certainly striking that only two of their crusading number in 1270, John de Vescy and Robert de Haulton, had stood against Henry III in the troubles of the 1260s.[203] The remainder were loyal, many of them staunchly so, acting as the linchpins of Henry's cause in the northern shires. That they then responded positively to the call to the crusade suggests that they also viewed its prospect more or less in common.

199 On these connections, see *The Complete Peerage by G.E.C.*, ed. V. Gibbs *et al.* 12 vols. (2nd edn., London, 1910–59), i. 236; iii. 169; iv. 196; vii. 629.

200 See e.g. the analyses of J. Longnon, *Les Compagnons de Villehardouin: Recherches sur les croisés de la quatrième croisade* (Geneva, 1978); H. van Werveke, 'La Contribution de la Flandre et du Hainaut à la Troisième Croisade', *Le Moyen Âge*, lxxviii (1972), 55–90.

201 For full listing, see appendix 4.

202 J. C. Holt, *The Northerners: A Study in the Reign of King John* (Oxford, 1961), *passim* but esp. p. 69.

203 For John and Robert, see below, pp. 131–2. B. Beebe, 'The English Baronage and the Crusade of 1270', *BIHR* xlviii (1975), 131–2, considers that John d'Eyville was another Northern *crucesignatus* who had been a rebel. I find no evidence that he took the Cross.

Some of their mutual ties may be briefly sketched out to reveal the type and degree of their regional association. They frequently witnessed each other's acts and charters. Many were present at York in September 1268 attesting a series of redemption agreements in accordance with the Dictum of Kenilworth. That between Robert Bruce V, a *crucesignatus*, and Walter de Fauconberg was witnessed by Alan de Lascelles, Eustace de Balliol, John de Romundeby, Robert Bruce IV, and Adam of Jesmond, *crucesignati*.[204] With the exception of Adam, the others also witnessed the agreement between Robert Bruce V and John de Meaux on the same day.[205] Adam, former castellan of Newcastle upon Tyne and sheriff of Northumberland, was linked with a number of Northern *crucesignati* through tenurial ties; some were closely dependent upon him. Ralph de Cotun, for example, had been granted the vill of Benridge and the park of Wythirley by Adam, part of a transfer of property from Roger Bertram of Mitford to Adam.[206] Ralph also received North Gosforth from Adam, following Henry III's grant of the wardship of William Surtees' lands in 1263; he sold it to his brother John de Cotun when he went on crusade.[207] The Cotuns were also connected to the Balliols, both brothers serving with Alexander de Balliol in the Welsh campaign of 1277.[208] Ralph acted as one of Alexander's executors on his death in 1278.[209] Eustace de Balliol was one of the pledges of Ralph de Cotun in a concord with Robert Bruce, concerning interests in Yorkshire, in February 1270.[210] Eustace, former castellan of Carlisle and sheriff of Cumberland, acted together on royal business with his counterpart in the north east, Adam of Jesmond, on a number of occasions.[211] As justices in eyre in 1267–8, they were joined with

204 *CPR 1266–72*, pp. 293–4.

205 John de Vescy and John de Ardern, with others, attested another agreement shortly afterwards. John de Goer, himself *crucesignatus*, was appointed one of Ardern's crusade attorneys in 1270: ibid. 282, 292, 294.

206 *CCR 1272–9*, pp. 44, 151; *CIPM* iii. 384; *CPR 1258–66*, p. 359.

207 *CIPM* i. 234–5; *CPR 1258–66*, p. 291.

208 *Parliamentary Writs and Writs of Military Summons, Edw.I–Edw.II*, ed. F. Palgrave, 2 vols. in 4 (London, 1827–34), i. 209. John was in receipt of 100*s*. from Balliol's mill at Bywell: *CCR 1272–9*, p. 200. Ralph witnessed at least one deed of Balliol and his wife concerning their property in Bywell: J. Hodgson, *A History of Northumberland*, 7 vols. (Newcastle, 1820–58), II. ii. 48–9. Another *crucesignatus*, Robert de Marton, performed part of the military service due from Lady Devorguilla Balliol in 1277. It is tempting to think that Nicholas de Marton, also *crucesignatus*, was his kinsman. Both were from Yorkshire: *Parliamentary Writs*, i. 208; *Rotuli Hundredorum Temp. Hen. III et Edw. I. in tur. Lond. et in curia receptae scaccarii West. asservati*, 2 vols. (Record Commission, 1812, 1818), i. 112.

209 'Three Early Assize Rolls for Northumberland', ed. W. Page (Surtees Soc. 88; 1891), 262, 304.

210 PRO, KB 26/197, m. 13d.

211 See e.g. *CR 1264–8*, p. 557; *Cal. Docs. Rel. Scotland*, i. No. 2496.

Richard de Middleton, royal chancellor, whose younger son Gilbert took out a crusader's protection in 1270.[212] Thomas de Fenwick, another man with interests principally in Tynedale, leased two of his manors to Richard de Middleton in 1270.[213] Thomas, with another neighbour, Walter de Cambo, was also connected to Roger Bertram of Mitford, at least before his fall, and Walter was to become intimately connected with John de Vescy, whose wide northern interests are well known.[214] Richard de Stiveton, whose centre of gravity lay further south in Yorkshire, bore the Cross of Peter de Percy vicariously to the Holy Land in 1270.[215] In 1255 he had accompanied the then sheriff, William le Latimer, to Scotland on the king's business, stood surety for him in 1259, and was closely associated with him in the 1260s.[216] William died in 1268; his son, another William, was the *crucesignatus*.[217] Richard also stood surety with William fitzRalph for John de Meaux's payment of his redemption fine to Robert Bruce V in September 1268.[218] Another of the witnesses to that agreement was the Yorkshire knight John de Romundeby who, like his father, was identified with the Bruce connection in the county.[219]

This is by no means an exhaustive catalogue of the different ties linking the Northern *crucesignati* of 1270, but it suffices to demonstrate the tendency for men of a particular regional society to act as a group on the basis of pre-existing ties. Collective action came naturally to them. The implications for recruitment to the crusade are apparent, but the potential of these bonds had to be realized and the trigger was provided by the connections with the crusade leaders. That all but

[212] *CPR 1266–72*, p. 160; *CR 1264–8*, p. 361.

[213] *CPR 1266–72*, p. 683.

[214] *CCh.R 1257–1300*, pp. 76, 119–20, 147, 265; *CPR 1301–7*, p. 363; *Parliamentary Writs*, i. 204; *CCR 1272–9*, p. 512. Walter may already have transferred to Vescy after Roger Bertram's death in 1267; he was certainly his seneschal after the crusade. See Hodgson, *Northumberland*, II. i. 283.

[215] *CR 1268–72*, p. 281; *CPR 1266–72*, p. 423. Both Richard and Peter were connected with the Bruces in Yorkshire. See e.g. *Yorkshire Deeds, VII*, ed. C. T. Clay (Yorkshire Archaeological Soc., Rec. Ser. 83; 1932), 179–80. In the 1280s Richard's heir held in Stiveton three and a half carucates of Walter de Fauconberg, and he of Bruce, and one carucate of the Percy fee: *Kirkby's Inquest. The Survey of the County of York taken by John de Kirkby, called Kirkby's Inquest*, ed. R. H. Skaife (Surtees Soc. 49; 1867), 24, 27. Peter de Percy, former sheriff, had been another key agent of Henry III in the North in the 1260s, before his death in 1267.

[216] *CR 1254–6*, p. 223; *CIMisc.* i. 161; *RF* ii. 317–18.

[217] Richard de Vescy, kinsman of John de Vescy, had been undersheriff to the elder William: *CPR 1266–72*, p. 243. William acted on his behalf in 1268 in a case versus the bishop of Durham concerning return of writs: PRO, JUST. 1/1050, m. 54. In 1275 William held substantial property of John de Vescy in Lincolnshire: *Rot. Hundred.* i. 244.

[218] *CPR 1266–72*, p. 294.

[219] See e.g. *Cartularium prioratus de Gyseburne*, ed. W. Brown, 2 vols. (Surtees Soc. 76, 89; 1889–94), ii. 335 n., 342–3, 344; *CPR 1266–72*, pp. 292–3, 294.

two of their number were loyal to Henry III in the 1260s is immensely revealing, but it was not only a question of ideology. The personal and material links, above all with the Lords Edward and Edmund themselves, counted for much. Some Northern *crucesignati* appear in close household service before the crusade. The knights Alan de Lascelles, Walter de Percy, and Laurence de St Mauro, for example, are to be found in Edmund's circle before 1270, and in receipt of lands and revenues from him. Alan de Lascelles, for one, was granted the manor of Felton (Northumberland) before July 1270; it had belonged to Roger Bertram of Mitford who had stood against the king at Northampton in 1264.[220] Alan is found witnessing charters of Edmund in 1271 and clearly intended to accompany his patron on crusade, rather than Edward, since he did not take out a protection until February 1271, shortly before Edmund's departure.[221] Even if they were not in household service, the careers of the northern *crucesignati* of 1270 reveal that most had been closely associated with Henry III or his sons, sometimes all three, in the years before; they had consequently done well for their various services. Here was prime material, of an overwhelmingly curial complexion, from which Edward and Edmund could recruit a crusading force from the northern shires, and if men of such considerable regional influence as Adam of Jesmond or Eustace de Balliol took the Cross, then quite naturally some of their dependants, kinsmen, and friends, within their regional society, would follow them.

Analysis of the different crusading forces recruited in England in the thirteenth century suggests that the precise personnel of each was largely a function of the interaction of the various ties of association discussed above. At the centre of each was a group of great lords who looked to men of their connection for support. They, in turn, could reasonably expect the aid of some of the individuals of their own affinity, thus extending the net of recruitment along the lines in which society was organized. Some were more susceptible than others, precisely because of the workings of those influences and factors, such as dynastic tradition, previously discussed, but the overall pattern of recruitment suggests that the crusade was approached in much the same way as men responded to other enterprises. Studies of William the Conqueror's invasion of 1066, or the initial Anglo-Norman invasion of Ireland in 1169–70, or royal campaigns of the thirteenth century have revealed the degree to which these enterprises were dominated and moulded by great lords, in the company of their

220 *CR 1268–72*, p. 215; *Fees* ii. 1115; *CPR 1258–66*, p. 316; 'Three Early Assize Rolls for Northumberland', ed. Page, p. 326.

221 *CPR 1266–72*, pp. 515, 588. The connection continued after the crusade.

kinsmen, friends, and dependants. They reflect in miniature the way in which society was organized; crusading forces were no exception.

It follows that the major problem lies in the decision of individual great men to respond favourably or not to the call to the crusade, but the precise reasons for an individual's response can never be asserted definitively. We can never see fully into the heart and mind of a Ranulf of Chester, Richard of Cornwall, or Lord Edward, although we can reconstruct the conditions in which they took their decisions; but it is certain that the inhabitants of the Latin East, their allies, and the papacy, in devoting their attention to the great men of society in their promotional drives, understood well the implications of social structure. To secure their commitment was critical to the dispatch of substantial aid.

4

THE CRUSADE OF 1270–1272: A CASE STUDY

SINCE space precludes detailed treatment of the recruitment, organization, and preparations of each crusading force to leave England in the thirteenth century, that of 1270–2 has been selected for detailed analysis as an example. It has been chosen primarily because the happy chance of an unbroken succession of the more important central government records for the years immediately preceding, during, and following the crusade allows a much fuller listing of participants than for any other force in the period. The same circumstance further allows the reconstruction of the careers, interests, and connections of the great majority of *crucesignati* to a degree which is probably impossible for any other significant crusading force, English or otherwise.[1]

Once raised, a force had then to be organized if it was not to become incoherent and ineffectual. Contracts, as an instrument of organization if not recruitment, had been applied to crusading forces in the past, as we shall see, but we have to wait until the crusade of 1270–2 to see an English force organized systematically by means of contracts. Since its leader, the Lord Edward, was accordingly responsible for much of the provisioning and transport of those following him, the crusade may also provide a useful vantage point from which to observe some of the features of crusade preparation and crusading in practice in the thirteenth century.[2]

RECRUITMENT AND ORGANIZATION

The formal origins of the expedition lie in Urban IV's declaration of a new crusade to the Holy Land in 1263.[3] England, however, was fast drifting into civil war, and promotion, if it was ever begun, seems to have been suspended until after the decisive battle of Evesham. In October 1266 Clement IV urged his legate Ottobuono to promote the crusade 'ferventius', which suggests that he had already taken up the cause again and lends credence to Clement's report to the patriarch of

[1] The results are tabulated in appendix 4.

[2] Preparations of individuals are discussed below, ch. 5.

[3] See above, ch. 1 n. 9.

Jerusalem in August 1266 that the Cross was then being preached in England.[4] The crucial breakthrough in recruitment occurred on 24 June 1268 at the parliament of Northampton, when the Lords Edward and Edmund, Henry of Almain, William de Valence, Gilbert de Clare, John de Warenne, and others took the Cross. They would provide the nucleus of the forces leaving England in 1270–1.[5] Since Edward was clearly marked out as the leader from this early date, and since his immense influence was bound to affect the response of so many, for reasons discussed in the previous chapter, his own motivation requires some discussion.

Edward's determination to take the Cross and then to fulfil it in person, notwithstanding the initial opposition of both Henry III and Clement IV, is probably explained by his circumstances as the heir apparent, his love of martial exploits, and the influence of Louis IX.[6] He had been granted a very extensive appanage in 1254 but his control therein was severely restricted by conditions attached to the grant, and Henry III frequently interfered in his son's administration and his uses of its revenues.[7] Edward clearly found the situation galling. Moreover, although he had played a leading role in national affairs, his openings for action were somewhat circumscribed by 1268 with the end of the clearing-up operations following the battle of Evesham. There was little prospect of large-scale campaigning in England and the settlement with Llywelyn ap Gruffydd in 1267 closed for the time being any opportunities for military glory against the Marchers' traditional foe.[8] The series of tournaments which

[4] *Reg. Clement IV*, Nos. 1110, 1146. Ottobuono had already promoted the crusade in Ireland, perhaps as early as Jan. 1266. For his role, see A. Lewis, 'The English Activities of Cardinal Ottobuono, Legate of the Holy See', MA thesis (Manchester, 1938), esp. pp. 140–3.

[5] John de Warenne did not sail. He became one of the guardians of the realm on Henry III's death, and nothing further is heard of his vow. Some suggestions concerning Earl Gilbert's vow are made in my 'Gilbert de Clare, Richard of Cornwall and the Lord Edward's Crusade', *Nottingham Medieval Studies*, xxx (1986), 46–66. Henry de Lacy, earl of Lincoln is said to have pledged himself to the crusade, but although the *Debate* with Walter de Bibbesworth, upon which this assumption depends, refers to Henry as earl and indeed signed with the Cross, he was granted the title only in 1272. Since there is no supporting evidence that he took vows before then, the surmise is to be rejected: M. D. Legge, *Anglo-Norman Literature and its Background* (Oxford, 1963), 348.

[6] On the opposition see below, pp. 231–2. This is not to say that other motives were absent. He may already have felt a certain devotion to the Holy Land, and he had strong dynastic reasons for responding to the call to the crusade. The poem in Edward's praise says he took the Cross wishing to perform service to Christ who had safely delivered him from the barons' wars: *The Political Songs of England, from the Reign of John to that of Edward II*, ed. T. Wright (Camden Soc. os 6; 1839), 130–1.

[7] J. R. Studd, 'The Lord Edward and King Henry III', *BIHR* l (1977), 4–19.

[8] Tout, in explaining why English forces were not deployed against Llywelyn at this time, argued that Edward had decided upon the crusade as early as Feb. 1267, but he

began in late 1267, after years of official prohibition, were but a poor substitute, keen contestants though Edward and other crusade leaders were.[9] Restless, chafing under restraints, the heir to the throne probably regarded the prospect of the crusade with relish. Louis IX also encouraged him. He had urged Henry III to fulfil his own outstanding vow of 1250 on a number of occasions in the 1260s,[10] and he probably promoted the cause ever more ardently among his Plantagenet kin after taking the Cross himself in March 1267. It is apparent from Clement IV's letter to Louis in January 1268 that Edward and Louis had already been in contact over the matter by late 1267.[11] Louis, perhaps, had been making overtures to Edward as early as this, a surmise strengthened by Henry III's observation in June 1272 that Edward had set out for the Holy Land at Louis's behest.[12]

Louis naturally turned to his own kinsmen and great vassals for support. On taking the Cross he proceeded to induce his brothers Alphonse of Poitiers and Charles of Anjou, his nephew Robert II of Artois, and the other great men of France to follow the lead of himself and his three sons.[13] Edward too was a kinsman and following the Treaty of Paris (1259) his duchy of Gascony was a direct fief of the French king. For his part, Edward was in urgent need of cash when he attended a council of the various leaders of the projected crusade at Paris in August 1269.[14] On 27 and 28 August Edward and Louis sealed the instruments which formally bound Edward to the Capetian's expedition. Louis would lend 70,000*l.* *tournois* to Edward: 25,000*l.* were reserved for Gaston de Béarn, his contingent of Gascons, and their passage overseas; the rest for Edward 'pur chevaus, pur viandes, pur nefs, e pur passage de celi Edward'.

adduced no evidence to that effect. More likely, the decision to settle with Llywelyn, and use the resulting cash, encouraged Edward and the Marchers to look to an entirely different theatre of war: the Holy Land. But Louis IX, before taking the Cross in Mar. 1267, may nevertheless have looked already to Edward for support: see *The Collected Papers of Thomas Frederick Tout with a Memoir and Bibliography*, 3 vols. (Manchester, 1932–4), ii. 88–97.

9 See above, p. 99.

10 *Royal and Other Historical Letters Illustrative of the Reign of Henry III*, ed. W. W. Shirley, 2 vols. (RS; 1862, 1866), ii. 304–5; *CR 1264–8*, p. 552.

11 *Reg. Clement IV*, No. 1288; *Thesaurus novus anecdotorum*, ed. E. Martène and U. Durand, 5 vols. (Paris, 1717), ii. No. 583.

12 *Foedera*, I. i. 494–5; also 'Continuation' of Gervase of Canterbury in *The Historical Works of Gervase of Canterbury*, ed. W. Stubbs, 2 vols. (RS; 1879, 1880), ii. 249; William Rishanger, *Chronica et annales, regnantibus Henrico tertio et Edwardo primo*, ed. H. T. Riley (RS; 1865), 60.

13 J. R. Strayer, 'The Crusades of Louis IX', in R. L. Wolff and H. W. Hazard (eds.) *A History of the Crusades* II, (Philadelphia, 1962), 509 ff.

14 See below, pp. 146–7.

Edward in return was to arrive at Aigues Mortes for embarkation no later than 15 August 1270, to accompany Louis wherever he might go, and obey him in good faith on crusade.[15] Strayer suggests that the primary purpose of the loan was to secure the participation of Gaston de Béarn and other Gascons, but the terms make it plain that the chief intention was to provide Edward with sufficient ready cash to cover transport, victuals, and horses for both his own force and Gaston's.[16] The money was to be paid over to those whom Edward should appoint to make purveyance in France against his passage; any outstanding sums were to be delivered when Edward joined Louis overseas.

The Paris agreement is best treated as a binding contract which formalized relations between Louis and Edward by laying reciprocal obligations upon the two parties, parallel to other agreements which Louis made around this time with other contingent leaders. The intention was not perhaps to encourage recruitment so much as to create a unified command structure through reinforcing the tendencies towards unity and discipline inherent in kinship and lordship bonds. As far as Edward was concerned he had now to ensure that he could meet his contracted obligations. The agreement does not specify the number of bannerets, simple knights, and other ranks whom he would lead, but it is difficult to see how the firm figure of 70,000*l.* was agreed without reference to actual numbers. Since we know that Edward duly contracted for 225 knights in England for the crusade,[17] it is tempting to see a connection with the 45,000*l.* earmarked for Edward's own force, Louis agreeing to a subsidy of 200*l.* per knight, although it is impossible to say whether a fixed number of knights, or a round sum of money, or both, was agreed at Paris. If a connection is allowed, then, at the same rate of 200*l.*

15 *Dipl. Docs.* i. No. 419. For repayment of the loan see J-P. Trabut-Cussac, 'Le financement de la croisade anglaise de 1270', *Bibliothèque de l'École des Chartes*, cxix (1961), esp. 114–24.

16 Strayer, 'The Crusades of Louis IX', p. 510.

17 See below. A comparison may be drawn with the treaty of 1201 between the Venetians and the counts of Flanders, Champagne, and Blois for the Fourth Crusade, when the sum of 85,000*m.* was presumably calculated after the envoys gave their erroneous estimate of likely numbers. See J. Longnon, *Recherches sur la vie de Geoffroy de Villehardouin* (Paris, 1939), 179–81, for the treaty; and D. E. Queller, 'L'évolution du rôle de l'Ambassadeur: Les pleins pouvoirs et le traité de 1201 entre les croisés et les Vénitiens', *Le Moyen Âge*, lxvii (1961), 479–501. Of Edward I's later contracts for service, that of 1297, whereby five earls contracted for 500 horse for £7691. 16*s.* 8*d.*, clearly indicates that they first thought of the number of troops. The contracts for the Gascon war of 1294–8 involved round numbers of both money and men, however, and the variations suggest that the number of men was fitted into the sums of money. See M. C. Prestwich, *War, Politics and Finance under Edward I* (London, 1972), 73, 76. I am indebted to Michael Prestwich for his suggestions concerning the 1269 agreement.

subsidy per knight, Gaston de Béarn's contingent would have comprised 125 knights, so Edward would have been overall commander of 350 knights drawn from the Plantagenet dominions. Moreover, since Edward paid 100*m.* to each of the 225 knights contracted in England in 1270, and if the same terms of 100*m.* per knight were made available to Gaston de Béarn's contingent, as seems probable, then Edward would have been obliged to find 12,500*m.* for Gaston. His farming of the customs of Bordeaux and other Gascon revenues in 1269–70 was perhaps intended to provide the cash required.[18]

The battle formation at Tunis in 1270 reveals that each division comprised those crusaders tied by bonds of lordship and regional association to individual commanders. The Navarrese, Champenois, and Burgundians served under Theobald, king of Navarre and count of Champagne, for example.[19] On this basis, Edward would presumably have commanded the Anglo-Normans of England and Ireland along with the Gascons. The Paris agreement clearly envisaged these two groups as being discrete though combined, Edward's Gascon vassals to serve under the immediate command of Gaston de Béarn, 'whom we retain, he and his people, in our [Edward's] company'. Gaston was present in Paris and put his seal to the documents, but it is unknown whether he and Edward then came to a more precise agreement concerning their relationship on crusade and the numbers to accompany Gaston.[20] Gaston, however, never sailed; he remained behind in Gascony. It has been suggested that he had every intention of sailing as late as October 1270,[21] but this is unlikely since Louis IX's crusade treasurer paid Edward 25,000*l.*, that presumably earmarked for Gaston out of the total 70,000*l.*, when he sailed for Tunis from Aigues Mortes in late September.[22] Ebles IV de Ventadour was one southern lord who certainly enlisted in Edward's force, perhaps transferring when it became clear that Gaston would be remaining behind, but he left the crusade at Tunis and in 1277 found himself

[18] *CPR 1266–72*, pp. 367, 396, 455; *Foedera*, I. i. 485. The amount, if raised, is unknown. See Trabut-Cussac, 'Le financement', esp. p. 121.

[19] 'Extrait d'une chronique anonyme', *RHGF* xxi. 125.

[20] Edward was eager, however, to establish closer relations with the troublesome Gaston, playing a leading role in the negotiations leading to the marriage of Henry of Almain and Gaston's daughter in June 1269. Gaston came to England for the nuptials before travelling to Paris with Edward, it seems: *CPR 1266–72*, p. 323; Wykes, *Chron.*, pp. 221–2; *De ant. leg.*, pp. 109, 111.

[21] J. Ellis, 'Gaston de Béarn: A Study in Anglo-Gascon Relations (1229–90)', D.Phil. thesis (Oxford, 1952), pp. 278–83; and less forgivably, S. D. Lloyd, 'The Lord Edward's Crusade, 1270–2: Its Setting and Significance', in J. B. Gillingham and J. C. Holt (eds.), *War and Government in the Middle Ages: Essays in Honour of J. O. Prestwich* (Woodbridge, 1984), 125.

[22] Trabut-Cussac, 'Le financement', p. 115.

pressed to redeem or fulfil his vow. Edward petitioned Pope John XXI on his behalf, reporting that Ebles had been 'de familia nostra' when he set out on crusade but, stricken by illness, had returned home with Edward's licence and on his business.[23] In April 1271 Ebles acknowledged that he owed Edward 500*l. tournois* for this release.[24] This may represent the fee for which Edward had retained him for the crusade.

If it is uncertain whether Edward used contracts to mould the Gascon forces to his service, it is plain that written contracts provided the backbone of the Anglo-Norman force. On the Pipe Roll of I Edward I is entered the account, up to 20 October 1272, of the three initial receivers of the twentieth granted in England for the crusade in 1269–70. It includes a list of eighteen crusaders who contracted to accompany Edward, each with a fixed quota of knights.[25] Altogether 22,500*m.* were paid out for this purpose, and as the rate was set at 100*m.* per knight, Edward accordingly raised 225 knights for his service on crusade by this means.[26] Most of the original contracts to which the Pipe Roll entries refer have vanished, but the one between Edward and Adam of Jesmond has survived and has been printed by Richardson and Sayles.[27] Fortunately, another has since come to light, whereby Payn de Chaworth and Robert Tiptoft contracted to accompany Edward with ten knights, five apiece according to the Pipe Roll, and remain in his service for one

[23] *Anc. Corr.* 13. 154, 154a; *Foedera*, I. ii. 542.

[24] *Gascon Register A (Series of 1318–19)*, ed. G. P. Cuttino and J-P. Trabut-Cussac, 3 vols. (London, 1975–6), i. No. 157. He was released from this sum in Nov. 1275: *CPR 1272–81*, p. 113. On his return Ebles was appointed seneschal of Périgord: J-P. Trabut-Cussac, *L'Administration anglaise en Gascogne 1254–1307* (Paris, Geneva, 1972), 181–2, 382.

[25] PRO, E 372/117, m. 6. Part of the account is printed in *Lancashire Lay Subsidies: An Examination of the Lay Subsidy Rolls, Henry III–Charles II, I (1216–1307)*, ed. J. A. C. Vincent (Lancs. and Cheshire Rec. Soc. 27; 1893), 100–5. The list of contractors was first printed by T. H. Turner, 'Unpublished Notices of the Time of Edward I', *Archaeological Journ.* viii (1851), 46. B. Beebe, 'The English Baronage and the Crusade of 1270', *BIHR* xlviii (1975), 142, omits Gilbert de Clare, whilst *Adam* de Monte Alto should be read for *Alan*.

[26] This figure postulates ninety-nine knights serving with Edmund, eleven with Hamo Lestrange, and nine with Gilbert de Clare, for only the payments to these men, and not their quotas, are recorded. Considering Edmund's remarkable landed power by 1270 the figure of ninety-nine need not be doubted. Edward's own household establishment should surely be added to the figure of 225. Peter de Castro Novo was one household knight, paid 100*m.* in part payment of Edward's debt to him, coming from Acre to England in 1271–2: PRO, E 101/350/5, mm. 1, 4. William of Tripoli, who completed his *De statu Saracenorum* at Acre, 1273, and in a good position to know the size of Edward's force there, states it amounted to 300 knights. See H. Prutz, *Kulturgeschichte der Kreuzzüge* (Berlin, 1883), 587.

[27] H. G. Richardson and G. O. Sayles, *The Governance of Mediaeval England from the Conquest to Magna Carta* (Edinburgh, 1963), appendix vi, pp. 463–5. Comparison with BL Cotton Charter xxix. 65 reveals certain omissions in the printed text.

year beginning 'at the next September passage', presumably when Edward should embark at Aigues Mortes. In return they were granted 1,200*m*. 'and passage, that is to say, hire of a ship and water for so many persons, and horses as befits knights'. Should they be prevented from serving, then substitutes were to be provided or the money repaid in proportion to the service owing. If Edward should die, they were bound to serve whomsoever he might appoint in his place.[28]

Since the terms of the two contracts were identical, we may conclude, with the additional evidence of the Pipe Roll account, that general terms for service on crusade were offered.[29] The terms, however, are lamentably vague and rudimentary in comparison to English contracts of later date. Nothing is said of the number of other ranks or the number or type of horses to accompany each knight, the means of payment to the knights in each contractor's *mesnie*, compensation for horses lost in service, bouche of court; nor whether Edward had full rights over spoils of war and if he was to provide arms and mounts.[30] Nevertheless, it is of considerable interest that Edward should make systematic use of contracts to organize his force and in some sense expand his household for the expedition, considering his tendency as king to prefer cavalry forces raised through contract as an alternative to the traditional feudal host.[31]

The contractors were men whom Edward had come to know and trust over the years. He had campaigned with most in the turbulent days of the 1263–7 period, and acted in affairs of state with many. Three were great lords in their own right and Edward's kin: Edmund, William de Valence, and Henry of Almain. Walter de Percy was one of Edmund's own knights, having earlier transferred from Henry

[28] BL Additional Charter 19829. For further information on this and other contracts, see Lloyd, 'The Lord Edward's Crusade', esp. pp. 125–8.

[29] The Pipe Roll reveals that the contractors, excepting only Gilbert de Clare, were paid on 26 July. The other contracts were probably drawn up on 20 July, at Westminster, the date of the two surviving ones.

[30] Various references suggest that *restor de chevaux* was included, at least for those in Edward's immediate household. Thus Gerard de St-Laurent was granted 40*m*. in 1272–3 for a horse lost in service, and 12*m*. for arrears of his wages 'de tempore quo stetit in servicio nostro in Accon': PRO, C 62/49, m. 6; E 403/20.

[31] J. E. Morris, *The Welsh Wars of Edward I: A Contribution to Mediaeval Military History* (Oxford, 1901), esp. p. 68, considered that Edward's reign was crucial in the development of a paid army, but it is now clear that he overstated his case. See, in particular, Prestwich, *War, Politics*, ch. 3. If Tout was broadly right in saying that the Lord Edward's household became the household of Edward I and largely correct in suggesting that the armies of Edward I were composed essentially of 'the household in arms', then the extended household crusade was evidently of great importance in suggesting the nucleus of Edward's later campaign forces: T. F. Tout, *Chapters in the Administrative History of Mediaeval England*, 6 vols. (Manchester, 1937), ii. 133, 138.

III's household. Adam de Monte Alto, Hamo Lestrange, Brian de Brampton, Robert de Munteny, and William de Huntercumbe were prominent royal servants. Robert Tiptoft, Richard de la Rochelle, Thomas de Clare, and Roger de Leyburn all appear in Edward's close circle before the crusade, whilst Payn de Chaworth, Adam of Jesmond, William fitzWarin, and Roger de Clifford were intimately associated with Henry III and his son. It was entirely natural that Edward should look to such men for support.

By means of these contracts Edward could assure Louis that he would be accompanied by a given number of knights bound to his service. They also placed men such as Edmund and William de Valence under Edward's command and thus acted to prevent what Louis and Edward feared: the disintegration of the crusade into a number of loosely cohesive forces. In this context the terms of the other agreement known to us are revealing. According to Richard of Cornwall's award of May 1270, Gilbert de Clare was to join the crusade in the passage following Edward's departure. Should he wish to lead an independent force on reaching the Holy Land he would be granted 2,000*m.* by Henry III, but if he were to be 'atendaunt e eydaunt' to Edward then the king would give him 8,000*m.* and a fitting ship for his passage.[32] The extra inducements made available to the mercurial earl of Gloucester underline that the unity of the English force under Edward's overall command was considered a high priority.

The network of contracts may be taken one stage further. Just as Edward looked to those of his connection for support, so the contractors sought the service of knights of their own acquaintance. Some, perhaps most, were already in the service of the contractor concerned, or closely connected to him in other ways. William Graundyn, for example, is identified as one of Roger de Leyburn's knights in November 1269, when he accompanied his lord to Gascony on Edward's business: it cannot be demonstrated that Roger subcontracted him for the crusade, but it is very likely.[33] Thomas de Sandwich may have been another of Roger's squadron. A former Montfortian, he had been received into the king's peace as early as November 1265, entering Roger's service no later than April 1266 when Roger committed the bailiwick and chamberlainship of

[32] For the award, and Gilbert's vow, see Lloyd, 'Gilbert de Clare'.

[33] *CPR 1266–72*, p. 397. He witnessed the dower settlement between Roger's widow and their son William in 1271: PRO, E 368/45, m. 3. Roger did not reach the Holy Land. From Nov. 1269 he was seneschal of Gascony, though he was back in England apparently from Jan. 1271: *CPR 1266–72*, pp. 397, 511, 596; *Reg. Gregory X*, No. 191. It looks as if William Graundyn accompanied Roger on his travels and did not sail on crusade either.

Sandwich to Thomas's keeping.[34] Geoffrey Gacelyn almost certainly accompanied William de Valence. A Welsh Marcher who rose to prominence in royal service in Gascony and on the March in the 1240s and 1250s, Geoffrey is frequently found in William's circle both before and after the crusade, and gaining due material reward. In a presentment of 1286 he was specifically identified as one of William's knights in connection with an offence in Kinver forest in 1277.[35] He died in 1282. Laurence de St Mauro surely sailed as one of Edmund's contracted knights. Although Laurence first took out a crusader's protection in May 1270, he renewed it and appointed attorneys in February 1271, when his patron sailed.[36] Laurence is found associated with Edmund time and again, either side of the crusade. Their close relationship is amply demonstrated by the fact that, after serving as steward, Laurence acted as Edmund's executor on his death in 1296.[37]

Many of the 225 knights effectively picked themselves by virtue of the sort of ties to the contractors outlined above, so it is not surprising that only limited traces of the process of subcontracting survive. It is entirely consistent that those that do relate to new or modified relationships stimulated by the demands of the crusade. In 1269 William de Munchensi, a former Montfortian rebel, was under a bond to pay 1,000*m.* to William de Valence, his brother-in-law, 'if by chance he should not cross with him to the Holy Land', and he does indeed appear to have forfeited and withdrawn from de Valence's *mesnie* for the crusade, for 500*m.* of the bond was remitted and terms agreed for payment of the remainder.[38] Lord Edmund was

[34] *CPR 1258–66*, pp. 497, 578. He was in office until 1268: *CPR 1266–72*, p. 208; *CLR 1267–72*, p. 40. He later became seneschal of Ponthieu. For his career see H. Johnstone, 'The County of Ponthieu, 1279–1307', *EHR* xxix (1914), esp. pp. 443–4. Since he too witnessed the Leyburn dower settlement in 1271, and witnessed a charter granted to Roger in July 1271, it is unlikely that he set out on crusade either: *CCh.R 1257–1300*, p. 175.

[35] 'Pleas of the Forest, Staffordshire, *temp.* Henry III-Edward I', trans. G. Wrottesley (William Salt Archaeological Soc., *Collections, 5*, part 1, 1884), 160. See further, for his specific connections with William, *CPR 1266–72*, p. 46; *CR 1264–8*, p. 297; *CPR 1272–81*, pp. 211–12, 317; *CCh.R 1226–57*, p. 462; *A Descriptive Catalogue of Ancient Deeds in the Public Record Office*, 6 vols. (London, 1890–1915). iv. Nos. A 7183,8096.

[36] *CPR 1266–72*, pp. 479, 588–9.

[37] J. R. Maddicott, 'Thomas of Lancaster and Sir Robert Holland: A Study in Noble Patronage', *EHR* lxxxvi (1971), 458. For his particular connection with Edmund see esp. *CPR 1258–66*, pp. 535, 615; *CPR 1272–81*, pp. 156, 251, 436, 440–1; *CPR 1281–92*, pp. 162, 228, 245, 264; *CR 1268–72*, p. 265; *CIPM* i. 260; BL Cotton Charter xii. 27; *The Stoneleigh Leger Book*, ed. R. H. Hilton (Dugdale Soc. Publicns. 24; 1960), 42–3.

[38] *CR 1268–72*, p. 241. De Valence had been granted de Munchensi's lands; for their redemption, see *CPR 1258–66*, pp. 352, 667; *CPR 1266–72*, pp. 32, 161, 181; *CR 1264–8*, pp. 506–7, 512. De Munchensi had been in Gilbert de Clare's household

accompanied by Robert de Turberville, a Marcher already in his service. He had been granted 20*l.* per annum from the issues of the manor of Minsterworth, but in February 1271, 'because he is about to cross the sea with him', Edmund granted the manor itself to Robert for a three-year term, after which he would receive his 20*l.* as before.[39] Shortly before, in January, Edmund had granted to Geoffrey de Langley junior, another of his knights, the manor of Kingshay and the mills of Hungerford, providing that Edmund would resume seisin if Geoffrey were assigned 20*l.* of land. His prospective service with Edmund on crusade doubtless lay behind this grant; one month later Geoffrey took out his crusader's protection.[40]

The most interesting case of all concerns Thomas de Clare, who contracted to serve Edward with nine knights. Most were probably found from the ranks of those already associated with Thomas,[41] but one, Nicholas de Sifrewast, a knight of Oxfordshire and Berkshire, and former sheriff of those counties (1265–7) does not appear to have had any connection with Thomas before the preparation for the crusade. In 1269–70 the two entered into a complex agreement. First, on 4 May 1269, Nicholas enfeoffed Thomas for life with his manor of Hampstead Norreys, a half knight's fee held of him in Bensington, one knight's fee in Pebworth, and certain services. In return, Thomas agreed to provide Nicholas for life with land of equivalent value to Hampstead Norreys, 10*l.* of arable land, and a payment of 100*m.* when Thomas should take seisin. Further, Thomas would give Nicholas 'se il veet od lui en la Tere Seinte a la primere monte ke serra ansi cum a un de ses bacheliers ke od lui irunt'.[42] Hampstead Norreys formed part of Nicholas's paternal inheritance along with the manors of Aldworth and Purley. These too Nicholas made over to Thomas in 1270, but this time in perpetuity, receiving Aldworth back for life along with certain rights in Purley.[43] In addition, on 11 January 1270, Thomas acknowledged that he

from 1267, and may, in 1270, have intended to crusade with him: M. Altschul, *A Baronial Family in Medieval England: The Clares, 1217–1314* (Baltimore, 1965), 113, 114, 118; *CPR 1266–72*, pp. 410, 412. If so, his release from prospective service with de Valence in 1269 makes sense.

39 *CPR 1266–72*, p. 515; 'eo quod nobiscum transfretaturus est': PRO, C 66/89, m. 21. Robert is frequently found in Edmund's circle; e.g. *CPR 1266–72*, pp. 502, 515; *CR 1268–72*, p. 265.

40 *CCh.R 1257–1300*, p. 162. For Geoffrey see above, Ch. 3, n. 172.

41 Ranulf de Ardern was probably one, identified as a knight of Thomas in Apr. 1272: *CPR 1266–72*, p. 643.

42 *CR 1268–72*, pp. 143–4; *CPR 1266–72*, pp. 474–5. The 100*m.* was probably a conveyance charge. In 1270 Thomas acknowledged that he was held to pay 45*m.* to Nicholas at Easter, perhaps the residue of the sum: PRO, E 159/44, m. 11d.

43 *Fees* ii. 843, 845, 851, 857; *CR 1268–72*, pp. 249–50.

was bound in 60*s*. per annum to Nicholas for life, and he further granted Nicholas, again for life, his lands in Cottesmore, Belaugh, Playford, Withersdale, and Weybread.[44] A final concord between the parties at Westminster in Trinity 1270 confirmed these landed transactions.[45]

It looks as though Thomas had retained Nicholas for life, his service to include crusading with Thomas as one of his bachelors; both received protections in July 1270.[46] If so, then this is of exceptional interest as a very early example of a life retainer, the more so since the relationship was initially stimulated by the needs of Thomas as a contracting crusader. Comparison with later indentures shows it to be a primitive agreement, tantalizingly vague in its terms, although not all the relevant instruments may have survived. There is little indication of what the retainer envisaged nor, alas, of the precise terms offered to Nicholas as one of Thomas's bachelors on crusade. Nevertheless, the very existence of the relationship lends support to suggestions that magnate use of indentures was already well-established by the early fourteenth century if not considerably earlier.[47]

The core of the English crusading force, then, consisted of a group of important lords intimately connected to the Plantagenet house, tied to Edward through a systematic use of contracts, and serving with their own knights raised for the expedition. They were accompanied by—indeed they partly formed—the single largest group of crusaders: men who were already in the service of Henry III, his sons, and their respective wives, either as close household members, in administrative and military positions beyond the household concerned, or with some significant curial connection. Of the 293

[44] *CPR 1266–72*, p. 474, probably to meet his promise to provide land to the equivalent value of Hampstead Norreys, along with 10*l*. of arable.

[45] PRO, CP 25(1), 283/17/470. See further on these transactions, below pp. 189–90.

[46] In 1273 and 1274 Nicholas appears making attorneys for Thomas and acting in a suit on his behalf: *CCR 1272–9*, pp. 56, 125, 131. The connection ended soon after. The lands granted him for life then reverted to Thomas. In 1276 Thomas surrendered the manors of Hampstead Norreys, Aldworth, Compton, and Alvescote, along with rents in Cottesmore, to Robert de Mucegros in an exchange: *CFR 1272–1307*, p. 66; *CCh.R 1257–1300*, p. 198; further, *CCR 1279–88*, p. 82, *CIPM* ii. 233. Purley, at least, reverted to the Sifrewasts: *VCH Berkshire*, iii. 420.

[47] See G. A. Holmes, *The Estates of the Higher Nobility in Fourteenth Century England* (Cambridge, 1957), 80; J. R. S. Phillips, *Aymer de Valence, Earl of Pembroke 1307–24* (Oxford, 1972), 255; Prestwich, *War, Politics*, pp. 61–2. Compare the agreement with the earliest permanent retainer thus far printed, that of Roger Bigod and John de Segrave, 1297, in N. Denholm-Young, *Seignorial Administration in England* (Oxford, 1937), 167. Compare also with those of Aymer de Valence and Thomas de Berkeley, 1297, and of Thomas of Lancaster and William Latimer, 1319: *Calendar of Documents Relating to Scotland Preserved in the Public Record Office*, ed. J. Bain, 4 vols. (Edinburgh, 1881–8), ii. No. 905; Phillips, *Aymer de Valence*, ch. 9, appendix ii; Holmes, *Estates*, pp. 71, 122–3.

crusaders tabulated in Appendix 4, 162 (55·3%) can certainly be classified in this way. A number of reasonably well-defined circles grouped around the leaders can be identified. Edward's own household on crusade included, amongst the *domestici*, his sumpter Russel, his cook William de Saundon, John de Osbeston, probably Edward's chamber usher on crusade, and Robert la Warre, perhaps already holding the position of pantler to the prince. Two of his chaplains are known: Nicholas de Attrabato and Stephen de London. Amongst an important group of clerics, clearly intended to bear the brunt of secretarial and administrative chores, were Antony Bek, Philip de Willoughby, and Thomas Gunneys, who administered Edward's wardrobe for most of the return journey from the Holy Land. Among the sergeants were the balister Richard de Saundon and Richard Foun, who may have been put in charge of Edward's stables on crusade, considering the horses bought from him at Acre and his later association with Edward I's studs. The highest ranks included *valetti* such as John de Gayton, and knights of the stature of Richard de la Rochelle, Edward's former justiciar in Ireland, Otto de Grandson, Luke de Tany, his admiral on crusade, and Hugh fitzOtto, probably his steward on crusade.[48]

Another group accompanied Eleanor of Castile: men such as John le Espeynol, her *valettus*, her knight and steward John de Weston, her tailor Richard de la Garderobe, her clerks William de Tackley and William de Yattinden. A third household group sailed with Edmund: knights such as Richard de Wykes, his steward, Alan de Lascelles, Hugh de Aungerville, and Laurence de St Mauro, *valetti* such as Roger de Conyers. Yet others appear to have been seconded to the crusade by Henry III and his queen, perhaps at the request of Edward and other leaders since it was common practice to switch men from the king's or queen's immediate service to their close kin on occasion. They included men of all ranks: knights such as William Belet, *valetti* such as William de Moleford, that group of six sergeants whose wages in arrears were to be paid speedily in May 1270 lest their departure be shamefully retarded, the queen's knight and steward Guy Ferre, the surgeon Hugh Sauvage, and a number of clerics with administrative expertise.

[48] Detailed accounts for the households of Edward and other crusade leaders do not survive, so it is not possible to reconstruct their household personnel exactly. PRO, E 101/350/5, for the period 54 Henry III–2 Edward I, covers payments from Edward's wardrobe going back to *c.*1266–7, but it is largely a record of disbursements to individuals coming to and going from Edward's household on specified business in the years immediately before and after his accession. E 101/350/7, related, is mostly destroyed. Little survives of Philip de Willoughby's account, as keeper of the wardrobe, 4 Nov. 1272–18 Oct. 1274, in E 101/350/8. The summary of the account is entered on Pipe Roll 5 Edward I, but it is very bald.

Traces of the households of lesser men also survive. Richard de la Rochelle, for example, was accompanied by his clerk John de Fifhide. John de Selston very probably sailed with John de Vescy; he had been presented to a moiety of the church of Rotherham by Agnes de Vescy, John's mother, in or before 1270. But regardless of the precise household in which individuals served, it is plain that they went on crusade in large part because their particular services—martial, clerical, or otherwise—were required, leaving aside any personal crusading enthusiasm. Moreover, analysis of the status and occupations of those making up the force shows that so far as papal policy was concerned it was of the preferred type: it was well-organized, tolerably well-financed, and it promised to be effective in the field. Of the 216 *crucesignati* whose profession is known, 168 were members of the military classes, mostly knights. A further thirty-seven were ecclesiastics, of whom nineteen were in Plantagenet service before the crusade. These, along with the surgeon Hugh Sauvage, the tailor Richard de la Garderobe, and merchants such as Alan de Castell, almost certainly participated because their professional services were required.

The workings of those regional ties of association discussed in Chapter 3 are no less apparent. Apart from the group of Northern crusaders previously considered, it is possible to identify a number of more or less discrete regional groupings. One was formed of Welsh Marchers, established both within and without Chester and Edward's other Welsh lordships: Roger de Clifford and his brother-in-law Roger de Leyburn; Peter de Ardern, Edward's justice of Chester (1253–8), and his son John; James de Audley, justice of Chester (1265–7), and his constable John de Baskerville; Jordan de Pulesdon, former sheriff of Chester (1265–7); Urian de St Petro and his brother-in-law William Patrick; Hamo Lestrange and his brother Robert; Adam and John de Monte Alto; Hervey, Patrick, and Payn de Chaworth, whose chief interests lay further south on the March, along with those of John de Verdun and Geoffrey de Geneville. They were accompanied by a significant number of their friends, tenants, and colleagues.[49] Another grouping consisted of men closely or wholly identified with the eastern counties of Essex, Hertfordshire, Cambridgeshire, Huntingdonshire, Norfolk, and Suffolk. They included Arnulf and Robert de Munteny, Baldwin de Bassingburn, Bartholomew de Brianso, Berenger le Moyne, Hugh fitzOtto, John

[49] Tout, 'Wales and the March', in *Collected Papers*, ii. 47–100, demonstrated the remarkable coherence of the Marchers as a political group in 1258–67. That a large number then took the Cross comes as no surprise. Edward, Edmund, and William de Valence had intimate ties with most of them.

and Robert Tiptoft, Richard Bruce, Robert de Ufford, and other notable figures. Yet, as the interests, connections, and careers of men like Payn de Chaworth or Robert Tiptoft reveal, it would be unwise to distinguish these regional groupings too sharply; they were not rigidly distinct. Above all, as far as the crusade was concerned, the majority of these men shared a common background of curial connections which transcended narrower ties. This is further impressed upon us by the fact that 121, of the total of 293 listed in Appendix 4, can be shown to have served Edward as king in some capacity (41.3%), and of these only twenty-six do not seem to have enjoyed close curial connections before the crusade. Again, although sixty-six of the 162 crusaders with demonstrable curial connections before the crusade do not afterwards appear in Plantagenet service, at least twenty-five of them are known to have died in or before 1277, and a significant number of the remaining forty-one were of advanced age by 1272 and appear to have retired from active public life thereafter.

Of the remaining crusaders beyond the core group of 162, thirty-two appear to have had connections with the Crown or important *curiales* before the crusade, although firm evidence that they were in royal service is lacking. They include kinsmen of members of the core group, such as William fitzRobert de Willoughby; relations of important non-crusading *curiales*, such as Walter Basset and William Pavely; men in receipt of privileges and grants from the king, which suggests a meaningful tie, such as Walter de Wigton; and men whose rapid appointment to important positions soon after the crusade argues for their prior service to the crusade leaders or *curiales*. John de la Bere, for example, was appointed constable of Bordeaux in 1274. His connections with Henry of Almain and Luke de Tany probably provided the initial opening to his career in royal service after the crusade. Of a further seventy-six crusaders little, or nothing, is known of their activities or careers before 1270–1, although some were later to serve Edward as king. The remainder consist of an assortment of ecclesiastics, a few Anglo-Scots, some who cannot be safely distinguished from other contemporaries of the same name, and a group of Montfortian rebels who are discussed below. When due allowance is made for the evident difficulties attached to statistics drawn from records of the type available, our conclusion must be that the 1270–2 crusading force was composed essentially of the kinsmen, dependants, friends, and acquaintances of the Lords Edward and Edmund.

It should, then, come as no great surprise to find that few former Montfortian rebels are known to have participated in the crusade, but recently Beebe has constructed an intricate argument around their general failure to respond to the call to the crusade, a failure all the more remarkable in his view, since he argues that the crusade was promoted as an integral part of the drive towards peace and stability after the outbreak of civil strife in 1264. In explanation of the fact that it was overwhelmingly royalists rather than rebels who reacted positively, Beebe presents arguments which focus upon the political and financial difficulties facing former rebels, and which emphasize the legal and financial benefits open to their former political opponents—a state of affairs openly upheld by the Crown.[50] Some comment is clearly called for in the light of the findings presented above.

The available evidence makes it abundantly clear, first, that both Urban IV and Clement IV authorized their respective legates to preach the crusade *against* the rebels as part of papal policy to aid Henry III in the troubles of the 1260s. Promotion of the crusade to the Holy Land was allowed to lapse, and only when peace was restored do we find it promoted again with vigour. Until then, the rebels, far from being the object of a recruitment campaign to entice them from England, were in fact the declared object of a 'political' crusade *within* the realm.[51] Second, Beebe's definition of 'rebel' and 'royalist' is unhappy, the more so since the distinction lies at the heart of his overall argument. Analysis of the sixteen former rebels whom he cites as taking the Cross reveals that any who sought admission to the king's peace, and pardon for their activities in the period of disturbance, are included. Yet even Edward himself, and men of the stature of John Giffard and Gilbert de Clare, found it advisable in the circumstances after the battle of Evesham to secure royal exoneration for certain of their activities.[52] Gilbert, it is true, is excluded on the grounds that he was often 'at odds' with the royal party, but then so were so many others.[53] Moreover, a substantial number followed their

[50] Beebe, 'The English Baronage'.

[51] The evidence for the application of crusade against the Montfortians is set out in Lloyd, "Political Crusades" in P. W. Edbury (ed.), *Crusade and Settlement: Papers Read at the First Conference of the Society for the Study of the Crusades and the Latin East and Presented to R. C. Smail* (Cardiff, 1985), pp. 116–17. The evidence Beebe cites to the effect that the crusade to the Holy Land was actively promoted in this period does nothing of the sort, e.g. no source supports the contention that John de Valenciennes's mission of 1263–4 was concerned with recruitment, and that he was thus engaged at Northampton, Apr. 1264: Beebe, 'The English Baronage', p. 129. Rather, John was sent by Louis IX to mediate between Henry III and his opponents: *CPR 1258–66*, p. 317; *Foedera*, I. i. 437; 'Contin.' of Gervase of Canterbury, ii. 234; further, *CPR 1258–66*, pp. 240, 308; *CR 1261–4*, p. 369. A connection with promotion of the crusade appears only in relation to John's activities in France, where apparently he was handling moneys, not recruiting men: *Reg. Urban IV*, Nos. 374, 393. He was indeed engaged in receiving moneys for the Holy Land from Henry III on the eve of the battle of Lewes: *CPR 1258–66*, p. 317.

[52] Beebe, 'The English Baronage', esp. pp. 131 and n. 6, 133, 136; Altschul, *A Baronial Family*, pp. 112–14.

[53] Beebe, 'The English Baronage', pp. 132–3.

lords' lead in political manœuvring. John de Ingoldthorpe, for one, is included as a 'rebel' by Beebe, yet we are informed that after the battle of Lewes he 'behaved faithfully to the king, the Lord Edward, and Gilbert de Clare in whose service he was'.[54] Should John be categorized as a 'rebel', whilst Gilbert is not? An altogether more satisfactory definition would designate as rebels those whose properties were confiscated by the Crown after Evesham and who were then obliged to redeem them according to the terms of the Dictum of Kenilworth, 1267. Excluding four crusaders whose identification with rebels of that name is by no means clear, thirteen crusaders can certainly be deemed rebels by this criterion, not at all the same as those tabulated by Beebe.[55]

To explain the low 'rebel' reponse, Beebe argues that many were openly opposed to a crusade anyway and were suspicious of papal intentions. There is certainly evidence to this effect, but its general application may be questioned since it refers only to the rebels in the Isle of Ely in February 1267, and one of their leaders, Nicholas de Segrave, later took the Cross. Moreover, their objections were shared by others of different political persuasion; they were not limited to any partisan group.[56] Beebe further argues that most rebels were financially oppressed through the devastation of their estates, fines for admission to the king's peace, and the costs of redeeming their estates, difficulties compounded by the legal problems and delays they encountered. Of course rebels faced severe problems, but close scrutiny of the evidence cited does not establish Beebe's case,[57] and it is well known that the estates of many royalists did not escape unscathed. Moreover, the case of Hugh de Neville, who suffered more than most, indicates that rebels could undertake a crusade if they really wished, notwithstanding their difficulties.[58]

Hugh's lands were taken into the king's hands after Evesham and

[54] *CPR 1266–72*, p. 516.

[55] See appendix 4. Many within the crusading force had, of course, identified with the cause of the Provisions and of Simon de Montfort at some point, like many of their contemporaries.

[56] Beebe, 'The English Baronage', p. 133; *Councils*, II. ii. 734.

[57] Beebe, 'The English Baronage', pp. 133–5. e.g. Nicholas de Yattinden is said to have 'appeared before the royal courts to argue a single claim in February and November 1269, November 1270 and February 1271.' But Nicholas was a royal justice, as the source cited shows: E. F. Jacob, *Studies in the Period of Baronial Reform and Rebellion, 1258–67* (Oxford, 1925), 164–5, apart from other references. Nicholas was not a crusader, and has presumably been confused with William de Yattinden, who was.

[58] For Hugh, see C. H. Knowles, 'The Disinherited, 1265–80', Ph.D. thesis (Wales, 1959), part iii, 88–90; id., 'The Resettlement of England after the Barons' War, 1264–67', *TRHS* 5th ser. xxxii (1982), 29, 36–7; 'On the Testament of Sir Hugh de Nevill, Written at Acre, 1267', ed. M. S. Giuseppi, *Archaeologia*, lvi, part 2 (1899), 351–70.

granted to Robert Walerand.[59] He responded by joining up with other die-hard Montfortians in the Isle of Axholme, and he was not admitted to the king's peace until June 1266, when he came to an agreement with Robert whereby a substantial proportion of his lands were restored. The remainder he quitclaimed to Robert.[60] Soon afterwards Hugh set out for the Holy Land, and during his absence he approached the papal Curia, unsuccessfully, for recovery of his alienated lands. His mother Hawisia refused to accept what she regarded as a piece of legal trickery and urged Hugh to approach the pope again for help. She further impressed upon him the need to return home quickly because, she wrote, nothing could be achieved during Hugh's absence 'for the great power your adversary has in the king's court'.[61] Apparently in response to this forceful appeal, which made him mindful of his responsibility to lineage and family interests, Hugh obtained absolution from his vow and set off home.[62] But he never saw England again, dying in Italy, apparently, in 1269, and his family never recovered the lands he had been driven to alienate.[63] Here was a rebel, his material substance severely depleted and his inheritance truncated, paying a high price for his political behaviour, yet still able and willing to go to the Holy Land. Nor was he a lone exception. John de Vescy, for example, agreed terms in Michaelmas 1267 with Count Guy of St-Pol for the payment of the huge sum of 3,700*m.* for the redemption of his lands by January 1272. It was a crippling short-term burden, but John had duly paid 3,000*m.* by Easter 1270.[64] The fine of 2,000*m.* which Nicholas de Segrave agreed with the Lord Edmund did not prevent him from departing on crusade, and the debt was not settled finally until 1295.[65] That Nicholas at the time of the crusade faced a severe cash crisis, which was exacerbated by his participation in it, is indicated by his debt to William de Valence in 1276 to the tune of at least 1,000*m.*[66] Contemporaries did not approach the prospect of a crusade simply on the grounds of financial buoyancy and economic rationalism; the honour and prestige alone to be gained through participation saw to that.

59 *Close Rolls (Supplementary) of the Reign of Henry III, 1244–1266*, ed. A. Morton (London, 1975), 45.

60 *CPR 1258–66*, pp. 608–10, 668. His London houses remained in John de Warenne's hands as late as Dec. 1266: ibid. 457, 468; *CPR 1266–72*, p. 14.

61 Giuseppi, 'On the Testament of Sir Hugh de Nevill', pp. 358–9. The reference is surely to Robert Walerand.

62 Ibid. 362–3. Much of the absolution, dated 26 June 1268, Acre, is illegible.

63 Ibid. 363; *RF* ii. 498; *CIPM* ii. 6, 89.

64 *Cal. Docs. Scotland*, i. No. 2456.

65 Knowles, 'The Resettlement', p. 35; F. M. Powicke, *King Henry III and the Lord Edward: The Community of the Realm in the Thirteenth Century*, 2 vols. (Oxford, 1947), ii. 554.

66 *CCR 1272–9*, p. 331.

The material circumstances of royalists in the period after Evesham were generally more favourable doubtless, but the argument that recruitment from amongst their ranks was positively encouraged by the various privileges accorded to *crucesignati*—and the Crown's partisan reinforcement thereof—may be rebutted.[67] One advantage, Beebe claims, was the continued possession of rebels' estates for the duration of the crusader's royal judicial protection, and he considers the number of royalists able to take advantage as being 'impressive'. But only twenty-eight, of the total of 230 crusaders listed by Beebe, are cited.[68] More importantly, detailed analysis reveals that fifty-three crusaders had at some point been in possession of rebels' properties, but of these ten appear as having been in possession of Michaelmas 1265 rents alone, or had illegally seized and retained lands in the period of disturbances and were later obliged to surrender them. Of the remaining forty-three, only twelve can be shown definitely to have been in seisin of the properties granted in accordance with the Dictum of Kenilworth when they took out their crusader protections. Whether ten others remained in seisin is unknown or unclear: it would be unwise to assume that they were. The rest can be shown to have begun the process of restitution, and most had already returned properties to their former rebel holders.[69] This reflects the conclusions of Knowles's exhaustive study of the subject as a whole; he has demonstrated that the bulk of redemption transfers were drawn up, if not completed, before 1272, and, moreover, that rebels were generally allowed entry to their lands immediately after the sealing of redemption recognizances.[70]

Beebe further argues that crusaders' lands would be protected by the Crown until their return, in accordance with royal protections, thus prolonging the gains of royalists at the expense of rebels. Beebe cites the cases of Luke de Tany and Robert de Ferrers by way of illustration.[71] The case against Luke concerned homicide, not property, and anyway no case had yet been brought against him upon receipt of his protection. With regard to the unfortunate Robert de Ferrers, earl of Derby, it must be shown that the delays he faced were a direct consequence of the crusader protections granted to Lord Edmund and Hamo Lestrange. However, Robert had already

[67] Beebe, 'The English Baronage', pp. 136–40.

[68] Ibid. 138, tables 2, 3, and appendices a, b. The figure of twenty-eight is inaccurate since it includes a number who do not appear in possession of rebels' estates at any point, and omits others who certainly were.

[69] See appendix 4 below.

[70] Knowles, 'The Disinherited', part iii, esp. pp. 77–8. The sources Beebe cites to support the assertion that crusaders exploited their privileges to sell or lease rebels' lands will not bear this interpretation.

[71] Beebe, 'The English Baronage', pp. 138–9.

brought an action against Edmund before his grant, so the protection would not apply, and nowhere in the extensive materials bearing upon the case do we find Edmund's attorneys pleading crusader status on their lord's behalf. It is difficult to agree that Edmund was aware that his protection would ensure his undisputed retention of Robert's estates.[72] Further, crusaders' need for ready cash, before, at, and after their departure, can only have speeded up the process of restitution so far as rebels' estates are concerned. And if the royalist crusader intended to alienate estates for cash, permanently or temporarily, then the lessee, gagee, or purchaser naturally sought to ensure that the transaction was entirely above-board in legal terms.[73]

The substantial fact remains: few rebels responded to the call to the crusade. The reason is probably that they were not, nor wished to be, nor were generally encouraged to be, closely associated with Edward and his crusading companions, their former political opponents so shortly before. Investigation of the circumstances of those rebels who *did* take the Cross strengthens this surmise, because most of them either had previously close connections to the royal house which were restored between 1265 and 1270–1, or had developed links with important *curiales* in that period, or had, in a career change, entered into close association with Edward and his kin by then. Hugh de Aungerville, in Henry III's service in the 1250s, became one of Edmund's knights between 1267 and 1270–1.[74] Robert de Staundon, destined to become a key man in Edward I's administration of North Wales in the 1280s and 1290s, was enfeoffed of lands by a fellow Marcher and royalist, Urian de St Petro.[75] Geoffrey de Scoftinton (Skeffington) is found as an attorney of James de Audley by 1268.[76] Robert de Cadamo was restored in 1271 to his annual fee at the Exchequer, first granted in 1253.[77] Of the more important rebel lords, John de Vescy, the son of a distinguished servant of Henry III, had

[72] Ibid. 139. For Ferrers, see Jacob, *Studies*, pp. 218, 388–94; *CR 1268–72*, pp. 398, 545–6, 565. On protections and their limitations, see below, pp. 165–7. The only certain way of assuring the integrity of one's properties during crusade was to come to agreement with opponents over disputed possession. As confiscated rebels' estates were an obvious source of friction at this time, it is scarcely surprising to find few crusaders still definitely in possession upon departure, or without having begun the process of restitution.

[73] See further below, p. 172.

[74] *CR 1253–4*, pp. 219, 302; *CCh.R 1257–1300*, pp. 161–2.

[75] *CIPM* ii. 92. Urian, in turn, had received them from Hamo Lestrange.

[76] *CR 1264–8*, pp. 525–6. Geoffrey held land of James: 'Extracts from Plea Rolls', trans. G. Wrottesley (William Salt Archaeological Soc., *Collections, 6*, 1; 1885), 81, 107, 123.

[77] *CPR 1247–58*, p. 246; *CLR 1251–60*, p. 279; *CLR 1267–72*, p. 153. The fee was apparently cancelled in 1262.

been in royal service until 1262. Captured at Evesham, he indulged in a final rebellious fling in the abortive Northern rising of 1267, but thereafter he was rapidly drawn into Edward's close circle and is found again in close association with loyal Northerners from 1268.[78] In that year he mainprised the only other Northern crusader known to have been a rebel, Robert de Haulton.[79] Nicholas de Segrave appears as a royal *valettus* in 1257.[80] The tie with the royal house had been re-established by the time of the crusade, notwithstanding his joining with desperadoes in the Isle of Ely and his association with Gilbert de Clare in the earl's occupation of London in 1267. His relationship with Lord Edmund was to be especially important for him; it was with Edmund that he sailed in 1271.[81]

The reabsorption of rebels into political and social life was not painless, but it was in the general interest that they be rapidly integrated once more within the fabric of society.[82] Edward himself appears to have appreciated the point; apart from some notable exceptions, he was generaly magnanimous towards former rebels.[83] Moreover, with their former lords dead or eclipsed, what were men like Roger de Reymes, once a *valettus* of Earl Robert de Ferrers, to do?[84] Royal service offered a well-trodden and potentially lucrative path, and service on crusade, with the heir to the throne or his close kinsmen and followers, could be expected to facilitate the hazardous process of rebuilding a shattered career: some grasped that opportunity.

78 *Flores Historiarum*, ed. H. R. Luard, 3 vols. (RS; 1890), iii. 6; Wykes, *Chron.*, pp. 197–8; 'Waverley', p. 365; *Cal. Docs. Scotland*, i. No. 2456.

79 *CPR 1266–72*, p. 286. Robert's reabsorption was doubtless aided by his former role as royal bailiff. He was also the brother of John de Haulton, sheriff of Yorkshire and of Northumberland in the 1260s: *Chartulary of the Cistercian Abbey of Fountains*, ed. W. T. Lancaster, 2 vols. (Leeds, 1915), i. 75, 293; *The Chartulary of the Cistercian Abbey of St. Mary of Sallay in Craven I*, ed. J. McNulty, 2 vols. (Yorks. Arch. Soc., Rec. Ser. 87, 90; 1933, 1934), i. 90. Robert entered royal service in the 1270s.

80 *CR 1256–9*, pp. 40, 143–4; *CLR 1251–60*, p. 387. See *DNB* xvii. 1140–1, for a summary of his career.

81 Edmund had been granted Nicholas's lands; they were restored by July 1267: *CPR 1266–72*, pp. 73–4; *CR 1264–8*, p. 333. As earl of Leicester, Edmund was now feudal lord of most of Nicholas's estates.

82 Knowles, 'The Disinherited', part iii, 101–18.

83 See Powicke, *Henry III*, ii. ch. 12; Knowles, 'The Disinherited', part i, 53–5; and the balancing remarks of Prestwich, *War, Politics*, pp. 25–6.

84 For the association, see *CIMisc.* i. 259. Roger witnessed confirmations of two of Edward's charters in Apr. 1269: HMC, *Lisle and Dudley MSS, I*, (London, 1925), 113. The witness list of one of Roger's charters, *c.*1260–5, suggests that relations with men close to Henry III and Edward played a part in his career change: A. L. Raimes, 'The Family of Reymes of Wherstead in Suffolk', *Suffolk Institute of Archaeology and Natural History*, xxiii (1939), 108–9.

Preparations and Crusading in Practice

The experience of the earliest crusades had revealed that careful planning and preparation were essential, notwithstanding the astonishing though unique success of the First Crusade. Of particular importance was the need to establish coherent organization of the forces involved, a clear command structure, and discipline. The problem was not peculiar to crusading armies, but with such a force, above all an international *passagium generale*, it was especially pressing: contingents might be drawn widely from the West, the total number of crusaders might run into many thousands, and the army might be absent on campaign for two, three, or more years. The consequent difficulties facing crusade leaders were as immense as they were intractable.

The fissiparous nature of crusading forces has recently been underlined by Schmandt, who observes, with particular reference to the Fourth Crusade, that 'the typical crusading army can best be described as a voluntary confederation of many small, quasi-independent fragments, the entourages of self-conscious, legalistic noblemen who exercised a highly personal kind of leadership involving limited discipline'.[85] The fundamental units, the households of individual crusading knights, possessed their own structure and discipline through the ties of service binding the members to the lord concerned.[86] The chief problem lay in combining and articulating these units to form a larger and effective division, and then to establish a firm command structure over the various divisions comprising the one army. In this process, ties of association had a major part to play at all levels. Edward, for example, was the natural commander of the forces of the Plantagenet dominions in 1270–2, just as Richard I and Philip II were the natural leaders of the forces from their respective dominions on the Third Crusade. But, as the events of the Third Crusade notoriously revealed, there was always the possibility that the leaders would fall out and unity disintegrate. Positive measures *before* departure were clearly required.

One obvious measure was to appoint a commander-in-chief, a *capitaneus*. Perhaps learning from the Third Crusade, the leaders of the Fourth Crusade may have first appointed, or accepted, Count Theobald III of Champagne as their commander.[87] On his death in

[85] R. H. Schmandt, 'The Fourth Crusade and the Just-War Theory', *Catholic History Review*, lxi (1975), 192.

[86] Those units might, of course, fragment in certain circumstances. See e.g. J. S. C. Riley-Smith, *The First Crusade and the Idea of Crusading* (London, 1986), 77–9.

[87] See, on this issue, E. E. Kittell, 'Was Thibaut of Champagne the Leader of the Fourth Crusade?', *Byzantion*, li (1981), 557–65. A *capitaneus* might be appointed on

1201 attempts were made to find a successor. Odo III of Burgundy was approached first, Villehardouin observing that the envoys promised to hand over to him the money for the crusade which Theobald had raised, with the further undertaking that 'we will swear to you on the Holy Gospels, and cause it to be sworn by others, that we will serve you in good faith as we would have served him [Theobald]'. The offer was rejected by Odo, and then refused again by Theobald I, count of Bar-le-Duc.[88] Thereupon Boniface of Montferrat was approached. He duly accepted 'la seingneurie de l'ost', amid emotional scenes, at a *parlement* of the crusade leaders at Soissons.[89] The leaders' persistence is revealing of their perception that a clear command structure, established before departure, should be a central part of their preparations.

When the *passagium generale* was led by a ruler of European stature, the matter of appointment of a commander did not arise. Frederick II was naturally the *capitaneus* of his crusade of 1228–9, just as his arrival in that role had been eagerly awaited at Damietta some years earlier. Louis IX was indisputably the overall commander of the forces participating in his two crusades later in the century. If Edward I had duly departed on crusade in the 1290s he would undoubtedly have been *capitaneus* of the multi-national force.[90] But the post of commander did not in itself, of course, ensure cohesion and discipline within the army concerned: the disastrous sequence of events and developments on the Fourth Crusade is proof, if proof is needed.

'Pay', observed Morris, 'produces discipline and naturally leads to a subordination of commands.'[91] He may have placed too much confidence in the effects of pay in these terms, but he was certainly correct to see the application of pay as perhaps the most effective means available at the time to remedy the problems of organization, command structure, and discipline within armies comprising discrete units. The use of pay in a crusading context was as old as the First Crusade. It is well known, for example, that Raymond of Toulouse offered large sums to Godfrey de Bouillon, Robert of Normandy, Tancred, and apparently other leaders, at Chastel Rouge in 1099.[92]

campaign, as when Theobald IV of Champagne was elected 'caput et ductor' of the French crusade in 1239 at Acre. See S. Painter, *The Scourge of the Clergy: Peter of Dreux, Duke of Brittany* (Baltimore, 1937), 111–12.

88 Geoffroy de Villehardouin, *La Conquête de Constantinople*, ed. E. Faral, 2 vols. (2nd edn., Paris, 1961), i. 39–40.

89 Ibid. 42, 44.

90 See below, pp. 152–3.

91 Morris, *Welsh Wars*, p. 68.

92 Raymond d'Aguilers, 'Historia Francorum qui ceperunt Iherusalem', *RHC Occ.* iii. 271.

His precise motives remain controversial, but light is shed upon the conditions attached by Raymond d'Aguilers's report that Tancred had been offered 'V. milia solidorum et duos farios optimos, eo pacto ut in servitio ejus esset usque in Iherusalem'.[93] Offers of pay made in the course of a crusade became entirely common. In part, they helped to maintain the strength of an army. On arrival at Acre in 1240 Richard of Cornwall is said to have proclaimed that no crusader should depart through lack of money, 'sed stipendiis ejus sustentandi morarentur Christo strenue militaturi'.[94] Richard of Devizes reports that fifty years earlier Henry of Champagne, running low in money and provisions, accepted Richard I's offer of 4,000 measures of wheat, 4,000 pig carcasses, and 4,000*l.* of silver.[95] There were, of course, strings attached. It sounds as if Henry entered into a short-term contract whereby he, and the forces tied to him, would serve under Richard for a stipulated period. Henry was not alone. Richard was prepared and able to outbid Philip II in their rivalry for leadership of the crusade, and when Philip offered pay of three besants per month to knights, Richard countered by proclaiming that he would find four, 'sub-conditione', for those knights who would be his stipendiaries.[96] The terms are not detailed, but their essence emerges from Richard of Devizes's observation that the bulk of the army, excepting only those few who stood by Philip, accepted Richard as their leader and lord.[97]

Such arrangements were the response in the course of a campaign to a prior lack of unity and overall command. Preventive measures, taken before an army's departure, were required, and the formal contract for service provided the means. It is likely that contracts were employed to this effect in the twelfth-century crusades, but there seems to be no certain proof thereof, although contracts were used to arrange shipping and transport.[98] Perhaps they were not committed to writing; as late as 1270 the will of Alphonse of Poitiers, some of whose written contracts *do* survive, refers to agreements with certain knights for their service on crusade 'par letres ou par paroles

[93] Ibid. 278.

[94] Paris, *CM* iv. 71; *Flores*, ii. 241.

[95] Richard of Devizes, *Chronicon Richardi Divisensis De tempore regis Richardi primi*, ed. and trans. J. T. Appleby (London, 1963), 42–3, reporting that this followed a mean and insulting offer from Philip II. Devizes, extremely hostile to Philip, may have exaggerated, but the substance of his report may be accepted.

[96] 'Itinerarium Peregrinorum et Gesta Regis Ricardi', in *Chronicles and Memorials of the Reign of Richard I*, ed. W. Stubbs, 2 vols. (RS; 1864, 1865), i. 213–14.

[97] Devizes, *Chron.*, pp. 42–3. In 1192 Richard again used offers of pay, but most who then flocked to him were 'inutiles': ibid. 81.

[98] For example, Philip II's contract with the Genoese, 1190, for transport and victualling, in A. Cartellieri, *Philipp August: König von Frankreich*, 4 vols. (Leipzig, Paris, 1899–1922), ii. 119–21.

certaines'.[99] In any event, we have to wait until the thirteenth century to observe the application of contracts. So far as English forces are concerned, it is just possible that Earl Ranulf of Chester employed contracts on the Fifth Crusade, for Eracles reports that 'he held 100 knights in the host for one year'.[100] The period of service and the round number of knights are suggestive. We are on altogether more certain ground with the crusade of Richard of Cornwall. The list of bannerets serving with Richard, William Longespee, and Simon de Montfort is especially interesting because Matthew Paris refers to them as being 'de familia comitis Ricardi'.[101] If written contracts were employed by Richard then they have not survived, but one intriguing instrument has come to light and is printed as Appendix 5. Thereby, John de Hulecote informed John de Neville that Philip Basset had agreed to accompany Neville to the Holy Land with two other knights and four horses. Philip would pay for his passage to the Holy Land but on arrival he would serve in Neville's *familia* and at his expense with the two knights. The instrument is undated, but it refers to terms being reached at Northampton, probably a reference to the council of crusade leaders held there in November 1239 when, according to Paris, arrangements were made for the forthcoming crusade.[102]

The document is of considerable interest, not least because it is a draft contract negotiated by three of John de Neville's close acquaintances on his behalf.[103] Their precise remit is unknown; perhaps they were authorized to enter into a number of agreements on Neville's behalf at the council. Nor, alas, does the final contract survive—assuming it was made—but the draft is the earliest evidence we have for the application of contracts for crusading purposes prior to departure. It was, however, Henry III's projected crusade which stimulated the earliest English crusading contract to have survived. On 14 April 1253 Peter of Savoy, by open letters which survive in the form of enrolment on the Patent Roll, bound himself by oath to set out with Henry at the time fixed for his passage, 24 June 1256, and not to undertake any business in the meantime which might impede his participation. In return, on 18 April, Henry solemnly bound himself

99 *Layettes du Trésor des Chartes: Inventaire et documents publiés par la Direction des Archives*, ed. A. Teulet *et al.* 5 vols. (Paris, 1863–1909), iv. No. 5712.

100 'L'Estoire de Eracles empereur et la conqueste de la Terre d'Outremer', *RHC Occ.* ii. 342–3. Henry III's letter to Frederick II in 1226 on Peter des Roches's behalf is more suggestive. It looks suspiciously as if Peter had hopes of a contractual arrangement with Frederick before his departure: *RLC* ii. 204. Frederick certainly offered money, provisions, and transport to crusaders: see T. C. Van Cleve, *The Emperor Frederick II of Hohenstaufen, Immutator Mundi* (Oxford, 1972) , 194.

101 Paris, *CM* iv. 43–4.

102 Ibid. iii. 620.

103 See appendix 5, n1.

to provide Peter with 10,000*m.* at Marseilles, a ship for his passage, with victuals and necessaries, and twenty war-horses on arrival in the Holy Land.[104] No other contract appears to have survived, but there is no reason to consider the agreement with Peter unique at the time. That William Longespee employed contracts for his second crusade seems most probable. Paris reports that when Louis IX marched from Damietta in 1250 he was accompanied by William 'cum suis qui ei adhaerebant associatis . . . simulque militibus et servientibus quos secum retinuerat stipendariis'.[105] Elsewhere he describes William as leader ('dux') of the English contingent, with around 200 knights.[106]

To see an English crusading force systematically organized by contract we have to wait until 1270. Whether Edward's force was the first to be organized thus must remain an open question until further evidence comes to light, but two points may be made. First, by expanding his household forces by means of those contracts Edward was following normal royal practice. The nucleus of Henry III's armies, for example, at home or abroad, was provided by the household knights and Walker has shown how the needs of campaign led to the contraction or expansion in the number of knights in service.[107] As king, Edward was to pursue a similar policy.[108] Second, English practice should not be isolated from the wider European development towards the common usage of contracts in the thirteenth century. It is, for example, well known that Louis IX and his brothers made extensive use of contracts for their crusades.[109] Typical of the 1270 contracts for immediate household service was that between Louis and Erard de Valéry. Erard was to serve Louis with thirty knights for one year in return for 8,000*l. tournois*, transport, and *restor de chevaux*, but he was not to receive bouche of court. Payment of the knights was Erard's responsibility; he was also to ensure that each banneret had two horses and each simple knight one horse, with a groom to each mount.[110] Altogether around 400 knights made up Louis's extended

[104] *Foedera*, I. i. 288; *CPR 1247–58*, pp. 188–9. Peter's service was presumably to last for the duration of the crusade. If so, and if the twenty horses suggest twenty knights, then the considerable sum of 10,000*m.* is put in perspective.

[105] Paris, *CM* v. 130–1.

[106] Ibid. 76.

[107] R. F. Walker, 'The Anglo-Welsh wars, 1217–67', D.Phil. thesis (Oxford, 1954), esp. pp. 67–81.

[108] See, esp. Morris, *Welsh Wars*; Prestwich, *War, Politics*, chs. 2, 3; J. O. Prestwich, 'The Military Household of the Norman Kings', *EHR* xcvi (1981), esp. pp. 1–6.

[109] From Paris, esp. *CM* v. 132–4, it looks as if Longespee formally entered Louis IX's service. Guy de Lusignan was another lord with English connections who was certainly bound by contract to Louis: see *Reg. Innocent IV*, No. 4054.

[110] *RHGF* xx. 305. Other contracts were essentially of this type, but some knights were granted bouche of court: ibid. xx. 305–8; *Layettes*, iv. Nos. 5674–5.

household for the crusade.[111] By comparison, the terms of Edward's contracts were vague indeed, but their very use in 1270 was probably suggested by contemporary practice. The *stimulus* for their systematic employment, however, was probably the agreement between Louis and Edward in August 1269, whereby Edward incurred obligations which he then had to meet: the employment of contracts naturally encouraged their usage by contingent leaders. Louis's second crusade provides us with the fullest picture of a *passagium generale* structured throughout by means of contracts.

Finally, with regard to Edward's contracts, it is apparent that the 100*m.* available for each contracted knight was scarcely a glittering inducement to join the crusade. Even allowing for the transport provided, 100*m.* could have gone only a little way towards the likely costs on crusade of each knight and his household. A measure of the value of the fee is suggested by the prices paid for horses at Acre in 1271–2: they reached as high as 50*m.*, presumably for a destrier.[112] Nor does the late date of the contracts, within weeks of departure, suggest that they were intended primarily as instruments of recruitment, though Edward had probably come to oral agreements with the main contractors beforehand.[113] The evidence for the contractors' raising of knights points to the same conclusion. As early as 4 May 1269 Thomas de Clare had agreed terms with Nicholas de Sifrewast, as far as his participation on crusade was concerned.[114] Edward's contracts were primarily a means of organization.

If Edward, in his use of contracts, was not departing from well-established practice, then neither does he appear to have been innovative in his other practical arrangements for his force. Only the broad thrust of those arrangements can be discerned for the most part, however; the finer details generally elude us. Whilst documentary survival allows the measures of such contemporaries as

[111] This helps to explain why 'Continuation' of Gervase of Canterbury, ii. 249, records Edward as promising in 1269 to accompany Louis 'quasi unus baronum et de familia sua'. See also Wykes, *Chron.*, p. 230; 'Continuation' of Florence of Worcester, *Chronicon ex Chronicis, with two continuations*, ed. B. Thorpe, 2 vols. (Eng. Hist. Soc.; 1848–9), ii. 203–4. It is revealing that they considered their relationship on crusade in these terms.

[112] PRO, E 101/350/5, m. 1; C 62/49, mm. 4, 6; C 62/51, mm. 8, 10, 11; *Anc. Corr.* 12. 7.

[113] The late date probably has to do with the raising of the twentieth, still being assessed in the spring and summer of 1270. The earliest surviving orders for its collection are dated 2 Apr., and only on 10 July were the receivers instructed to lay up the proceeds at the New Temple against future disbursement: see S. K. Mitchell, *Taxation in Medieval England*, ed. S. Painter (New Haven, 1951), esp. pp. 47–8; *CPR 1266–72*, p. 439. There was also disagreement, involving Gilbert de Clare and others, concerning the terms and conditions for the crusade: below, pp. 143–4.

[114] See above, pp. 122–3.

Louis IX and Alphonse of Poitiers to be traced with considerable precision, we possess nothing of comparable value for Edward, nor, indeed, for the other leaders of thirteenth-century English crusading forces. Their private archives have largely disappeared, leaving only fragmentary indications of the measures they took; but sufficient survives to allow some discussion.

The Paris agreement of August 1269, and the terms of the surviving contracts, reveal that it was incumbent upon Edward to provide for much of the victualling and transport of the force accompanying him, and that it was for him to make appropriate arrangements so that his force would be ready to embark at Aigues Mortes on or before 15 August 1270. These responsibilities were the logical consequence of what was, in its essentials, an extended household operation. Edward originally intended to visit Gascony before departing on crusade, probably to pick up men and supplies, combine his force with Gaston de Béarn's contingent, and affirm arrangements for the governance and security of his duchy during his absence.[115] Accordingly, he travelled first to Portsmouth in early August 1270 for embarkation. However, he was already very pressed for time if he was to reach Aigues Mortes within the term agreed, for his original date for departure, 24 June, had been postponed largely because of the crisis in relations with Gilbert de Clare. When contrary winds kept him in Portsmouth, he accordingly cancelled the projected visit to Gascony and moved to Dover to sail across the Channel.[116] He was still there, awaiting favourable winds, on 24 August, but he managed to reach Aigues Mortes by 28 September, for on that day he issued letters patent at the port.[117]

There must have been considerable activity on the part of Edward and his officials in 1269–70 as they negotiated for shipping, and purchased and laid up all manner of military stores, but few traces of those preparations survive. However, unlike Richard I for the Third Crusade, Edward did not intend to raise a large fleet and dispatch it to the Latin East; nor did he plan to ship large quantities of stores and supplies from England. He preferred instead to hire the ships he required at Marseilles and other ports, to purchase the supplies he needed in southern France, and to lay them up at Aigues Mortes. It was probably agreed at Paris in August 1269 that Edward would enjoy victualling privileges in the lands of Louis IX and his brothers,

[115] *De ant. leg.*, p. 125, who also reports Edward's intention of journeying to Castile to speak with Alfonso X, doubtless concerning Gascony's security.

[116] Ibid.; 'Winchester', p. 109; 'Worcester', p. 459. Wykes, *Chron.*, p. 236, and *Chronicle of Bury St. Edmunds, 1212–1301*, ed. A. Gransden (London, 1964), 47, are in error.

[117] *CR 1268–72*, p. 290; *Gascon Reg. A*, No. 251.

Alphonse of Poitiers and Charles of Anjou, but the surviving evidence suggests that practical steps were taken only in spring 1270. In April, Alphonse instructed his seneschals of Toulouse, Albi, and the Venaissin to permit Edward's men to take away 'ad opus vie transmarine' victuals and other necessaries bought, or to be bought, to the value of 1000*l.* in each bailiwick.[118] John de Grailly was specially delegated to the task of fitting out the force: in August 1275 he was acquitted of all receipts and expenses incurred in his capacity as 'deputed purveyor of the king's passage into the Holy Land'.[119] When he began that task is unclear, but it was in April 1270, again, that 1000*m.* was delivered to him for purveyances made, and to be made, in Gascony for the crusade.[120] In June, another of Edward's servants, John Hardel, was sent to Marseilles to make purveyances against Edward's arrival.[121]

During the crusade Edward seems to have made arrangements as expediency dictated. In September 1270, following the decision to winter in Sicily, Charles of Anjou instructed the citizens of Marsala and Mazzara to assign fitting quarters to him, Eleanor of Castile, and those accompanying them, and to allow them to obtain all necessaries in the towns' markets.[122] In December, Charles instructed his officials to furnish Edward and his men with fodder and other necessaries when travelling through the kingdom.[123] Since William de Valence was permitted to purchase corn, meat, and other supplies shortly afterwards, and since John II of Brittany was given leave in January 1271 to take corn to ship to Acre, it is probable that Edward too was taking steps to provision his force for the coming spring passage to the Holy Land.[124] Wykes reports that *en route* the fleet called in to Cyprus for revictualling, but of Edward's arrangements during his stay in the

[118] *Correspondance administrative d'Alfonse de Poitiers*, ed. A. Molinier, 3 vols. (Paris, 1884–1900), ii. Nos. 1419, 1824.

[119] *CPR 1272–81*, p. 102.

[120] *CLR 1267–72*, p. 123; Trabut-Cussac, *L'Administration anglaise*, p. 373. It was fitting that John, seneschal of Gascony, 1266–8, be entrusted with this business. He was doubtless aided by Roger de Leyburn, appointed Edward's lieutenant in Gascony, 1269: ibid. 38–9, where it is suggested that one of Roger's duties was the raising of Gascon auxiliaries for the crusade—more specifically, perhaps, Gascon crossbowmen, whose qualities were renowned.

[121] *CLR 1267–72*, p. 126.

[122] *Foedera*, I. i. 485. Edward did not apparently follow Alphonse of Poitiers in making prior purchase of stores and victuals in Sicily and Apulia in 1269: *Corr. admin. d'Alfonse de Poitiers*, ii. No. 1755. Nor did he follow Louis IX's example in building up stocks in Cyprus prior to his first crusade: see W. C. Jordan, *Louis IX and the Challenge of the Crusade: A Study in Rulership* (Princeton, 1979), 76–7.

[123] *Foedera*, I. i. 487.

[124] *I Registri della cancelleria angioina ricostruiti*, ed. R. Filangieri di Candida *et al.* (Naples, 1950–), vi. Nos. 974, 1003. This, of course, is evidence that the more important leaders sailing with Edward made certain of their own arrangements.

Latin East little is known.[125] One particular problem facing Edward in Acre is plain, however: a shortage of horses, a difficulty which confronted so many crusading forces. He paid considerable sums for horses purchased in Acre, or taken from certain of his companions, and it is of some interest that John Hardel was granted safe conduct to take palfreys and other necessaries to the Holy Land for his master's use in 1272.[126] The costs incurred in shipping them over such a considerable distance indicates that the shortage of suitable horses had become critical by that time.[127]

John Hardel may have been the agent employed by Edward to hire ships when he was sent to Marseilles in June 1270, but no documentation survives to shed light on Edward's arrangements for shipping at this point. According to an Italian source, Edward arrived at Tunis in ships of Genoa and Provence, whilst Guisborough reports that he later landed at Trapani with thirteen ships, perhaps the same in which he had sailed from Aigues Mortes.[128] It was at Trapani, in January 1271 or shortly before, that Edward's admiral Luke de Tany contracted on his behalf for the service of at least nine ships of Genoa and Marseilles to take his force East.[129] But one can only speculate as to Edward's arrangements for transport back to Sicily in 1272, when he was doubtless afforded further hospitality by Charles of Anjou.[130]

Edward took the precaution of seeking protection and safe conduct for his force in the dominions through which they would pass. This was a sensible safeguard for all crusade leaders, but it was rendered the more desirable at this time since papal protections were unavailable because of the vacancy following the death of Clement IV in

125 Wykes, *Chron.*, p. 244. PRO, E 101/350/5, 350/7, 350/8, record the purchase and delivery of various items—foodstuffs, military equipment, and other supplies—but it is not apparent that they were procured in the East. Some, indeed, hark back to the siege of Kenilworth, 1266, and others refer to Edward's long stay in France on return from crusade.

126 PRO, E 101/350/5, m. 1; C 62/49, mm. 4, 6; C 62/51, mm. 8, 10, 11; *Anc. Corr.* 12. 7 (for horses); *CPR 1266–72*, p. 674 (for John Hardel).

127 John then accompanied Edward back to France and thence England, acting as purveyor and keeper of his palfreys: PRO, C 62/50, mm. 7, 8; E 101/350/5, mm. 1, 3. Further supplies were probably taken out by those recorded as going to Edward in the Holy Land, 1270–2: E 101/350/5, mm. 1, 5; C 62/50, mm. 4, 6.

128 'Oberti Stanconi, Iacobi Aurie, Marchisini de Cassino et Bertolini Bonifatii Annales', *MGH SS* xviii. 268; Walter of Guisborough, *The Chronicle of Walter of Guisborough, Previously Edited as the Chronicle of Walter of Hemingford, or Hemingburgh*, ed. H. Rothwell (Camden Soc., 3rd ser. 89; 1957), 207.

129 The shipowners' quittance is printed in *Archives de l'Orient Latin*, ii (1884), 407–9. The original contracts do not apparently survive. This alone makes it impossible to estimate the size of Edward's force at this point with any accuracy, but see above, n. 26.

130 Charles certainly ordered an honourable reception for Edmund and John II of Brittany should they pass through Sicily: *I Registri*, viii. Nos. 315–16.

November 1268. It was only in July 1272 that Gregory X issued a protection for Edward.[131] Edward may have obtained safe conduct for himself and his force from Louis IX at Paris in August 1269, for he then promised that neither he nor his companions would injure the lands of the king and his brothers, both within and beyond the French realm, whilst passing through them on crusade.[132] The truce agreed in September 1269 with Theobald, king of Navarre and count of Champagne, to last for five years from Easter 1270, also accorded him a measure of security. It was agreed, *inter alia*, that if Edward were to pass through Theobald's lands he would enjoy safe conduct therein.[133] Edward almost certainly travelled through part of Champagne on his way to Aigues Mortes in 1270.[134]

The safe conduct which Edward secured from Charles of Anjou in November 1270 for his stay in Sicily has fortunately survived.[135] Therein, Charles promised Edward and all his followers 'full security and safe conduct in both persons and possessions' during their sojourn in Charles's dominions, and in going and returning. No less important, Charles further granted that Edward should exercise full justice over his followers.[136] Unfortunately, nothing further is known of this matter of internal jurisdiction and discipline within Edward's force. He perhaps drew up ordinances to regulate conduct, like those instituted by Richard I in 1190.[137] It is apparent only that in Sicily he was responsible for disciplining his own followers, although the terms of the Paris agreement suggest that this responsibility extended to the passage of the force through the lands of Charles's brothers as well.

Safe conducts and protections, papal or otherwise, did not of course guarantee immunity and safe passage in practice, as Richard I so rudely discovered on return from the Third Crusade. Crusaders had

[131] *Foedera*, I. i. 495. The scandalous treatment of Richard I in 1193–4 was surely still fresh in Plantagenet memories.

[132] *Dipl. Docs.* i. No. 419.

[133] *Foedera*, I. i. 482; *Layettes*, iv. Nos. 5579–80.

[134] Edward's itinerary through France cannot be reconstructed in detail, but he presumably travelled to Paris, then down one of the roads along the Seine, or one of its tributaries, into Champagne and Burgundy, and thence to the Rhône–Sâone corridor. Whatever the route, it cannot have been so different from that taken by Richard of Cornwall in 1240. See Paris, *CM* iv. 45–6. The exact routes cannot have been dissimilar to the itineraries through France, as far as Lyons, provided by Paris in his famous London–Apulia itineraries. See K. Muller, *Die ältesten Weltkarten*, 3 vols. (Stuttgart, 1895), iii. 84-90, for the itineraries and identification of place-names.

[135] *Foedera*, I. i. 486–7.

[136] Ibid. 487.

[137] Roger of Howden, *Chronica Rogeri de Houedene*, ed. W. Stubbs, 4 vols. (RS; 1868–71), iii. 36, 58–9; id. (Benedict of Peterborough, attrib.), *Gesta Regis Henrici Secundi Benedicti Abbatis*, ed. W. Stubbs, 2 vols. (RS; 1867), ii. 110–11, 129–32. Paris, *CM* iv. 47, reports that Richard of Cornwall 'classem totam ordinavit et oneravit' at Roche-en-Mer, the entrance to the port of Marseilles, in 1240.

cause always to be wary. The Rhône Valley, an area of particular political fragmentation in the twelfth and thirteenth centuries, seems to have posed especial dangers. Even Louis IX was obliged to lay siege to the castle of La Roche-de-Glun in 1248 because its lord, Roger de Clérieu, had the audacity to demand tolls from those travelling down the Rhône, Louis's crusaders included, notwithstanding their exemption in canon law.[138] At Avignon and Marseilles further trouble ensued between the citizens and Louis's forces. According to Paris, open warfare was narrowly averted.[139] Paris also records that Richard of Cornwall ran into trouble at Vienne *en route* for Marseilles in 1240. The citizens seized the boats in which he intended to sail down the Rhône to Arles, only restoring them to Richard at Beaucaire.[140] Considering these and other past outrages, Edward may not have been entirely surprised when some of his men, passing the castle of Tournon on their way to Aigues Mortes, were set upon by William de Tournon himself. Edward took his revenge on his return in 1273. Amongst other things, William undertook in his submission never again to molest English pilgrims passing through his lands.[141]

In planning his crusade, it is not surprising that Edward does not appear to have departed radically from established practices: he had the experience of generations of crusaders to guide him. His uncle, Richard of Cornwall, seems especially to have given him advice and guidance, doubtless based upon his own experience of the difficulties involved in organizing, supplying, and shipping a crusading force.[142] Richard, indeed, came to play the leading counselling role in the months before Edward's eventual departure on crusade. It is reported that after long discussion at the Hoketide parliament of 1270 'de vicesima et itinere crucesignatorum', the magnates agreed to refer the entire business to Richard's arbitration, but Gilbert de Clare and others dissented and the affair was prolonged until after Midsummer. The magnates met again in London at some point in July to discuss the outstanding business.[143] Richard's award of May 1270 was the

138 'Historia Albigensium, auct. Guillelmo de Podio Laurentii', *RHGF* xxi. 771; Nangis, in ibid. 356. See further E. L. Cox, *The Eagles of Savoy: The House of Savoy in Thirteenth Century Europe* (Princeton, 1974), pp. 190–1.

139 Paris *CM* iv. 23–4.

140 Ibid. 45.

141 *Foedera*, I. ii. 504; and the comments of Powicke, *Henry III*, ii. 613.

142 For their discussions in Aug. 1269, see *De ant. leg.*, pp. 110–11; also Wykes, *Chron.*, pp. 224–5. Space precludes discussion of Richard's own plans but Edward's arrangements differed little in their essentials. See esp. N. Denholm-Young, *Richard of Cornwall* (Oxford, 1947), 224–5.

143 'Winchester', p. 108; 'Worcester', p. 459. Royal letters refer to the magnates and prelates meeting in the parliament 'to provide concerning money and other necessaries' in connection with the crusade, and to discuss arrangements for the realm's security

most striking outcome of his active involvement, but it was probably Richard also who provided a comprehensive settlement of the terms and conditions for participation in the crusade. The contracts, as we have seen, were not drawn up until 20 July, and it is unlikely to be coincidence that the bulk of royal letters of protection and attorney, and licences to alienate properties held in chief were issued to crusaders in a pronounced burst of Chancery activity in the weeks immediately after 10 July. That Richard played a major role in the matter of alienations is plain. In a letter of August 1272 Henry III recalled that it had been provided, on the counsel of Richard and others, that all crusaders of the realm might demise their lands for four years.[144] As an elder statesman, experienced arbitrator, and former crusader, it is not surprising that Richard's counsels informed much of the practical thought concerning his nephew's crusade, but Edward may also have drawn upon the projected crusading plans of his father in the 1250s, and he was probably influenced by Louis IX and other experienced leaders.[145] Certainly, he would not have been short of useful and informed advice.

The precise cost of Edward's crusade cannot be computed, but it was clearly considerable and placed a severe strain upon royal finances for some years. The burden of expense would primarily have been Edward's, of course, since he was responsible for most of the provisioning, transport, and possibly sustenance of a very large number of those accompanying him. Moreover, he may have contracted with additional crusaders following the death of Louis IX at Tunis and the disintegration of the army. Edward alone among the leaders proceeded to the Holy Land, and his force from the Plantagenet dominions was joined by others wishing to fulfil their vows. Erard de Valéry and John II of Brittany, for example, are among a number of crusaders, formerly serving on contract with Louis, who are known to have sailed with Edward from Sicily in 1271, possibly at his pay.[146]

upon the crusaders' departure: *The Register of Walter Giffard, Lord Archbishop of York, 1266–79*, ed. W. Brown (Surtees Soc. 109; 1904), 161; *Historical Papers and Letters from the Northern Registers*, ed. J. Raine (RS; 1873), 24.

[144] *CR 1268–72*, p. 500. It was probably at this time, *c.*1269–70, that measures were taken 'de consilio regni nostri', to speed the swift recovery by crusaders of debts owed to them: BL Additional MS 38821, fo. 37 (register of writs, apparently early Edward I). I am indebted to Dr Paul Brand for drawing my attention to this.

[145] For Henry's plans see below, pp. 212–13.

[146] A French source records that, following Edward's request, some of the French joined Edward at Tunis with Philip III's licence and at his pay: 'Extrait d'une chronique anonyme', *RHGF* xxi. 126. Enguerrand de Balliol may have been one such. At Messina, 1271, he received 290*l.tournois* of Philip's special grace for himself and his knights. He had been in Louis IX's household on crusade. See 'Documents divers relatifs à la croisade de saint Louis contre Tunis (1270)', ed P.G.G., *Les Cahiers de Tunisie*, xxv (1977), appendix 2b; *RHGF* xx. 308.

Erard de Valéry was certainly granted an annual fee of 100*l.* by Edward at or shortly after this time.[147] It is tempting to think that Erard's service on crusade lies behind the grant.[148] Probably, too, some of the contracts drawn up in July 1270, specifically for one year's service, were extended to run further from September 1271, whilst Edward must have spent large sums in constructing fortifications and hiring mercenaries in the Holy Land.[149] These considerations help to explain both the massive borrowings which Edward made at Acre and elsewhere from the Temple, Hospital, Riccardi of Lucca, and others, and also his continued insolvency on his return to England.[150]

Edward, like all crusaders, sought to raise what he could from his personal resources, but in his capacity as leader he also received, and crucially, aid from the Church and the proceeds of taxation voted in England both before and after the crusade.[151] To help defray his costs, the English Church contributed with the grant of a biennial tenth in 1273, and in due course the papacy granted him moneys raised from the redemption of vows, and gifts and legacies for the Holy Land. The rationale behind these grants was of course that Edward would subsidize those crusaders dependent upon him: the logical consequence, in terms of funding, of an extended household operation. For this reason, this aspect of crusading finance may usefully be considered apart from the private arrangements made by individual crusaders to raise cash.[152]

The twentieth of 1269–70, the fifteenth of 1275, the clerical biennial tenth of 1273, and the application of moneys from the Holy Land subsidy have been exhaustively studied in the past and so do not in

[147] PRO, C 62/50, m. 5. Erard had been long associated with Henry III and Edward. In or before June 1261 he had been granted an annual fee of 80*m.*, but the grant appears to have lapsed after 1263. There is no indication that the 100*l.* fee was granted before Edward's crusade. See *CPR 1258–66*, p. 163; *CLR 1260–7*, pp. 44, 90, 115.

[148] For Erard joining Edward, see 'Extraits de la chronique attribuée à Baudouin d'Avesnes', *RHGF* xxi. 178. For John II of Brittany, see *Mémoires pour servir de preuves à l'histoire ecclesiastique et civile de Bretagne*, ed. H. Morice (Paris, 1742), i., cols. 152–3, 1007–8, 1186.

[149] *Flores*, iii. 29, reports that on returning Edward dismissed stipendiaries at Acre. For the tower he built there, see *CPR 1272–81*, p. 296.

[150] For some of these loans, see *Royal Letters*, ii. 347–51; *Cart. Gen. Hosp.* iii. Nos. 3445, 3465; *CPR 1272–81*, pp. 131–2; PRO, C 62/50, m. 7. R. W. Kaeuper, *Bankers to the Crown: The Riccardi of Lucca and Edward I* (Princeton, 1973), 81–2, points out that the Riccardi's services were crucial at this juncture, and from then dates that close relationship with Edward which lasted until 1294.

[151] See generally on finance, Powicke, *Henry III*, ii. 563–9; Prestwich, *War, Politics*, pp. 169–70.

[152] For those arrangements, see below, esp. pp. 175–94.

themselves require detailed treatment here.[153] However, with regard to papal support it should be stressed that Edward did not apparently receive any aid at all from this source before 1272–3. This helps to explain not only the considerable strain upon Edward's available resources, but also certain of his actions before and after the crusade. It was only in and after September 1272 that Gregory X prevailed upon the English clergy to grant a tenth, ordered the collection and deposit of moneys arising from legacies and the redemption of vows, and instituted proceedings concerning grants made from the crusading subsidy during Clement IV's pontificate.[154] Edward's failure to procure papal support beforehand is partly explained by the long papal vacancy between November 1268 and March 1272, although Clement had plenty of time to grant moneys to Edward between his assumption of the Cross in June 1268 and the pontiff's death in November. Clement, however, felt that the English Church was already overburdened following the demands of the tenth imposed by the Montfortian regime in 1264–5, the triennial tenth of 1266 designed to relieve the king, and the twentieth on behalf of the Disinherited in 1267. He would not countenance any direct taxation of the Church in support of Edward's projected crusade.[155] Yet he was prepared to make grants to others from the crusading subsidy. In April 1268 he instructed Ottobuono to assign to Edmund an appropriate sum from legacies and redemptions in England if Edmund should go on crusade in Henry III's place 'with a fitting company'.[156] Sums from the same source were also granted to Payn de Chaworth, Robert Tiptoft, and Roger de Leyburn.[157] Since they were very close to Edward and probably received the Cross when he did, Clement's lack of support for Edward is all the more remarkable.

The reason probably lies in the uncertainties consequent to Edward's vow. Would Henry III be going on crusade; if so, would he be accompanied by his sons? To whom, then, should moneys be entirely or chiefly assigned? Henry, it should be observed, did not

[153] See esp. Mitchell, *Taxation*, esp. pp. 47–52, 104–5, 149–50, 218–20; W. E. Lunt, *Financial Relations of the Papacy with England to 1327* (Cambridge, Mass., 1939), pp. 230–8, 446–8; id., 'The Consent of the English Lower Clergy to Taxation during the Reign of Henry III', in *Persecution and Liberty: Essays in Honor of George Lincoln Burr* (New York, 1931), esp. pp. 160–4; Powicke, *Henry III*, ii. 562–9.

[154] *Reg. Gregory X*, Nos. 186, 190–1, 193, 232, 350, 830, 920, 967; *Reg. W. Giffard*, pp. 39–41.

[155] See his letter to Louis IX, Jan. 1268: *Reg. Clement IV*, No. 1288; *Thesaurus*, ii. No. 583. See *Councils*, II. ii. 798–800, for the English clergy's own objections, on similar grounds, to the twentieth in 1269.

[156] *Reg. Clement IV*, No. 609.

[157] *Reg. Gregory X*, Nos. 191, 232. Only Roger, apparently, received any cash before 1272–3.

formally set aside his Cross until 4 August 1270.[158] Clement was also hostile to Edward's crusading plans, at least back in January 1268, and in April he made quite plain his wish that Henry should stay in England, considering the political uncertainties there.[159] There was, then, much to negotiate in the months before Clement's death, and it is likely that no final agreement had been reached when the pope died, notwithstanding Ottobuono's lobbying on Edward's behalf.[160] Significantly, Edward is not known to have claimed later that Clement had promised or granted him anything. Edward, then, would have had to await the election of a new pope before he could hope for a grant.

Such a circumstance would help to explain the severe financial difficulties facing Edward on crusade and beforehand. Lunt estimated that Edward ultimately received around £22,000 from the clerical tenth of 1273, and an unknown sum, though surely considerable, from legacies, gifts, and the redemption of vows.[161] The overall total must have compared favourably with the sum of over £31,488 received from the proceeds of the twentieth by October 1272.[162] But until Edward received moneys from the crusading subsidy he inevitably faced something of a crisis, especially as there were still difficulties attached to the grant of the twentieth in 1269–70, and cash immediately available was in very short supply because of the wretched state of Crown finances.[163] Hence Edward's readiness to borrow from Louis IX in August 1269 on the security of his Gascon revenues. If Edward was to make his preparations then he needed ready cash in large quantities, and quickly.

Edward's rather shabby treatment of his brother on their return is

[158] *CPR 1266–72*, p. 452; *Foedera*, I. i. 485. At the same time Henry conferred the proceeds of the twentieth upon Edward. After the Paris agreement of 1269 there can have been little doubt that Henry would be staying at home, and the protracted negotiations over the grant of the twentieth was probably due largely to wranglings concerning taxation which was clearly in aid of the king's son, since Henry alone as king was entitled to such an aid. He perhaps deliberately refrained from setting aside his Cross in an attempt to neutralize objections.

[159] *Reg. Clement IV*, No. 609.

[160] 'Letters of Cardinal Ottoboni', ed. R. Graham, *EHR* xv (1900), 87–120, No. 26.

[161] Lunt, *Financial Relations*, pp. 236–7, 446–7.

[162] For the receipts from the twentieth, see Mitchell, *Taxation*, pp. 48, 51. A considerable amount remained to be paid after Oct. 1272.

[163] As late as 1270, indeed beyond, the state of royal finances was pathetic. It is nowhere better revealed than in the letter of the treasurer and chamberlains of the Exchequer to Henry III in 1270. See 'Exchequer and Wardrobe in 1270', ed. L. Ehrlich, *EHR* xxxvi (1921), 553–4. In 1267 Henry had even been obliged to pledge the Crown and Westminster jewels. See generally on finance, Jacob, *Studies*, esp. pp. 248–75; Powicke, *Henry III*, ii. 558–9. Royal credit rating was very low indeed, as the 1270 letter reveals, until the twentieth came to be paid.

also more easily understood if Edward had received no papal grants prior to his departure. Gregory X included Edmund in his request for a subsidy from the English Church, but it availed Edmund little because Edward, in the face of protest, appropriated all or most of the proceeds of the biennial tenth.[164] He allowed Edmund only what Henry III had granted him towards his crusade.[165] Yet Edward could fairly claim that he had already subsidized Edmund from the twentieth by 10,000*m.*, the sum granted to him as a contractor in July 1270, and he doubtless felt that since he had borne the brunt of expenditure on crusade he should receive whatever might be forthcoming upon his return.

Finally, the aid ultimately extended to Edward by Gregory X should be located within a broader context since, by 1270, it had become entirely normal for the papacy to subsidize crusaders from moneys raised for the Holy Land. The potential value of such grants is indicated by some intense lobbying known to have taken place both in England and at the papal court. For example, William Longespee apparently went to Rome in 1247 to petition for a subsidy for his second crusade, whilst Earl Gilbert Marshal is said to have paid 200*m.* to secure subsidy in the late 1230s.[166] However, grants were not commonly made to English crusaders, at least, until the late 1230s and 1240s. Before then, moneys collected in England do not seem to have been disbursed to individual crusaders, but forwarded to the Holy Land or the papal Curia.[167] Thus there is no indication that any English participant in the Fifth Crusade received any subsidy. The triennial tenth of 1215 imposed upon the clergy for the crusade was certainly collected, but the bulk of the proceeds, some 20,000*m.*, were shipped from the realm by July 1220.[168] Nor, apparently, were grants

164 Lunt, *Financial Relations*, pp. 230–1, 235–6. The grant made conditionally to Edmund in Apr. 1268 appears to have been suspended. Edmund did not crusade in Henry's place, and he is not known to have received moneys from the crusading subsidy before his departure.

165 PRO, C 62/51, m. 7, with reference to the 2600*m.* granted from the profits of justice in 1271: see *CPR 1266–72*, p. 514; PRO, E 368/45, m. 4d. In 1270 Edmund was also granted profits of justice arising in his own lands: E 159/44, mm. 2d, 6. Since he received 80*m.* from his burgesses of Leicester for the twentieth 'given to him by the lord king', it is also likely that he was granted the proceeds of the tax arising elsewhere in his lands. See *Records of the Borough of Leicester*, ed. M. Bateson, 3 vols. (Cambridge, 1899–1905), i. 128, No. 39.

166 Paris, *CM* iv. 135–6, 629–30.

167 Richard I appears to be the sole exception, receiving redemptions of vows on Clement III's authority: Howden, *Chron.* iii. 17; Devizes, *Chron.*, p. 6.

168 Lunt, *Financial Relations*, pp. 242–7; C. R. Cheney, *Innocent III and England* (Stuttgart, 1976), 267–8. If disbursement was made in the East to English crusaders, there is no evidence to this effect. See Cheney, *Innocent III*, pp. 268–9, notwithstanding Honorius III's observations on this matter of subvention generally in 1220: *Epistolae selectae saeculi XIII*, ed. C. Rodenberg, *MGH Ep.* i. 89.

made from the moneys arising from the redemption of vows, legacies, or gifts.[169] In short, it seems that English crusaders in the earlier part of the thirteenth century were thrown back entirely upon their own financial resources.[170]

The decisive development came with that notable shift in policy in and after 1234, when the securing of funds emerged as a central feature of promotion of the crusade in England.[171] The first crusade leader to benefit was Richard of Cornwall. In April 1238 Gregory IX assigned him the proceeds collected in England from redemption of vows, gifts and legacies to the Holy Land, the clerical thirtieth of 1237 and, significantly enough, from what remained of the clerical twentieth of 1215.[172] That the grant was without precedent is suggested by the comments of contemporary chroniclers and Matthew Paris's report that William Longespee, in petitioning for a subsidy in 1247, expressly grounded his request upon the favours previously extended to Earl Richard.[173] In June 1247 Innocent IV granted him 1,000*l.* from redemptions, extended in March 1248 to 2,000*m.*[174] He was not the only beneficiary: Walter Cantilupe, bishop of Worcester, was assigned the redemptions, gifts, and legacies arising within his diocese;[175] William de Valence was promised 2,200*m.*;[176] Simon de Montfort was granted 4,000*m.* in June 1248.[177] These, together with other grants and references to disbursement of moneys, reveal that by the late 1240s subsidization of crusaders was becoming conventional practice.

It is not easy to determine how far down the social scale direct grants normally extended, but there are strong reasons for supposing that subsidies were primarily granted only to the crusade leaders and their more important commanders, to help meet both their expenses

[169] Bishop William Brewer of Exeter received royal and papal support in 1226–7 in securing 4,000*m.* deposited with the Temple by his uncle, but this legacy was purely of a private nature and not a grant from the crusading subsidy: *Reg. Gregory IX*, No. 24; *PR 1225–32*, pp. 89–90.

[170] Later, the sources are full of references to grants from the subsidy, claims that grants had been made, and wranglings over payment. The silence at this juncture is deafening.

[171] See above, pp. 18–21.

[172] *Reg. Gregory IX*, No. 4268. See also Lunt, *Financial Relations*, pp. 194–5, 432–4.

[173] Paris, *CM* iv. 629–30.

[174] *Reg. Innocent IV*, Nos. 2758–9, 3723–4, 4474, 4484.

[175] Ibid., No. 4873, confirmation of an earlier grant.

[176] Reference to the papal authorization is made in the materials relating to the payments: see, esp. *CR 1253–4*, pp. 217, 292, 303; *Rôles Gascons*, ed. C. Bémont, 3 vols. (Paris, 1896–1906), i. Nos. 3014, 3586.

[177] C. Bémont, *Simon de Montfort, Earl of Leicester, 1208–1265*, trans. E. F. Jacob (Oxford, 1930), 72, and n. 2. His kinsman, Robert de Quenci, was promised an unspecified sum in Dec. 1247: *Reg. Innocent IV*, No. 3475.

and those of their followers.[178] Thus Innocent IV explicitly stated that the 4,000*m*. granted in 1248 to Simon de Montfort was 'for himself and others whom he shall lead in his company'.[179] Again, in 1295 and then in 1302, Otto de Grandson was assigned moneys 'for his own necessities and those of his company and the subvention of other faithful men'.[180] Such examples suggest that papal financing of crusading forces was consciously dovetailed to fit the way in which armies were organized around a number of contingent leaders. If so, the tendency was given sharper point by the attempts of the greater men to secure the bulk of the available proceeds for themselves. Some light is shed upon the effects of this by a mournful passage in the letter which Hugh de Neville, then in the Holy Land, received from his mother, *c.*1266–8. Hawisia advised Hugh not to place much hope in receiving his grant of moneys: 'For many great lords of England will go on crusade, by what they say, and they will carry away whatever shall be raised of the crusade by what certain friends make me to know.'[181] Hugh and his mother were small fry in the murky business of securing, and holding on to, funds. When Hugh drew up his will at Acre in 1267 he still awaited satisfaction to the tune of 500*m*.

The amounts and the units of assignation varied according to the recipient's position and status. Moneys might be assigned from any part of the subsidy when expedient, but it is clear that bannerets and simpler knights were generally granted only redemptions, legacies, and gifts, and then on a narrowly tenurial basis. Thus, in August 1238, Hugh Wake, who sailed as one of Simon de Montfort's bannerets in 1240, was assigned the redemptions arising from his own lands and fees.[182] Such grants might extend to the lands of one's kinsmen. In November 1247 Robert de Quenci was granted both the redemptions and legacies arising from his own lands and those collected from the lands of his kinsmen, the earls of Winchester and Derby, providing these two were not themselves *crucesignati* and providing that no prejudice would arise to those of their vassals who were.[183] Crusade leaders were distinct in that they received additionally part, or all, of

178 For general discussion, see M. Purcell, *The Chief Instruments of Papal Crusading Policy and Crusade to the Holy Land from the Final Loss of Jerusalem to the Fall of Acre, 1244–1291* (Leiden, 1975), 145–9.

179 Bémont, *Simon de Montfort*, tr. Jacob, p. 72 n. 2. The precise sums granted were presumably, as Purcell, *Papal Crusading Policy*, p. 148, suggested, tied to the number of crusaders expected to accompany the beneficiaries.

180 *Reg. Boniface VIII*, Nos. 826, 830, 4490.

181 Giuseppi, 'On the Testament of Sir Hugh de Nevill', pp. 358–60. Hawisia advised Hugh to apply to the pope. Ottobuono, it appears from the letter, had granted moneys to Hugh, but of them 'little have we ever found, except that they are in the hands of such as themselves would go into the Holy Land'.

182 *Reg. Gregory IX*, No. 4509.

183 *Reg. Innocent IV*, No. 3475.

clerical taxation on behalf of the Holy Land, which explains why their grants were normally made from moneys collected within integral ecclesiastical units. In February 1237, for example, the Anglo-Norman Henry de Trubleville, a former seneschal of Gascony who was to have been the leader of the Gascon contingent on Richard of Cornwall's crusade, was granted the proceeds of the twentieth of 1215, the thirtieth of 1237, and the redemptions arising within the provinces of Bordeaux and Auch, for himself and his company.[184] *Capitanei* of crusading forces received grants of moneys collected within integral political units. Richard of Cornwall, again, appears as the first to receive a grant of this type; his award of April 1238 embraced moneys arising from throughout the kingdom of England. Significantly, the grant was made 'in your [Richard's] aid and [that of] all *crucesignati* of England'.[185] This helps to explain why the other English crusade leaders, Simon de Montfort, William Longespee, and William de Forz, were not granted moneys at this time on the same scale as Richard.[186]

A decade later Henry III hoped that Guy de Lusignan would lead the English *crucesignati* preparing to follow Louis IX. He petitioned Innocent IV that the passage of the English be deferred until after the French had sailed and that Guy be appointed their 'dux'. His further request that moneys for the crusade collected in England be assigned to Guy was clearly related to that hope.[187] Grants of the type made available to *capitanei* would inevitably cause problems if particular moneys had already been assigned to individual *crucesignati*, and in refusing Henry at this time Innocent stressed that the executors of the Cross had previously been instructed to assign moneys as they saw fit. This commission he would not revoke because of the scandal which he feared would result.[188] The problem emerged again when Henry himself took the Cross in 1250. Now the natural *capitaneus* of the prospective English force, expecting to be followed by many of his subjects, many doubtless at his pay, Henry sought to lay his hands upon as much of the moneys as possible.[189] In April 1250 Innocent obliged by granting him a clerical triennial tenth from England and his other dominions, but he adamantly refused to assign Henry all

[184] *Reg. Gregory IX*, No. 3528. Henry died shortly after the crusaders' council at Northampton, 1239. For his plans, see Paris, *CM* iii. 620, 624.

[185] *Reg. Gregory IX*, Nos. 4268–72.

[186] They may have been granted redemptions, legacies, and gifts arising within their own lands.

[187] *Reg. Innocent IV*, Nos. 4054–6.

[188] Ibid., No. 4054, and Nos. 2843, 3838, for the commission to distribute moneys, and its renewal in Apr. 1248.

[189] See, in general, Lunt, *Financial Relations*, esp. 255 ff., 439.

moneys on deposit deriving from redemptions, gifts, and legacies.[190] He agreed only to a grant of those moneys collected from these sources, in Henry's various dominions, after 6 March 1250, when Henry took his vow.[191] Any grants made before this date were to be respected.[192] As *capitaneus* of the prospective crusade, however, Henry enjoyed considerable powers over disbursement of the moneys granted to him. He was careful to ensure that the proceeds were duly put on safe deposit, and monitored very closely any promise, or actual delivery, of the proceeds to individual *crucesignati* who would be sailing with him.[193]

Edward would have been fully aware of these precedents at the time of his own crusade, and Gregory X's grants of 1272–3 were surely made in acknowledgement of his role as *capitaneus* of the crusading forces of the Plantagenet dominions. Moreover, his eventual receipt of all the redemptions, legacies, and gifts outstanding from Clement IV's pontificate, coupled with his treatment of Edmund regarding the tenth of 1273, suggests that he, like his father, enjoyed considerable authority over the application of the proceeds. The evidence, though limited, suggests that he respected only prior assignations made from redemptions and legacies by Clement IV to Payn de Chaworth and others.[194]

The position of *capitaneus*, and the overall financial support which he should enjoy, reached its fullest development with the later crusading plans of Edward. Once he had taken the Cross again in 1287 he could reasonably pose as the *capitaneus* of a new *passagium generale* to restore the Holy Land. Accordingly, he petitioned in 1290 for all moneys for the crusade arising in the lands of those lords who would not themselves be going.[195] Nicholas IV agreed, and did what he could to support Edward once he had set his departure date at 24 June 1293.[196] This was in addition to the previous grant of the sexennial

190 *Foedera*, I. i. 272; see further *Reg. Innocent IV*, No. 6400; *Foedera*, I. i. 280, for the specification of Wales, Ireland, and Gascony as those other dominions.

191 *Foedera*, I. i. 274.

192 In Oct. 1250 Innocent IV confirmed, on the petition of the *crucesignati* of England, that grants made prior to 6 Mar. would be completed: *Reg. Innocent IV*, Nos. 4880–1. For Henry's acceptance of the ruling, at least concerning William de Valence and Stephen Longespee, see *CR 1247–51*, p. 522; *CR 1253–4*, pp. 217, 292, 303.

193 See e.g. his sharp instructions to the executors of the Cross in Nov. 1252. No disbursement was to occur without his knowledge: *CR 1251–3*, p. 272.

194 Beebe, 'The English Baronage', p. 141, regards the grants to Payn de Chaworth and Robert Tiptoft as evidence that Ottobuono had 'supplied some of the funds distributed by Edward—or at least in two instances was prepared to match the prince's grants'. But the contracts of July 1270 were financed solely from the twentieth, entirely distinct from the Holy Land subsidy.

195 *Foedera*, I. ii. 705.

196 In addition to the grant of a new sexennial tenth in 1291, Nicholas assigned him 100,000*m*. from the 1274 tenth collected outside England: see *Reg. Nicholas IV*, No. 6668; *Foedera*, I. ii. 750.

tenth of 1274 in Edward's dominions, along with moneys from redemptions and other sources.[197] By this time Nicholas IV regarded Edward as a *capitaneus* who should be subsidized on an international basis, but the idea was perhaps most succinctly expressed in one of the submissions to the council of the Canterbury clergy in February 1292, called in response to Nicholas IV's request for advice on the best ways and means to recover the Holy Land. If foreign kings and princes were willing to go on crusade, then they should be assigned the proceeds of the tenths of 1274 and 1291 from their own lands; if not, then a suitable leader should be elected and to him all moneys should be assigned. But if 'such a man will not be found in those parts, the tenths of those parts should be assigned to the king of England, who with the favour of divine clemency is about to set out overseas'.[198] In his formal reply to the pope, Archbishop Pecham was more circumspect in that he did not indicate the king of England himself, but he argued much the same course. Kings and princes should be urged by the pope to constitute a 'principalis capitaneus exercitus christiani', and to enjoin the *crucesignati* of their lands to obey that commander.[199] Surviving requests from foreign lords eager to enlist in Edward's force, and at his pay, suggest that the English clergy were not alone in regarding their king as the appropriate *capitaneus*.[200]

This grand design came to nothing, but the projected scheme reveals the extent to which practical crusading thought had evolved by the end of the thirteenth century. It may also be added that the claim that small-scale expeditions came to be preferred in the later thirteenth century appears tenuous. More probably, it was the papacy's failure to secure Edward's due commitment to a new *passagium generale* between 1275 and 1287 that led, by default, to the dispatch of only a series of smaller forces to the Latin East in the later thirteenth century.[201] Any change in strategy is more apparent than real: Edward I was to have been a *capitaneus* of the old school, but financed altogether better than any other in the past.

197 See, generally, Lunt, *Financial Relations*, ch. 6, and pp. 448–57.

198 Other moneys should be similarly assigned: see *Councils*, II. ii. 1105–6. The Norwich clergy held to the traditional yet anachronistic notion that as the emperor, by virtue of his office, was the proper leader of the Christian forces, a new emperor should be elected to command the crusade: ibid. 1104–5.

199 Ibid. 1111. If he should die, or be otherwise indisposed, then another *capitaneus* should be appointed lest the crusade disintegrate, 'as is known to have happened to others'.

200 *Foedera*, I. ii. 760, 787, 798; *Anc. Corr.* 20. 117, 118; *CCR 1288–96*, p. 266.

201 For Edward's negotiations with a series of popes in this period, see below, pp. 232–6.

5

CRUSADERS' PREPARATIONS: MEASURES, CONTEXT, AND EFFECTS

THE weeks, months, even years, preceding the departure of a crusading force were marked by intense activity as crusaders prepared for their great adventure. Their efforts have left an abundance of traces in the records, and from these it is possible to build up a picture of the measures commonly taken. The aim of this chapter is to elucidate and examine those measures, with particular reference to their social and economic context, and with regard to some of their effects. It is not easy to gain a balanced impression of an individual's preparations, however. No contemporary writer felt compelled to provide an account of the measures typically taken; there is regrettably no English equivalent to Jean de Joinville's famous description of the preparations for his crusade in 1248.[1] Even Matthew Paris, so voluble on many aspects of his contemporary world, says little on the subject. This is not altogether surprising, for the humdrum preparations of crusaders were scarcely headline news in a society which had become entirely accustomed to them. They lacked intrinsic interest for observers largely concerned with the events of crusades, if they were bothered with the business of the Cross at all. The coverage accorded in the literary sources consists largely, then, of snippets of information and vague general statements, only occasionally rising above the banal.

These limitations are paralleled by the difficulties attached to the documentary evidence. First, the private archives of crusading lords such as Earls Ranulf of Chester and Richard of Cornwall have disappeared, and the royal records are not as illuminating as they surely would be had one of the thirteenth-century kings duly departed for the East. Second, although crusaders' acts have certainly left an abundance of relevant materials in the records, those materials offer something less than a comprehensive view. There is a consequent danger that our perception of crusaders' preparations will be unduly biased towards measures for which there is most evidence. Moreover, there is a relative paucity of evidence for the sort of measures taken by

[1] Jean de Joinville, *Histoire de Saint Louis*, ed. J. Natalis de Wailly (Paris, 1872), 62–4, 68–70.

lesser folk; generally we know only of this or that property transaction in isolation. Of the acts of their social superiors we are predictably much better informed; necessarily, then, discussion will centre upon crusaders drawn from the higher levels of society. For these we are dependent in large measure, if not to an inordinate degree, upon the royal records for evidence: our vision of the subject is unavoidably coloured as a result. The available material, then, will only take us so far, and its flaws and limitations must be borne in mind with regard to what follows.

In making their preparations all crusaders faced the same broad challenges. These were, fundamentally, the need to settle their affairs satisfactorily and arrange for the safeguarding and administering of their interests during their absence, to raise the liquid cash required to meet expenses incurred and anticipated, and to take care for the state of their souls. Qualifications need to be made, of course: the type and range of measures varied, the particular individual making what arrangements he deemed appropriate according to his immediate circumstances, profession, and place within society, and not least his prudence and anticipation of difficulties which might arise during his absence. Moreover, the higher up the social hierarchy a crusader stood, the greater the range of business requiring attention. The simple English freeman of the thirteenth century, possessing only a few acres and as likely as not engaged for the crusade in a lord's service, was free of many of the cares which weighed upon the lord concerned. The latter's greater material interests and responsibilities required more extensive and careful consideration, and it was for him to arrange for such matters as the shipping and provisioning of the men in his train. Finally, although it is convenient to distinguish between spiritual and material acts, the two cannot be sharply separated, for the spiritual needs of crusaders informed certain of their material preparations, as we shall see.

Spiritual Measures

Crusaders were pilgrims and penitents as well as warriors, engaged in an extremely hazardous enterprise from which they might not return; there was considerable risk of death through disease, shipwreck, or other mishap, apart from the dangers of combat. Naturally, then, crusaders were acutely conscious of their spiritual needs as participants in a collective holy enterprise which was also an act of individual piety, and as mortals whose death might be imminent. Amongst other things, they required intercessory measures on their behalf, notably prayers; they further needed to take steps to eradicate any taint of sin which might jeopardize the safety of their souls should they die, steps which in any event were required for the success of their venture, considering contemporary conceptions of the bearing of sin upon the outcome of human affairs. Since such concerns, and the measures flowing from them, did not abruptly cease once a crusader had left his homeland, coverage will be extended here to their actions both *en route* and upon their return.

The perceived efficacy of prayer on behalf of crusaders is well illustrated by the graphic account in the Dieulacres chronicle of how Earl Ranulf of Chester and his company escaped death through shipwreck on their return from Damietta in 1220.[2] Their ship sailed into a terrible tempest but Ranulf remained unperturbed, nonchalantly advising the sailors that they should work until midnight when, he trusted, God would provide aid and the storm would cease. He then returned to his cabin. As midnight approached, the ship's captain advised Ranulf that he should prepare himself for death; the storm was increasing and all were in imminent peril. Ranulf then deigned to leave his cabin to help the terrified sailors with the rigging and tackle; shortly afterwards the storm ceased. Next day the captain asked Ranulf why he had not leapt to action until almost midnight, and why then he had got through more work than anyone else on board. Ranulf replied that at midnight

> my monks, and other religious whom my ancestors and I have founded in various places, arise to chant divine service and remember me in their prayers, and I hoped that God, because of their prayers and intercession, would give me the fortitude which I had lacked. And he caused the storm to cease as I predicted.

It is difficult to believe that Earl Ranulf acted quite like this in the circumstances, and the anecdote is primarily intended both to demonstrate the efficacy of the prayer of the monks of Dieulacres and to celebrate the special relationship between a monastic community and its founder. Nevertheless, there is plenty of evidence to show that crusaders considered prayer to be a vital insurance policy. They could, of course, like Ranulf, count on the prayers of the communities established or patronized by themselves or their ancestors. They also enjoyed the fruits of the prayers and suffrages offered generally for the well-being of the Holy Land and those who went in its defence.[3] But many individuals took more specific steps. Particularly illustrative of the spiritual concerns of a crusader before, during, and on return from

[2] Printed in *Monasticon Anglicanum*, ed. W. Dugdale; new edn., ed. J. Caley, H. Ellis, and B. Bardinel (London, 1817–30, repr. 1846), v. 627–8. Ranulf transferred Dieulacres from its original site at Poulton (Cheshire) in 1214. See J. W. Alexander, *Ranulf of Chester: A Relic of the Conquest* (Athens, Ga., 1983), 39–41.

[3] See above, pp. 51–2, for some indication of this liturgy in England.

his passage are the actions of Richard of Cornwall. *Flores historiarum* reports that he commended himself to the prayers of all the religious of England before he sailed in 1240,[4] but Matthew Paris suggests that he was more discriminating. He observes that Richard came to St Albans and begged that he be allowed special participation in the benefit of the brethren's prayers, Paris adding, characteristically, that he sought the same at some of those other houses where the sanctity and discipline of the order was especially regarded.[5] Probably, like Richard I for one before him, Earl Richard undertook a tour of selected shrines in England as part of his preparations. *En route* for embarkation at Marseilles, Richard stopped off at Cîteaux and St-Gilles and perhaps other famous houses, since it appears to have been customary for crusaders, at least of his social rank, to take the opportunity to visit shrines on or near the route in question. It was at Cîteaux, in July 1240, that he humbly commended himself to the prayers of the general chapter and bestowed 20*m*. annual rent upon the abbot and convent, in support of the general chapter, from his mills of Boroughbridge or, failing that, his manor of Knaresborough.[6] In addition, surely at the same time, he granted the church of South Stainley for the expenses of the general chapter.[7] Whether any property transactions resulted from Richard's visit to St-Gilles does not appear, but he went there, says Paris, to secure the saint's favour 'that he might more safely pass through the dangers of the sea'.[8]

Richard returned from the East via Sicily and Italy.[9] He went to Rome, and doubtless paid his respects to SS Peter and Paul and offered prayers for his safe passage across the Mediterranean. Since his return was plainly leisurely and unhurried, he perhaps took the opportunity to indulge in some sightseeing and visits to shrines in the fashion of William II de Mandeville, earl of Essex, in 1177–8.[10] On

[4] *Flores Historiarum*, ed. H. R. Luard, 3 vols. (RS; 1890), ii. 241. He further fortified himself with a series of papal bulls in accordance with the spiritual privileges accorded crusaders in canon law. See N. Denholm-Young, *Richard of Cornwall* (Oxford, 1947), 39–40.

[5] Paris, *CM* iv. 146, also 43–4. *Flores* and Paris both emphasize that his safety on crusade, more specifically in face of the perils of the sea, resulted from the efficacy of those prayers.

[6] *Yorkshire Deeds, III*, ed. W. Brown (Yorkshire Archaeological Soc., Rec. Ser. 63; 1922), 8, confirming Paris, *CM* iv. 46.

[7] *Yorkshire Deeds, III*, p. 136, without date. Richard followed his uncle's example. At the start of the Third Crusade, Richard I granted the church of Scarborough to support the Cistercian abbots during their general chapter: ibid. 104–6.

[8] Paris, *CM* iv. 46.

[9] His itinerary from Cremona to Dover, which he reached in Jan. 1242, cannot be reconstructed: Denholm-Young, *Richard of Cornwall*, pp. 43–4.

[10] 'Tewkesbury', p. 120; Paris, *CM* iv. 146–8; Wykes, *Chron.*, pp. 86–7. For Earl William's return from the Holy Land, see *Monasticon*, iv. 143–4.

his return to England Richard was received by Henry III, Queen Eleanor, and others at Dover; in London, where the streets were decorated with banners and hangings of silk, he was welcomed with all pomp and ceremony, 'quasi angelus', and led in solemn procession to St Paul's. Later the same day, he was received in liturgical procession at Westminster.[11] A banquet given by Henry followed. In thanksgiving for his brother's safe return, Henry offered forty halfpence of musc at Westminster, and a cloth which Richard had brought from the Holy Land was edged with green and red sandal and worked with gold before being presented.[12] Whether Richard was received liturgically elsewhere, and whether he granted gifts to other houses of his particular connection does not appear.

Perhaps the most illuminating account of an English crusader's return is the Walden chronicle's report of that of Earl William II de Mandeville in 1177–8.[13] To all churches of his fee, we are told, he presented silks to be made into chasubles or altar cloths.[14] Walden, founded by the infamous Geoffrey II de Mandeville, received one of the best, as was fitting. It was also fitting that one of William's first acts upon his return was to visit the abbey. To the chant of the *Benedictus* he was received in liturgical procession, and amidst great joy, prostrate at the great altar, was blessed by the prior. Then, rising up, he presented a fine reliquary containing the relics which he had acquired in the Holy Land and received as gifts from the Byzantine emperor and from his friend and crusading companion, Count Philip of Flanders, the man indeed who had belted him a knight.[15] Following the *Te Deum laudamus*, William entered the chapter house to be greeted by the brethren, their joy being sealed with the kiss of peace which William gave to, and received from, each. In the conversation which followed William doubtless recounted some of his adventures and caught up on the convent's news, before a splendid meal was served up to him and his *familiares*. On his departure, we are told, he went to visit his kinsmen and friends, celebrating his safe return like the monks, and carefully took stock of all his interests.

[11] 'Waverley', p. 329; Paris, *CM* iv. 180.

[12] *CLR 1240–5*, pp. 121, 205.

[13] *Monasticon*, iv. 143–4.

[14] Oriental textiles appear to have been favourite souvenirs. Among further examples, William Marshal brought back silk cloths in which he wished to be buried: *Histoire de Guillaume le Maréchal, comte de Striguil et de Pembroke, régent d'Angleterre (c.1140–1219)*, ed. P. Meyer, 3 vols. (Société de l'Histoire de France, 1891–1901), lines 18,243–60.

[15] *Monasticon*, iv. 143. Other examples of the donation of relics from the Holy Land procured by crusaders include Edward I's gift to Vale Royal on the occasion of its first foundation, 1277, and Peter des Roches's presentation of a foot of St Philip on his return to Winchester in 1231: ibid. v. 705–6; 'Winchester', p. 85.

This joyous homecoming contrasts with William's departure, as far as the brethren of Walden were concerned. The chronicle reports that he was harsh in his dealings with them, and relations were decidely cool.[16] The evidence suggests that normally crusaders were at pains to avoid such a state of affairs, a crusade being a classic occasion to act out the part of the solicitous and contrite patron or benefactor, whilst also securing spiritual support and removing cause of sin through reparation of injury. In April 1270, for example, the crusader Walter de Wigton, a Cumbrian knight, came to terms with Abbot Henry of Holm Cultram concerning his detention of certain beasts belonging to the abbey. The dispute had been taken to law, but now Walter entered into a comprehensive settlement of the underlying issue, rights of pasture.[17] There are many cases of this type, the timing of the settlement of which clearly owed much to the prospect of imminent departure on crusade, although the proximate motive is rarely made explicit.[18] Especially noteworthy is the ending to the long-running dispute over lands in the 1220s and 1230s between Peter II de Brus, who went on crusade in 1240, and Guisborough priory, a Brus foundation. In 1239, probably at the prior's bidding, Peter issued a very precise and detailed confirmation of the grants made to the priory over the years by men of the Brus fee and those holding otherwise of the family. Over eighty separate donations were confirmed, relating to some 140 distinct properties.[19] It may be safely presumed that in many such cases the crusader received a sum of cash in return for his concessions.

A great deal of property plainly passed to the church as a consequence of the spiritual needs of crusaders. In a few instances a crusade was even the occasion to establish a monastic house, hospital, or similar institution and to endow it with property. Vale Royal (Cheshire) owed its establishment to the decision of Lord Edward to make good his original vow, taken back in 1263–4, to found a Cistercian house in gratitude for being spared shipwreck whilst crossing the Channel in a perilous storm. The foundation charter, whereby Edward's estate at Darnhall was made over to a colony of monks from

[16] William complained that since his father had granted all churches of the fee to them, he had none to give his clerks. He was disinclined to grant the house further possessions. See *VCH Essex*, ii. 111. Relations warmed only following his return from crusade.

[17] *Register and Records of Holm Cultram*, ed. F. Grainger and W. G. Collingwood (Cumberland and Westmorland Antiquarian and Archaeological Soc., Rec. Ser. 7; 1929), 43, and further pp. 42, 45.

[18] For a clear example, see the settlement between Nostell priory and Henry de Lacy, cited by W. E. Wightman, *The Lacy Family in England and Normandy, 1086–1194* (Oxford, 1966), 82–4.

[19] *Cartularium prioratus de Gyseburne*, ed. W. Brown, 2 vols. (Surtees Soc., 76, 89; 1889, 1894), i. 94–8; ii. 198–9; and see i. 102–12, esp., for the dispute.

Dore, was granted on 2 August 1270, about three weeks before Edward's departure on crusade.[20] Considering a crusader's urgent need to raise cash, and that it was also on 2 August that Edward appointed attorneys to oversee his interests during his absence,[21] the foundation provides an excellent indication of the importance of the spiritual in a crusader's preparations: to set sail with such a solemn vow unfulfilled was to court disaster. Similarly, a crusade could be the occasion to gain absolution from a prior vow to make a foundation. Thus, in 1239, Ralph de Thony, shortly before his departure, granted three granges to the Cistercian house of Cumhyr to support thirteen monks who were to serve in perpetuity for his soul and those of others of his line. In return, the abbot bound the convent to obtain from the Cistercian general chapter absolution of Ralph's outstanding vow to found an abbey from a moiety of his manor of South Tawton, that being insufficient to support the thirteen monks required for a new foundation.[22]

The conscience of the benefactor was only one factor. Well aware of social conventions and crusaders' spiritual needs, many religious probably regarded the prospect of a crusade as an excellent opportunity to pester landowners into granting them properties particularly prized by the house in question. *Crucesignatus*, the landowner could fairly be expected to be more pliable and responsive to their representations. A splendid example of this way of thinking is surely afforded by the way in which the Cistercians of Meaux were enabled finally to establish a grange at Croo, in Holderness.

Like many granges, that at Croo could be established only following the consolidation of a group of separated lands. More particularly, the monks' intent depended upon their tenure of a large area of property at Beeford, neighbouring Croo, part of the estate of Geoffrey Bryto.[23] In the early thirteenth century Geoffrey's heiress, Emily, sold all of the property excepting two mills and a close to the monks, but Platt points out that it was precisely this close that was

[20] *Monasticon*, v. 704; *VCH Cheshire*, iii. 156–7. The monks moved to Vale Royal in 1277. For a hospital founded by a departing crusader, see *Registrum Antiquissimum of the Cathedral Church of Lincoln*, ed. C. W. Foster and K. Major (Lincoln Rec. Soc. 3; 1935), Nos. 792–4, for Richard de Argentein's establishment of Little Wymondley (Herts.) shortly before his departure, 1218–19.

[21] J. R. Studd, 'The Lord Edward's Lordship of Chester, 1254–72', *Transactions of the Historic Soc. of Lancashire and Cheshire*, cxxviii (1979), 16–17 has noted the coincidence.

[22] *The Beauchamp Cartulary Charters 1100–1268*, ed. E. Mason (Pipe Roll Soc. NS 43; 1980), Nos. 382–3; and for the background, E. Mason, 'Timeo barones et donas ferentes', in D. Baker (ed.), *Studies in Church Hist.* xv (1978), 69–70.

[23] For this case, see C. Platt, *The Monastic Grange in Medieval England: A Reassessment* (London, 1969), 53–4, and maps, pp. 50, 57.

needed to establish the demesne lands of the prospective grange since it abutted on the lands already possessed by the monks in Dringhoe. Emily married one Roger of Greensby and it seems that for some years the family refused all offers to sell, but ultimately Peter, the grandson, sold up: not to the monks, however, but to William II de Forz, count of Aumâle and lord of Holderness. There can be little doubt that in the period preceding William's crusade the brethren leaned heavily upon him. In 1240–1, William, conveniently the abbey's chief patron, duly obliged by granting the close for an annual pittance just before his departure for the Holy Land, and within a few years Croo grange was established.[24] William may have been persuaded to part with the close in due course anyway, but it was nevertheless the prospect of his crusade which saw the crucial transaction, enabling thereby the final completion of a lengthy process of selected land acquisition with a long-term aim in mind. William surely gained additional, or at least more fervent, prayers as a result.

It was not just landed property which might be at issue. For example, in June 1270 Prior Guy of Grandmont wrote to Lord Edward urging that he restore to the cell of Luc, near St-Macaire, the tithes of bread taken from the castles of Benauges and St-Macaire. Guy stressed that by precept of the order's general chapter mass was celebrated by each and every brother that God protect Edward in the Holy Land and direct his acts. Through their assiduous prayers they interceded for him and his crusading company, but, Guy observed, should Edward accede to his request then Christ would look favourably on his passage and give him victory over the infidel. In Guy's mind, here was an unambiguous quid pro quo.[25]

Grants were frequently made by crusaders once they had left England. On 2 May 1241, for example, William Peverel confirmed to the Templars the manor of Sandford which his uncle, Thomas, had previously donated.[26] Since he almost certainly sailed for home with Richard of Cornwall from Acre the following day, it looks as if the fear of the return sea-passage lay behind the grant.[27] When John de Lacy, at Damietta in 1218, made donation to the church of All Saints, Pontefract, the souls of members of his family and the welfare of his people were in mind. The properties conveyed were for the purpose of enlarging the church's burial ground, the construction of a charnel

24 *Chronica monasterii de Melsa*, ed. E. A. Bond, 3 vols. (RS; 1866–8), ii. 47–8, and i. 164–7.

25 *Gascon Register A (Series of 1318–19)*, ed. G. P. Cuttino and J-P. Trabut-Cussac, 3 vols. (London, 1975–6), ii. No. 286. Whether Edward relented is unclear.

26 *The Sandford Cartulary*, ed. A. M. Leys, 2 vols. (Oxfordshire Rec. Soc. 19, 22; 1938, 1941), i. No. 4.

27 Earl Richard provides 3 May as the departure date in his letter preserved in Paris, *CM* iv. 138–44.

house, and the erection of a chapel (aptly enough in honour of Holy Sepulchre and Holy Cross) for the souls of all the faithful.[28] If a man was close to death on crusade his thoughts naturally turned to home and to measures for his salvation. John de Harcourt, 'in extremis agens in exercitu Damete', was one: he granted 10*l.* of land in Roelay in free alms to the Templars in 1218–19.[29]

Regrettably, few wills of English crusaders have survived: they would surely have allowed greater amplification of the pattern of behaviour which emerges from other evidence. A rare exception is the will of Hugh de Neville, drawn up at Acre in 1267.[30] He left various items of his personal property to his companions and followers, rewarding past and present services and in some cases, at least, providing for the return passage of the beneficiary to England. For the humblest of his household this must have been a great relief. Other items and sums of cash were left to institutions in Acre. The poor and the sick of Acre were remembered also, while Walter, his chaplain, was to receive 8*m.* to chant for Hugh's soul every year, and 15*m.* were left 'to do my service on the day of my obit'. Having provided for what he hoped was a laudable end, Hugh instructed that he be buried in the sepulchre of St Nicholas, presumably in Acre.

'To effect this testament and acquit my debts I will and devise that my horses and my armour and all my other things be sold.' Hugh's concern about unpaid debts was typical;[31] but the serious matter of debt encumbrance also occupied many crusaders before their departure. Henry III for one spelled out the spiritual reasons for this in July 1270, when he granted Lord Edmund the notable privilege of allowing his executors or creditors to hold the lands Edmund held in chief for seven years, from the day of his death, to pay off his debts and others he might incur in the course of his crusade:

Nos, attendentes periculosum esse anime sue si, eo taliter recedente [on crusade], debita sua, que non nisi de exitibus terrarum suarum possent exsolvi, remaneant in incertis, cum major pars terrarum suarum ad nos devolvi debeat si eum sine herede de corpore suo decedere contingeret . . .[32]

28 *Chartulary of St. John of Pontefract (c.1090–1258)*, ed. R. Holmes, 2 vols. (Yorkshire Archaeological Soc., Rec. Ser. 25, 30; 1899, 1902), i, 36–7.

29 *RLC* i. 402b. The later memory of the grant was faulty. See *Fees* ii. 1280.

30 'On the Testament of Sir Hugh de Nevill, Written at Acre, 1267', ed. M. S. Giuseppi, *Archaeologia*, lvi, part 2 (1899), 351–70.

31 In his will drawn up at Acre in 1272, Lord Edward empowered his executors to repay his debts from his goods and, if necessary, from the issues of his lands: *Foedera*, I. i. 495.

32 PRO, C 66/88, m. 8. The calendar in *CPR 1266–72*, p. 448, partly misses the point. The grant was extended in Jan. 1271 by the stipulation that escheats and other appurtenances might also be held by his executors or creditors: ibid. 511.

Edmund was naturally seeking to protect his estates from the royal bailiffs should he die on crusade, and, as things stood in 1270, the Crown would be his heir as Henry noticed.[33] But it is quite apparent that the spiritual motive was just as important. Indeed, Edmund drew up a will before his departure, in which, we learn, he made arrangements for the payment of his debts.[34]

The privilege accorded Edmund was both rare and highly prized. Not surprisingly it was limited to crusaders who were either royal kinsmen or close to the king in other ways.[35] Normally, the Crown allowed the executors of a crusader's will to have free administration of the dead man's goods to execute his will, providing they acquitted any debts owed to the king.[36] Nevertheless, some crusaders, at least, took pains to pay back specific debts before their departure, notwithstanding the privileges which they enjoyed in canon law in this matter and the financial pressures under which they laboured.[37] Before his crusade, in 1240, Robert de Fraxineto even paid off all his debts to Aaron and Ursello, Jews of Colchester. They were instructed to deliver all relevant instruments to Oliva, Robert's wife, but 'maliciose' they had kept one back, we learn, and were seeking to defraud her.[38] In this and other cases, concerns other than the safety of the crusader's soul were doubtless involved, but it would be unwise to dismiss the spiritual motive. The line, frequently thin, between the spiritual and the material is here blurred to the point that sharp differentiation is as difficult as it is undesirable. The same may be said of those measures taken by crusaders to make reparation for injuries and to restore properties wrongly or dubiously held. Such actions earned merit in the eyes of God and man, but they also went some way towards establishing the security of a crusader's interests during his absence by removing a prime cause of grievance and friction.

Security and the Settling of Affairs

It is a commonplace that assurances as to security were critical to the raising and dispatch of crusading forces, for crusaders of all degrees were naturally fearful lest their interests be compromised, disturbed,

[33] In Apr. 1269 he married Avelina de Fortibus, then aged only about ten years.

[34] *CPR 1266–72*, p. 511. It does not survive.

[35] See, generally, J. M. W. Bean, *The Decline of English Feudalism, 1215–1540* (Manchester, 1967), 34–7, who cites some examples of crusaders. Others could be added.

[36] Amongst a host of cases, see that concerning Hamo Pech, who died on the 1240–1 crusade, in *RF* i. 363.

[37] See J. A. Brundage, *Medieval Canon Law and the Crusader* (Madison, Milwaukee, London, 1969), 179–93.

[38] *CR 1237–42*, p. 489.

or even lost during their absence. Accordingly, a crucial element of the prudent crusader's preparations consisted of measures designed to provide for that security.

His anxieties were to some extent allayed by the privileges he enjoyed in canon law. These are well known and do not require extensive discussion here, but it should be emphasized that by the time of the Fourth Lateran Council (1215) a coherent set of privileges had emerged, automatically available upon an individual's assumption of the Cross, and designed to free him from any obstacle which might hinder or prevent the fulfilment of his vow, whilst also enabling him, judicially and financially, to accomplish his passage the more easily.[39] Close monitoring was, of course, essential to ensure that these various privileges were duly implemented and upheld, the burden of responsibility being thrust upon individual prelates.[40] In addition, conservators were appointed with the specific task of upholding crusader privileges, and popes themselves might intervene on behalf of particular crusaders.[41] In many respects the ecclesiastical authorities were fully capable of protecting crusaders, but with regard to privileges such as debt respites, exemption from tolls and taxes, or the right to essoin in secular courts, the Crown's attitude was critical. The Church might take the primary responsibility for protecting the crusader, but the effective realization of privileges in practice frequently demanded the co-operation of the secular power.

A comprehensive study of the relationship between canon law and English common law regarding the crusader is still wanting, but the evidence indicates that the Crown and the royal courts responded positively to the needs and privileges of crusaders, upheld ecclesiastical protections, and reacted favourably to the representations of bishops and others on behalf of individual crusaders.[42] There were important qualifications and limitations. If legal proceedings had been initiated before the crusader departed then the essoin would be refused.[43] If a crusader committed crimes whilst wearing the Cross then neither canon law nor common law would normally extend

[39] Brundage, *Medieval Canon Law*, esp. chs. 5, 6.

[40] Commonly, they delegated to members of their clergy. See e.g. *The Registers of Walter Bronescombe and Peter Quivil, Bishops of Exeter*, ed. F. C. Hingeston-Randolph (London, 1889), 63–4.

[41] The sort of measures taken can be traced in the papal and episcopal registers. Earl William de Ferrers was one crusader on campaign who appreciated the measures taken on behalf of himself and his men. See *Royal and Other Historical Letters Illustrative of the Reign of Henry III*, ed. W. W. Shirley, 2 vols. (RS; 1862, 1866), i. 24.

[42] Brundage, *Medieval Canon Law*, ch. 6, *passim*.

[43] Henry de Bracton, *De Legibus et Consuetudinibus regni Angliae*, ed. T. Twiss (RS; 1878–83), v. 164, 166–8.

protection to him.[44] Third, no essoin would be allowed to crusaders in common law with regard to pleas of novel disseisin, although on occasion the king might grant respite of his special grace. Within these limits, however, the crusader's essoin was almost always upheld in the royal courts. If it was overruled then it was because the privilege was seemingly being abused.[45] Crusaders were nevertheless well advised to avail themselves of privileges available from the Crown. Considering the rules governing all essoins, procedural technicalities in general, and the pitfalls facing the unwary and unlearned at law, the wise crusader invested in royal letters of protection and attorney, for they afforded an altogether more certain security during a crusader's absence. But, like all privileges, they cost money, and this helps to explain why it was generally crusaders higher up the social order who availed themselves. Their greater material possessions gave them good reason, and they could more easily afford it.[46]

Royal protections were of two kinds, simple and judicial.[47] Simple protection did little beyond safeguarding a man's lands, rents, men, and possessions, but the judicial promised much more in addition because it anticipated action in the courts and came, in the thirteenth century, to exempt the recipient from all litigation during his absence excepting those pleas outlined above.[48] Like the protections for men in royal service upon which it was formally modelled, the crusader's protection evolved slowly.[49] Initially there was no standardized

[44] See M. Purcell, *Papal Crusading Policy: The Chief Instruments of Papal Crusading Policy and Crusade to the Holy Land from the Final Loss of Jerusalem to the Fall of Acre, 1244–1291* (Leiden, 1975), 167; Brundage, *Medieval Canon Law*, pp. 171–2.

[45] See Brundage, *Medieval Canon Law*, p. 174.

[46] In 1199 the fee for a simple protection was fixed at 2*s*., but it was often exceeded: *Foedera*, I. i. 75–6. The cost of a judicial protection and letters of attorney in the 13th c. is unclear, but in July 1259 the bishop of Ely was charged 20*m*. for the grant of both: *CPR 1258–66*, p. 221. In 1299 the prior of Holy Trinity, York, paid 10*m*. for letters of attorney: *Select Cases in the Court of King's Bench 1272–1422*, ed. G. O. Sayles, 7 vols. (Selden Soc. 45, 47, 48, 74, 76, 82, 88; 1936–71), I. xcvii, n. 3.

[47] For what follows, see esp. J. S. Critchley, 'The Early History of the Writ of Judicial Protection', *BIHR* xlv (1972), 196–213.

[48] It is not clear when the first individual crusader protections were granted, but Richard I committed himself to the general principle in 1189 at Nonancourt. He and Philip II declared that the goods of those going to Jerusalem were to remain intact, royal officials remedying injury: Ralph of Diceto, *Opera historica*, ed. W. Stubbs, 2 vols. (RS; 1876), ii. 73–4; *Foedera* I. i. 50. The earliest enrolled protections date from early in John's reign: see *RLP* 11b, 22b.

[49] Crusader protections developed from two distinct principles. The first, ecclesiastical, was concerned with the interests of the crusader *per se*. In early grants of royal protection this influence was often made explicit: see e.g. the terms of the grant to Peter des Roches in July 1227, in *PR 1225–32*, p. 135. In form and exact substance, however, the protection plainly owed much to the Crown's desire to support men in royal service, esp. when they were beyond the realm.

formula; terminology, phraseology, and substance varied considerably.[50] For the Lord Edward's crusade, however, a stereotyped protection was available. That granted to John Tiptoft in July 1270 may stand for all.[51] In the form of letters patent, it declared that since John was about to depart as a crusader to the Holy Land in the company of the king and Edward, the king took John, his men, lands, rents, and all possessions into royal protection. Accordingly, John and his possessions should be maintained, protected, and defended, no injury permitted. Should he suffer injury then it was to be rectified at once. The protection was to run for four years from Easter 1270. This was the simple protection; in addition came the *Volumus* clause granting judicial protection. Thereby, John was declared quit from the time of his departure for the remainder of the term, or until he returned, of all pleas and *querelae*, excepting pleas of dower *unde nichil habet*, novel disseisin, and darrein presentment. Altogether some 243 crusaders are known to have taken out protections in this form in 1270 and 1271.[52] There were variations according to the term of the protection, but the nature of the protection afforded was constant.[53] Additional privilege required further letters. Thus some obtained exemption from all common summonses before justices in eyre and justices of the forest, others from suit of court at county and hundred courts.[54] But the standard 1270 protection acted as the model for those later granted to crusaders in the reign of Edward I. The only substantial development was the addition of pleas *quare impedit* to those of *unde nichil habet*, novel disseisin, and darrein presentment, to which judicial protection did not apply.[55]

50 The pleas covered, and the terms for which protections should run varied considerably: see e.g. those in *PR 1216–25*, pp. 147, 151, 158, 161, 301; *PR 1225–32*, pp. 126, 129, 130, 135, 196, 323, 390; *CPR 1232–47*, p. 106; *CPR 1247–58*, p. 18. Nevertheless, the attempt to apply canonical principles is apparent. Some crusaders contented themselves with simple protections.

51 *CPR 1266–72*, p. 440; *Foedera*, I. i. 483.

52 Most, but not all, were enrolled. Master John Pute's attorney presented his letters in an assize mort d'ancestor in Aug. 1270: *Somersetshire Pleas, Civil and Criminal, from the Rolls of the Itinerant Justices*, ed. C. E. H. C. Healey and L. C. Landon (Somerset Rec. Soc. 11, 36, 41, 44; 1897–1929), ii. 134. No protection for John is recorded on the Chancery rolls.

53 Some ran from a date prior to the crusader's departure, or from Easter 1271 for those sailing the following year. The vast majority were for four years, but those for Lord Edward and one or two others were for five: *CPR 1266–72*, pp. 403, 479, 395.

54 See e.g. the exemptions granted to Nicholas de Segrave, John de Verdun, and Robert de Turberville in *CPR 1266–72*, pp. 421, 448, 513. Ralph de Cotun seems to have been alone in obtaining a protection 'with the clause that he be quit of the three pleas', presumably *unde nichil habet*, novel disseisin, and darrein presentment, in Nov. 1271. In June 1270 he received a standard judicial protection: *CPR 1266–72*, pp. 479, 604.

55 See e.g. the letters of protection presented on Otto de Grandson's behalf in a *quo*

Protections did not in themselves guarantee the immunity of a crusader's interests from injury; nor did they necessarily prevent the initiation of legal proceedings against him. The Crown might take action on hearing of injury, as when Lord Edmund was dispatched in November 1270 to attach the men of Earl Robert de Ferrers who had forcibly entered Roger de Leyburn's manor of Stonyford in disregard of his crusader's protection, but in such cases it is probable that action only followed upon representations to the king on the crusader's behalf.[56] For a protection to be more than a reassuring deterrent, and for a crusader to be tolerably sure that his interests would indeed be effectively upheld during his absence, representatives with duly authorized and well-defined powers at law were essential. It was for them to act should injury threaten or actually occur, and to initiate proceedings in the interests of their crusader principal.

Crusader attorneys first appear in the records in the late twelfth century.[57] Initially they were seemingly admitted by the Crown to represent their principals in specific suits or interests only.[58] Rarely, in this early period, does it appear that more general powers were granted.[59] Only later, when the general right to employ attorneys was regularized and extended, were crusaders, as other men, enabled routinely to appoint attorneys for prosecution and defence in hundred, county, and royal courts.[60] Crusader attorneys with general powers became more common about 1250,[61] but it was once again the 1270 crusade which saw the system reach maturity. Chancery enrolments and surviving letters of attorney reveal that a common

warranto case, 1293: *Placita de Quo Warranto, Edward I–Edward III in curia receptae scaccarii Westm. asservata*, ed. W. Illingworth (London, 1818), 354. The protection, for a three-year term, the norm after the 1270 crusade, was enrolled: *CPR 1292–1301*, p. 17.

56 *CPR 1266–72*, p. 497.

57 See e.g. *Pipe Roll 2 Richard I: The Great Roll of the Pipe for the second year of the Reign of Richard the First*, ed. D. M. Stenton (Pipe Roll Soc. NS 2; 1925), 82, for Robert de Federestan's attorning of William de Derefeld. Much earlier, the *Leges Henrici Primi*, ed. and trans. L. J. Downer (Oxford, 1972), 15, 61 had already observed that anyone going to Rome, Jerusalem, or distant parts should appoint someone to look after his affairs.

58 See e.g. Earl William de Ferrers's attornments in 1218, at the Exchequer and in a plea against the citizens of London: PRO, E 368/1, m. 1d.

59 Robert le Sauvage, who died on the Fifth Crusade, may have been one, but the evidence is inconclusive: see *RLC* i. 397b, 399b. Peter des Roches appears to have left his seneschal, Roger Wascelin, and his clerk, John de Heriet, to look after his interests on his departure in 1227: *RLC* ii. 201b, 211b; *CRR 1227–30*, pp. 126, 161, 189, 276.

60 I am indebted to Dr Paul Brand for his advice on these matters.

61 The 1240–1 expeditions perhaps saw this first on a large scale, judging from a few references to attorneys' activities, but the loss of the Close Rolls for 23 Henry III, and the Patent Rolls for 23 and 24 Henry III, means that any enrolled letters of attorney escape us.

form had evolved. Attorneys were appointed in Chancery with general powers to appear on behalf of their principals for prosecution and defence in all manner of suits in all manner of courts, with the additional power to substitute or present other attorneys as expedient, for a fixed term normally of four years unless the crusader returned meanwhile.[62] Around sixty grants of this type have been collected, but a close search of the unpublished plea rolls would probably reveal more.[63]

In most cases, two attorneys were appointed. There was a tendency for one to be a kinsman or close friend of the crusader, acting in conjunction with another, probably trained or experienced in the law and its workings. Thus, in July 1270, Geoffrey de Monte Alto was admitted as an attorney of his brother, Adam, with Hugh de Insula; Master Henry Lovel for John Lovel, with Martin de Suthmere, a close associate of John; Guichard de Charron for Adam of Jesmond, his neighbour, friend, and colleague in royal service.[64] In many such cases we probably see a crusader empowering individuals not only to represent him at law, or cause him to be represented, but also to act as his general attorneys or executors during his absence. For those with more limited interests, especially, such a modest arrangement would have sufficed, but those crusaders who were at the top of the ladder of status, power, and wealth, and those whose affairs were more complicated, required more elaborate plans involving more personnel. Hugh de Neville, for example, who departed for the Holy Land under a cloud of anxieties, as we have seen, attorned Richard de Gibbecrake and Hugh William de Waleis in 1266 to act for him in all litigation.[65] He authorized his mother, Hawisia, and John, his brother, to farm out his lands for five years to his advantage, and, somewhat optimistically, to receive back the lands he had forfeited for his rebellious activity.[66] He further appointed John, and William de Moyne, to take custody of all escheats falling to him during his absence.[67] By yet another deed he appointed Richard de Gibbecrake and James de Royng as custodians of his lands and 'negotia'.[68] The

62 For an original grant, see BL Additional Charter 19828 (dated 12 May 1270), on behalf of Thomas Mauduit and enrolled: see *CPR 1266–72*, p. 484.

63 For a good picture of a crusader's attorneys at work, presenting their letters to court and pleading their master's case, see PRO, KB 26/191, m. 11, for the attorneys of Giles de Fenes in 1270.

64 *CR 1268–72*, pp. 281, 289; *CPR 1266–72*, p. 443.

65 See above, pp. 128–9, for Hugh.

66 *CR 1264–8*, p. 254.

67 PRO, DL 25/1, L 176. If either died, John le Bretun and (?Hugh) William le Waleis were to be substituted.

68 PRO, DL 25/1, L 173. The prior of Waltham was to allow them to have copies of all charters and writings in his keeping for doing Hugh's business.

terminology may be imprecise, hiding a clear division of responsibilities in practice between Hugh's appointees, but it is plain that his attorneys at law were charged with only part of his affairs.

The arrangements made by Lord Edmund in 1271 are much clearer. A royal scion of immense power and landed wealth distributed throughout the realm, Edmund more than most needed to take care for the governance and security of his vast possessions and interests.[69] On 13 January 1271 he declared that he had committed his place and honour in England, 'locum nostrum et potestatem', to his mother, Queen Eleanor of Provence, for the duration of the crusade.[70] She was to enjoy supreme authority over all his seneschals, attorneys, bailiffs, constables, receivers, and other ministers, with the power to appoint, remove, or change them as and when seemed expedient to her. She might also present to vacant churches of his advowson; confer, sell, assign, or farm his lands, together with wards, marriages, escheats, and other appurtenances; grant or sell his woods and venison; contract loans for Edmund's use and oblige him, his heirs, and possessions; in short, 'to do everything which we would or ought to do if we were present'. To execute any of these things Eleanor might appoint attorneys for herself as expedient.[71] This is the clearest statement of the powers of a crusader's general attorney that has survived, but there is no reason to consider it exceptional.[72] In the case of Queen Eleanor and of others, it may be presumed that the attorney or a close associate was given custody of the crusader's seal, a vital matter for concern, but in some instances, such as the Lord Edward's, a seal of absence was manufactured and left behind to authenticate the acts of attorneys.[73]

[69] In 1271 he was earl of Lancaster, earl of Leicester, and lord of the honours of Derby and Monmouth amongst other lordships, already holding most of the fees, 263 and a fraction, in demesne or as overlord, recorded in his inquisition post mortem, 1296. See W. E. Rhodes, 'Edmund, Earl of Lancaster', *EHR* x (1895), 40. He had hopes then of even further influence following his marriage in 1269 to Avelina de Fortibus, heiress of William III, count of Aumâle and lord of Holderness, and of Baldwin de Redvers, earl of Devon.

[70] PRO, C 66/90, m. 7, *inspeximus* of 28 July 1272. The calendar in *CPR 1266–72*, p. 668, omits many important details. The attorneys Edmund appointed on 27 Jan. 1271 were plainly intended to represent him only at law: ibid. 587.

[71] Bishop Roger Longespee of Coventry/Lichfield, Gilbert Talbot, and John de Oketon were associated with Queen Eleanor, acting on Edmund's behalf, by Aug. 1271: ibid. 566.

[72] Similar powers were assuredly granted by Otto de Grandson to Robert Burnell, bishop of Bath and Wells in 1291: see, esp. *Rôles Gascons*, ed. C. Bémont, 3 vols. (Paris, 1896–1906), iii. No. 1924; *CPR 1281–92*, pp. 362, 363, 371, 440, 462, 496, for Robert's discharging of some of his responsibilities.

[73] Lord Edward's seal of absence was entrusted to Robert Burnell, one of his attorneys from Aug. 1270. See J. R. Studd, 'The Seals of the Lord Edward', *Antiquaries Journ.* lviii (1979), 310–19. Richard I did much the same: T. F. Tout, *Chapters in the*

Arrangements for the governance and safeguarding of his interests during his absence helped to mollify his fears, but it was also incumbent upon the crusader himself to take precise action to order affairs before his departure. If he held an office it was for him to appoint a substitute, if he was so allowed.[74] If he feared prosecution for any misdemeanour then he might seek pardon in anticipation. John de Ardern, for example, was pardoned for all trespasses in the forests of Essex and Galtres in May 1270.[75] William de Valence was pardoned more generally in July of that year for all trespasses committed in the royal forests, parks, hays, and rivers.[76] Alternatively, a crusader might secure a stay in anticipated proceedings against him. In July 1270 Henry III granted that if Luke de Tany, or any of his household, going to the Holy Land, be appealed for the deaths of certain fellows, then they would neither suffer outlawry nor lose their lands, the appeals to be heard upon their return.[77]

Debt encumbrance occupied many. Leaving aside the moral question, it is plain that many sought to free themselves, or were tied down to make payment, before departure. Arrangements for debt repayment were, of course, being made all the time, but the prospect of a crusade clearly stimulated a flurry of activity, notwithstanding crusaders' privileged status in law. The 1270–2 crusading forces again provide some illuminating examples. Thus, Richard de la Rochelle, before departing, acknowledged a debt of 60*m.* to the executors of Thomas de Ippegrave, and agreed terms for repayment against the security of his lands 'notwithstanding any protection of the lord king granted to him or his men, as to a *crucesignatus* or in any other way'.[78] In April 1270 William de Valence bound himself to pay Thomas de Clare 3,500*m.* in instalments by Midsummer 1271, 'all remedy of law either civil or canon being hereby renounced'.[79] William was one crusader whose financial relations with the Crown also came under scrutiny. In August 1270 the barons of the Exchequer were instructed

Administrative History of Mediaeval England, 6 vols. (Manchester, 1937), i. 148; also L. B. Larking, 'On the Heart-shrine in Leybourne Church: A letter', *Archaeologia Cantiana*, v (1863), 133–92, for the likelihood that Roger de Leyburn had a second seal made for his projected crusade, 1269–70.

[74] e.g. John de Neville, chief forester of England, appointed Ralph de Neville to discharge his duties in the counties of Northampton, Oxford, Buckingham, and Huntingdon for four years from Easter 1240. He raised £120. per annum towards his crusading expenses thereby: PRO, DL 25/1, L 180.

[75] *CPR 1266–72*, p. 426.

[76] Ibid. 449.

[77] Ibid. 442.

[78] *CR 1268–72*, p. 286.

[79] *CCh.R 1257–1300*, pp. 138–9. In another case involving two crusaders, Payn de Chaworth agreed to pay 100*m.* to John Lovel by 24 June 1270, the date originally set for the departure of Edward's force: *CR 1268–72*, p. 266.

to provide a general statement of account of the king's debts to William and vice versa.[80] Of course, the king might of his special grace remit certain debts and it is not surprising, considering the curial complexion of the 1270–2 crusading force, to find many examples of the royal largesse being extended in this matter.[81] But the fact that the debtor was a crusader seems itself to have influenced the king. Amongst other examples, Henry III's quittance to Alexander Luterel in July 1270, for all account required of him for the keeping of the body and lands of his brother Geoffrey, explicity mentions that Alexander is going to the Holy Land with the Lord Edward.[82]

The prudent crusader also took steps to clarify his rights of tenure. Like Peter des Roches in 1227, he might seek a general confirmation of his property rights from the Crown, in the form of a royal *inspeximus*.[83] More commonly, it seems, he sought confirmation of a particular right. Geoffrey de Langley junior is one of a considerable number who secured an *inspeximus* of a grant made by the crusader's immediate lord. On 8 February 1271 his seisin of the manor of Kingshay and the mills of Hungerford, granted by Lord Edmund's charter of 12 January, was confirmed by Henry III.[84] Some crusaders, assuredly leaning on their curial connections, managed to convert the nature of their tenure of certain properties. In September 1270, for example, Henry III granted that the lands Ellis de Rabeyn held of the king within the manor of Milbeston, ancient demesne of the Crown, along with lands of the inheritance of his wife, Maud, and those of his purchase, be held in chief, quit of suit of court of hundred and county, and quit of tallage.[85]

[80] *CR 1268–72*, p. 216.

[81] Some debts were long-standing. Geoffrey Gacelyn was acquitted the scutage he owed for the Gannoc campaign of 1245: ibid. 347. See also the cases of William le Latimer and Richard de Rus for clear evidence of quittance as a reward for past service. See ibid. 175; *CPR 1266–72*, pp. 371, 411.

[82] *CPR 1266–72*, p. 447. Peter des Roches perhaps did best in this matter, explicitly as a crusader as well as for his service to John and Henry III. See the pardons granted to him, before and during his crusade, in *RLC* ii. 189b, 190b; *Pipe Roll 14 Henry III: The Great Roll of the Pipe for the Fourteenth Year of the Reign of Henry III, Michaelmas 1230*, ed. C. Robinson (Pipe Roll Soc. NS 4; 1927), 194, 197. Earl Ranulf of Chester received quittances totalling 423*m*. on the point of his departure in 1218. The writ does not specify his crusade as a reason for this, but rather his expenses in keeping the king's castles: PRO, E 368/1, m. 7d.

[83] *CCh.R 1226–57*, pp. 29–30: confirmation of John's charter to Bishop Peter, confirming the rights of the church of Winchester. See *RLC* ii. 179b, for royal mandates to ensure the confirmation was upheld.

[84] *CCh.R 1257–1300*, p. 162.

[85] *CPR 1266–72*, p. 458. See also *CCh.R 1257–1300*, p. 143, for the grant to Eleanor of Castile in May 1270 that she hold certain manors in fee, held previously for life, term of years, or at will.

A further crop of confirmations indicates that many crusaders were also prepared to accord to others the security which they craved themselves. In part, this earned merit since, conventionally, no crusader or pilgrim should depart possessed of anything which was not rightfully his. The other party, of course, was naturally eager to secure concession from the crusader before he departed: the situation at law might be immeasurably more difficult should the crusader die in possession. Further, the crusader surely knew that the best way of ensuring the integrity of his possessions lay in removal or compensation of grievances against him; he certainly knew from the terms of his protection that particular actions at law might yet be brought against him during his absence. Here, too, was a means of raising some badly needed cash. Thus Lord Edmund, shortly before his departure, confirmed to the prior and convent of Bridlington the vill of Little Kelke. He raised £80. thereby.[86] The monks of Fountains abbey gave John II, duke of Brittany and earl of Richmond £40. 'of their charity, towards his journey to Jerusalem' for his confirmation in October 1269 of the vill of Aynderby to hold in free alms.[87] More broadly, as far as the 1270–2 crusaders are concerned, we have already seen how most of those who had been granted rebel properties in the aftermath of the barons' wars had begun or completed the process of restitution to their former owners or their heirs by the time of their departure for the East.[88] Again, the crusader's urgent need for cash probably helped to speed up the process as the time for departure neared. Hamo Lestrange, for example, had been granted, amongst other properties, the lands of the rebel William de Birmingham; in 1270 Roger de Somery, the chief lord of William's fee, bound himself to pay 80*m.* to Hamo by Whitsun for all William's lands.[89]

As dynasts and family men, crusaders were anxious to provide for their wider family interests. This might involve settlements between kinsmen, as when Amaury de St-Amand, who sailed as a banneret of Simon de Montfort in 1240, received royal confirmation in October 1239 of the quitclaim made to him by his brother, William, of all lands and rents lately held in England by their kinsman Ralph fitzWalter de Verdon and by their brother, Guy. In consideration of this, Amaury

[86] *Abstracts of the Charters and Other Documents Contained in the Chartulary of the Priory of Bridlington in the East Riding of the County of York*, ed. W. T. Lancaster (Leeds, 1912), 168, and dated 20 Feb. 1271 in Edward I's confirmation: ibid. 171.

[87] *Chartulary of the Cistercian Abbey of Fountains*, ed. W. T. Lancaster, 2 vols. (Leeds, 1915), ii. 11.

[88] See above, p. 130.

[89] *CR 1268–72*, p. 249.

granted William the manors of Cleyndon and Exning.[90] Some were concerned to contract marriages for their heirs before sailing East. In February 1240 John de Neville and Earl Roger de Quenci of Winchester agreed terms for the marriage and endowment of John's son, Hugh, and Roger's daughter, Isabel.[91] Again, in June 1239 the royal assent was secured for the union of Ralph de Thony's heir, Roger, with Alice, daughter of the earl of Hereford and Essex, on the eve of Ralph's departure for the East.[92] Alternatively, where no particular match was to mind, the crusader might secure the privilege whereby his executors were enabled to provide for the marriage and keeping of the heirs should the crusader die before his return.[93] A man would seek to pre-empt his lord's rights of wardship if circumstances permitted.

Crusaders commonly endowed members of their families with properties before their departure.[94] In many cases, probably, no further motive than the wish to provide for kinsmen was involved, although he might raise some cash in this way, but in others it looks as if the crusader was seeking to safeguard the inheritance against all likely eventualities, especially when his heirs were minors. In June 1270, for example, Roger de Reymes granted all his property in Wherstead, Ipswich, Caldwell, Westerfield, 'and everywhere' to his son William, and the heirs of his body, to hold in fee as of inheritance for the life of Roger, rendering £40. per annum for all services, and rendering after Roger's death the services due to the chief lords of the fee. If William died without issue then the property was to remain to Richard, Roger's other son, and his heirs. If Richard, too, died without heir, then the whole was to revert to Roger's heirs principal. Roger further attorned Lucy, daughter of William fitzRoger de Berholt, to receive the £40. on Roger's behalf until his return from the Holy Land 'which will be, God granting, within four years'. She was

90 *CCh.R 1226–57*, p. 247; and see further *Feet of Fines for Oxfordshire, 1195–1291*, ed. H. E. Salter (Oxfordshire Rec. Soc. 12; 1930), 235–6. Earl Simon himself finally secured the formal renunciation of his brother Amaury's claim to the earldom of Leicester in Apr. 1239, shortly before Amaury's departure on crusade and Simon's the following year. See C. Bémont, *Simon de Montfort, Earl of Leicester, 1208–1265*, trans. E. F. Jacob (Oxford, 1930), 4–7, 59.

91 BL Cotton Charter viii. 7.

92 *RF* i. 327.

93 e.g. Robert Tiptoft in July 1270. See *CPR 1266–72*, p. 441; ibid. 451, for William de Valence. Such privileges were rare: Bean, *Decline*, pp. 27–8.

94 For an example of the endowment of sons, see *RLC* i. 423b, 432b, 441, 457, for Saher de Quenci's grants before departure in 1219. For a grant to a mother, see *CIPM* ii. 445–7, for John de Vesci's conveyances to Agnes in 1270. For temporary demise of land to a wife, see *CR 1231–4*, p. 248, for William de Ardern's grant to Avicia.

also granted the wardship of William, with the property, for that term. If he did not return from the East then Lucy was to have the property for her life.[95]

Whatever the precise steps taken, the crusader had to be wary of legal pitfalls and the possibility that the kin so endowed would challenge the terms of the grant. John de Vescy, for example, upon his return from the Holy Land, was obliged to bring a writ of covenant against his mother in 1275. Only then did she acknowledge the manors granted her for life in 1270 to be of John's right.[96] When, on the other hand, Hamo Lestrange assigned his manor of Stretton to his sister Hawise before his departure, he required her, with the consent of her husband, to declare that she would restore it to him when he returned from the East.[97] Yet Hamo was one of a number of crusaders who caused later difficulties for his kin by failing to secure due authority for his conveyances, falling foul in this case of the requirement for tenants-in-chief to secure royal licence to alienate properties held in chief. Hawise and one brother, Robert, were certainly compromised, another brother, Roger, probably so.[98]

The thoughtful crusader sought to protect his family from the intrusion of royal bailiffs on other grounds. Before sailing in 1227 William Paynel appointed his wife, Alice, and Hugh de Sandford to pay 20*m*. per annum for three years at the Exchequer in part payment of his debts to the king.[99] It was a wise precaution, but frequently, it appears, insufficient thought was given to the possible predicament of a crusader's kin during his absence, especially should he die leaving outstanding debts. In August 1220 Margery, the widow of Earl Saher de Quenci, found herself pressed in the midst of her grief by royal bailiffs seeking the chattels and corn in the lands of her own inheritance, as well as Saher's, to meet his debts to the king. She had to provide security that she would reply for those debts at the Exchequer.[100] Nor had Saher assigned Margery her dower before he

[95] See the instruments printed in A. L. Raimes, 'The Family of Reymes of Wherstead in Suffolk', *Suffolk Institute of Archaeology and Natural History*, xxiii (1939), 110–11. Lord Edward's dispositions for the safeguarding of his children against possible eventualities—their rights to the throne included—and the governance of his interests are the best-known arrangement: *Dipl. Docs.* i. no. 423.

[96] *Feet of Fines for the County of York, 1272–1300*, ed. F. H. Slingsby (Yorkshire Archaeological Soc., Rec. Ser. 121; 1956), 5; *CIPM* ii. 445–7. The action may have been preliminary to levying a fine, however.

[97] R. W. Eyton, *Antiquities of Shropshire*, 12 vols. (London, 1853–60), x. 274–5, prints the deed fragment.

[98] For Robert's problems, see *CFR 1272–1307*, p. 48; *CIMisc.* i. 298; *CCR 1272–9*, p. 203; *CPR 1272–81*, p. 81. For Roger, see *CFR 1272–1307*, p. 21; *CIMisc.* i. 295. For Hawise, see *CFR 1272–1307*, p. 4.

[99] *RF* i. 167. He committed the manor of Bampton for this purpose.

[100] Ibid. 50–1, 52.

departed, a cause for further anguish. In July 1220 she was given temporary custody of the manor of Eynesbury until the matter was settled.[101] Many a crusader's widow found herself facing considerable hardship through this failure to assign dower in advance.[102] In some instances this led to unseemly family rows at law, as when Eleanor, Roger de Leyburn's widow, clashed with their son William in 1271.[103] Furthermore, a crusader's cash raising, combined with legal pitfalls, might even bring his widow to the point of destitution. Before the justices in Wiltshire in 1249 Christiana, Walter le Tayllur's widow, claimed a messuage in New Sarum as her dower against Matthew de Caddeleigh. He claimed he ought not reply because Walter, before going to the Holy Land, sold him the property, Christiana being present and agreeing to the sale. The point was that the custom of Salisbury held that if a woman, in full court with her husband, consented to a gift or sale by him, she lost any claim to it as dower. Christiana, poor woman, could not deny that she had indeed been present so she lost the case.[104] Plainly, the different demands upon a departing crusader were not always compatible, consequent difficulties resulting either from lack of care or foresight, hurried arrangements, perhaps from a calculated gamble, or simply bad counsel.

Raising of Cash

Since crusades were extremely costly enterprises, it is scarcely surprising that the thirst of many crusaders for cash was virtually unquenchable. Every crusader needed a fund of cash for his journey and he needed it quickly, so the urgent quest for coin was inevitably central to a crusader's preparations, but the exact expedients to which he might resort naturally depended upon his precise circumstances: for example, his position in society, the quantity and nature of his assets and his ability to realize them, his relationship to his lord and others who might be prevailed upon to make gifts or loans against his passage. Each case has to be investigated in its own terms.

101 *RLC* i. 424b. Saher's executors, however, were to have the earl's chattels to execute his will.

102 See e.g. the enforced ejection of Hugh de Dutton's widow from the manor of Nesse, which she entered on Hugh's death, of which neither she nor any other on her part was to have the administration: *RF* i. 356.

103 See the enrolled agreement in PRO, E 368/45, m. 3.

104 *Civil Pleas of the Wiltshire Eyre, 1249*, ed. M. T. Clanchy (Wiltshire Rec. Soc. 26; 1971), Nos. 465, 483. For a case involving a widow higher up the social scale, see *CRR 1237–42*, p. 320, for the difficulties of Petronilla de Thony in 1241, when seeking dower in property farmed by Ralph de Thony in 1239.

Crusading lords especially felt the pinch because the onus of crusade financing rested primarily upon them as a function of the way in which crusading forces were organized around them. Some support, of course, was available in the form of grants from the crusading subsidy, at least from the 1230s, and from the proceeds of taxation in the case of the 1270–2 crusade,[105] but even those fortunate enough to receive a direct grant, or to be subsidized indirectly by a greater lord, found in practice that the moneys went only a little way towards meeting their expenses.[106] Moreover, the English lord could not expect a customary aid from his men as of right towards his crusade, unlike his thirteenth-century French peers at least.[107] Cap. 15 of Magna Carta (1215) laid down that the king would not give his permission for a lord to take an aid from his free men except to ransom his body, knight his eldest son, and marry his daughter once. Admittedly, this clause was omitted from later reissues, and the king frequently made requests to lords' tenants to grant aids on a variety of grounds thereafter.[108] Only four men, however, are known to have secured royal letters requesting their respective tenants to make an aid specifically to meet crusade expenses, all of them before the definitive reissue of Magna Carta of 1225: Bishop Sylvester of Worcester in 1218, and John de Lacy, Philip Daubeny, and Bishop Peter des Roches in 1221.[109] Thereafter there is silence in the records, although in some cases requests for aid which do not specify the reason for debt may hide a crusader's petition. Quite possibly a lord's tenants might have willingly made a contribution to his crusade expenses, but, if so, there is apparently no record of any such grant.[110] Any conclusions *e silentio* can only be tentative, but it does not appear that aids contributed significantly towards financing English crusades in the thirteenth century, excepting the extraordinary grant of a twentieth towards Lord Edward's crusade. Neither can tallage be shown to have made a contribution, but the picture concerning tallage is even less clear than for aids.[111]

[105] See above, pp. 148–51.

[106] See above, p. 138. For evidence that estimates of anticipated expenses were made, see amongst other examples the papal licence for Richard of Cornwall to commute his vow in 1238 for 'expensas quas esses in eundo ad Terram Sanctam, morando ibidem et redeundo facturus': *Reg. Gregory IX*, No. 4608.

[107] See, briefly, on the French crusading aid, F. Lot and R. Fawtier, *Histoire des institutions françaises au moyen âge, II* (Paris, 1958), 169–71.

[108] J. C. Holt, *Magna Carta* (Cambridge, 1965), 204, 219; and see S. Painter, *Studies in the History of the English Feudal Barony* (Baltimore, 1943), esp. pp. 141–6.

[109] *PR 1216–25*, pp. 143, 284, 318–19.

[110] On the question of voluntary aids, see in particular S. K. Mitchell, *Taxation in Medieval England*, ed. S. Painter (New Haven, 1951), esp. pp. 159–64; G. L. Harriss, *King, Parliament and Public Finance to 1369* (Oxford, 1975), chs. 1, 2.

[111] See Painter, *Studies*, pp. 168–9; C. Stephenson, 'The seignorial tallage in

Crusaders could nevertheless look more broadly to men of their connection for support. The notion that all members of a particular social group should club together and subsidize the pilgrimage or crusade of one of their number is perhaps best indicated by the rules and regulations of confraternities and gilds. Amongst other examples, the gild of Tailors, Lincoln, stipulated that any member making a pilgrimage to the Holy Land was to receive one penny from every gildsman and gildswoman.[112] Crusaders beyond the confines of such institutions could look to their kinsmen, their friends, and their lords. Lord Edward received 100*m*. 'de dono nostro' from Archbishop Walter Giffard of York in 1270, the closeness of their relationship amply evidenced by Walter's appointment as one of Edward's attorneys for the crusade.[113] At the other end of the social scale was one Spiriot 'setting out to the Holy Land', who was granted 12*d*. of the archbishop's alms, whilst Richard de Glen, 'our beloved *familiaris*', received 20*m*.[114] It was probably these grants to which Walter referred in a letter to the papal Curia around this time, in which he moaned of the financial burdens under which he laboured. Amongst other things he specified 'donaria quae sibi [Lord Edward] ac aliis nobilibus consanguineis ac aliis cum eo transeuntibus oportuit exhibere . . .'[115] Considering especially his financial hardship at the time, it seems that Walter felt obliged to support crusaders of his acquaintance and connection. Perhaps too, as a churchman, he was particularly moved by the notion long stressed by the papacy: that since the crusade concerned the common good of the Church, all should contribute to the cause. And, so far as ecclesiastical support more generally is concerned, it is interesting to see Gregory X deploying another argument when he urged the English prelates to grant aid to Lords Edward and Edmund. He recalled the accumulated debt of the English Church to the princes' ancestors, appealing to the prelates to remember how they had endowed their churches and fortified them with liberties and privileges. Should they not now respond generously and sustain the princes in their moment of such great need as a result of their crusade expenses?[116]

England', in *Mélanges d'histoire offerts à Henri Pirenne par ses anciens élèves et ses amis à l'occasion de sa quarantième année d'enseignement à l'Université de Gand*, 2 vols. (Brussels, 1926), 465–74.

112 *English Gilds: The Original Ordinances of more than One Hundred English Gilds*, ed. L. T. and T. Smith (Early English Text Soc., os 91; 1870), 182.

113 *The Register of Walter Giffard, Lord Archbishop of York, 1266–79*, ed. W. Brown, (Surtees Soc. 109; 1904), 123.

114 Ibid. 116, 124; and see *CPR 1266–72*, p. 589, for Richard's crusader status.

115 *Reg. W. Giffard*, pp. 244–5. From the Cinque Ports Edward received a 'courteous' sum in aid of his crusade. This would not serve as a precedent: *CPR 1266–72*, p. 513.

116 *Reg. W. Giffard*, p. 41; *Reg. Gregory X*, No. 920.

The royal records of Henry III's long reign provide the best illustration of how one man responded to the crusades of men of his connection, even if the scale and substance of his largesse was exceptional by virtue of the unique powers of royal lordship. To his close kinsmen Henry was naturally most generous. For Richard of Cornwall's crusade the English Jewry were 'persuaded' to grant 3,000*m.* in 1237; a further 1,000*m.* owed to the king by certain Jews of York was made over in June 1240.[117] Shortly before Richard's departure 400 lb. of wax were delivered to him, and £100. which he had lent Henry for work on the Tower was repaid.[118] In 1238 arrangements were made for the shipment to Paris of 6,000*m.*, from the proceeds of the thirtieth of 1237, against Richard's departure.[119] He was further granted the profits of justice arising from the eyre in Cornwall, Devon, Rutland, the honour of Berkhampstead, and probably elsewhere, between 1238 and 1241.[120] To speed him on his way, Henry instructed the bailiffs of Dover to find sufficient ships to convey Richard, William Longespee, and their households across the Channel in June 1240.[121] Once Richard had sailed, Henry quickly intervened to hasten the collection, and then dispatch to Acre, of the proceeds from redemption of vows and legacies to the Holy Land granted to the earl by Gregory IX.[122]

Royal servants could also hope for assistance. Very occasionally wardships and other sources of revenue were made available. In July 1270, for example, Roger de Clifford, close to the Plantagenets for so many years, was granted the first wardship falling to the king worth £500. per annum; he could even have it if it was worth £700. It was explicitly because he was going to the Holy Land with Edward and as a reward for his past service that this particularly generous grant was

[117] *CPR 1232–47*, p. 173; *CR 1234–7*, p. 410; *CR 1237–42*, pp. 4, 197. The claim of R. C. Stacey, *Politics, Policy, and Finance under Henry III 1216–1245* (Oxford, 1987), 126, that Henry III spent over 16,000*m.* in support of Richard's crusade, Feb.–May 1238, is without firm foundation. It is very unlikely that Henry III had the crusade in mind when he dispatched 8,000*m.* to aid Frederick II in 1238. The 1,500*m.* granted to the Hospitallers, and the 750*m.* for Baldwin II of Constantinople, had nothing at all to do with Richard's crusade.

[118] *CLR 1226–40*, pp. 448, 472.

[119] *CPR 1232–47*, p. 222.

[120] *CR 1237–42*, pp. 58, 70, 233, 259, 270.

[121] *CLR 1226–40*, p. 473. Henry also paid for his return passage across the Channel: *CLR 1240–5*, p. 103.

[122] *CPR 1232–47*, p. 250. The probability must be that Richard received even more than the above: the Close Rolls for 23 Henry III, and the Patent Rolls for 23 and 24 Henry III are lacking. Lords Edward and Edmund also did well some thirty years later: see in particular *CPR 1266–72*, pp. 540, 546; *CLR 1267–72*, pp. 123, 126; PRO, E 368/44, m. 5d. Edmund received the profits of justice from various sources: see above, ch. 4 n. 165.

made.[123] More typical were outright grants of cash in hand. Amaury de St Amand, for example, royal steward and a key royal agent in the Welsh Marches in the 1230s, was granted 50*m.* of the royal gift in 1240 to make his crusade.[124] The grant may stand for countless others made throughout Henry III's reign, but particular mention may be made of the liberality afforded Philip Daubeny, that long-serving and faithful servant of John and Henry, since it is especially revealing of the workings and extent of royal largesse in the matter of the crusade. Philip himself received gifts of at least £120., 500*m.*, and 50*m.* respectively towards his crusades of 1222, 1228, and 1235.[125] But in addition his standing in the king's regard helped to secure support for some of those accompanying him. Thus in 1235 Oliver Daubeny, his nephew and anyway a royal household knight, received 100*s.*, whilst William de Chany, one of Philip's own knights and also a kinsman, was granted 5*m.*[126] Henry further agreed to the transfer of a royal wardship from Philip to William, at Philip's instance we are told.[127] To be associated with a crusader who basked in his lord's favour was plainly advantageous.

Loans were also employed. Guy de Lusignan was one such, receiving a loan of £1,000. before he sailed for the Holy Land in addition to gifts and privileges.[128] He was further licenced to raise another loan of £1,000. on the security of his annual fee from the king, and 1,000*m.* at least was duly raised from a merchant of Siena.[129] Exchequer fees were an obvious source of ready cash for their recipients who were setting out on crusade, and Henry commonly obliged by allowing advances, especially in the earlier part of the reign. Typically, the advance was for two or more years, presumably for the anticipated absence of the crusader.[130] Those lower down the hierarchy of royal service were not forgotten either. Amongst other examples, Semeine,

[123] *CPR 1266–72*, p. 448.

[124] *CLR 1226–40*, p. 471. He was one of those privileged few to receive Lord Edward from the baptismal font in 1239: Paris, *CM* iii. 540.

[125] *RLC* i. 511, 515; *CLR 1226–40*, pp. 93, 249.

[126] *CLR 1226–40*, p. 249.

[127] *CPR 1232–47*, p. 107.

[128] *CPR 1247–58*, p. 84. A loan of 500*l. tournois* in Dec. 1247, to buy war-horses, was probably part of his preparations. He also received £900. of Henry's gift in 1247, to be paid by Michaelmas. For these and further grants, see ibid. 4, 504, 511; *CR 1247–51*, pp. 27, 218, 326; *CLR 1245–51*, pp. 159, 160, 167; and H. S. Snellgrove, *The Lusignans in England, 1247–1258* (Albuquerque, 1950), esp. pp. 36–7.

[129] *CPR 1247–58*, p. 5; *CR 1247–51*, p. 218.

[130] Amongst other examples, Robert de Musters received £60. against his annual fee of £20. for three years in 1239: *CLR 1226–40*, p. 379. Less frequently, it appears, crusaders might quitclaim their annual fees in return for a sum of cash. In Apr. 1270, e.g., Guy de Lusignan quitclaimed his £300. fee, and all arrears thereof, for 1,000*m.*: *CPR 1267–72*, p. 121; *CPR 1266–72*, p. 513.

the king's crossbowman from as early as 1220, was granted 10*m.* in aid of his crusade in 1233.[131] But generally men of the lower ranks only received satisfaction for the arrears of their wages: thus, on 27 May 1270, urgent instructions went to the Exchequer that the arrears of a group of six sergeants be paid by 15 June at the latest, lest their journey to the Holy Land with Edward be retarded through default of the cash, some £120. in all.[132]

It may well be that those crusaders associated with the king enjoyed a significant advantage over others when it came to crusade financing.[133] However, the case of Archbishop Walter Giffard is suggestive of the kind of support which might be offered by others, and it is most likely that great lords of immense wealth, like Richard of Cornwall—whom we know to have been sympathetic to the crusading cause—played an especially significant role in subsidizing the crusades of their followers and acquaintances.[134] But whatever sources of external support the crusader might look to, and from whomsoever, he still needed to fall back upon his own resources and ingenuity to raise the cash he required.

One obvious response was to secure repayment of any outstanding debts, and the records are sprinkled with references to crusaders seeking satisfaction.[135] Some secured the debtor's recognizance that he would repay the sum within a fixed term or by agreed instalments, and occasionally the term was fixed with a crusading passage specifically in mind.[136] Inevitably, others were obliged to begin legal proceedings. Just two days after receiving his crusader's protection in January 1271, Urian de St Petro appointed attorneys to

[131] *CLR 1226–40*, p. 217.

[132] *CR 1268–72*, pp. 195–6. This followed previous orders, not acted upon, to supply the cash to pay the men by 28 Jan. 1270: PRO, E 159/44, m. 9d.

[133] Edward I could be as generous as his father. See e.g. his grants and debt quittances to Otto de Grandson in 1290: *CPR 1281–92*, p. 373; *CCR 1288–96*, pp. 78, 80. See also PRO, E 36/201, pp. 56, 61, 64, for grants in the year 1286–7 to three of his palfreymen, a knight, and a citizen of Bayonne going to the Holy Land, illustrating the social range of the recipients of his largesse. But it looks as if Henry was altogether more generous. Fewer men went East during Edward's reign, but M. C. Prestwich, 'Royal patronage under Edward I', in P. R. Coss and S. D. Lloyd (eds.), *Thirteenth Century England I: Proc. of the Newcastle upon Tyne Conference 1985* (Woodbridge, 1986), 41–52, has stressed Edward's limited liberality in comparison to other rulers.

[134] For Richard, see above, pp. 92–3. He certainly lent money to Edward and Edmund in 1271: *CPR 1266–72*, pp. 545, 567.

[135] The task for some was eased by the consideration that it was held to be only proper for debtors to make restitution to crusaders before their departure. See *Royal Letters*, i. 15, for Earl William de Warenne's observations on this score in 1218.

[136] In 1282 Hugh Despenser agreed to pay the final instalment of a debt of 1,600*m.* to Earl William of Warwick by Midsummer 1283, if William went to the Holy Land, and by Martinmas following if not: *CCR 1279–88*, p. 184.

recover a debt of 50*m*.[137] Whilst William Belet, who had previously bound Ralph Perot to pay £40. by 1 November 1269, brought a plea of debt against Ralph in early 1270 upon his default.[138] The king himself might intervene on behalf of those close to him. Thus, in January 1250, Henry III instructed Aymer de Valence to pay 2,000*m*. to Geoffrey de Lusignan, in aid of his crusade, in four instalments beginning at Easter.[139] There can be little doubt that references in the royal records evidence but a fraction of a much wider process of debt recovery stimulated by crusading passages.

Another source of cash lay in the ardent desire of men eager to secure a particular right or privilege in the crusader's gift. Townsmen, especially, seem to have been quick to appreciate the chance offered to them by the prospect of a crusade. So far as their liberties are concerned, many towns had already secured their charters by 1216, but one thirteenth-century example of how a crusade might occasion a grant is supplied by the burgesses of Poole. It was probably in 1248, when preparing for his second crusade, that William Longespee granted them a charter for 70*m*.[140] There were other possibilities. In 1239, when actively preparing his crusade, Simon de Montfort ceded rights of pasture to the burgesses of Leicester, and it was probably around the same time that he granted them further privileges for which they were prepared to pay.[141] Altogether different was the situation of London after its involvement in the barons' wars. Lord Edward received custody of the city in Lent 1269, the elective mayoralty and sheriffs suspended, but at Whitsun 1270 Edward restored the offices. Their liberties recovered, the citizens granted him 500*m*. towards his crusade expenses, surely a quid pro quo occasioned by Edward's forthcoming passage.[142]

Burgesses could also gain from their crusading lord's connections with the Crown. It was at Ellis de Rabeyn's instance that his burgesses of Lyme were granted immunity in February 1270 from being attached for any debts of which they were not sureties or principal debtors in England, Ireland, and Gascony.[143] Others could benefit too. In July 1270 William de Valence secured quittance

[137] *CR 1268–72*, p. 392.

[138] PRO, KB 26/197, m. 16d. William also brought a plea of debt against Richard de Seyton and his wife: ibid. m. 20.

[139] *CPR 1247–58*, p. 58.

[140] See J. Sydenham, *The History of the Town and County of Poole* (Poole, London, 1839), 78–80, and 154–7, where the charter is printed.

[141] Bémont, *Simon de Montfort*, tr. E. F. Jacob, pp. 21–2.

[142] *De ant. leg.*, p. 124; G. A. Williams, *Medieval London: From Commune to Capital* (London, 1963), 240–2. Edward not only raised a tidy sum but further defused political tension by this act.

[143] *CPR 1266–72*, p. 412.

from the tallage of 1260 for himself and his men of Corbridge.[144] Adam of Jesmond was one of a number of crusaders, shortly before departure, to secure the grant of a weekly market and annual fair on one or more of their manors.[145] On the day that Gerard de Grandson received his crusader's protection, he and his men were exempted from murage and other customs in the city and county of Lincoln.[146] There can be little doubt that in such cases the beneficiaries paid handsomely for the crusader's efforts on their behalf. One notorious individual who certainly seized the chance presented by a crusader's thirst for cash was the monk of Reading, excommunicated and imprisoned by the abbot for his many arrears as cellarer and custodian of manors. In 1270 he sent £100. of silver, 'de mammona iniquitatis', to Lord Edward for his crusading passage, that he might escape the abbot and his prison. Plainly grateful in his need, Edward instructed on his departure that the monk be provided with a vacant abbey or priory, and in due course he was sent to be presented as prior of Dover.[147]

Useful though they were, such sums were by their nature windfalls. A more certain source of cash lay in the realization of assets and the disposal of property, and it was through these measures that the crusades exerted probably their greatest impact on local society and economy. The subject is a vast one which cannot be explored comprehensively here. Instead, attention will centre upon the crusading lords, for whom, predictably, the evidence is most satisfactory.

Although recourse might be had to all manner of disposable assets, it seems that the sale of timber was a typical and especially favoured device for raising cash. It was an asset easily and quickly realized, timber being a commodity in great demand. One of Richard of Cornwall's first moves on taking the Cross in 1236 was to cut down and sell his woods,[148] and it was perhaps his appreciation of their value which led Richard in 1270 to amend the terms of his award between Gilbert de Clare and Lord Edward whereby Gilbert might sell the woods, vines, and parks appurtenant to his castles of Tonbridge and Hanley against his own passage. This was in response

144 *CPR 1266–72*, p. 204.

145 In Adam's case, Cramlington (Northumberland): see *CCh.R 1257–1300*, p. 149. In May 1227, on the eve of his departure, Peter des Roches even secured a mandate to the sheriff of Berkshire to cause the bishop's market at Wargrave to be proclaimed and held notwithstanding the prohibition of markets instituted since 1216 in the county: *RLC* ii. 185; *CLR 1226–40*, p. 31.

146 *CPR 1266–72*, pp. 513, 588.

147 'Continuation' of Gervase of Canterbury, *The Historical Works of Gervase of Canterbury*, ed. W. Stubbs, 2 vols. (RS; 1879, 1880) ii. 267–8.

148 Paris, *CM* iii. 368–9.

to Gilbert's petition on the matter.[149] A further indication of the contemporary perception of the value of timber to help meet crusade expenses is Simon de Montfort's sale in 1240 of the greater part of his forest of Leicester.[150] In 1261 or 1262 Simon sought to relate this sale to his financial hardship at the time, especially since Henry III raised 500*m*. from his estates on the eve of his departure on crusade: 'I had to sell part of my land and of my forest.'[151] Only in the case of Simon de Montfort do we have any inkling of the sums raised (according to Paris it was about £1,000[152]), but there is every reason to think that sales of timber contributed significantly to the finances of many. Dossat has shown how important they were to Alphonse of Poitiers, for one, in the preparations for his second crusade.[153]

If, in their disposal of timber, crusaders were following a conventional resort of men in need,[154] then nor were they doing anything out of the ordinary in gaging, leasing, or selling their estates. The evidence for this activity is varied: surviving deeds, or more commonly copies thereof, in episcopal registers, cartularies, and other archives; occasional seigneurial licences for tenants to alienate property; accounts of transactions in chronicles, letter-books, and other sources. The bulk of the material lies in the Crown's records: licences for tenants-in-chief to alienate properties held of the king, and action consequent to unlicensed alienation; royal confirmations and enrolments of transactions; final concords made between the crusader and another party before the royal justices. Since much of this material does not in fact relate to properties held in chief, we are probably aware of only part of a much wider process of alienation. In many cases we know only a few dry facts, to the effect that a crusader alienated a certain property, or was licensed to do so, but fortunately there is sufficient material of a much more informative kind to allow some assessment of the impact of crusaders upon the contemporary land market.

It appears that crusaders did not alienate their lands permanently through sale if they could avoid it. Conscious of their duties to family

[149] See my 'Gilbert de Clare, Richard of Cornwall and the Lord Edward's Crusade', *Nottingham Medieval Studies*, xxx (1986), 58, 60, 65, 66.

[150] 'Dunstable', p. 151; Paris, *CM* iv. 7.

[151] C. Bémont, *Simon de Montfort, Comte de Leicester* (Paris, 1884), 333; tr. Jacob, pp. 60–1. The crusader might otherwise farm his woods. See e.g. Paris, *CM* v. 98, for Roger de Monte Alto. If woods were held in fee, then licence to alienate was required. See e.g. *RLC* i. 383b, 385, 404b, 429, for the case of Enjuger de Bohun and then of his executors, 1218–20.

[152] Paris, *CM* iv. 7.

[153] Y. Dossat, 'Alfonse de Poitiers et la préparation financière de la croisade de Tunis: Les ventes de forêts (1268–70)', in *Septième Centenaire de la mort de saint Louis* (Paris, 1976), 121–32.

[154] See Painter, *Studies*, pp. 165–6, on timber sales; and specifically for the Crown's sales, C. R. Young, *The Royal Forests of Medieval England* (Philadelphia, 1979), esp. ch. 6.

and lineage, most preferred to raise the money they needed through loans raised on the security of their property, but some were either driven to sell or for some reason preferred this course of action. Since the resulting transactions led to permanent changes in the tenurial structure it is appropriate to consider these initially.

The case of Hugh fitzHenry, a Berkshire knight, is especially illuminating of the social and economic context within which such transactions occurred. Hugh took the Cross in or before 1247, becoming a Templar at some point thereafter. He determined to sell his entire estate, even though he had a son. His one hide in Hill in Leamington Hastings (Warwickshire) held of Abingdon abbey and rated as one-sixth of a knight's fee, was sold to Robert Hastang for 24*m.*, the transaction completed by a final concord of 3 February 1248.[155] In Oxfordshire he held a half fee of the honour of Wallingford.[156] By final concord dated 23 June 1247, Hugh recognized the property, a carucate in Alkerton and two virgates in neighbouring Balscott, to be the right of Master Simon de Walton, who gave him 300*m.*[157] These properties were 'outliers', for the core of Hugh's holdings lay in Berkshire, and it was from their sale that he did best.[158] Abingdon abbey, the lord of Hugh's fee, eventually purchased the estate, but since the convent consequently found itself in serious difficulties, the detailed account of the transaction was entered in one of the abbey's letter-books at the end of the thirteenth century as a cautionary tale which future monks should heed.[159]

Hugh's one knight's fee[160] comprised, we are told, two carucates and a virgate in Abingdon,[161] a hide in Dry Sandford with eight

155 *Warwickshire Feet of Fines*, ed. E. Stokes *et al.* (Dugdale Soc. 11, 15, 18; 1932–43), No. 679. See further *Fees* ii. 1278. The abbot acknowledged Hugh's right in 1245–6, probably a preliminary to the sale: *Warwickshire Feet of Fines*, No. 625. Hugh's hide, with that held by William de Curly, comprised the Abingdon estate in Hill. Significantly, Robert Hastang, once he secured Hugh's holding, married William's co-heiress and united the two parts of the abbey's estate in his own hands: *VCH Warwickshire*, vi. 152.

156 *Fees* ii. 823.

157 *Feet of Fines for Oxfordshire, 1195–1291*, p. 141. On 27 May 1247 Hugh, for 11*m.*, secured Michael de Wroxstane's quitclaim to the Balscott property, plainly in preparation for its sale to Simon: ibid. 141. Simon, notable curialist, justice, and future bishop of Norwich, was active in the land market. More particularly, he already held land in Balscott and neighbouring Tysoe (Warwicks.) before this purchase: *VCH Oxfordshire*, ix. 177.

158 On at least one occasion Hugh was identified as 'of Abingdon': *Fees* ii. 823.

159 BL Cotton Julius A. ix, fos. 166–7; printed, but with important omissions and misreadings, in R. Hill, *Ecclesiastical Letter-Books of the Thirteenth Century* (privately printed, no date), 269–72, and briefly discussed on p. 36.

160 See *Fees* ii. 845, 848; *VCH Berkshire*, iv. 342. The letter-book reveals that Hugh also enjoyed liberty of waif and stray, observing that it was in repentance for his savage exploitation of this right that he took the Cross.

161 Confirmed by PRO, CP 25(1), 8/16, No. 1.

virgates in East Drayton, one virgate in Babhanger, along with a spacious house, moated and defensible, in Abingdon itself. It was an attractive estate, as the letter-book account is at pains to stress, compact and centred on Abingdon, lucrative and well-appointed. When news reached the royal court that Hugh had put it on the market, several nobles eagerly sought to purchase, notably Richard of Cornwall. To the monks the prospect of a great magnate ensconced on their fee at the heart of their territorial interests was understandably alarming. The obvious response was to buy out Hugh themselves, but there was insufficient cash to hand and a substantial number of the brethren argued against purchase largely for this reason. They were overruled, however, the greater part of the obedientiaries being swayed by the political argument for purchase. Abbot John de Blosmeville gave his consent,[162] and the monks dispatched as their proctor to negotiate with Hugh one Nicholas of Headington, a man 'exceedingly skilled and circumspect in secular affairs'. The deal hammered out must have taken the monks' breath away: they were to purchase for little short of 1,000*m.*, Hugh insisting that he be paid in new not old coin, the coinage being renewed in 1247.[163] The cash was to be delivered by Easter 1248, 300*m.* to be paid by Michaelmas 1247 when the convent should take seisin of the estate. As security, the convent's vill of Shippon was to pass to Hugh until Easter 1248, but if the convent then defaulted in its payment the vill would remain forever to Hugh or his assigns. In addition, the convent was to find, at their expense, a chaplain to celebrate for Hugh's soul for ten years, and to institute two corrodies, for Hugh and his son, for the rest of Hugh's life.

There were further murmurings within the convent over these terms, but the transaction went ahead and Prior Walter duly arrived with other brothers at Hugh's house in Abingdon on Michaelmas Day to take seisin. But Hugh, 'intending to frustrate their intention had prepared a great party [*magnum convivium*] for several knights and magnates in his house that day'. This was seen as a ruse, Hugh seeking to delay livery by claiming that the demands of hospitality prevented him from handing over seisin until the following day. Clearly suspecting that Hugh was about to back out, and perhaps arrange another deal, the monks dispatched their proctor Nicholas to expostulate with Hugh. All day they argued, Nicholas countering Hugh's 'lies and falsehoods' and doubtless threatening legal action as well. Around Vespers, with his guests arriving for dinner and a great

[162] *Chronicle of the Monastery of Abingdon, 1218–1304*, ed. J. O. Halliwell (Berkshire Ashmolean Soc.; 1844), 6.

[163] The kitchener was bound to supply the cash, duly weighed and computed.

crowd gathering outside to hear and see what was happening, Hugh at length gave in and handed over seisin, making his way with his household and his 300*m.* to his new temporary home at Shippon, just one mile from Abingdon. The party had to be cancelled, the assembled company, naturally disappointed, seemingly dispersed with some difficulty by the monks. Following this scare the abbot and convent wisely determined to procure 'to their greater security' a final concord in the royal court, but this only added to the considerable costs. That concord, made before the justices in eyre at Gloucester, reveals that Hugh acknowledged his property in Abingdon to be the right of the abbot for 800*m.* of silver.[164] Since it does not concern Hugh's other properties elsewhere in Berkshire, the total price for Hugh's fee, as the letter-book indicates, was probably not far short of 1,000*m.*,[165] leaving aside the costs incurred in the provision of a chantry and two corrodies, the fees of Nicholas of Headington, the journey to Gloucester for the final concord, conveyance charges, and other overheads.

In consequence the monks got into serious difficulties. They were obliged to mortgage some of their lands and rents, and borrowed what they could.[166] Special internal arrangements had to be made. Hugh's estates were initially made over to the kitchener along with the debt, but the burden was too much and had to be shared, notwithstanding the marked development towards departmental autonomy at Abingdon which had led, in 1245, to the regulation that no office was to bear the burdens of another. Each obedientiary was now obliged to make regular payments against the debt, and only by cutting back on the normal expenditure of each.[167] The monks were in for a lean time, and it is no wonder that the affair of Hugh

164 Dated fifteen days after Easter 1248: PRO, CP 25(1), 8/16, No. 1. It is a measure of their sense of urgency and suspicion of Hugh that the monks did not wait until the justice, Roger Thirkelby, was at Reading and Wallingford in July 1248. He was at Gloucester, 3 May–4 June. See *Records of the General Eyre*, ed. D. Crook (PRO Handbook, No. 20; London, 1982), 106–10. Like the monks of Westminster, e.g., those of Abingdon probably did not enter the crucial stages of a final concord until they knew they could complete payment, and Hugh doubtless wanted to see the colour of his money. See B. Harvey, *Westminster Abbey and Its Estates in the Middle Ages* (Oxford, 1977), 174.

165 *Chron. Abingdon*, p. 6, says the cost was 900*m.* A much later list of Abbot John's acquisitions states that 800*m.* was the price for *all* Hugh's lands in Abingdon and Berkshire: 'A Chronicle Roll of the Abbots of Abingdon', ed. H. E. Salter, *EHR* xxvi (1911), 731.

166 The squeeze was such that they had even to refuse a loan to their daughter-house of Colne. See BL Cotton Julius A. ix, fo. 159.

167 See G. Lambrick, 'Abingdon Abbey Administration', *Journ. of Ecclesiastical Hist.* xvii (1966), esp. pp. 172–3, and citing Chatsworth MS 71E, fos. 8v. 63v. The letter-book also mentions this exceptional arrangement.

fitzHenry's estate was entered in the letter-book many years later. Its effects and its memory remained to needle.

Hugh's various sales suggest a great deal concerning the context in which crusaders' transactions need to be firmly located and they suggest something of the potential scale of their consequences. Most obviously, they underline the buoyancy of the English land market in the thirteenth century, suggesting that as a general rule crusaders found little difficulty in finding a buyer, even if the asking price, as in the case of Hugh's Berkshire lands, was seemingly very high. According to Guibert of Nogent, writing of the First Crusade, prices then fell spectacularly as so much property came on to the market in the stampede to sell.[168] Very different was the situation in thirteenth-century England with its developing land-hunger, a feature too well-known to require further discussion here. Crusaders, as others, could expect to do well when disposing of their land. It was a seller's market.

One reason why Hugh was able to drive so hard a bargain for his Berkshire estates was that there were prospective buyers other than the monks. Richard of Cornwall alone is named, but the letter-book explicitly states that others were interested. The entire tale suggests that Hugh was playing off potential purchasers against one another, open to bid and counterbid, with Earl Richard and the monks the front runners. Local political and tenurial factors go a long way towards explaining why these two in particular should have been the leading bidders. Richard of Cornwall, of course, was an active land speculator and shrewd businessman with a vast income at his disposal, but in this case his appetite was doubtless whetted by his tenure of the honours of Wallingford and St Valery and his other landed interests in Oxfordshire, Berkshire, and Buckinghamshire.[169] Hugh's estates would nicely expand those regional holdings. As far as Abingdon abbey is concerned, Hugh was one of their tenants and at Abingdon, as at many other houses, a policy of recovering fees became established in the thirteenth century.[170] Under Abbot John de Blosmeville, Abingdon recovered not only Hugh's fee, by far the

[168] 'Gesta Dei per Francos', *RHC Occ.* iv. 140–1; see also Orderic Vitalis, *Historia Ecclesiastica*, ed. M. Chibnall, 6 vols. (Oxford, 1969–80), v. 16.

[169] See Denholm-Young, *Richard of Cornwall*, esp. pp. 162–70; and S. Raban, 'The Land Market and the Aristocracy in the Thirteenth Century', in D. Greenaway *et al.* (eds.), *Tradition and Change: Essays in Honour of Marjorie Chibnall* (Cambridge, 1985), 244–6, for Richard's dealings.

[170] See e.g. Harvey, *Westminster Abbey*, ch. 6, esp. pp. 164–7; S. Raban, *The Estates of Thorney and Crowland: A Study in Medieval Land Tenure* (Cambridge, 1977), esp. pp. 62–5; E. King, *Peterborough Abbey, 1086–1310: A Study in the Land Market* (Cambridge, 1973), esp. pp. 53–4, 66–9; J. A. Raftis, *The Estates of Ramsey Abbey: A Study of Economic Growth and Organization* (Toronto, 1957), ch. 4.

largest single purchase, but the manor of Sunningwell, properties in Abingdon, and other holdings.[171] A variety of motives lay behind the acquisitions of Abingdon as other houses, but in the case of Hugh's property we find firm evidence of what may be suspected in other instances: action consequent to the fear of encroachment by outsiders on the fee of a monastic overlord.[172] The argument that prevailed in the initial conventual discussions was to the effect that the monks had no choice but to put in a bid for Hugh's lands, considering their location and the regional influence of Richard of Cornwall, even though it was a high-risk venture and sufficient liquid cash was not to hand. Indeed, the letter-book reports that it was Richard whom 'all the English [or at least the monks] feared more than his own king'. For the monks the stakes were high, and a potent symbol of Richard's regional power, Wallingford castle, was uncomfortably close to them. It is not without interest that they do not seem to have been concerned to purchase Hugh's holdings further away in Oxfordshire and more distant Warwickshire.

If the purchaser felt no pressing necessity to buy up a crusader's property, he nevertheless bought for precise reasons. Most commonly, it seems, he saw the opportunity to expand his interests in the locality concerned. Master Simon de Walton's purchase of Hugh fitzHenry's holding in Balscott is one of many examples.[173] Since Simon thereby became lord of the manor it may also be that the curial cleric's desire to improve his social standing was involved. It was a personal consideration that certainly played a part in the landed investments of many merchants and bourgeoisie, and a crusader's needs could provide an opening for such men.[174] Again, consolidation of local interests was often involved. For instance, the London mercer Philip le Taylor began to acquire property beyond the city walls in 1259.[175] He already held a stake in the neighbouring Crayford and Erith areas of Kent when he purchased the manor and church of Crayford, and leased that of Erith, from the crusader John de St John in 1270.[176] Across the Thames, in Essex, Robert de Munteny's sale in late 1269 of Elmdon manor for £200. to John le Ferun, another Londoner, expanded John's prior interests in the county.[177]

171 'A Chronicle Roll', ed. Salter, p. 731.

172 See esp. S. Raban, *Mortmain Legislation and the English Church, 1279–1500* (Cambridge, 1982), esp. pp. 147–8.

173 See above, p. 184.

174 On this point, concerning Londoners, see Harvey, *Westminster Abbey*, p. 190.

175 For Philip, see Williams, *Medieval London*, pp. 59, 332–3.

176 Ibid., and specifically *CPR 1266–72*, p. 464; *CR (Suppl.) 1244–66*, p. 44; *CIMisc.* i. 227. For his Kentish property on his death, see further *Select Cases in the Exchequer of Pleas (1236–1304)*, ed. H. Jenkinson and B. Formoy (Selden Soc. 48; 1931), 155.

177 PRO, KB 26/191, m. 6d (enrolment of the deed). Robert regained Elmdon,

In the case of Richard Hotot's purchase of Clapton (Northants.) local and personal factors of a different complexion were involved, for Clapton had been part of the ancestral Hotot estate, fragmented between 1175 and 1190, which Richard was determined to restore. Between 1213 and his death, *c.*1250, he spent 413*m.* acquiring the different fragments. 170*m.* went on Clapton, purchased from Hugh de Ringstone in 1242. Hugh had previously bought the holding for 100*m.* in 1240 from his brother Ralph, who accompanied Richard of Cornwall's crusade. In 1248 Richard Hotot finally attained his goal by purchasing the remaining portion of the original estate for 160*m.* The especial point of interest from our perspective is that a crusader's need for cash initiated further transactions which allowed one man to realize his dream, and Richard Hotot's preparedness to pay 170*m.* for a property which just two years earlier had sold for 100*m.* indicates his determination in the matter.[178]

In none of the cases mentioned thus far is there any suggestion that the crusader concerned was experiencing anything more than short-term liquidity problems arising out of a crusading intention, but Nicholas de Sifrewast was probably one whose affairs were in crisis before he took the Cross. For him, perhaps, the prospect of the crusade prompted him to sell up and to enter the service of Thomas de Clare.[179] There are definite hints of difficulties. In 1239 his father William leased the manor of Aldworth for twenty years, and since we also know that William was indebted to a Jew in 1255, it looks as if Nicholas inherited some financial difficulties.[180] In 1257 Nicholas leased Hampstead Norreys for eight years.[181] Men did not usually lease their patrimonies as a matter of course, and Hampstead Norreys indeed appears to have been the *caput* of the Sifrewast estates.[182] It is not without significance that in 1272–3 Nicholas found himself hard pressed to pay back to the king debts outstanding from his period of shrieval office.[183] Thomas de Clare's territorial ambitions probably explain why Nicholas and he came together, for in the late 1260s

enfeoffing his son with it before his death in 1287: *CIPM* ii. 386. For John's further interests in Essex, acquired before his death in 1273, see *CCR 1272–9*, pp. 26, 50–1; *CIPM* ii. 278–9, 510; *CFR 1272–1307*, p. 7.

178 For the details of this intriguing tale, and comment, see 'Estate Records of the Hotot Family', ed. E. King, in *A Northamptonshire Miscellany*, ed. E. King (Northamptonshire Rec. Soc. 32; 1983), 8–9, 44–6; id., *Peterborough Abbey*, pp. 47–8.

179 See above, pp. 122–3, for details of their transactions, 1269–70.

180 *CCh.R 1226–57*, p. 245; *VCH Berkshire*, iv. 3; *CR 1254–6*, p. 102.

181 *CPR 1247–58*, p. 546; *VCH Berkshire*, iv. 73.

182 It was known as Hampstead Syfrewaste in the 13th and 14th c. before its descent to the Ferrers and then Norris families: *VCH Berkshire*, iv. 74.

183 PRO, E 368/45, mm. 6, 6d; E 159/47, m. 12d. The sheriff of Oxfordshire and Berkshire was to inquire in full county court of Nicholas's goods in the county.

and early 1270s Thomas was developing an interest in the Thames valley. In particular, West Drayton and East Ilsley came into his hands on the fall of the Montfortian Gilbert de Elsfield; he was still in possession in 1276.[184] Thereby, Thomas and Nicholas became neighbours, for East Ilsley is only some five miles from Hampstead Norreys, four miles from Aldworth, and two from Compton. If Nicholas was indeed in difficulties then here was a splendid opportunity for Thomas to step in and consolidate his local interests, as well as securing the services on crusade of one of those nine knights for whom he had contracted with Lord Edward. Nicholas, on the other hand, had hooked a powerful patron whose star was then in the ascendant, nationally and locally. This looks to have been a deal which admirably suited the immediate circumstances and likely prospects of both parties.

One further case may be cited here because it demonstrates how investment in a crusader's property could effectively initiate a long-term policy on the part of the purchaser which would stretch over centuries. By 1252 the bishops of Norwich already held some land in Terling (Essex), but their interest was limited.[185] In May 1270, however, the crusader Herbert de Boyville was licensed to sell his manor of Terling to Bishop Roger Scarning (1266–78), who presumably saw possibilities there.[186] For 500*m.* he bought out Herbert's interests, some 160 acres of arable and 30*s.* rent, rated at one fee.[187] The Neketon family held rather more in Terling, some 360 acres forming two fees held of the Bruces and one in chief.[188] By 1276 William de Neketon seems to have been in some financial trouble, and this may have been the opportunity for Bishop William Middleton (1278–88).[189] In 1280, at any rate, he bought out John de Neketon, William's heir.[190] Thereby the bishops of Norwich dominated the locality and continued to expand. By 1318 they held not just Terling but a slice of the

[184] *CCR 1272–9*, p. 270; *VCH Berkshire*, iv. 342. For his interest in nearby Checkendon (Oxfordshire) by 1268, see *A Descriptive Catalogue of Ancient Deeds in the Public Record Office*, 6 vols. (London, 1890–1915), A 3181. He seems to have sold out to Adam de Stratton: ibid. A 3178–80.

[185] *CCh.R 1226–57*, p. 404. In the survey of 1232–3 they did not apparently possess property there: see *Fees* ii. 1464.

[186] *CPR 1266–72*, p. 425.

[187] *CCh.R 1257–1300*, p. 146, which reveals that Herbert was granted this by John Mauduit. The inquisition post mortem for John's father in 1261 reveals the details of the property: *CIPM* i. 136.

[188] *CIPM* i. 166, but compare with *Rotuli Hundredorum temp. Hen. III et Edw. I in tur. Lond. et in curia receptae scaccarii West. asservati*, 2 vols. (Record Commission, 1812, 1818), i. 161.

[189] *CCR 1272–9*, p. 430.

[190] *CPR 1272–81*, pp. 374, 375, 422; *CCR 1279–88*, p. 89.

honour of Hatfield Peverel, of which Terling was once part, and the neighbouring manor of Legh.[191] In Terling itself they continued to hold three knights' fees as late as 1428.[192] A crusader's need for cash had provided the occasion for a policy of expansion in the chosen area.

The local and personal factors considered above help to explain why ecclesiastical corporations, *curiales*, merchants, and local knights and magnates were chiefly the purchasers of crusaders' properties. Otherwise, crusaders' kin appear often to have stepped in, an arrangement which kept the property in the family whilst providing the crusading member with badly needed cash.[193] These considerations also help to explain why the Jews, a traditional source of capital, apparently played only a minor role in crusade financing. But there were other reasons. It is well known that in the course of the thirteenth century their capacity to act in the land market was seriously affected by savage royal taxation and repressive legislation. More specifically, at times of crusade, we find the king earmarking block sums to subsidize the expeditions of his kinsmen, as we have seen.[194] Under such immediate and intense pressure it may be that many Jews were unable to meet the needs of lesser crusaders.[195] In any event, they must frequently have been ruled out by limiting clauses which prevented the individual from conveyancing property to Jews or others, and the lord of a fee might certainly intervene to prevent the entry of an individual to whom he was opposed.[196] Perhaps, too, the Jews became a less attractive proposition with the development of the more sophisticated international banking system and the rise of the merchant bankers of Italy and elsewhere. From the 1240s and 1250s these bankers came to play an increasing role in the world of finance, and with their local branches in both the West and Latin East many

191 *CCh.R 1300–26*, p. 395.

192 *Feudal Aids: Inquisitions and Assessments Relating to Feudal Aids, with Other Analogous Documents Preserved in the PRO, 1284–1431*, 6 vols. (London, 1899–1920), ii. 215.

193 Amongst many examples, Ralph de Cotun sold North Gosforth (Northumb.) to his brother John before departing on Lord Edward's crusade: *CIPM* i. 234–5.

194 See above, p. 178, for Richard of Cornwall. Lord Edward was granted 6,000*m.* from the Jews in 1270: *CPR 1266–72*, pp. 545–6.

195 The almost complete silence on this score in the records would suggest that they were not, but since unredeemed gages leave most trace it may be that Jews, at least in the first half of the century, played a larger role than now appears, their crusader clients duly redeeming their pledges. See *CPR 1232–47*, p. 173; *CR 1234–7*, p. 410, for Henry III's distraint of Jews as early as Nov. 1237 for payment of the 3,000*m.* granted to Earl Richard.

196 On these points, see Raban, *Mortmain Legislation*, esp. pp. 12–13; P. A. Brand, 'The Control of Mortmain Alienation in England, 1200–1300', in J. H. Baker (ed.), *Legal Records and the Historian* (London, 1978), 29–40.

English crusaders saw the advantages of making over some of their property or revenues to them against loans.[197] It is well known that Lord Edward's crusade came to depend in large measure upon the facilities provided especially by the Riccardi of Lucca.[198]

Thus far we have been concerned largely with sales of property, but the evidence suggests that crusaders avoided selling up permanently if they could, certainly their entire estates.[199] Naturally, they preferred instead to borrow, meeting a short-term need by a short-term expedient. It was, then, in the short-term that crusaders exercised the greatest impact on the land market and the tenurial structure as they strove to raise cash. Forms of gage and lease were the devices chiefly employed. Mortgage was apparently the most common form of pledge used by twelfth-century crusaders, but the evidence suggests that in England, at any rate, the vifgage was altogether more typically employed by crusaders in the thirteenth century.[200] Part of the explanation may be that only a few potential mortgagees could raise the cash in one sum at short notice without risking financial difficulties for themselves; if they could, then outright purchase would have been a better investment from their point of view. Equally, mortgage must often have appeared unattractive to the crusader since, following his expenditure on campaign, he then needed to raise the cash to redeem his pledge whilst out of possession of the property in question, risking possible forfeiture if he could not. The vifgage was more appealing because, in contrast to mortgage, the principal was repaid from the revenues of the property whilst in the gagee's hands. It may be that the developing land-hunger in thirteenth-century England frequently enabled crusaders, as suppliers of land, to secure the more favourable terms of the vifgage.

[197] Guy de Lusignan is an early example. See above, p. 179. The military orders, of course, continued to be important.

[198] See esp. R. W. Kaeuper, *Bankers to the Crown: The Riccardi of Lucca and Edward I* (Princeton, 1973), esp. pp. 78–82, and more generally on their wider role in England, pp. 1–35. Their role in crusade financing, as in other ventures, may have been much greater than appears, for there survive no recognizances of debt from certain clients known otherwise to have had significant dealings with them: ibid. 31, and n.

[199] That such a drastic step was considered unusual, at least at this social level, is indicated by Henry III's observation, in a grant of wardship to Robert Charles in 1270, that he had been moved to pity to hear that Robert had sold 'totam suam terram' to accomplish his crusade: PRO, C 66/88, m. 13.

[200] The thirteenth-century crusader utilized that device appearing most appropriate in the particular circumstances. This is quite apparent from the terms of royal licences to alienate. For the twelfth century, see esp. G. Constable, 'The Financing of the Crusades in the Twelfth Century', in B. Z. Kedar *et al.* (eds.), *Outremer: Studies in the History of the Crusading Kingdom of Jerusalem Presented to Joshua Prawer* (Jerusalem, 1982), esp. pp. 72–3. The subject of financing through gage and lease requires further study. I am indebted to Dr Paul Brand for his help and suggestions.

So far as leases are concerned, it would at first sight appear that such transactions scarcely met the crusader's need to secure lump sums quickly, but it is probable that in many instances the lease in fact disguised a loan. Too much should not be made of formal distinctions, especially since it was not uncommon in lease arrangements for an initial premium to be paid as well as a regular rent. In any event, much would depend upon the respective circumstances and bargaining positions of borrower and creditor. Typical of the sort of arrangement which often resulted was that agreed in May 1235 between Philip Daubeny, preparing for his last crusade, and Bishop Jocelin of Bath and Wells. Philip pledged his manor of South Petherton (Somerset) to Jocelin for £280, but even the bishop of one of the wealthiest of English sees could or would not find the sum at once. He made an initial payment of £120. and bound himself to pay £40. per annum for four years from Easter 1239. He paid a further £40. for all the corn sown in the manor in 1235, and £19. 10*s*. for rent of the manor in the current term and its stock. Jocelin would receive all profits and issues until the end of the seven-year term, but if he received more than £280. he was to apply the surplus to support of the Holy Land or other pious uses. This looks to have been a considered compromise, combining elements of lease and vifgage, in which the crusader's need for ready-cash was tempered by the circumstances of the creditor. Typically, one or other of the parties secured royal confirmation of the transaction.[201]

With lease and gage as well as sale much of the interest lies in explaining why a crusader disposed of one property but not another, and why the investor concerned was interested in securing that particular estate.[202] There was a clear tendency to dispose of acquisitions or 'outliers' rather than the core of the patrimony: a wife's marriage portion, estates granted in wardship or otherwise *de ballio*, or holdings which had come to the family only recently.[203] This pattern, reminiscent of the monastic benefactions of many, is what we would expect of a society in which men tenaciously retained their

201 *CCh.R 1226–57*, p. 203. Jocelin later demised the manor to his steward, William de Wethamstead, for the term. Should William die, the dean and chapter of Wells were to have it for the remainder of the term: ibid. 226. This, and other examples, suggests active speculation on the part of the lessee or gagee.

202 Judging from royal licences to alienate, only a very few considered alienating all their properties, and even then these were probably precautionary general licences against possible future need.

203 Limiting clauses, again, prevented alienation of some properties. The 1270 crusader, William le Graunt, for example, granted the manor of West Allington (Leics.) for life in 1268, was prohibited from alienating the whole or part of it, permanently or in the short term, to hinder its reversion to the grantors: *Final Concords of the County of Lincoln 1244–1722*, ed. C. W. Foster (Lincoln Rec. Soc. 17; 1920), 226.

patrimonies if they could.[204] Philip Daubeny may be cited by way of general illustration. In 1235 he was granted royal licence to alienate four manors held of the king, each *terra Normannorum*, a recent acquisition, but he is not known to have realized cash from his other estates.[205] Moreover, study of the local tenurial context of each reveals that it was alienated to a creditor already with some interest in the area. South Petherton was snapped up by Bishop Jocelin of Bath and Wells, as we have seen.[206] Chewton (Som.) was leased by Hugh de Vivona, whose landed power was concentrated in the county.[207] Bampton (Oxon.) went to the abbot of Cirencester.[208] Wighton (Norf.) was demised to Richard of Cornwall, whose East Anglian interests were centred not so far away on Eye.[209]

However much cash a crusader might cobble together himself, or receive from other sources, he could still find himself hard pressed during a crusade and upon his return. At Acre in 1271–2, for example, Roger de Clifford, Hamo Lestrange, John de Grailly, John de Vescy, Otto de Grandson, John II of Brittany, and Lord Edmund were obliged to borrow considerable sums from creditors locally on the security of their landed estate.[210] Not surprisingly, Payn de Chaworth and Robert Tiptoft, at least, were lobbying the papal Curia by 1273 for moneys owed from the Holy Land subsidy, whilst Edward and Edmund petitioned for clerical subsidy in England almost as soon as Gregory X ascended the papal throne.[211] Edward's finances were such that he was compelled to turn to his subjects for a grant of taxation; meanwhile creditors such as the Riccardi of Lucca kept him

[204] See e.g. the comments, and material cited, of E. Mason, 'Timeo barones', pp. 70–1.

[205] *CPR 1232–47*, pp. 74, 93. Significantly, Philip had already utilized these manors, in different ways, for his crusades of 1221 and 1228: *PR 1216–25*, p. 287; *PR 1225–32*, p. 175.

[206] Philip was granted the manor by 1223, receiving it in fee in 1231: *RLC* i. 534, 541b, 554; *CCh.R 1226–57*, p. 142. He used it first to support his nephew Ralph, and initially was licensed to pledge it to him in Feb. 1235, before then alienating it to Bishop Jocelin: *CPR 1232–47*, p. 93; *CR 1234–7*, p. 25.

[207] *CPR 1232–47*, p. 106. On Philip's death, it seems, Hugh was granted it *de ballio: CCh.R 1226–57*, p. 211. Philip had an interest there in 1221. It was assigned to him, with others, in 1223; by 1226–8 he appears in sole possession: *RLC* i. 550b; *PR 1216–25*, p. 287; *Fees* i. 377.

[208] *CR 1234–7*, pp. 68, 390; *Fees* i. 614. Philip was granted it in 1227: *CCh.R 1226–57*, p. 54.

[209] *CR 1234–7*, p. 385; *Fees* i. 591. Philip was granted it in 1227: *CCh.R 1226–57*, p. 57; *Fees* i. 388, 402.

[210] *The Antient Kalendars and Inventories of the Treasury of His Majesty's Exchequer*, ed. F. Palgrave, 3 vols. (London, 1836), 80. At Lord Edward's instance, the master of the Temple paid their debts. Edward bound himself as security, along with their lands, against repayment to the Temple.

[211] *Reg. Gregory X*, Nos. 232, 920; *Reg. W. Giffard*, p. 41.

solvent.[212] Edmund was one crusader whose attorneys acted to raise more cash during his absence. It was doubtless Queen Eleanor who requested Henry III to grant 2,600*m.* to his use in 1271.[213] She certainly arranged a loan of 1,000*m.* from Richard of Cornwall, and by her powers as Edmund's attorney pledged Leicester, with the borough farm, and other properties to Edmund of Cornwall for four years in July 1272 for 3,500*m.*[214] Once again a crusader's kin are found rallying around in a time of need.

There are some spectacular examples of immediate poverty resulting from a crusade. For instance, Matthew Paris records that Guy de Lusignan arrived back in England from Egypt around Christmas 1250 in such straits that he travelled on foot and turned out of his way to beg hospitality from the abbot of Faversham. He requested the abbot to provide him and his few companions with horses to take them to London, declaring on oath that he would return the mounts. According to Paris, however, the despicable Poitevin returned neither thanks nor horses to his host.[215] Not for the first time Guy was able to sponge off his half-brother. Within days Henry III was arranging emergency relief for Guy, including four manors in wardship.[216]

Guy's immediate plight was real enough, but there is no indication that it was anything more than short-term. How different was the predicament of Thomas de Fenwick, a Northumbrian knight, upon his return from Lord Edward's crusade. Shortly before his departure Thomas leased his manors of Fenwick and Matfen for six years to Richard de Middleton, but we learn that in October 1272 Thomas and his men had lately ejected William, Richard's son and heir, from Fenwick.[217] Perhaps Thomas wanted his home back, but other evidence reveals that he was in financial difficulties. In 1274, for 70*m.* borrowed from Alan de Swinburn, he conveyed to the lender four of his men, their chattels, and land, in Great Heaton. In the same year he conveyed a further two carucates to Alan, for £100. 'which he has given me in my great necessity'. Ultimately, by final concord in Michaelmas Term 1275, he acknowledged Alan's right to the entire

[212] See above, p. 145, and n. 150.

[213] See above, ch. 4 n. 165.

[214] *CPR 1266–72*, p. 566; PRO, C 66/90, m. 7. The terms of the pledge are slightly misrepresented in *CPR 1266–72*, pp. 668–9. Attempts were also made to secure a loan of £3000. from the goods of Richard of Cornwall: *Register of Bishop Godfrey Giffard, 1268–1301*, ed. J. W. Willis-Bund, 2 vols. (Worcestershire Hist. Soc.; 1898, 1902), i. 51.

[215] Paris, *CM* v. 204. The sheriff of Kent received 20*m.* in compensation for the assistance he gave to Guy on landing, partly confirming Paris's tale: *CR 1247–51*, p. 326.

[216] *CPR 1247–58*, pp. 83, 84.

[217] *CPR 1266–72*, p. 683.

manor, with appurtenances.[218] Thomas died shortly afterwards, his property, apparently, by now mostly sold or leased.[219] There is seemingly no indication that he faced financial crisis before his crusade.

It may be suspected that many more found themselves obliged to act like Thomas, for there are plenty of recorded debts owed by returned crusaders. Rarely, however, can it be positively demonstrated that the motive for alienation was the need to raise cash to pay off debts incurred specifically by reason of crusading. It looks further as if the exercise of royal patronage, as in the case of Guy de Lusignan, or other support from kinsmen, friends, or lord frequently helped many over the worst. This would help to explain why alienation of property by returned crusaders did not occur as frequently or to the extent as may have been expected. Alexander de Balliol, for example, had returned from the East by February 1272. His elder brother Hugh had meanwhile died in 1271, leaving Alexander his heir. In February 1272 Henry III, responding to Alexander's urgent request that he be put in seisin of his lands, regretted that this could not be done immediately since the inquisition and extent of Hugh's lands had not yet been completed, but he obliged him to the extent of instructing that the inquisition be completed hastily, that the escheator answer to Alexander for all the issues of his lands, and that Alexander be allowed to sow and cultivate his estates before livery.[220] Within a month Alexander was seised, and Henry graciously pardoned his relief fine.[221] Alexander was obviously feeling the pinch, and Henry responded as far as custom and procedure allowed. That Alexander was married to Eleanor of Geneva, a close relation of the queen, doubtless had something to do with it, but more important was the lobbying which Lord Edward is said in the royal letters to have done on Alexander's behalf.

Alexander's finances remained precarious. In 1275 he owed 200*m.* each to William de Valence and Master Roger de Seyton, in 1276 a debt of £80. 3*s.* 8*d.* to two Florentine merchants, and in 1278 a further 110*m.*[222] In 1278 he also found himself pressed to pay £300. still owing from the relief fine of his brother Hugh.[223] It is not

[218] J. Hodgson, *A History of Northumberland*, 7 vols. (Newcastle, 1820–58) II, i. 212–13; III, ii. 1–3; National Register of Archives, *Swinburne (Capheaton MSS)*, Part I (1962), pp. 88, 92.

[219] *Northumbrian Pleas from De Banco Rolls 1–19*, ed. A. H. Thompson (Surtees Soc. 158; 1950), 80–1.

[220] *CPR 1266–72*, p. 628; *CIPM* i. 270, for the inquisition.

[221] *CR 1268–72*, p. 472.

[222] *CCR 1272–9*, pp. 248, 251, 431; *Calendar of Documents Relating to Scotland Preserved in the Public Record Office*, ed. J. Bain, 4 vols. (Edinburgh, 1881–8), ii. 26.

[223] *Cal. Docs. Rel. Scotland*, ii. 26.

surprising, then, that he leased his manor of Whittonstall (Northumb.) and other properties in 1272, nor that he alienated the rent of his mill at Bywell, on the Tyne, before July 1275.[224] But he and his family were fortunate, because Edward I partially came to the rescue on Alexander's death in 1278 by granting very reasonable terms for the payment of his debts to the Crown, his friends Otto de Grandson and the Lord Edmund apparently using their influence.[225] No extensive sale or lease of assets, it appears, was ever necessary, and the records do not suggest that his son John was in any great difficulty after Alexander's death. Finally, it should be stressed that Hugh, whom Alexander succeeded, was already in great debt to the king when he died in 1271.[226] It is a warning that we should never assume that a crusader's debts on his return were necessarily a sole consequence of his crusading, nor that any subsequent property transactions were prompted by his expenses on crusade. Each case must be investigated in its own terms if we are to appreciate a crusader's acts, both before and after his expedition.

224 Hodgson, *Hist. of Northumberland*, VI, 52 n.; *CCR 1272–9*, p. 200.

225 *CFR 1272–1307*, pp. 105, 106. In 1277 he was allowed temporary respite for payment of those debts: *CCR 1272–9*, p. 379.

226 See esp. *RF* ii. 532–3.

6

HENRY III, EDWARD I, AND THE CRUSADE

HAD either Henry III or Edward (as king) departed on crusade, he would undoubtedly have led a considerable number of his subjects beneath his banner, by virtue of the immense influence which the king could exert in thirteenth-century England. This consequence of the king's position in society was fully recognized by the inhabitants of the Latin East, their Eastern allies, and the papacy;[1] however, despite their persistent and intensive lobbying, and the positive declarations of both kings, neither Henry nor Edward set out personally on crusade. This failure requires explanation, not least because of its direct bearing upon the overall level of English participation in the crusade during their reigns. The following discussion aims largely to provide a framework within which each king's responses to the crusade should be located, and suggests that political considerations of some complexity provide much of the explanation, especially with regard to Henry III's second, controversial vow of 1250, around which much of the discussion revolves.

It is doubtful if Henry or Edward ever considered the crusade simply with concern for the fate of the Holy Land and their own souls in mind. For Plantagenets who were also kings in an intensely competitive Western political scene, the crusade and the crusading vow possessed much wider significances. As Plantagenets, first, both must have been acutely aware of dynastic precedents, especially that set by Richard I on the Third Crusade. His deeds were naturally a source of great pride, and both Henry and Edward doubtless basked in the reflected glory of their illustrious predecessor. The poem in praise of the young Edward I, for example, explicitly compares him to the Lionheart; Edward indeed 'shines like a new Richard', and it was Richard the crusader which the poet clearly had in mind.[2] John of Howden goes further in his *Rossignol*. He associates Edward's name not only with the crusading deeds of Richard (and those of Robert

[1] See above, esp. pp. 31, 85–92, 105–6.

[2] *The Political Songs of England, from the Reign of John to that of Edward II*, ed. T. Wright (Camden Soc. os, 6; 1839) 128, l. 6. It was apparently composed before Edward's return to England from the Holy Land.

Curthose), but also with those of such famous figures as Godfrey de Bouillon, Bohemund I of Antioch, Tancred, and Louis IX, and the feats of heroes of epic and romance.[3] However, dynastic precedent was something of a two-edged sword. Although it added lustre and prestige to the dynasty's name and inflated the pride of its later members, it also imposed a certain burden of emulation. Henry III was left in no doubt of this, both popes and Eastern princes seeking unambiguously to engage his honour as a member of the Plantagenet line and successor, more specifically, to Richard I. It was incumbent upon him to seek to emulate the deeds of his noble ancestors.[4]

That Henry was proud of those deeds, and eager to emphasize the prestige they imparted, is indicated by the works which he commissioned by way of commemoration. On 5 June 1251 he ordered Edward of Westminster to cause painting of the 'history of Antioch in the chamber of the king's chaplains in the Tower of London'.[5] Next day, the sheriff of Hampshire was instructed to arrange the painting of Rosamund's Chamber in Winchester castle with the same subject.[6] Shortly after, as part of the works in progress at Clarendon, the sheriff of Wiltshire was ordered to paint in the king's chamber under the chapel 'the story of Antioch and the duel of King Richard'.[7] Yet a fourth Antioch chamber was being painted simultaneously in the palace of Westminster.[8]

The 'duel of King Richard' clearly refers to the single combat in which he was supposed to have fought Saladin, an accretion to the Lionheart's legend which Henry evidently wished to celebrate. Apart from the painting, tiles almost certainly depicting the duel were found *in situ* at Clarendon during excavations in 1936, whilst the famous decorated tiles of Chertsey which illustrate the combat were very probably produced under Henry's influence.[9] The 'story of Antioch' is problematical. Borenius, quite reasonably wishing to see a

[3] L. Stone, 'Jean de Howden poète anglo-Normand du XIIIe siècle', *Romania*, lxix (1946–7), esp. pp. 509–13, lines 3969–4048. See also J. Vale, *Edward III and Chivalry: Chivalric Society and its Context* (Woodbridge, 1982), 20–1.

[4] See above, pp. 32–4.

[5] *CR 1247–51*, p. 454.

[6] *CLR 1245–51*, p. 358.

[7] Ibid. 362.

[8] *CR 1247–51*, p. 464. Henry cannot have been alone in commissioning such works. Humbert of Romans, for one, noted that the decoration of nobles' palaces with paintings of the deeds of warriors of old was customary: *Tractatus Solemnis Fr. H. de Praedicatione Sanctae Crucis*, ed. P. Wagner (Nuremberg, *c.*1495), cap. 16. As exempla they led men to fight the Saracens, he thought. Wall-hangings doubtless depicted similar scenes, but very little survives for the 13th c. Some fragments may depict holy warriors. See A. G. I. Christie, *English Medieval Embroidery* (Oxford, 1938), 65, 141–2.

[9] See, now, E. S. Eames, *Catalogue of Medieval Lead-Glazed Earthenware Tiles in the Department of Medieval and Later Antiquities, British Museum*, 2 vols. (London, 1980), i. 144–5, 192–3. See ibid. 193–4, for other combat tiles almost certainly depicting crusaders, some related closely to the Clarendon tiles.

connection with Richard, considered that it concerned events of the Third Crusade, but this is very unlikely, since Antioch, as he recognized, 'was not one of the main pivots of action', and Richard went nowhere near it.[10] More probably, Henry had in mind events of the First Crusade and the deeds of Robert Curthose, duke of Normandy, his ancestral kinsman. C. W. David showed that Robert rapidly became a legendary crusading hero in the twelfth century, the memory of his supposed exploits remaining strong throughout the thirteenth.[11] Naturally, he was celebrated most enthusiastically by Anglo-Normans, many writers regarding him as the pre-eminent crusade leader. He may even have been the hero of a lost Anglo-Norman epic cycle.[12] Here it will suffice to note that Robert emerged as the hero of the battle of Dorylaeum, 1097, and was developed as the triumphant victor of Kerbogha, the crusaders' greatest foe, in single combat at Antioch: in Anglo-Norman eyes the First Crusade equivalent to Richard's legendary duel with Saladin. It was probably this episode which Henry commemorated in his Antioch chambers.[13] Whether Henry sought otherwise to commemorate the crusading deeds of members of his dynasty is not clear.[14]

As members of a noble dynasty with a reputation to respect and nurture, Henry and Edward could not ignore the crusade in an age which regarded combat with the infidel as an admirable means of winning prestige and honour, for their line as well as themselves. But they were also crowned kings with a peculiar dignity to uphold, and kings above all men were under a moral prescription to sustain the interests of Christendom. The point was widely aired in the thirteenth century, and even if it was theoretical it was no less influential for that.[15] Moreover, crusading kings could expect to improve their

[10] T. Borenius, 'The Cycle of Images in the Palaces and Castles of Henry III', *Journ. of the Warburg and Courtauld Institutes*, vi (1943), 45. He omits the painting in Rosamund's Chamber, Winchester castle.

[11] C. W. David, *Robert Curthose, Duke of Normandy* (Cambridge, Mass., 1920), pp. 190–202.

[12] G. Paris, 'Robert Court-Heuse à la première croisade', *Comptes Rendus des Séances de l'Académie des Inscriptions et Belles-Lettres*, xviii (1890), 190–215.

[13] Curthose's legend was probably fostered by the Plantagenet kings. Wace, e.g., highlights Robert's supposed role on crusade in his *Le Roman de Rou*, commissioned by Henry II. It is noteworthy, considering his close connections with the royal court, that John of Howden refers explicitly to Robert's deeds at Antioch in his *Rossignol*.

[14] I know of no evidence that Edward I acted in similar fashion, but Edward II commissioned paintings of the life of Edward I in 1324, for the lesser hall of Westminster palace, which possibly included scenes of his crusading adventures. The wars of Edward I were included in scenes of the king's life commissioned by Bishop Walter Langton for the episcopal palace, Lichfield: R. A. Brown, H. M. Colvin, and A. J. Taylor (eds.), *The History of the King's Works, I : The Middle Ages* (London, 1963), p. 508; Vale, *Edward III*, p. 93.

[15] Among examples, see Honorius III's appeal to Henry III, 1223: *Reg. Honorius III*, No. 4262; *Foedera*, I. i. 172–3.

standing in the West, a point frequently stressed by popes in their appeals, none more succinctly than Innocent III in his exhortation to John in 1215:

although there is an almost countless host of crusaders manfully girding themselves to succour the Holy Land, all will look to you as a leader pre-eminent; and so the praise of your name will be spread more widely, and He in whose hands are kings and kingdoms in reward for your devotion will on earth secure and confirm the throne of your kingdom to you and your heirs, and in heaven the righteous judge will give you a crown of glory that fadeth not away.[16]

In the desperate circumstances of 1215 Innocent must have known that John would have been relieved to hear of these assurances, but contemporary appraisals of Richard I, Louis IX, or Edward I demonstrate that these were not empty pronouncements as far as the image of the *rex crucesignatus* was concerned. Innocent reflected the perceptions of an age. Not surprisingly, then, appeals from the East sometimes underlined the contribution of a crusading record to a king's reputation. In 1263, for example, the legate Thomas and his co-respondents vigorously stressed the fame and acclamation which would accrue to Henry, as a king, if he sent aid or, better still, hastened his own departure,[17] whilst in 1261 the bishop of Acre pandered to Henry's sense of his personal standing as well as his regal dignity by holding up the glorious prospect of his being considered a new Godfrey de Bouillon, should he provide support in such dark times.[18]

Behind such honeyed words lurked a further compulsion. Matters of honour and prestige, as these petitioners knew well, operated in a comparative framework, and ever since the precedent set by Louis VII and Conrad III on the Second Crusade it had become conventional for the crusader's badge to be included among the regalia of kings. The trend was given sharper point and political purpose by the rivalries between the royal houses themselves, and for this reason no king could with impunity allow his rivals to steal a march over him in expressions of commitment to the crusade. The point is well illustrated by the competition between the Plantagenet kings and their especial rivals, the Capetian kings of France. Their struggles took place as much over prestige and status as disputed territory and conflicting political goals, and kings of both dynasties seem to have approached the matter of the crusade with an eye to the potential political capital to be realized.

16 *CLI*, No. 1010; *Selected Letters of Pope Innocent III Concerning England (1198–1216)*, ed. C. R. Cheney, trans. W. H. Semple (London, 1953), No. 78.

17 *Dipl. Docs.* i. No. 385; *Anc. Corr.* 55. 2; *Foedera*, I. i. 395 (misdated).

18 *Dipl. Docs.* i. No. 343; *Anc. Corr.* 47. 27.

In one respect Henry III and Edward I were at a very marked disadvantage in this connection. They could boast of nothing comparable to the Capetians' past crusading record; leaving aside the crusades of Plantagenet cadets there was only Richard to set beside Louis VII, Philip II, Louis VIII, and then Louis IX before Edward's crusade of 1270–2. Moreover, the Capetians were heirs to the earlier record of the Merovingians and Carolingians in holy war, a point remorselessly pushed home in an interesting panegyric on the *virtù* of French kings up to and including Louis VIII.[19] The poet was particularly concerned to stress the long and proud tradition of royal participation in holy war. For him, combat with the infidel was an essential ingredient of regal dignity. Yet he passes over the deeds of Charlemagne and ignores the recent past crusades of Louis VII, Philip II, and Louis VIII; perhaps he felt they were too well-known to require special mention. He fastens instead upon the triumphs in holy war, historical or legendary, of earlier kings, especially those of Charles Martel and of the Merovingians, notably Clovis, Lothar, Dagobert, and Chilibert. This emphasis suited well the poet's overt attempt to demonstrate that through time the kings of England were totally eclipsed by their French rivals. The poem begins sharply:

> Honis soit li rois d'ingleterre!
> Rois francois ont faite mainte gerre
> As Sarrasins per lor vertu.

The figure of Charlemagne nevertheless towered over all others in the pantheon of French kings. It is well known that it was with him and his cult that the Capetians, his heirs, were most closely identified, and from this association that they derived so much of their lustre and prestige. Henry III's enthusiasm for the crusading deeds of Richard I has surely to be seen partly in this context. To whose memory could Henry otherwise appeal? Indeed, it is tempting to think that he positively fostered the cult of Richard partly in the attempt to set him up as a royal Plantagenet counterpart to the figure of Charlemagne. We may certainly see a connection with Henry's revival of the cult of Edward the Confessor and his veneration of St Edmund, king and martyr, the jewels in a rival pantheon of English royal saints whose names Henry recited on a famous occasion before Matthew Paris in 1257.[20] Here, at least, the king of England could compete with his Capetian rival on very favourable terms.

[19] BL MSS Harleian 4333, fos. 100v–101v, composed shortly after Louis VIII's death in 1226, and copied *c.*1250.

[20] Paris, *CM* v. 617. For another context see M. T. Clanchy, 'Did Henry III Have a Policy?', *History*, liii (1968), esp. p. 214. It is of considerable interest in the context of Capetian–Plantagenet rivalry that in 1254 Henry III displayed Richard I's shield at the Paris Temple: Paris, *CM* v. 480.

The honour of the realm and its subjects must also be taken into consideration, since royal crusades and crusading deeds touched the standing of a king's subjects by virtue of the commonly held notion that the holiness of a king reflects upon his kingdom.[21] Richard I himself drew out the point when he sought to take political advantage of Philip Augustus's withdrawal from the Third Crusade. From Jaffa in October 1191 Richard reported his own famous victory over Saladin's forces at Arsuf and then roundly condemned the Capetian for deserting the crusade: he had scandalously forsaken his vow against God's will, to the 'eternal shame of himself and his kingdom'.[22] If kings thought thus it is scarcely surprising that popes occasionally linked the prospect of a royal crusade with the honour which would accrue thereby to king and kingdom alike.[23] Since, moreover, the overall notion was seen to operate comparatively, it must have been extremely irksome for the king of England and his subjects, increasingly conscious of their 'national' identity, to know that the king of France was generally accredited by the mid-thirteenth century as 'most Christian king', his people the most devout.[24]

The operation of this compound of dynastic pride, regal dignity, and 'national' honour, set within an intensely competitive atmosphere, helps to explain the great pride and joy displayed by Henry III and Edward I in relics from the Holy Land which they acquired. None were more eagerly sought or highly valued than those associated with Christ himself, but in this connection the Plantagenets laboured under a marked disadvantage ever since Louis IX pulled off the greatest *coup* in the period under consideration. Between 1239 and 1241 he purchased various relics of the Passion from his impecunious kinsman, Baldwin II, Latin Emperor of Constantinople, the haul including a portion of the Cross, the Lance, the Sponge, and the Crown of Thorns, the *pièce de résistance*.[25] The relics dramatically boosted the prestige of Capetian monarchy and the pride of its

[21] See esp. J. R. Strayer, 'France: The Holy Land, the Chosen People, and the Most Christian King', in T. K. Rabb and E. Seigel (eds.), *Action and Conviction in Early Modern Europe* (Princeton, 1969), 3–16.

[22] Roger of Howden, *Chronica Rogeri de Houedene*, ed. W. Stubbs, 4 vols. (RS; 1868–71), iii. 129–30; also echoed in id. (attrib. Benedict of Peterborough), *Gesta Regis Henrici Secundi Benedicti Abbatis*, ed. W. Stubbs, 2 vols. (RS; 1867), ii. 182–3.

[23] See e.g. Innocent IV's responses to Henry III on hearing of his assumption of the Cross, 1250: *Foedera*, I. i. 272.

[24] As Strayer, 'France: The Holy Land', p. 6, observes, even Matthew Paris admitted this. See esp. Paris, *CM* v. 480, 606.

[25] For a list of Louis's acquisitions, and valuable discussion, see K. Gould, 'The Sequences *De Sanctis Reliquiis* as Sainte-Chapelle Inventories', *Medieval Studies*, xliii (1981), 315–41.

subjects,[26] and it is no wonder that Louis should have built Sainte-Chapelle specifically to house them.

An excellent measure of the contemporary estimation of the acquisition is provided by the *De Susceptione Coronae Spinae* of Gautier Cornut, archbishop of Sens, composed at Louis's request and delivered as a sermon on 11 August 1240, the anniversary of the translation of the Crown of Thorns.[27] Gautier highlights the inestimable honour and glory which the precious relic bestows on both king and kingdom. It is, he says, a cause of great joy to all, regardless of sex, dignity, and status, that France has been specially chosen to receive the Crown, it being Christ's will that it be translated from East to West, from Greece to France. Thus God 'terram nostram incomparabili thesauro ditavit, genti et regno nostro quasi summum post multos accumulavit honorem. Laetetur in iis sacris solemniis Ecclesia Gallicana, et tota gens Francorum . . .'

The balance of prestige between kings and kingdoms had been dramatically upset. Henry III, so sensitive in such matters, can only have been acutely conscious of the fact and determined to counter the French *coup*. The balance was partly redressed in 1247 when a vase containing some of the Holy Blood was presented to Henry by the community of Outremer.[28] To Henry it was a very important development; he would present his precious acquisition to his beloved Westminster abbey with all due reverence and solemnity. The day chosen for the grand event was, predictably, the Translation of Edward the Confessor (13 October), his dearest patron saint, and all magnates of the realm were summoned to witness in person so glorious and historic an occasion, in effect a celebration of English and royal honour. After devoutly keeping vigil, Henry himself bore the precious relic in liturgical procession from St Paul's to Westminster where he took it on a triumphant circuit around the church, the

[26] This was fully acknowledged by Paris, *CM* iv. 90–2, who regarded the Cross as taking pride of place. Gould, 'The Sequences', p. 334, draws attention to Innocent IV's bull of 1244, which equated the Crown of Thorns with the Crown of France. Some of the sequences composed for the reception of the Crown of Thorns echo this. The political implications are apparent.

[27] Established by N. de Wailly in 'Récit du XIIIe siècle sur les translations faites en 1239 et en 1241 des saintes reliques de la Passion', ed. N. de Wailly, *Bibliothèque de l'École des Chartes*, xxxix (1878), 401–15, who also printed an account of the reception of the other relics in 1241. Gautier's work is printed in *RHGF* xxii. 26–32. See ibid. xxiii. 399–400, for another account from Rouen closely based upon it. Extracts from twenty-six sources are in *Exuviae sacrae constantinopolitanae*, ed. P. Riant, 2 vols. (Geneva, 1877, 1878), ii. 241–59, a measure of the excitement and pride generated. See also Paris's account, in *CM* iv. 90–2.

[28] For what follows see Paris, *CM* iv. 640–4. The 1247 acquisition, compared to Louis's, was a poor showing. A portion of the Blood was but one of his acquisitions.

palace, and his own chambers, before reverently presenting it to his beloved Confessor.

Walter Suffield, bishop of Norwich, delivered a sermon that day extolling the virtues of the relic. Probably composed at Henry's request, it is of considerable interest in the context of thought which we have been tracing, for Walter observed that in possession of this great treasure England might experience as much glory and joy as did France in its acquisition of the Holy Cross. Moreover, it was on account of the great reverence and holiness of the king of England, known to be the most Christian of all Christian princes, that this priceless relic had been sent from Outremer, so that it might be honoured more in England than Syria, now almost desolate; for faith and holiness flourished in England more than anywhere else, as the world knew. Robert Grosseteste made much the same set of points in his own discourse on the Blood, but it is particularly significant, in the context of Anglo-French rivalry—both of peoples and kings—that he was at pains to stress that if the Cross, Crown of Thorns, and other relics of the Passion were holy on account of their contact with Christ's body, then how much holier was the Blood of the Saviour himself.[29] The English, then, were to understand that the relic acquired by their king outshone the collection amassed by Louis IX. Matthew Paris was surely correct to comment that in this business Henry was overtly following the example of Louis, his rival.[30] Indeed, it looks very much as if he was seeking to trump the Capetian in the game of international prestige.[31]

The process continued. In 1249 Henry presented to Westminster abbey a slab of white marble which bore the imprint of Christ's foot at the point of his ascension.[32] Not that other houses of the royal connection were forgotten: in 1277 Edward I donated a portion of the Cross to his own foundation of Vale Royal.[33] In 1282 Edward reverted to

29 Ibid. vi. No. 72.

30 Paris says he was present at Westminster and was instructed by Henry to record the events of that day lest they be lost to posterity. The Blood and the coronation regalia were the most precious in the Westminster collection. The Blood was promoted hard as an attraction to pilgrims: by 1272 some twenty-two prelates had offered indulgences. I am indebted to Miss B. F. Harvey for this information. The process began with Walter Suffield on the day of the presentation; he granted indulgence of six years and 140 days to those coming to venerate the Blood, according to Paris.

31 This is not to say that Henry's interest was purely political. His veneration of relics is well attested. Particular mention should be made of his interest in that other relic from the Holy Land, the Rood of Bromholm, for which see esp. F. Wormald, in 'The Rood of Bromholm', in *Journ. of the Warburg Institute*, i (1937–8), 31–45.

32 Paris, *CM* v. 81–2.

33 *Monasticon Anglicanum*, ed. W. Dugdale; new edn., ed. J. Caley, H. Ellis, and B. Bandinel, 6 vols. (London, 1817–30, repr. 1846), v. 74–6; further, *VCH Cheshire*, iii. 156–7. Edmund of Cornwall purchased another portion of the Blood in 1267; the cadet

Westminster, following a *coup de grâce* which reflected more upon king, realm, and subjects than on Plantagenet and dynasty. In the course of the second Welsh war he captured one of the most famous of Welsh relics, the Cross of Neath, which, like the Stone of Scone for Scotland, could be construed as symbolizing the vigour, pride, and very independence of the Welsh. In purely political terms, then, its capture by the conquering king of England was highly significant; no wonder that Edward should seek to make much of it, as he would of his possession of the Stone of Scone. However, the Cross of Neath was also a potent relic of some fame; brought from the Holy Land by a Welsh priest, it had performed many miracles. On 4 May 1285 Edward accompanied Archbishop Pecham in solemn procession from the Tower of London to Westminster abbey, where the Cross was ceremonially presented, to join Arthur's Crown, brought back from Wales in 1282. The subjugation of the Welsh to the successor of Edward the Confessor was symbolically complete.[34]

Lest the question of the crusade be lost in this fascinating interplay of honour and prestige, personal and dynastic reputation, and 'national' pride and rivalry, it should be remembered that participation in holy war/crusade was a central part of the claim of the kings of France to be considered as 'most Christian kings'. It was a reputation with which other royal dynasties had to live, and an accolade to which they had to respond. For Louis IX, the Sainte-Chapelle was to be the focus and very receptacle of those things which symbolized Capetian and French prestige, and Jordan has plausibly suggested that as a building it paralleled Louis's crusading zeal. Its very windows, depicting a pilgrim penitent, illuminated that *rex Christianissimus* in whose glory all his subjects could bask; the relics of the Passion it would contain acted as a symbol of the earthly Jerusalem which Louis, *crucesignatus* from 1244, sought to recapture.[35] Henry III intended Westminster abbey to be the great reliquary and necropolis of the Plantagenet kings of England, partly the functional counterpart

Plantagenet branch was not to be outdone. Significantly enough, he donated part of it to his father's abbey of Hailes on Holy Rood Day, 1270, shortly before his own departure on crusade: *Monasticon*, v. 686 n.

[34] Bartholomew Cotton, *Historia anglicana, necnon ejusdem Liber de archiepiscopis et episcopis Angliae*, ed. H. R. Luard (RS; 1859), 166; 'Waverley', pp. 401–2; 'Dunstable', p. 37; *Flores historiarum*, ed. H. R. Luard, 3 vols. (RS; 1890), iii. 59, 63; William Rishanger, *Chronica et annales regnantibus Henrico tertio et Edwardo primo*, ed. H. T. Riley (RS; 1865), p. 104; *Chronicon de Lanercost 1201–1346*, ed. J. Stevenson (Bannatyne Club, 1839), p. 112; 'Annales Londonienses', in *Chronicles of the Reigns of Edward I and Edward II*, ed. W. Stubbs, 2 vols. (RS; 1882, 1883), i. 93, a measure of the contemporary interest the acquisition generated.

[35] W. C. Jordan, *Louis IX and the Challenge of the Crusade: A Study in Rulership* (Princeton, 1979), 107–9.

of Sainte-Chapelle. If Branner is right, it was to be an architectural image of the king of England's prestige, underscored by the abbey's association with Edward the Confessor, its role as the coronation church, and its proximity to the royal palace of Westminster.[36] The decorative scheme of the complex is no less significant, and Henry's commissioning of one of his Antioch chambers for the royal apartments, when the king himself was *crucesignatus*, gains added interest as a result. Moreover, and this leads us directly back to the question of the contemporary crusade, Louis IX presented his relics of the Passion to the people in Sainte-Chapelle on the eve of his departure on crusade in 1248.[37] It was, surely, no coincidence that in March 1254 Henry III expressed his intention of dedicating his own new edifice of Westminster abbey, now fortified with relics, before he set out on crusade in 1256. The date was to be St Edward's Day 1255, when, he declared, he would publicly wear his Crown.[38] For both Henry and Louis the crusade could not be divorced from the wider image of the royal persona; there is no reason to suppose that Edward I thought very differently.

Neither Henry nor Edward, then, could simply ignore the crusade in this intensely competitive environment. Both appreciated the necessity of matching their rivals, and of responding to the ideal of participation in the crusade, so deeply embedded in the conventions of their age, regardless of their personal inclinations and enthusiasms. Plainly, the vows of neither can be regarded simply as a free expression of their solidarity with the crusading cause. Moreover, we must also make allowances for papal policy and strategy concerning the affairs of Christendom, both East and West. Whilst Edward I, as we shall see, was consistently encouraged in his plans to return to the Holy Land, papal policy towards the crusading vows of Henry reveals other priorities, frequently at odds with the interests of the Latin East.

Henry III

Henry took three separate vows in the course of his long reign. The last, taken in April 1271 following an illness which nearly killed him, was probably but an act of conventional piety by a man naturally

[36] R. Branner, 'Westminster Abbey and the French Court Style', *Journ. of the Soc. of Architectural Historians*, xxiii (1964), 3–18. See also F. M. Powicke, *King Henry III and the Lord Edward: The Community of the Realm in the Thirteenth Century*, 2 vols. (Oxford, 1947), i. 240; ii. 571; P. Brieger, *English Art 1216–1307* (Oxford, 1957), esp. pp. 109–10.

[37] Jordan, *Louis IX*, pp. 108–9.

[38] *CPR 1247–58*, p. 281; *Rôles Gascons*, ed. C. Bémont, 3 vols. (Paris, 1896–1906), i. No. 2469.

preoccupied with the hereafter.[39] He appeared serious, by taking measures designed to reduce expenditure against his departure, but the personal fulfilment of this vow was no more than a dream which necessarily required a degree of public posturing.[40] As recently as February 1271 Henry had urged Edward, then wintering in Sicily *en route* for the Holy Land, to return home: his plea was largely based upon the possible consequences of his selfsame illness for the safety of the realm. Edward should heed the example of Louis IX's son, Philip III, who had returned to the governance of his realm following his father's death at Tunis.[41]

Henry's first vow is of greater interest. His assumption of the Cross was no expression of his own free will, nor of concern for the Holy Land. He was just nine years old when he took this vow at the time of his coronation in October 1216. Forey has argued that it arose from his obligation to fulfil his father's outstanding vow of March 1215.[42] This may be so, but there are strong reasons for supposing that his vow, taken apparently at the legate Guala's bidding, was fundamentally a device intended to bolster the young king's position in the exceptionally perilous circumstances of the time.[43] Following the breakdown in relations between John and his baronial opponents after Magna Carta of June 1215, and the Capetian invasion led by Prince Louis in May 1216, there was the very real prospect that the Plantagenets would be swept from the English throne. Innocent III and then Honorius III threw their full weight behind John and then his young son, and at some point before 7 October 1216, at the latest, the Plantagenet cause had been declared a crusade.[44] Since the crusade had been declared before John's death on 19 October, Henry's first crusading vow may, then, be considered an instrument of a continuing papal policy which sought to preserve Plantagenet

[39] *Foedera*, I. i. 488; *CPR 1266–72*, p. 531. Henry claimed that his health recovered miraculously from the moment he received the Cross.

[40] *CPR 1266–72*, pp. 574, 622; *CR 1268–72*, p. 585. Perhaps Henry felt pangs of conscience regarding his failure to depart on crusade in the past, his illness a divine reprimand for his dereliction of duty. His vow may also have been intended to fortify his political position in his uncertain last years.

[41] *Foedera*, I. i. 487; *CR 1268–72*, pp. 397–8.

[42] A. J. Forey, 'The Crusading Vows of the English King Henry III', *Durham University Journ.* lxv (1973), 229–30. Paris, *CM* v. 327; and 'Burton', p. 349, provide additional support for this argument.

[43] For what follows see S. D. Lloyd, '"Political Crusades" in England, *c.*1215–17 and *c.*1263–5', in P. W. Edbury (ed.), *Crusade and Settlement: Papers Read at the First Conference of the Society for the Study of the Crusades and the Latin East and Presented to R. C. Smail* (Cardiff, 1985), 113–16, where the evidence is set out more fully.

[44] In a papal bull of 7 Oct. Savaric de Mauléon is described as 'crucesignatus pro defensione Regni Angliae': *Reg. Honorius III*, No. 50; BL Additional MS 15351, fo. 27.

rule in England.[45] A crusading force in young Henry's support was created by offering crusader privileges to those who took the Cross to fight against the king's enemies, and by applying the vows for the Holy Land previously taken by royalists. Guala was empowered to suspend the fulfilment of all such vows until the political situation improved, and to urge royalists to remain at home to fight in their king's cause. Critical was Guala's success in retaining in England Earl Ranulf of Chester, a linchpin of the Plantagenet cause.[46]

The point requiring emphasis here is the evident fact that the papacy considered the peaceful settlement of England to be the priority at this stage, and was prepared to relegate the interests of the Holy Land to that end. Nowhere in papal sources, however, do we hear of formal commutation of vows for the Holy Land to the English theatre, only their deferment until peace and Plantagenet authority were restored.[47] Individuals such as Earl Ranulf duly departed to join the Fifth Crusade at Damietta in the years following, and Henry III's own vow also remained binding. The papacy's long-term intention was probably to secure Henry's fulfilment of his father's vow in the East, but only at some suitable future time. Until then his Cross would function as a political support.[48] If so, this would explain Honorius III's expressed pleasure that Henry had taken up John's Cross, and the timing of his exhortation that Henry duly aid the Holy Land. For on 13 April 1223 Honorius formally declared his royal ward to be of legal age in most respects; just two weeks later the pope exhorted him to set out for the East in person.[49] This is unlikely to be pure coincidence, especially since the realm by then was altogether more stable.

[45] This is not to say that John took the Cross purely for political reasons: there is some evidence that he intended to fulfil his vow. In June 1216 he granted a ship to Henry fitzReginald of Winchelsea, that he might sail in it with John to Jerusalem: *RLP* 86b. In Mar. 1216 William fitzRocelin agreed to pay 200*m.* to John within two years from Easter, unless John went to the Holy Land before then: *Rotuli de oblatis et finibus in Turri Londinensi asservati*, ed. T. D. Hardy (London, 1835), 589. See also ibid. 562–3; *Dipl. Docs*. i. No. 54, for further indications that John was considering a passage to the East. None of this denies the political uses to which he put his vow in the crisis of 1215–16.

[46] *Foedera*, I. i. 146; *Reg. Honorius III*, No. 274; *RHGF* xix. 623–4; *Royal and Other Historical Letters Illustrative of the Reign of King Henry III*, ed. W. W. Shirley, 2 vols. (RS; 1862, 1866) i. 527–9.

[47] *Reg. Honorius III*, No. 244; *Royal Letters*, i. 527; *RHGF* xix. 623–4. Compare with Walter of Coventry, *Memoriale fratris Walteri de Coventria: The Historical Collections of Walter of Coventry*, ed. W. Stubbs, 2 vols. (RS; 1872, 1873), ii. 235, who does talk in terms of commutation.

[48] For this aspect see e.g. *Reg. Honorius III*, Nos. 247, 524; *Royal Letters*, i. 529; *RHGF* xix. 625, 629. The point was being stressed as late as 1220: *Royal Letters*, i. 536–7.

[49] *Foedera*, I. i. 172–3. There is silence before this concerning a royal crusade to the Holy Land.

This weighing of the interests of the Holy Land with the papacy's political goals in the West continued, albeit in different forms, to determine the thrust of papal crusading policy regarding Henry for most of the rest of his life. Careful scrutiny of the papal letters to Henry concerning the crusade reveals that, after the 1223 appeal, he was urged to take the Cross only twice, in 1234 and 1245.[50] Even after the fall of Jerusalem in 1244 his participation was not especially sought; in 1245 he was but one recipient of Innocent IV's general appeal to the princes of the West. His intended role was altogether more lowly than personal participation. It consisted primarily of providing the conditions for successful recruitment amongst his own subjects.[51] Above all, he was urged time and again to make peace with Louis IX since their rivalry, in papal eyes, threatened to dash recruitment in both realms. This particular exhortation runs as a continuous thread through the relevant correspondence of Honorius III, Gregory IX, and Innocent IV, just as Anglo-French peace had occupied their predecessors as far back as the 1170s and 1180s. Even the appeal to both kings in 1234 to take the Cross was concerned primarily to secure a lasting peace between them.[52]

The major determinant of the papacy's attitude was undoubtedly its long and savage struggle with the Hohenstaufen. Faced by the more or less constant threat of Frederick II and then his sons, from *c.*1227, the papacy sought to retain both Louis and Henry in reserve should they be required to provide aid. So far as this affected their crusading aspirations, Innocent IV spelt out the papal view quite candidly in April 1250 on hearing that Henry had taken the Cross for a second time. He applauded the king's pious intention, but equally he impressed upon Henry that the absence of both himself and Louis would jeopardize the peace and dangerously threaten papal prospects in the West. Should both be absent together, he warned, Mother Church, which depended so much on both kingdoms, would be prey to the plundering and ravaging of its enemies, a barely veiled reference to the forces of Frederick II.[53] Innocent was entirely consistent in agreeing only reluctantly to support Louis's crusade, which departed in 1248, and in seeking to divert resources away from the Holy Land to a crusade against the Hohenstaufen foe.[54] It was a policy shared by Innocent's immediate predecessors, faced by the

50 *Reg. Gregory IX*, No. 2187; *Foedera*, I. i. 254–5.

51 For instance, his co-operation was sought in the removal of domestic obstacles to recruitment. See e.g. *Foedera*, I. i. 173, concerning tolls demanded from *crucesignati*.

52 *Reg. Gregory IX*, Nos. 2186–9; *Royal Letters*, i. 557.

53 *Foedera*, I. i. 272.

54 M. Purcell, *Papal Crusading Policy: The Chief Instruments of Papal Crusading Policy and Crusade to the Holy Land from the Final Loss of Jerusalem to the Fall of Acre, 1244–1291*

same menace. However desirable, the recovery of the Holy Land was not the overriding goal to which all resources should be directed. Henry, for one, was to understand this and delay his departure accordingly.

The disastrous battle of Mansourah in February 1250, followed by Louis IX's surrender in April, forced a change. Innocent could scarcely sit idly by, especially in the face of the great wave of consternation which swept through the West in the aftermath of the disaster. Among other developments, Innocent now warmed towards Henry's crusading intentions.[55] Already signed with the Cross, Henry was the obvious candidate to mount a new crusade. But the timing of this sharp change in attitude is also significant because Frederick II died in December 1250 and Innocent, with great relief, evidently considered that the Hohenstaufen threat was emasculated, temporarily at least.[56] He could, then, devote more attention and more resources to the affairs of the Holy Land. To aid Henry, Innocent issued a stream of mandates and indults in the years 1251–3: protections for the king, his family, and dominions, liturgical activities on behalf of Henry and his crusading companions, a reinvigorated promotional campaign, and measures designed to raise moneys for the crusade.[57] The contrast between this flurry of papal activity and the very sparse measures following Henry's assumption of the Cross in 1250 is striking. The heavily qualified applause of Henry's crusading intention had given way under force of changed circumstances, in both East and West, to positive and practical encouragement. Moreover, Innocent now began to stress the deeds of Henry's predecessors in the Holy Land, notably those of Richard I, in his attempts to secure Henry's due departure.[58]

Henry's expedition never sailed. Instead, his vow became tied to a combined Plantagenet–papal policy towards Sicily from 1254. This has inevitably coloured assessments of Henry's commitment to the crusade. Indeed, his very intentions in taking the Cross in the first

(Leiden, 1975), 73–9. Innocent's accession to Henry's request at this point that English *crucesignati* be compelled to remain till Henry should himself depart is also consistent with papal policy: Paris, *CM* v. 103–4, 135; vi. Nos. 97–8; 'Tewkesbury', p. 141; *CPR 1247–58*, p. 79; and see E. Berger, *Histoire de Blanche de Castille, reine de France* (Paris, 1895), 382.

[55] See the bull urging Henry's departure in Oct. 1251, in 'Burton', pp. 293–5; also Paris, *CM* v. 274. But Innocent's measures in late 1250 and early 1251 reveal Henry already under pressure: PRO, *Lists and Indexes*, XLIX (London, 1923), 237.

[56] On Frederick's considerable successes before his death, and Innocent's reactions, see T. C. Van Cleve, *The Emperor Frederick II of Hohenstaufen, Immutator Mundi* (Oxford, 1972), 525–30.

[57] See esp. *Reg. Innocent IV*, Nos. 5946, 5979–80, 6035–6, 6072, 6985; *Foedera*, I. i. 279–80, 285–7, 292–3; 'Burton', pp. 293–5, 298–9.

[58] 'Burton', pp. 293–5, 298–9; *Reg. Innocent IV*, No. 6072; *Dipl. Docs.* i. No. 268.

place have been interpreted on the dubious premise that since he never went to the Holy Land he never planned to do so. The benefit of hindsight, acceptance of the scathing comments of certain contemporaries, and preconceptions about Henry's character have combined to produce a jaundiced tradition, Denholm-Young going so far as to declare that 'Henry III took the Cross with great ceremony but quite obviously with no intention of going abroad'.[59] Since such a view has obvious implications for any assessment of Henry's motives in assuming the Cross, and his later preparedness to see the diversion of his vow, it will be well initially to consider the claim that he never intended to sail.

Pace Denholm-Young, the evidence suggests that between 1250 and 1254 Henry was entirely sincere in his declarations of intent to depart for the East, but not, it should be noted, to sail before 1256. According to the intelligence report sent from France in April 1250 from the chaplain Philip to his master Alphonse of Poitiers, then in Egypt, Henry had taken the Cross 'a movoeir a sis ans'.[60] There is no reason to doubt the truth of this neglected report of Henry's long-term intentions, for Philip was well-connected and well-informed, and his intelligence is confirmed by Henry's public declaration, on 14 April 1252, that he would sail for the Holy Land on 24 June 1256.[61] It is no surprise, then, that Henry did not take any practical measures against his departure in the two years after his assumption of the Cross,[62] but he did play an active role in the promotional campaign, and took measures to stimulate recruitment to his crusade.[63]

It might be argued that Henry was merely seeking in cynical fashion to raise as many men and as much money as possible, to be applied to enterprises other than the crusade, but it would be difficult to reconcile this interpretation with the very practical preparations which Henry began to take in 1252 after his declaration of 14 April. In June 1252 he requested the masters of the Temple, the Hospital, and the Teutonic Knights in the Holy Land to prepare their best ships for his use. They were to send them a year in advance of his passage to take horses and supplies to the Holy Land, where the merchandise should be safely stored. The ships should then return in

59 N. Denholm-Young, *Richard of Cornwall* (Oxford, 1947), 73; also W. Stubbs, *The Constitutional History of England*, 3 vols. (4th edn., Oxford, 1906), ii. 67. Powicke, *Henry III*, esp. i. 231, 367–8, gave credence to Henry's preparations to depart on crusade, but he did not consider Henry's expressed enthusiasm convincing. For a more favourable view see Forey, 'The Crusading Vows', pp. 235–6.

60 'Lettre addressée en Égypte à Alphonse, comte de Poitiers, frère de Saint Louis', ed. T. Saint-Bris, *Bibliothèque de l'École des Chartes*, i (1839–40), 400.

61 *Foedera*, I. i. 282; *CPR 1247–58*, pp. 157–8.

62 Compare Forey, 'The Crusading Vows', pp. 235–6.

63 See above, pp. 21, 44–5, 58–9.

the year following to convey Henry and his force to the East.[64] By September he was preparing to send royal agents to the Holy Land and Mediterranean ports to make arrangements against his departure—probably the purchase and storage of foodstuffs and other necessaries, and the hire of ships.[65] He summoned to England certain men of Marseilles, the chosen port of embarkation, to discuss the details of his passage; and in the attempt to determine the shipping required, estimates were sought in May 1253 of the total number of *crucesignati* from Ireland and Scotland, and perhaps elsewhere, who would be accompanying him.[66] He also began the process of drawing up contracts, as we have seen.[67] Moreover, in a letter of January 1253, which has not received the attention it deserves, Henry requested Innocent IV to cause preaching of the Cross 'per cetera regna Christicolarum', to publicize the king's fixed departure date, and to admonish all *crucesignati* of different realms to set out with him at that time, for 'one prince should not bear the weight of so great a business alone'.[68] These were strange measures for a man to take if he had no intention of sailing.

There are other signs that Henry most certainly had set his heart upon accomplishing his vow. He apparently sought to reduce expenditure against his departure; according to Paris, this was why he did not distribute robes in the customary way during the Christmas festivities of 1250.[69] The timing of the important statutes concerning the Jews, promulgated in January 1253, is unlikely to have been just coincidence. Such measures were entirely consistent with the mentality of a royal *crucesignatus* seriously planning to liberate the Holy Land from other 'enemies of Christ'.[70] Likewise, the selection of

[64] *Foedera*, I. i. 282; *CPR 1247–58*, p. 158. Concurrent letters informed the powers of the Latin kingdom and the communes of Genoa, Pisa, and Venice of the day appointed for Henry's passage.

[65] *Foedera*, I. i. 285.

[66] Ibid. 289; *CPR 1247–58*, p. 191.

[67] See above, pp. 136–7.

[68] *CR 1251–3*, p. 448; *Foedera*, I. i. 288. In Sept. 1252 Innocent mandated the *crucesignati* of Henry's dominions to prepare to set out with the king: *Reg. Innocent IV'*, No. 5979.

[69] Paris, *CM* v. 199, and also p. 114; further, 'Dunstable', p. 184.

[70] *CR 1251–3*, pp. 312–13. See H. G. Richardson, *The English Jewry under Angevin Kings* (London, 1960), 191–2. Powicke, *Henry III*, i. 313, observed that Henry's attitude was probably always affected by Louis IX's aversion to the Jews. Louis's own crusading passage in 1248 was preceded by measures concerning the Jews, and in 1253–4 he enacted some drastic ordinances: see Jordan, *Louis IX*, esp. pp. 84–6, 154–5. Is it coincidence that Edward's crusade of 1270 was preceded by the statute of 1269? The expulsion of the Jews from Gascony in 1288, and from England in 1290, was in the view of Powicke, *Henry III*, ii. 731–2, directly connected with Edward I's crusading plans at the time.

crusading subjects for the decoration of Henry's Antioch chambers in 1251 suggests a man looking to the past for inspiration and to dynastic models for his own anticipated deeds in the East.

If such deeds were to be duly accomplished then Henry, like all *crucesignati*, would need to ensure the integrity and security of his dominions during his absence. This requirement helps to explain why Henry intended to delay his departure for six years after taking the Cross.[71] His attempts to settle the affairs of Gascony, if not stimulated by his assumption of the Cross, certainly gained a greater urgency as a result.[72] The marriage of his daughter Margaret to Alexander III of Scotland in December 1251 may also have owed something to Henry's wish to establish stable relations with a traditional foe before his departure.[73] And it cannot be coincidence that on 8 March 1250, just two days after taking the Cross, Henry empowered Richard of Cornwall and Peter of Savoy to renew the truce with Louis IX for six years. Significantly, the truce had been extended only a few months at a time since September 1248.[74] Finally, the gold treasure which Henry began to amass in a big way after 1248–9 was intended precisely for use on his projected crusade, and Henry was extremely reluctant to see it diverted to finance the Gascon expedition in 1253–4.[75]

Collectively, this body of material helps to dispose of the view held by some contemporaries, and echoed by certain later historians, that Henry took the Cross solely as a means of obtaining money.[76] It is an unconvincing argument for other reasons. Henry certainly went to great lengths to secure funds for his passage, but that should be no

[71] He would also need time to complete his other arrangements. Long delays prior to departure were common. Richard of Cornwall took the Cross in 1236, departing in 1240; Louis IX spent four years (1244–8) preparing for his first crusade. Edward I took the Cross in 1287; he was to have sailed in 1293.

[72] Powicke, *Henry III*, i. 230–1.

[73] Paris, *CM* iv. 489, included Anglo-Scottish relations as one of the reasons for Henry's discouragement of Waleran of Beirut from preaching the Cross in England in 1245. Relations were certainly bad. In 1249 Alexander II, significantly, promised not to enter into any alliance hostile to Henry. See in general F. M. Powicke, *The Thirteenth Century, 1216–1307* (2nd edn., Oxford, 1962), 587–9.

[74] For Henry's instructions in 1250, see *Dipl. Docs.* i. No. 261; *CPR 1247–58*, p. 62; *Royal Letters*, ii. 59–60. Alphonse of Poitiers's chaplain directly linked Henry's assumption of the Cross with the meeting at Melun of Richard of Cornwall and Queen Blanche to renew the truce: 'Lettre addressée en Égypte', ed. Saint-Bris.

[75] D. A. Carpenter, 'The Gold Treasure of King Henry III', in P. R. Coss and S. D. Lloyd (eds.), *Thirteenth Century England I: Proc. of the Newcastle upon Tyne Conference 1985* (Woodbridge, 1986), 68–73.

[76] See esp. L. Dehio, *Innozenz IV und England: Ein Beitrag zur Kirchengeschichte des 13 Jahrhunderts* (Berlin, 1914), 42 ff.; E. Berger, *Saint Louis et Innocent IV: Etude sur les rapports de la France et du Saint-Siège* (Paris, 1893), esp. pp. 222–3.

cause for suspicion.[77] It is difficult to think of a prospective crusade leader of Henry's time who did not make the urgent quest for funds a central part of his preparations, and if Henry sought grants from the papacy *before* assuming the Cross, that was only prudent.[78] The Lord Edward, for one, did precisely the same before he took his vow in 1268, yet none has argued that he assumed the Cross out of avarice.[79] But then Edward duly fulfilled his vow; Henry did not, and he came to apply much of the moneys raised to enterprises other than the crusade: here is the bone for sceptics and cynics to gnaw at. Furthermore, it is almost inconceivable that Henry was so simple-minded and ill-advised that he did not appreciate that the retention of moneys granted would depend upon the fulfilment of his vow, and that votive obligations would be incurred from the moment he took the Cross.[80] And with regard to Matthew Paris, whose views inform the opinion that Henry took the Cross for financial reasons, it must be remembered that he wrote in part with the benefit of hindsight, interpreting motives in the light of later developments. His notorious antipathy to financial exactions of any kind, by whomsoever, needs no emphasis here.

If, then, Henry was sincere when he took the Cross in 1250, and if in the years immediately following he had every intention of fulfilling his vow personally in the Holy Land, that does not mean that he was motivated purely with the fate of the Latin East and his own soul in mind. It is, of course, impossible to pronounce upon the exact reasons lying behind his assumption of the Cross, but the unfolding story of his second vow, from its genesis, is fully comprehensible only if it is set firmly within the context of thought outlined previously.[81] More specifically, Henry's compulsive urge to match his particular rival, Louis IX, in the competition for prestige, combined with their long struggle over territory and conflicting political goals, both within and beyond France, helps to explain much of the story of that vow.

[77] See, on this, the wise words of W. E. Lunt, *The Valuation of Norwich* (Oxford, 1926), 55–8; Forey, 'The Crusading Vows', 231–7.

[78] Henry's lobbying at the papal Curia in 1247 for crusading moneys in England has frequently been considered sinister, but as Lunt, *Valuation*, p. 54, observed, Henry's intention was surely to secure funding for the separate English crusade which, he hoped, his half-brother Guy de Lusignan would lead. The relevant materials in *Reg. Innocent IV*, Nos. 4054–6, should be read together; cf. Forey, 'The Crusading Vows', pp. 232–3.

[79] See above, p. 146, and below p. 232.

[80] See Forey, 'The Crusading Vows', pp. 236–7, on this point; cf., in particular, Berger, *Saint Louis*, pp. 222–3.

[81] I leave aside as given, here, the general motivating force of the plenary indulgence and other privileges, and the specific ties of Henry to the rulers of the Latin East, for which see above, pp. 31–2.

That Henry should have taken the Cross is not surprising; it is the timing of his vow which invites discussion. Since the fall of Jerusalem in 1244, Henry had been under some pressure to aid the Holy Land, the object of a diplomatic offensive which began in earnest with the arrival of Bishop Waleran of Beirut and Arnulph in 1245.[82] But there is no indication that Henry was moved to consider taking the Cross himself; domestic considerations and the security of his dominions weighed more heavily in these years.[83] Yet he would be left out in the cold if he simply ignored the crusade. Of his fellow monarchs, Haakon IV of Norway had been signed with the Cross since 1237; Eric XI of Sweden supported the crusade against the Estonians in 1248; the kings of Aragon and Castile were actively engaged in the *Reconquista* in Spain; and Frederick II was declaring by 1250 that he too hoped to depart on crusade, but that papal malice prevented him for the time being. Above all, Louis IX had taken the Cross in 1244, inspiring and inducing a considerable number of the great lords of France to follow his example. The eyes of all Christendom were focused upon his expedition when it sailed in 1248. Were he to succeed, especially against the background of recent failures in the East, the Capetians' prestige would soar as the Plantagenets' would sink, a royal dynasty apparently incapable or unwilling to succour the Holy Land in its hour of greatest need following the loss of Jerusalem in 1244.[84]

If such considerations held force at the Plantagenet court in the late 1240s this would help to explain Henry's petitions to Innocent IV in 1247: that the departure of English *crucesignati* be deferred until one year after the passage of Louis and the French; that Guy de Lusignan, Henry's half-brother, be appointed their 'dux'; and that the moneys for the crusade raised in England be made available to them.[85] This, surely, was in part an insurance policy. If Louis should score an outstanding success in the East, then at least a distinct English contingent could share in the glory. Henry could claim that he had

[82] See above, pp. 29–30, and below, appendix 2. The dispatch of the Blood in 1247 was probably part of that offensive. Like all gifts, for it does not appear to have been a purchase, it imposed certain obligations upon the recipient.

[83] See e.g. Paris, *CM* iv. 489. Welsh, Scottish, and Gascon affairs took up much of Henry's time and treasure. He also continued to oppose taxation for the crusade imposed in 1245. See Forey, 'The Crusading Vows', p. 231.

[84] The powers of the Latin East considered that the Capetians and Plantagenets represented their best hope for salvation in this period: see e.g. *Anc. Corr.* 5. 56; *Dipl. Docs.* i. No. 386; *Foedera*, I. i. 396. They surely knew that their end of securing Plantagenet support was well served by playing on the rivalry of Louis and Henry. See e.g. their flattery of Henry in 1254: 'Burton', pp. 368–9; *Foedera*, I. i. 308.

[85] *Reg. Innocent IV*, Nos. 4054–6. Carpenter, 'The Gold Treasure', pp. 70–1, plausibly suggests that the build-up of Henry's gold treasure from 1246–7 was intended to support an English crusade.

done his bit. Louis's initial success in Egypt, however, necessitated reconsideration. News of his capture of Damietta and, more, rumours of his conquest of Cairo had reached the sharp ears of Matthew Paris, for one, by the autumn of 1249.[86] As Lunt suggested, this news was probably responsible for the undoubted revival in England of interest in the crusade.[87] Henry's hand, then, was being forced, and Lunt was most likely correct in supposing that Henry's vow of 6 March 1250 was the product of his wish to emulate Louis.[88] That he should first have sought papal subsidy before assuming the Cross was entirely reasonable.[89] That he should thereafter have attempted to prevent the independent departure of English *crucesignati* was also reasonable, especially since they would be joining and aiding Louis, Henry's 'capitalis inimicus' as Paris puts it.[90]

Henry was doubtless shocked by the news of Mansourah and Louis's capture. He probably shed many tears, in characteristic fashion, but many may have been crocodile tears. As the full import of the calamity dawned, Henry, it seems, began to regard himself as the only possible saviour of the Latin East. He was egged on by Innocent IV, who also, as we have seen, came to appeal in 1251 and 1252 to the memory of Plantagenet crusading deeds, those of Richard I specifically. It was, surely, under the impact of those suggestions and Henry's own dreams that his Antioch chambers were commissioned in 1251. Henry would indeed be a new Lionheart.

Louis's discomfiture in the East provided distinct possibilities for Henry in the context of the Plantagenet–Capetian struggle, especially since Louis did not return to France on his release in May 1250. He sailed instead for Acre where he remained for nearly four years, attempting to bolster the position of the Latin kingdom. Without considerable reinforcement from the West, however, only modest goals were attainable, so it is not altogether surprising that Louis turned to Henry for aid once it became apparent that further support

86 Paris, *CM* v. 87, 118; vi. No. 87; and *De ant. leg.*, pp. 15–16. Wider dissemination of the news is suggested by the copying of the newsletter in a Tewkesbury abbey register: BL Cotton Cleopatra A. vii, fos. 103v–104.

87 Lunt, *Valuation*, p. 55, and n. 3.

88 Ibid. n. 3: 'Jealousy may have been his motive.'

89 Henry took the Cross some six months after Louis's initial success became known in England, but he had been negotiating before this with Innocent IV for papal subsidy: *Foedera*, I. i. 272. He probably delayed taking the Cross to await Innocent's reply. This need not, then, cast doubt on the view that he took vows in response to Louis's success: cf. Forey, 'The Crusading Vows', p. 237.

90 Paris, *CM* v. 135; and see Forey, 'The Crusading Vows', pp. 231–2. See further, above, p. 91. The chaplain Philip reported that many considered that Henry took the Cross to prevent the departure of English *crucesignati*, who would otherwise aid Louis: 'Lettre addressée en Égypte', ed. Saint-Bris, pp. 400–1. Henry was well aware in Mar. 1250 of their planned departure.

on a large scale from France would not be forthcoming. At some point before October 1251 Louis exhorted Henry to fulfil his vow, urging that the two kings act in concert in the Holy Land.[91] Louis's predicament was Henry's opportunity. His reply to Louis's proposal does not survive, but he alluded to it when he informed Louis in June 1252 that his departure on crusade was fixed for 24 June 1256.[92] He went on to observe that he might anticipate that date should Louis restore the lost Plantagenet lands in France. Concurrent letters to Queen Margaret of France and the leaders of Outremer added to the pressure upon Louis in this piece of crude blackmail. Paris reports that Louis indeed offered to meet Henry's territorial demands, providing Henry came to his aid in the East, but that French baronial opposition killed off the plan.[93] Paris also reports that Louis's reputation suffered badly following his failure in Egypt, and here too Henry could hope to score points. In the selfsame letter of June 1252 he brought Louis's esteem directly into play by observing that he might hasten his crusade 'to the increase of the honour of the said king of France'. The crusade of the new Richard, then, would be the means of restoration of Louis's tarnished reputation; the Plantagenet would rescue the Capetian and give him back his pride. Who, one wonders, would be entitled in such an event to the accolade 'most Christian king'?

Henry cannot be rescued from the charge of opportunism in the matter of the crusade. He took the Cross only when it became convenient, or necessary, to do so, and his crass attempt to exploit Louis's predicament after Mansourah reveals blatant expediency of a particularly unsavoury type. Indeed, Henry had attempted to take advantage of Louis even before he departed on crusade in 1248 by playing upon the Capetian's anxieties concerning the security of France during his absence. Although the truce of 1243 was renewed at Louis's request in 1246 to run until Michaelmas 1248, it was then extended only until 31 December 1248.[94] In addition, Henry threatened force to regain the Plantagenet lands, his sabre-rattling backed up by diplomatic pressure.[95] He became more conciliatory after taking the Cross in 1250, as we have seen, but by 1253 he was again

[91] The proposal appears in Innocent's letter of Oct. 1251 to Henry: 'Burton', pp. 293–5.

[92] *Foedera*, I. i. 282; *CPR 1247–58*, pp. 157–8.

[93] Paris, *CM* v. 280–1.

[94] *Layettes du Trésor des Chartes: Inventaire et documents publiés par la Direction des Archives*, ed. A. Teulet *et al.* 5 vols. (Paris, 1863–1909), ii. No. 3075; iii. No. 3713.

[95] Paris, *CM* iv. 506; v. 71, who also reports that Frederick II and his son, Henry, urged Louis in 1250 to restore the Plantagenet lands. Alphonse of Poitiers remained at home in 1248 against threats to Capetian security: *RHGF* xx. 356, 372.

threatening force, although an attack did not materialize.[96] Opportunism is also to be seen in the parallel negotiations into which Henry entered in 1254, with a view to the commutation of his vow into an assault upon North Africa in the company of Alfonso X of Castile, or upon the Hohenstaufen in Sicily.[97] However, the pressures and influences which lay behind Henry's preparedness to allow his crusading vow to become an instrument of his wider foreign policy have not always been sufficiently appreciated. Once again, Plantagenet–Capetian rivalry, albeit in a different form, would appear to provide much of the rationale behind developments.

Like his father John, Henry III refused to accept the loss to the Capetians of Normandy, Brittany, Anjou, Poitou, and their satellites in the opening years of the thirteenth century. The attempt to recover them was the central element of Henry's foreign policy until the 1250s, but neither military expeditions (in 1225–6, 1230–1, and 1242–3) nor diplomacy had succeeded in wresting those lands from the Capetians. Indeed, by 1250 the chances of recovery must have seemed slight. Louis IX had already taken considerable strides towards the consolidation of Capetian authority and influence throughout France following the disintegrative tendencies of his long minority. This was complemented by the installation of Louis's brothers in their appanages. So far as the Plantagenet lands are concerned, Charles was invested with Anjou and Maine in 1246, whilst Alphonse of Poitiers's vast appanage was finally assembled in 1249 when he succeeded to the county of Toulouse on the death of Count Raymond VII. Thereby, Plantagenet Gascony was effectively hemmed in to the north and east. Nor had Henry succeeded in his attempts to block Capetian ambitions elsewhere. In particular, he failed to prevent Provence falling under Capetian influence in the person of Charles of Anjou, who married the heiress in 1246. The terms of the Treaty of Beaucaire (1248), an interim settlement between Charles and the dowager countess, Beatrice, underlined that Henry's hopes had been effectively dashed.[98]

96 Paris, *CM* v. 434. Louis is said to have returned to France on hearing that attack from England as well as Germany was imminent: *RHGF* xx. 17, 386. The French feudal host was indeed summoned in Sept. 1253: ibid. xxiii. 730–1. In May 1253 Louis empowered Alphonse of Poitiers and Charles of Anjou to enter into, and confirm, the truce with Henry, if expedient: *Layettes*, iii. No. 4052.

97 Amongst others, Powicke, *Henry III*, i. 241; id., *Thirteenth Century*, p. 120, argued that Henry was guilty of deception in his negotiations with Alfonso. Forey, 'The Crusading Vows', pp. 238–45, presents a strong case for thinking that Henry, far from having set his heart on Sicily, was waiting upon events. The basic charge of opportunism remains.

98 See esp. E. L. Cox, *The Eagles of Savoy: The House of Savoy in Thirteenth-Century Europe* (Princeton, 1974), 145–63. A comprehensive settlement was reached only in 1257: ibid. 282.

Prospects for Gascony, the sole remaining Plantagenet territory in France, had never been bleaker than in the late 1240s. The political situation within the duchy was chaotic, the administration in utter disarray, a circumstance which inevitably encouraged intervention on the part of those with a claim to the lordship or otherwise hostile to the Plantagenet presence. Invasion was considered to be not so much likely as imminent in circles close to Henry III at the time. Amongst the conditions which Earl Simon de Montfort laid down for his appointment as seneschal of Gascony in 1248 was the requirement that Henry accept responsibility for any war over the duchy which might break out against 'the four neighbouring kings'.[99] The reference was to the kings of France, Castile, Navarre, and Aragon. With regard to the Capetians, Earl Simon later declared that he considered Gascony to be in imminent peril in 1248 from that quarter, and in 1249 the viscount of Fronsac was indeed accused before Henry III of plotting with Alphonse of Poitiers to betray the duchy to the Capetian.[100] Of the remaining hostile kings, Theobald I of Navarre certainly lent his support to Gascon rebels in 1248, the latest episode in a long-standing conflict over rival jurisdictional claims, whilst James I of Aragon had inherited a claim to Gascony via the rights of his queen.[101] Above all, Alfonso X of Castile revived his inherited claim to Gascony on his accession in 1252. Considering the close relationship between the royal houses of France and Castile, most obviously personified by the indomitable Blanche of Castile, Louis IX's mother and regent of France, and considering the alienation and turbulence following the dispatch of Earl Simon to quell the duchy in 1248, it is scarcely surprising that Alfonso's threat was taken seriously at the Plantagenet court.[102]

[99] C. Bémont, *Simon de Montfort, Earl of Leicester, 1208–1265*, trans. E. F. Jacob (Oxford, 1930), 75–6. The other conditions, and the seven-year term of Simon's appointment, indicate that the task of pacifying Gascony and establishing its wider security was considered esp. difficult. Henry's agreement to Simon's conditions is a measure of his perception of the situation. For conditions in Gascony, and its external relations, see J-P. Trabut-Cussac, *L'Administration anglaise en Gascogne, 1254–1307* (Paris, Geneva, 1972) , xxvi–xxxvii.

[100] *CR 1247–51*, pp. 343–4; Bémont, *Simon de Montfort*, tr. Jacob, pp. 75, 84.

[101] See Powicke, *Henry III*, i. 191–4, 214–15; Jordan, *Louis IX*, p. 43; Bémont, *Simon de Montfort*, tr. Jacob, pp. 73–4, 81–2.

[102] Powicke, *Henry III*, esp. i. 230–6, considered Alfonso's claim frivolous, intended to force Henry into negotiations, and the scare of Castilian invasion in 1253–4 a sham, which Henry turned to his advantage in England. Forey, 'The Crusading Vows', pp. 237–44, argues convincingly that Alfonso was in earnest, and that there was real fear of invasion. Negotiations were certainly more difficult than Powicke allowed. See also J. O. Baylen, 'John Maunsell and the Castilian Treaty of 1254: A Study of the Clerical Diplomat', *Traditio*, xvii (1961), 482–91; Trabut-Cussac, *L'Administration*, xxxiv–xxxvi.

A Plantagenet initiative was by now essential. Henry decided upon a policy of appeasement towards Alfonso. This was sensible; he could not fight all his opponents at once and it was vital to prevent their combination. He was helped by Alfonso's further claim, in 1252, to the overlordship of Navarre, for this led to an alliance between James of Aragon and Theobald II of Navarre against Castile.[103] Nevertheless, the strife within Gascony remained virulent, the stance of the kings of Aragon and Navarre a cause of anxiety. In short, Henry could not be confident in 1253–4 that Gascony and its borders were secure, nor that the threat of an alliance between his Castilian, Gascon, and Capetian foes had been scotched.

These uncertainties, combined with Henry's failure to recover his other French lands, help to explain the emergence of a grandiose Plantagenet foreign policy in the late 1240s and 1250s, a policy to which Henry's crusading vow would ultimately become tied. Henry apparently considered that if he could not recover his position in France, then he would look further afield in the hope of compensation. If this was the motive, the opportunity was presented by Innocent IV's deposition of Frederick II in 1245 and the prospect of disintegration and collapse of Hohenstaufen power in Germany and the Mediterranean. In the course of the next decade, as events unfolded, Henry would seek to grasp the constituent parts of the Hohenstaufen inheritance for members of the Plantagenet line. But Henry was not alone in seeking to capitalize on the Hohenstaufens' demise. In particular, the Capetians—more specifically, Charles of Anjou—and Alfonso X of Castile clearly recognized the possibilities. Henry, then, was under some compulsion to act through competition in the extremely volatile international situation which developed.

This is particularly apparent with regard to the kingdom of Sicily. To Richard of Cornwall the papal invitation to become king may have been akin to being offered the moon, to paraphrase Paris's famous words.[104] To Henry, however, the prospect was altogether more enticing, and he must have been fully aware that in August 1252 Innocent IV offered the throne to Charles of Anjou as well as Richard.[105] In the circumstances facing him, could Henry afford to stand back and watch Charles seek to acquire Sicily, especially as he was now count of Provence, well placed to launch an invasion? Should Charles accept the offer and take Sicily, his dynasty would dramatically extend its power and influence, depressing Plantagenet

[103] Powicke, *Henry III*, i. 235, and n.

[104] On Richard's reactions see Paris, *CM* v. 346–7, 361, 457. Richard may have been offered Sicily as early as 1249–50. See Van Cleve, *Frederick II*, pp. 524–5; Denholm-Young, *Richard of Cornwall*, pp. 81–2.

[105] On the two sets of negotiations see Berger, *Saint Louis*, esp. pp. 398–408.

prestige still further. Its proverbial wealth, notwithstanding Frederick II's savage exploitation in recent years, coupled with its strategic position, rendered Sicily a prize of massive potential value to whoever could seize it.[106] In 1252, then, Henry's hand was being forced by the appearance of Sicily on the open market, and he had little option but to press Richard to accept the throne, for if the Plantagenets did not grasp the nettle then the Capetians, it appeared, would. Charles took the offer very seriously and only dropped the project in late 1253, largely as a result of the prospects that opened up for him in Hainault and Flanders in the course of that year.[107]

At this stage Henry's projected crusade to the Holy Land remained apart from the matter of Sicily. The king envisaged two distinct expeditions: he would complete his crusade to the East; his brother would invade Sicily. This is made quite plain in his letter of 28 January 1253 to Innocent IV, in which Henry responded to the pope's request that he afford aid and counsel to Richard in the matter of Sicily. Henry agreed to do what he could, but on condition that the grants he had received, or would receive, to prosecute his crusade should not be compromised. His agreement to a grant of moneys to Richard from the English clergy, in these circumstances, is striking evidence of his desire that Richard should proceed with the Sicilian project.[108] On the very same day, as we have seen, he requested Innocent to cause the Cross to be preached throughout the West, and to publicize the date fixed three years hence for his passage to the Holy Land.[109] However, these plans came to nothing because Richard refused Innocent's offer of Sicily and remained impervious to Henry's pressure: Henry would have to find an alternative candidate. Edmund, his younger son, was the obvious choice from among Henry's immediate kin, and when Charles of Anjou finally withdrew in late 1253, Edmund was left alone in his candidacy. On 12 February 1254 Henry appointed proctors to receive the kingdom of Sicily on behalf of his son; on 6 March Henry's wish was fulfilled. In May the grant was confirmed by Innocent.[110]

106 History demonstrated this, as the council of Brindisi impressed upon Lord Edmund in 1257: *Dipl. Docs.* i. No. 295.

107 Charles probably broke off negotiations in Sept. 1253. See R. Sternfeld, *Karl von Anjou als Graf der Provence, 1245–1265* (Berlin, 1888), 92–6. The war of the Flemish succession was Charles's opportunity. Following the battle of Walcheren, July 1253, Margaret of Flanders offered Hainault to Charles in return for his help against John of Avesnes, her rival. Isolated, John turned, predictably, to Henry III. The matter ultimately had some bearing on Richard of Cornwall's imperial candidature, in succession to William of Holland, John's ally. See H. S. Lucas, 'John of Avesnes and Richard of Cornwall', *Speculum*, xxiii (1948), esp. pp. 91–5.

108 *CR 1251–3*, p. 449; *Foedera*, I. i. 284.

109 *CR 1251–3*, p. 448; *Foedera*, I. i. 288.

110 *Reg. Alexander IV*, No. 3036; *Foedera*, I. i. 297, 301. Henry's anxiety to secure Sicily is

Henry's crusading vow still remained apart from Edmund's elevation at this juncture. The papal envoy, Albert of Parma, had been empowered to commute Henry's vow in support of Edmund in 1253 but, significantly, Henry did not avail himself of the offer judging by the materials which survive.[111] By spring 1254, however, Henry had come round to the idea: to launch both an invasion of Sicily and a crusade to the Holy Land would place impossible strains on Plantagenet resources. But when Henry accordingly sought commutation he met with an ambivalent response. On 31 May 1254 Innocent replied that Conrad's death (21 May) had removed many of the obstacles to the settlement of Sicily, and very pointedly he further observed that once Sicily had been won the Holy Land could be more easily succoured. Accordingly, he would permit commutation only with the greatest reluctance.[112] Henry should continue with his crusade to the East.

Innocent's change in heart may be explained by his reassessment of the fluid political situation in Italy and Germany. Since Frederick II's death in 1250 he had adjusted his policy to accord with the realities of the moment and the comparative strength of the papal and Hohenstaufen parties. As far as Sicily was concerned, Innocent oscillated between a policy of direct papal overlordship, when the Hohenstaufen cause appeared on the wane (with a *rapprochement* with Frederick's sons an option), and one which looked to external support when the papacy seemed in peril. Conrad's death in May 1254 brightened the prospects once more for direct papal overlordship; inevitably, Innocent's enthusiasm for Edmund waned as a consequence.[113] Hence, too, he could look again to Henry to fulfil his vow in the Holy Land, and when the next Hohenstaufen, Manfred, surrendered Sicily to Innocent in October 1254, Plantagenet prospects must have seemed bleak indeed. Yet within weeks the situation

further indicated by his preparedness to overthrow his nephew, Henry (1238–54), the son of Frederick II and Isabella Plantagenet. He was to have succeeded his half-brother, Conrad, in the Empire and Sicily. Paris, *CM* iv. 613, says Henry III was overjoyed when the Sicilians rendered homage to Henry in 1247, and Henry apparently favoured the Plantagenet connection: ibid. v. 71, 432, 448. Perhaps Henry III originally intended that Henry be the vassal of the Plantagenet king of Sicily? See further above, pp. 14–15.

111 *Reg. Alexander IV*, No. 3036; *Foedera*, I. i. 297, 301: cf. Cox, *Eagles of Savoy*, pp. 242–3.

112 *Foedera*, I. i. 304, 308. cf. W. E. Lunt, *Financial Relations of the Papacy with England to 1327* (Cambridge, Mass.; 1939), 265, and n. 3, with Powicke, *Henry III*, i. 370–1; and see Forey, 'The Crusading Vows', pp. 238–9, 241.

113 E. Jordan, *Les Origines de la Domination angevine en Italie* (Paris, 1909) remains the best survey of the background to papal policy in this context. Forey, 'The Crusading Vows', pp. 238–41 and Cox, *Eagles of Savoy*, pp. 242–5 underline the ambiguity in the papal position even when Sicily was granted to Edmund in 1254.

changed radically again, for the accord between Innocent and Manfred collapsed and the papal forces were in utter disarray by the time of Innocent's death in December. No wonder, then, that Alexander IV turned again to Henry for support in 1255.[114] In May he empowered his nuncio Rostand and Archbishop Boniface of Canterbury to commute Henry's vow to Sicily, and in October Edmund was solemnly invested as king of Sicily.[115]

The sequence of events which followed with regard to Sicily is well known, but certain points, in so far as they touch upon Henry's crusading vow, should be stressed. First, as Forey has noticed, the proposal to commute that vow to Sicily appears originally to have been a papal initiative rather than a response to Henry's petition, although Henry had come to appreciate by 1254 that commutation suited his purpose.[116] Second, Henry's interest appears more reasonable, his actions less incoherent, if due weight is given to the wider background of Plantagenet prospects in the West, especially in relation to the Capetians, and the changing directions of papal policy in the 1250s.[117] Henry was not a free agent; he had to react to developments as did the pope. The pressures upon him at this time obliged him to gamble heavily, and once he had begun to play his hand it was not easy to turn back. Third, these considerations help to explain the significant fact, established by Forey, that Henry never formally commuted his vow to Sicily, notwithstanding papal permission. On the contrary, he continued to proclaim his intention to fulfil his vow in the Holy Land once the affairs of Sicily had been satisfactorily resolved,[118] partly perhaps because it was by no means clear in 1254–5 that Sicily would indeed be granted to Edmund. If the papacy was not yet committed to a single policy, then, it may be argued, Henry also

[114] Already, in Nov. 1254, Innocent had sent strong and unambiguous signals to Henry that he urgently send a representative to take over the government of Sicily: Jordan, *Les Origines*, esp. p. xiii.

[115] *Foedera*, I. i. 319–20.

[116] Forey, 'The Crusading Vows', esp. pp. 243–5.

[117] Powicke, *Thirteenth Century*, pp. 121–2 also observed that the propects in Sicily in 1254–5 were by no means hopeless. Charles of Anjou, of course, ultimately succeeded in conquering Sicily in the 1260s. M. T. Clanchy, *England and Its Rulers 1066–1272* (Glasgow, 1983), 235–7, argues that Henry's mistake lay in accepting the papal terms, and not in bidding for Sicily as such. The narrowly Anglocentric view of Henry's foreign policy, well-represented by R. F. Treharne, *The Baronial Plan of Reform, 1258–1263* (2nd edn., Manchester, 1971), esp. pp. 49–50, fails to allow for the influences bearing upon Henry at the time, and the way in which international politics were perceived and conducted. Cox, *Eagles of Savoy*, and Clanchy, *England and Its Rulers*, pp. 230–40, provide a convincing antidote.

[118] Forey, 'The Crusading Vows', pp. 238–46.

was keeping his options open. If he should be denied Sicily, then the Plantagenet position in the West required that he should look elsewhere in hope of compensation.[119]

When Sicily was put on the market by Innocent IV, and Henry decided to grasp the opportunity, other possibilities came into consideration. The conquest of Sicily would undoubtedly have expedited Henry's crusade to the Holy Land for logistic and strategic reasons, as Innocent IV impressed upon him in May 1254 and then the council of Brindisi in 1257.[120] But Henry's thoughts seemingly stretched further to contemplate the establishment of Plantagenet power in the east Mediterranean as well as Sicily. In itself the idea was not absurd: Charles of Anjou, after all, succeeded initially in his bid for a new Mediterranean empire based on Sicily, and with further ambitions in the direction of Byzantium and the Latin kingdom of Jerusalem. In 1277, indeed, he assumed the title of king of Jerusalem after purchasing the rights of Maria of Antioch, and until the Sicilian Vespers of 1282 the Angevin presence in the Latin kingdom was a very real one. There was logic in Charles's opportunism. The Angevin conquest of Sicily followed upon the crushing defeat of Conradin, the last Hohenstaufen ruler, at the astonishing battle of Tagliacozzo in August 1268, but Conradin was also the last of his line to be king of Jerusalem (1254–68). If Charles saw the logic in seeking to supplant the Hohenstaufen in both Sicily and Jerusalem, then so, it appears, did Henry III before him. Indeed, Henry went further, in his energetic support of Richard of Cornwall's candidature for the German part of the Hohenstaufen inheritance following the premature death of William of Holland in January 1256. Richard's election as king in January 1257 took place in the face of stiff opposition from his rival, Alfonso X of Castile, backed by Louis IX, and Alfonso further envisaged the conquest of Sicily. He

119 The negotiations with Alfonso X for the commutation of Henry's vow to North Africa may be set partly within this context. See Forey, 'The Crusading Vows', pp. 239–44. The timing of Henry's embassy to Rome in Sept. 1254, to seek that commutation, following upon Innocent's *rapprochement* with Manfred, is surely no coincidence. See *Foedera*, I. i. 308, 331; *CR 1253–4*, pp. 275, 316.

120 *Foedera*, I. i. 304; *Dipl. Docs.* i. No. 295. Alexander IV took the same line, seeking in 1256 to fix a new date for Henry's crusading passage and to extend the term within which he should dispatch a force to Sicily: *Foedera*, I. i. 347, 348, 350; *Reg. Alexander IV*, No. 1543. For the strategic importance of Sicily to the launching of Holy Land crusades, and the application of crusade to secure Sicily as a friendly base in these terms, see esp. Purcell, *Papal Crusading Policy*, esp. pp. 76, 87–8, 113; N. Housley, *The Italian Crusades: The Papal–Angevin Alliance and the Crusades against Christian Lay Powers, 1254–1343* (Oxford, 1982), esp. pp. 62–9.

too approached the Hohenstaufen inheritance in Germany and Sicily from a single perspective.[121]

That Henry was at least toying with the idea of extending Plantagenet power into the east Mediterranean is suggested most strongly by the negotiations being conducted in 1256 with a view to a marriage alliance between the Plantagenets and their distant kin, the Lusignans of Cyprus. When those negotiations began is unclear, but there are indications in Henry's reply to the letters of the bishop of Bethlehem in September 1256 that they had been in progress for some time.[122] They concerned the proposal that the Lord Edmund marry Queen Plaisance of Cyprus, and that her son marry Beatrice, Henry III's daughter.[123] Henry observed that he could not yet make firm reply since such a weighty matter required discussion amongst his counsellors, and as yet he had been unable to consult with all those he wished: he would make a definite response once his deliberations were complete.[124] This does not sound like a polite rejection of the proposed alliance,[125] and if Henry indeed took the matter seriously then this is all the more significant because in June 1256 active

[121] See Powicke, *Henry III*, i. 242–4; Forey, 'The Crusading Vows', p. 244, n. 115. The Plantagenet approach to Germany was again shot through with fears concerning the Capetians and Alfonso. See esp. Henry III's instructions to William Bonquer, his envoy in Rome, in Mar. 1256: *CR 1254–6*, pp. 408–9. Richard's candidature, fully endorsed by Henry, seemingly emerged from this fear, his intentions first becoming apparent in June 1256. See, now, H-E. Hilpert, 'Richard of Cornwall's Candidature for the German Throne and the Christmas 1256 Parliament', *Journ. of Medieval History*, vi (1980), 185–98.

[122] In Aug. 1255 Alexander IV pronounced against Plaisance's marriage to Balian d'Ibelin: see H. E. Mayer, 'Ibelin *versus* Ibelin: The Struggle for the Regency of Jerusalem 1253–1258', *Proc. of the American Philosophical Soc.* cxxii (1978), 46. Negotiations with Henry probably began around that time.

[123] *CR 1254–6*, pp. 445–6. The letters were brought by Plaisance's nuncio, Roland: ibid. 354; *CLR 1251–60*, p. 319. Henry's reply suggests that Plaisance initiated the proposal, but it is impossible to be sure. Neither her own letters nor her instructions to Roland are known.

[124] The bishop was Godfrey de Prefectis, appointed in Jan. 1245: *Reg. Innocent IV*, No. 956. He may have met Henry III in 1247, when he went to Scotland as papal legate: Paris, *CM* iv. 602. He probably had dealings with him concerning the collection of alms in England for the church of Bethlehem, authorized in 1248: *Reg. Innocent IV*, No. 4044. A passage in Henry's letter of 1256 suggests they had met in the past. By 1253 Godfrey was in the East, and in Sept. 1255 his consecration the following Advent was authorized: *Reg. Alexander IV*, No. 756. He would, then, have been in the East long enough to act for Queen Plaisance, and if he had met Henry his choice as negotiator is largely explained. I am indebted to Dr Bernard Hamilton for his help and information.

[125] Another reply was sent 'Eodem modo albo cardinali', apparently Master John Tolet, an English Cistercian and then cardinal priest of S. Lorenzo in Lucina: Paris, *CM* iv. 306, 354, 578–9. This suggests that the negotiations were supported at the highest levels at the papal Curia. Is it coincidence that in Sept. 1256 Alexander IV sought a new date for Henry's crusading passage?: *Foedera*, I. i. 347.

consideration was being given to the proposal that Edmund marry the daughter of Manfred of Sicily and that Manfred grant the kingdom to Edmund once the union occurred.[126] Since many of the practical and financial obstacles to the Plantagenet take-over of Sicily would have been solved at a stroke, it may be presumed that some glittering prospect for the Plantagenets in the east Mediterranean was being advanced.

When Henry I of Cyprus died in 1253, leaving an only child Hugh II as a minor, the regency of the kingdom fell to Plaisance in accordance with the *bailliage* rules.[127] Were Edmund to have married Plaisance he could have expected to enjoy effective exercise of the regency on her behalf, lasting until Hugh II came of age in 1267, and he could also have hoped for children by Plaisance for she was still young, born sometime in the late 1230s. As half-brothers or half-sisters to the Lusignan king they would have provided the foundations for a lasting Plantagenet influence in Cyprus. The second marriage would have worked in the same direction, for Beatrice would have become queen consort of King Hugh II and any children would have ruled in Cyprus. There was a further possible prospect. Since 1242 the Cypriot Lusignans had acted as regents of the Latin kingdom of Jerusalem on behalf of the absentee Hohenstaufen, beginning with Queen Alice of Cyprus (1242–6) and then her son Henry I (1246–53), but on his death John of Arsur (Ibelin) was chosen as regent as Hugh II's claim was not then pressed. In due course, however, first Plaisance and then other kin acted on Hugh's behalf as regent after 1258, and ultimately in 1268–9 the Lusignans inherited the throne of Jerusalem upon the extinction of the Hohenstaufen. In 1256, contemporaries could not have been able to predict many, perhaps any, of these developments. Nevertheless, at the time of the marriage proposals the Cypriot Lusignans had a stake in the Latin kingdom, and Henry III must have known it. Nor, considering his maintenance of proctors at foreign courts and the close communications with the Latin East, can Henry have been unaware that there were definite possibilities for a determined outside power following the collapse of the Hohenstaufen administration in 1242 and subsequent developments.[128] Mayer has observed that a power vacuum 'without precedence or parallel in the history of the kingdom' developed after the death of Henry I in 1253, the return to France of Louis IX in 1254, and then the death of

[126] *Dipl. Docs.* i. Nos. 282–3; *Foedera*, I. i. 360. Manfred would hold Taranto of Edmund.

[127] I am indebted to Dr Peter Edbury for his information and suggestions concerning what follows.

[128] P. Jackson, 'The End of Hohenstaufen Rule in Syria', *BIHR* lix (1986), 23–6, establishes 1242 as the most likely date.

Conrad. His heir, Conradin, was aged only two in 1254 and would not come of age until 1267; in any case, Hohenstaufen influence in the East was negligible by the early 1250s.[129] Nor should it be forgotten that the Crown of Jerusalem carried immense prestige, and it still remained a lucrative prize in the 1250s.

If these were the prospects which led Henry III to take the Cypriot marriage proposals seriously, then his own fantasies and his dynasty's traditions may have propelled him in the same direction. The new Richard surely remembered that his great-great-grandfather, Fulk of Anjou, had established the Angevin line of kings who ruled Jerusalem between 1131 and 1185 in the direct line; that the throne of the kingdom had been allegedly offered to his grandfather, Henry II, in 1185; and that Richard I had been instrumental in establishing the Lusignan kingdom of Cyprus on the Third Crusade.[130] He was surely aware, too, of the tradition that Robert Curthose had been offered the throne of Jerusalem in 1099 before Godfrey de Bouillon, for the tale is found frequently in Anglo-Norman sources of the thirteenth century.[131] If, perhaps, Henry was seeking in a sense to reconquer Sicily from the Hohenstaufen and restore it to the heirs of the Normans, as Clanchy has suggested, then was he also pondering an attempt to recover the kingdom of Jerusalem for the Plantagenets and bring Cyprus once more into their orbit?[132] Henry's failure to take up the papal offer to commute his vow to Sicily, at first sight puzzling, and his continuing proclamation of intent to depart for the Holy Land begins to become more comprehensible. With Edmund duly installed in Sicily, and with Plantagenet influence established in Cyprus too, the Holy Land might indeed be the more easily secured.

Queen Plaisance's consideration of a marriage alliance in 1256

[129] Mayer, 'Ibelin *versus* Ibelin', esp. pp. 42–3. Geoffrey de Sargines was left in charge of the contingent maintained in the East by Louis IX, becoming marshal, then seneschal, of the kingdom: ibid. 51. Henry was probably concerned to counter this Capetian influence, strong ever since Louis landed in 1250, a response to what Richard has identified as a shift in the 'politique orientale' of the Capetians. Thereby, after 1254, they became 'les protecteurs réguliers' of the crusader states: J. Richard, 'La politique orientale de saint Louis: la croisade de 1248', in *Septième centenaire de la mort de saint Louis* (Paris, 1976), pp. 197–207.

[130] It may have been only antiquarian fantasizing, but Walter of Guisborough, *The Chronicle of Walter of Guisborough, Previously Edited as the Chronicle of Walter of Hemingford or Hemingburgh*, ed. H. Rothwell (Camden Soc., 3rd ser. 89; 1957), 208, reports that when Lord Edward requested the Cypriots' service in the Holy Land in 1271, they replied 'dicentes se teneri mandatis ipsius pro eo quod antecessores sui dominabantur olim terre illorum et se debere regibus Anglorum semper esse fideles'.

[131] See David, *Robert Curthose*, pp. 197–200. Paris, *CM* v. 602, refers to it in relation to the offer of the German throne to Richard of Cornwall in 1257.

[132] Clanchy, *England and Its Rulers*, p. 236.

suggests that she thought it likely that the Plantagenets would indeed seek to become a Mediterranean power and that Henry's crusade might shortly occur.[133] Her thinking was echoed by the hopes of others in Outremer concerning Henry's crusade. Following Louis IX's departure for France in April 1254, all turned to Henry as the leader of the next prospective crusade, their hopes forcefully expressed in the letter sent in the name of the community of Jerusalem in September 1254 imploring Henry to accelerate his passage.[134] But the Cypriot marriage negotiations suggest further that Plaisance had more particular objectives in mind concerning Henry, especially since this is the earliest evidence for the Cypriot Lusignans seeking to intermarry with any Western royal house. (The first such union occurred only in 1317 when Henry II of Cyprus married Constance of Aragon.) Moreover, the fact that the intended partners were Plantagenets was tantamount to a major diplomatic volte-face since Henry I of Cyprus had been a leading member of the party opposed to the Hohenstaufen in the East, and the Plantagenets had been identified with the Hohenstaufen because of their connections.[135]

When Henry I died in 1253 the claim of his infant son, Hugh II, to the regency of Jerusalem was not then presented and the Lusignans lost their tenure of the office. Mayer has argued that Hugh was deliberately excluded, first by John of Arsur (Ibelin), who married his son Balian to Queen Plaisance shortly after Easter 1254, it appears (in the hope either of preventing Hugh from pressing his claim or of benefiting otherwise from the relationship), and then by his kinsman and supposed rival John of Jaffa, who replaced him as regent in August 1254.[136] According to Mayer, John of Jaffa then sought to undermine the marriage of Plaisance and Balian since that would strike at John of Arsur's position, and Alexander IV duly ruled against the union in August 1255 on the grounds of

[133] In Apr. 1252 Henry had informed many leaders of Outremer, including Plaisance's brother, Bohemund VI of Antioch, of his 1256 departure date: *Foedera*, I. i. 282; *CPR 1247–58*, pp. 157–8. Considering sheer distance and logistics, it is exceedingly unlikely that Plaisance would have sought to negotiate with Henry unless there was a real prospect that he might materially affect the situation in the East. In Sept. 1256 Alexander IV sought a new departure date for Henry's crusading passage: *Foedera*, I. i. 347.

[134] 'Burton', pp. 368–9; *Foedera*, I. i. 308. This, and the other letters and missions to Henry in the mid-1250s, must also have been inspired by the fear that he might commute his vow elsewhere. The timing of the Cypriot marriage proposals may have been related to this consideration.

[135] I am indebted for this information to Dr Peter Edbury. In the Holy Land itself, Richard of Cornwall had recently been associated closely with the imperial party during his crusade of 1240–1.

[136] Mayer, 'Ibelin *versus* Ibelin', esp. pp. 43–7.

consanguinity.[137] The political situation remains very unclear and Mayer's arguments in this connection are highly speculative.[138] Nevertheless, annulment suited Plaisance's purpose of loosening the Ibelin hold upon the regency, but if she was to reassert the Lusignan tenure of the office she would need powerful support to counter the immense Ibelin influence. Her brother, Bohemund VI of Antioch, who sided with her when she sought annulment, duly came to her aid.[139] In February 1258 he arrived at Acre with Plaisance and Hugh, presenting Hugh's claim to be heir to the kingdom and Plaisance's claim to the *bailliage* by virtue of her son's minority.[140] But it looks further as if both had previously looked to Henry III's projected crusade as an instrument to be used to their advantage in this business. It cannot be entirely coincidence that the only request for aid known to have been sent from Bohemund to Henry was dispatched in May 1255,[141] and within months the marriage negotiations between Plaisance and Henry were under way. If Henry indeed contemplated the establishment of Plantagenet power in the east Mediterranean then his crusade, in conjunction with the Cypriot marriages, would be crucial. Equally, if Plaisance and Bohemund could secure his support on crusade then the Lusignan claim to Jerusalem, upon which Henry's hopes partially rested, would be altogether more easily realized.

In the event, of course, the marriage alliance with the Cypriot Lusignans did not materialize, nor did the proposed union between Edmund and Manfred's daughter. Henry did not set out on crusade and Edmund was not enthroned in Sicily. None of Henry's ambitions with regard to the Hohenstaufen inheritance was realized, although Richard of Cornwall did what he could to establish himself in Germany; but that, here, is not the point. Out of Henry's failure to restore the Plantagenet inheritance in France was born the perceived necessity to compensate for that failure elsewhere. It is most unlikely that Henry started with the precise intention of supplanting the Hohenstaufen and gathering up their inheritance in Plantagenet hands, but as events unfolded after Frederick II's deposition in

[137] Mayer, 'Ibelin *versus* Ibelin', pp. 46–7.

[138] See esp. P. W. Edbury, 'John of Ibelin's Title to the County of Jaffa and Ascalon', *EHR* xcviii (1983), 115–33; and Mayer's reply, 'John of Jaffa, his Opponents, and his Fiefs', *Proc. of the American Philosophical Soc.* cxxviii (1984), 134–63; J. S. C. Riley-Smith, *The Feudal Nobility and the Kingdom of Jerusalem, 1174–1277* (London, 1973), esp. pp. 215–16, concerning the regency.

[139] Riley-Smith, *Feudal Nobility*, p. 216.

[140] G. F. Hill, *A History of Cyprus*, 3 vols. (Cambridge, 1940–52), ii. 150–1. In Feb. 1258, significantly, Alexander IV again pronounced against the marriage of Plaisance and Balian.

[141] 'Burton', pp. 369–71; *Foedera*, I. i. 321.

1245, and as opportunities opened up in different directions, something of a grand design appears to have emerged, slowly and piecemeal, under the force of competition from others, notably the Capetians and Alfonso X of Castile. The new Plantagenet empire, so envisaged, would be immeasurably more powerful than that of old. It would dominate both Eastern and Western Christendom, and the Capetians, to return to the old rivalry, would be totally overshadowed. If Matthew Paris can be believed, Henry even regarded the establishment of this new polity as a means to the restoration of the former Plantagenet greatness in France. He reports, *sub anno* 1255, that Henry considered that his French lands could be regained, by force if necessary, 'because between Apulia and England, France would be crushed as if between two millstones'.[142]

Henry's crusading vow was taken coincidentally at the point when the problems posed by the Hohenstaufen legacy began to emerge as the central issue in the power politics of Christendom. The crusade may even have been something of an unwelcome distraction in 1250, partly forced upon Henry by his compulsion to match Louis IX in the game of status and prestige, as we have seen. In the course of the next few years, however, Henry's projected crusade began to take on a very different complexion as events unfolded, emerging as just one element of an elaborate foreign policy. The story of Henry's vow in the 1250s is fully comprehensible only if it is set within the context of that developing foreign policy and the rationale upon which it was based.

Henry's votive obligations remained binding following the collapse of those wider schemes, but in the 1260s papal policy and Plantagenet interests combined once again to militate against his departure for the Holy Land.[143] The circumstances, however, were distinctly different, since the baronial movement of reform in 1258 ushered in a period of prolonged civil instability. From 1263 England slid into civil war with gathering momentum, and until peace was restored there was simply no possibility that Henry could or would fulfil his vow. Even after the battle of Evesham no attempt was made by Clement IV to secure the fulfilment of that vow. Realistically, the papacy considered that Henry's role should consist not in crusading but in settling the realm.

This attitude equally affected the Lord Edward, eager to accompany Louis IX on his second expedition to the East. Both Clement IV

142 Paris, *CM* v. 516.

143 Only once apparently, in 1263, was Henry, along with other English *crucesignati*, urged by the papacy to fulfil or redeem his vow: 'Continuation' of Gervase of Canterbury, *The Historical Works of Gervase of Canterbury*, ed. W. Stubbs, 2 vols. (RS; 1879, 1880), ii. 231–2.

and Henry himself were united in opposing Edward's intention. Indeed, in April 1268 Clement authorized his legate Ottobuono to release Henry from his vow if he sent not Edward but Edmund in his stead.[144] This was probably Clement's response to Henry's petition; thereby Edward, the heir to the throne, would be retained at home against any further outbreak of strife. Clement's thinking at this time is revealed by his letter to Louis IX in January 1268. He noted that Edward had recently sought papal counsel concerning his crusading plan and had requested financial subsidy to enable him to proceed. Clement strongly advised against Edward's intention, arguing that the political situation remained a cause for concern, and that it would be unsafe and irresponsible to leave the ageing Henry in such straits. He had therefore rejected Edward's request for aid.[145] The peaceful settlement of the realm was the overriding priority, taking precedence over Edward's personal wishes and over the interests of the Holy Land.

Edward I

Edward's failure to set out on crusade as king is an altogether less complex affair, for his second vow, taken in 1287, did not become engulfed in grandiose schemes and ambitions in foreign policy.[146] It simply remained unfulfilled for the remaining twenty years of Edward's life.

Precisely because he alone of the major leaders of Louis IX's second crusade completed his passage to the East, Edward won an enviable international reputation and thereafter was regarded widely as the potential leader of a new *passagium generale*, for the time being supplanting the Capetians as the expected saviour of the Holy Land. The hope projected upon him is patently clear from that long sequence of newsletters, appeals, and embassies dispatched to him from the East throughout his reign,[147] an effort complemented by an equally long series of papal appeals, for Edward, unlike his father, was regarded from the outset of his reign as a potential crusade leader who should be encouraged.[148]

144 *Reg. Clement IV*, No. 609; and further above, pp. 146–7.

145 *Reg. Clement IV*, No. 1288; *Thesaurus novus anecdotorum*, ed. E. Martène and U. Durand, 5 vols. (Paris, 1717), ii. No. 583.

146 See Lunt, *Financial Relations*, p. 338 n. 9, for the problem of dating Edward's vow precisely.

147 See above, pp. 23–31, 34, and appendix 1.

148 The combined pressure was intense. Of all the Plantagenet kings, his support for the crusade was the most eagerly sought.

This marked shift in papal policy is probably explained by the destruction of the Hohenstaufen cause in the West and the establishment of Charles of Anjou in Sicily after 1268, for the extinction of the Hohenstaufen not only liberated the papacy but freed the English king from papal restraints determined by the threat of the hated dynasty.[149] The appeals began even before Edward had returned to England from his crusade. In November and December 1273 Gregory X sought his personal attendance at the Council of Lyons II, planned to begin in May 1274 and concerned chiefly with the affairs of the Holy Land and the launching of a new crusade.[150] Edward did not attend, but Gregory continued to urge the crusade upon him and his persistence was duly rewarded by Edward's declaration, at some point before November 1275, that he would take the Cross.[151] This commitment, however vague, led a succession of popes thereafter to press Edward to make good his intention. The climax was reached under Honorius IV and Nicholas IV; by then Edward had again taken the Cross, and never, upon the fall of Tripoli in 1289 and then Acre in 1291, was his help more desperately needed.

In the process culminating in Edward's second vow, negotiations over the grant of moneys for the crusade, and the timing of their release to the king, loomed large. This, combined with Edward's eventual use of those funds for domestic policies, has led some historians to assert that the king's chief interest in taking the Cross lay in his wish to secure those moneys to sustain his position at home.[152] This may perhaps be a partly defensible assumption, though little more, concerning Edward's intentions in the critical and difficult last period of his reign, from *c.*1291, but it is an unwarranted slur upon

149 Angevin Sicily proved as difficult to control as Hohenstaufen Sicily, but an era in papal policy which had looked to the English king as a protector in reserve had come to an end.

150 *Reg. Gregory X*, Nos. 327–9. Edward's refusal to heed Gregory's plea that he reschedule his coronation, planned at the very time of the council, is evidence of the conflict between royal interests and the crusade at this early date: see P. A. Throop, *Criticism of the Crusade: A Study of Public Opinion and Crusade Propaganda* (Amsterdam, 1940), 220–1. The proposals in Edward's council for the briefing of proctors to attend at Lyons further underline the point: *Councils*, II. ii. 811–14.

151 See *Reg. Gregory X*, Nos. 945, 960. He was considering the crusade again as early as Jan. 1275, judging by a letter to the Mongol khan: *Foedera*, I. ii. 520; *CPR 1272–81*, p. 116. See also *Foedera*, I. ii. 522, for the letter of May 1275 to Alfonso X of Castile, alluding to negotiations with Gregory X.

152 For example, Purcell, *Papal Crusading Policy*, p. 156. Edward ultimately did well, certainly: see Lunt, *Financial Relations*, esp. pp. 335–6, 342–65; also, J. H. Denton, *Robert Winchelsey and the Crown, 1294–1313: A Study in the Defence of Ecclesiastical Liberty* (Cambridge, 1980), 64–6. Powicke, *Henry III*, ii. 729, made strenuous efforts to defend Edward's actions. Undoubtedly Edward's finances, rather than the Holy Land or the Holy See, benefited most, but to postulate from this prior motives and intentions on Edward's part is a perilous and dubious exercise.

his sincerity and intent in the 1270s and 1280s. The fact is that following the pestering of Gregory X, Innocent V, and perhaps Adrian V, Edward empowered his envoys in December 1276 to bind himself or his brother Edmund to set out at the next *passagium generale* to the Holy Land.[153] If Edward's only, or chief, interest lay in securing moneys and then utilizing them for his own ends, why did he propose his brother as substitute for himself? He would gain nothing thereby. Neither John XXI nor Nicholas III, however, would accept the proposal; it was Edward's departure on crusade they wished to secure, not Edmund's in lieu.[154] But it is a measure of Edward's commitment that he persisted with the nomination of Edmund, dispatching embassies to both Nicholas III and Martin IV and persuading the archbishops of Canterbury and York to lobby the papal Curia concurrently. In August 1280 Archbishop Wickwane sent a total of twenty letters, warmly recommending Edmund, to Nicholas III, the cardinals, and curial notaries, a remarkable offensive.[155] Shortly afterwards, Archbishop Pecham wrote to Nicholas in similar vein, depicting Edmund in glowing terms.[156] An almost identical letter was rushed off to Martin IV in April 1281 following receipt of the news of Nicholas's death.[157]

The popes remained unmoved by these representations. After yet another attempt by Edward to secure endorsement of his plan in 1282, Martin IV killed it off.[158] In January 1283 he expressed his deep sorrow that Edward did not intend to set out at the next *passagium generale* and urged him to reconsider. He would not accept Edmund in his place; the moneys for the crusade would remain on deposit.[159] Edward reluctantly accepted Martin's ruling in what had become a tiresome wrangle, and in late 1283 or early 1284 he announced his willingness to take the Cross.[160] There followed a long

[153] *Foedera*, I. ii. 532, 537; *CPR 1272–81*, p. 186.

[154] This is quite plain from the negotiations, 1276–80. See esp. *Reg. Nicholas III*, Nos. 961, 1110–11; *Foedera*, I. ii. 560–1. Nicholas was prepared to make concessions to secure Edward's vow: 25,000*m*. from the proceeds of the tenth would be advanced when he took the Cross. Gregory X had expressly stipulated that nothing would be paid until Edward should have sailed: *Reg. Gregory X*, No. 945.

[155] *The Register of William Wickwane, Lord Archbishop of York, 1279–85*, ed. W. Brown (Surtees Soc. 114; 1907), 184–7; *Historical Papers and Letters from the Northern Registers*, ed. J. Raine (RS; 1873), 63–4.

[156] *Registrum Epistolarum Johannis Peckham Archiepiscopi Cantuariensis (1279–92)* , ed. C. T. Martin, 3 vols. (RS; 1882–5), i. 140–1.

[157] Ibid. 190–1.

[158] For the 1282 negotiations see *Foedera*, I. ii. 606–7, 610; *CCR 1279–88*, p. 187.

[159] *Reg. Martin IV*, No. 286; *Foedera*, I. ii. 624; *CCR 1279–88*, pp. 235–6.

[160] *Reg. Martin IV*, No. 569; *Foedera*, I. ii. 641–2. The papacy's inflexible stance throughout probably owed most to the conviction that the reputation of a prospective crusade leader exerted a highly positive influence on recruitment. Both Pecham and Wickwane hint at this consideration in their letters. See nn. 156, 157 for refs.

and tedious period of negotiation concerning the exact terms and conditions upon which Edward would take the Cross and be granted subsidies. In June 1287 he formally took crusading vows and by May 1290 the negotiations concerning his passage were complete: his departure was fixed for 24 June 1293 and arrangements made for the prior payment of moneys in 1291 and 1292. At last, it seemed, the long-awaited liberator of the Holy Land would be setting sail.[161]

Edward's obvious reluctance to commit himself personally to the crusade before 1283–4, and then his subsequent failure to fulfil his second vow, is quite satisfactorily explained by the pressures upon him at home, in France, and further afield. Faced initially by the demands of his position as a new king, and a reforming one at that, and then by the deterioration of relations with Llywelyn ap Gruffydd which led to the Welsh wars of 1277 and 1282–3, Edward seems genuine enough in the excuses he put forward in the 1270s and 1280s.[162] The fact that he only agreed to commit himself personally once the second Welsh war had been brought to a successful close points to the same conclusion, and Edward consistently expressed his firm intention of setting out for the East thereafter, and then of fulfilling his obligations in person once he had taken his second vow. His sincerity is suggested by the energetic and varied measures which he took to prepare for his passage, set for 24 June 1293.[163] As Powicke indicated, so many of Edward's initiatives can be related to his eagerness to order business which might hinder his passage.[164] But the matter of the Scottish succession initiated a sequence of developments which unhinged all plans for departure at the appointed time. With gathering momentum a protracted crisis engulfed Edward in the affairs of Scotland, France, England, and Wales: his passage had to be postponed. By 1296, even more by 1300, it was out of the question for the foreseeable future.

161 On the negotiations see esp. Powicke, *Henry III*, ii. 728–9; Lunt, *Financial Relations*, pp. 337–40. Edward formally sealed the agreement with Nicholas IV on 25 Oct. 1290: *Foedera*, I. ii. 747.

162 Edward's reactions to Alfonso X's requests for aid against the Saracens of Spain and North Africa in this period provide an illuminating comparison. At first, in 1275–6, Edward was amenable, allowing his subjects to go in aid of Alfonso, ordering the construction of galleys at his cost in Gascony to be sent to Castile, and urging the citizens of Gascon ports to help out. The deepening Welsh crisis forced a halt. In 1277 and again in 1282 he turned down Alfonso's request for further aid because of his involvement in Wales: *Foedera*, I. ii. 522, 531, 540, 606–7; *CPR 1272–81*, pp. 128, 137, 155, 176.

163 Powicke, *Henry III*, ii. 729, commented that 'Cynicism is easy in reflection about Edward's second crusade, but it is not just.' The contrast to his treatment of Henry III's 1250 vow is striking.

164 Powicke, *Thirteenth Century*, esp. pp. 266–8; id., *Henry III*, ii. esp. pp. 731–3.

Edward continued to proclaim his intention of aiding the Holy Land throughout this stormy period. *In abstracto* he was probably sincere, but his genuineness in continuing to state that he hoped soon to depart may be questioned.[165] At best, it was a fervent though hopelessly unrealistic wish; at worst, it may have represented a crude attempt to retain the moneys for the crusade which, by then, he had appropriated. For those who held the cause of the Holy Land dear, Edward's declarations were perhaps a sad deception, although it must be emphasized that it was the papacy which had refused to countenance substitution for Edward's intended role as *capitaneus exercitus Christiani*. The hope which had resided with him for so long proved to be unjustified. Like his father, though for different reasons, Edward too died with his crusading vow unfulfilled. If Henry's three vows reveal the influence and workings of papal policy as much as the pressures of Plantagenet interests in the West, then the constant prevarications of his son admirably demonstrate the very real obstacles in the path of an aspiring crusader king.

This last point may be usefully expanded to provide a wider context for the vows of Henry and Edward. It has already been observed that without exception all of their royal Plantagenet predecessors took the Cross, yet the failure of all but Richard I to fulfil their vows in person indicates that he alone was willing to risk Plantagenet interests in the West for the cause. In magnified form this illustrates a primary restraint upon all men so far as personal participation on crusade is concerned: the fear that their interests or ambitions, however humble or great, would be compromised, disturbed, or lost during their absence. It was part of a wider dilemma, for there were always matters to attend to at home, and always other interests to occupy a man's thoughts and energies. A degree of tension between the pull of the crusade and the demands of family, dynasty, or crass self-interest was unavoidable. At the highest levels of society the problem was naturally more acute since so much more was at stake; for kings, by virtue of their status, it was most pressing. The call to the crusade forced them to confront fundamental questions of the most searching kind: were they first and foremost leaders of that wider community of Christendom, or were their loyalties and obligations altogether more narrow in the last analysis? Would the

[165] Edward's justification for continued delay became tortuous. In Apr. 1306 he went so far as to claim that Archbishop Winchelsey's continuing presence in England was then the chief obstacle to his departure: *CCR 1302–7*, p. 430; and see the comments of Denton, *Robert Winchelsey*, pp. 220, 233. Among many letters promising departure in this period, see *CCR 1302–7*, pp. 77–8, 208, 348; *Foedera*, I. ii. 949, 974; *Anc. Corr.* 14. 84, 85. The communications he received from prospective crusading companions in the early 1290s indicate that some, at least, considered him serious: see above, ch. 4 n. 200.

security of their realms be jeopardized if they went on crusade? The words which Paris puts into the mouth of Henry III by way of reply to Bishop Waleran of Beirut's request to preach the crusade in 1245 capture something of the essence of the problem:

I am surrounded by my enemies. I suspect the king of the Franks. I suspect the king of the Scots still more. The prince of Wales is openly opposed to me. The pope protects those who rise against me. I do not wish that my land, emptied of its knighthood and money, should be deprived of its strength.[166]

On this occasion, the demands upon the *rex Angliae* took precedence over the pressures upon him as *rex crucesignandus*, and, as the passage indicates, if secular rulers felt themselves insecure or threatened, they were more likely to seek to restrain from crusading those subjects whose services they required. Edward I solved the dilemma simply: the crusade consistently took second place. Keen to crusade though he was, he never forgot that his first priorities were those of a king of England. His stance is neatly encapsulated in the terms of that famous vow taken in the twilight of his long career in 1306. He swore with his knights first to go against Robert Bruce and then, on the conclusion of that business, but only then, to go to the Holy Land, never to bear arms against Christians again.[167]

This attitude was reinforced by a related restraint, though of different complexion: the conventional duty of a king towards his subjects. The dialectic which this involved in relation to the crusade is perhaps best illustrated by Henry II's rejection of the appeal by the patriarch of Jerusalem in 1185. Henry summoned a council to discuss the matter at length at Clerkenwell. Of the various accounts of the proceedings, that penned by Ralph of Diceto is the most interesting from the present perspective. He reports that the magnates rested their case for outright rejection of the appeal on the king's coronation oath, for therein Henry had promised to protect the Church, establish and maintain the peace, prevent rapine and all manner of iniquities, and render justice to all. Thus, 'it seemed preferable to all, and more in the king's spiritual welfare, that he should govern his realm with due care, and protect it from the incursions of *barbari* and from foreign peoples, than take care for the deliverance of the Orientals in his own

166 Paris, *CM*, iv. 489.

167 *Flores*, iii. 131–2; Nicholas Trevet (Trivet), *Annales sex Regum Angliae, 1135–1307*, ed. T. Hog (English Historical Soc.; 1845), pp. 408–9. This attitude is echoed in certain of Edward's letters. In May 1304, e.g., he explained to the master of the Temple that wars at home had thus far prevented his passage; he would sail 'with all speed, when the wars have been composed': *CCR 1302–7*, p. 208. When wintering in Sicily *en route* for the Holy Land in 1270–1, Edward made plain that he would abandon his crusade, if, *inter alia*, his father should die or war break out in England: *De ant. leg.*, p. 131.

person'.[168] Nothing could better express the obligations and restraints upon the king, as the protector and defender of the realm and his subjects, than this appeal to the coronation oath, raising imperatives which were fundamentally at odds with the very notion of crusade.[169] The objection to royal crusading in these terms occasionally surfaced in the thirteenth century. Peter Langtoft, for example, observed with regard to the Scottish question in 1293

> And if King Edward had gone towards Acre
> Greatly would the kingdom and royalty have been in peril.[170]

Langtoft's sense of priorities was shared by the Melrose chronicler in his account of Edward's crusade of 1270–2.[171] Edward is first contrasted favourably with Charles of Anjou, that 'proditor Christianismi' who diverted the crusade to Tunis, and he notes with evident approval Edward's declaration that he would never return home until he had fulfilled his vow and done his utmost to succour the Holy Land and confound the pagans. But then, he reports, Edward heard news of Henry III's death, and so 'he had of necessity to return home to be crowned, to succeed his father in the kingdom'. The chronicler was in no doubt at all that Edward had got his priorities right.[172] No matter how laudable participation in the crusade was perceived to be, and how much prestige and glory rubbed off on king and kingdom as a result, the narrower interests of king and subjects had to come first.

How far, and to what extent, such views were shared by contemporaries cannot be gauged, and Louis IX's determination to press ahead with his second crusade in the face of opposition from some, at least, of his subjects indicates that a great deal depended upon the charisma, force of will, and commitment of a *rex crucesignandus*. Nevertheless, it may be suggested that in thirteenth-century England,

[168] Ralph de Diceto, *Opera historica*, ed. W. Stubbs, 2 vols. (RS; 1876), ii. 33–4. See also Gerald of Wales, *Opera*, ed. J. S. Brewer *et al.* 8 vols. (RS; 1861–91), viii. 207–9; Gervase, *Chron.*, i. 325; William of Newburgh, 'Historia Rerum Anglicarum', in *Chronicles of the Reigns of Stephen, Henry II and Richard I*, ed. R. Howlett, 2 vols. (RS; 1884, 1885), i. 247; Howden, *Gesta*, i. 335–6; id., *Chron.*, ii. 299–301. See further B. Z. Kedar, 'The Patriarch Eraclius', in B. Z. Kedar *et al.* (eds.), *Outremer: Studies in the History of the Crusading Kingdom of Jerusalem Presented to Joshua Prawer* (Jerusalem, 1982), esp. pp. 191–4. Whether Henry was entirely ingenuous in summoning the council or not, the fact that he was reminded of his coronation oath suggests that it was considered an entirely credible reason for rejecting the approach.

[169] It could be objected that Eraclius's appeal involved rather more than crusading, temporary by definition, if the throne of Jerusalem was on offer.

[170] *The Chronicle of Pierre de Langtoft in French verse*, ed. T. Wright, 2 vols. (RS; 1866, 1868), ii. 267.

[171] *Chronica de Mailros*, ed. J. Stevenson (Bannatyne Club, 50; 1835), 218–19.

[172] The magnates urged Edward to return with all speed, in the interests of the realm, on Henry's death: *Foedera*, I. ii. 497.

under the impact of the rapidly developing concept of the community of the realm and the application of the notions of consultation and consent to royal action, royal participation in the crusade came to be considered as a matter about which his subjects' advice should be sought. A king would certainly have been well advised to take their views into account, for his subjects' support, in person or specie, would be critical to the successful fulfilment of a crusading vow, and a crusade was in a sense a species of that genus of foreign policy about which the community of the realm had a great deal to say.[173]

Support for the Crusade

The vows of Henry III and Edward I, then, remained as residual tokens. Nevertheless, there were other ways to aid the cause, and it was through these means that both kings sought to meet their obligations as kings, Plantagenets, and Christians.

Perhaps their most valuable service lay in the support they afforded their crusading subjects, easing their preparations and enabling them to fulfil their vows in the ways which we have seen,[174] but of their own direct contributions, the most important was probably the reservation of money. This took many forms. There were, first, the occasional grants made directly to the rulers of Outremer. The chief beneficiary was probably John de Brienne, king of Jerusalem, who came to England in 1223 seeking aid. The precise yield of the poll tax levied on his behalf is unknown, but there is every reason to consider that it was considerable, even though it was a voluntary grant.[175] According to the Barnwell annalist, John returned home loaded with silver and gold donated by the king, prelates, earls, and barons.[176]

The military orders and other institutions intimately connected with the Latin East were major recipients of royal patronage. Some grants were *ad hoc*. In January 1238, for example, Henry III granted 500*m*. to the master of the Temple for the ransom of

173 It is significant in this context that Henry III cited the advice of his subjects when conferring his Cross upon Edward in Aug. 1270: *Foedera*, I. i. 485; *CPR 1266–72*, p. 452.

174 See above, Ch. 5 *passim*.

175 Mitchell, *Taxation*, pp. 138–9, seems to suggest that 800*m*. was the overall total on the basis of two royal mandates concerning disbursement of the proceeds. But these may have been the only two enrolled. See generally, ibid. 19–20, 35–6, 67; and *RLC* i. 516b, 518b, 567, 567b; *PR 1216–25*, pp. 512, 527.

176 Coventry, *Memoriale*, ii. 252; also Ralph of Coggeshall, *Chronicon Anglicanum*, ed. J. Stevenson (RS; 1875), 193–4, but compare with 'Dunstable', pp. 80, 85.

Templars captured in battle in the principality of Antioch.[177] In April 1242 another 500*m.* was delivered to the master of the English Temple in aid of the Holy Land.[178] These are random examples; the aggregate total sum granted under Henry III and Edward I must have been very considerable. In addition were the regular annual payments to the orders. The Templars received the so-called 'Templars' mark', taken from the revenues of each shire from at least 1156. Under Henry III and Edward, the master of the English Temple received an annual fee of 50*m.* at the Exchequer, for the purpose of maintaining one knight in the Holy Land.[179] In 1235 Henry III granted the Teutonic Knights an annual fee of 40*m.*, perhaps with the same intention; it very probably owed something to the marriage of Frederick II, their great patron, to Isabella Plantagenet in that year.[180] After a lapse in payment from *c.*1261, 'ex certa causa', Edward renewed the grant in 1279.[181] The Order of St Lazarus was another to receive fixed alms, the sum again of 40*m.* first being granted by John, it seems, in 1212.[182] Curiously enough, neither the English confraternity of St Edward, Acre, nor the Order of St Thomas of Acre, the sole English military order, attracted much direct patronage from Henry and Edward.[183] Reference should also be made to the miscellaneous grants made to all orders touching their establishments in England, but survey of these matters lies beyond the scope of this work. The Temple appears to have been especially favoured.[184]

[177] *CPR 1232–47*, p. 207. Sometimes money was lent. See e.g. ibid. 209; 1,000*l.* for the prior of the Hospital to take East.

[178] *Rôles Gascons*, i. No. 920.

[179] See e.g. *CLR 1251–60*, pp. 53–4, 482. The last payment recorded under Henry III is dated 23 Oct. 1259: ibid. 484. In Nov. 1280 Edward instructed resumption of the payment: *CCR 1279–88*, p. 70; *CCh.R 1257–1300*, pp. 237–8. The lapse from 1259 probably resulted from baronial conciliar decisions.

[180] See P. Riant, 'Privilèges octroyés à l'Ordre Teutonique', *Archives de l'Orient Latin*, i (1881), esp. p. 417; *CCh.R 1226–57*, p. 200.

[181] *CCh.R 1257–1300*, p. 214.

[182] *RLC* i. 125b. Payments may be traced in the Close Rolls, to 1226, then Liberate Rolls. Again, the payment lapsed from *c.*1261, Edward restoring it in Oct. 1281: *CCR 1279–88*, p. 100.

[183] On the confraternity, probably founded by Edward I during or after his crusade, see J. S. C. Riley-Smith, 'A Note on Confraternities in the Latin Kingdom of Jerusalem', *BIHR* xliv (1971), 303. Richard I played an important part in the foundation of the Order of St Thomas, but his successors displayed little interest. In 1261 Bishop Florence of Acre underlined the liberality afforded by contrast to the Temple and Hospital by Henry III: *Dipl. Docs.* i. No. 343; *Anc. Corr.* 47. 27. On the Order, see A. J. Forey, 'The Military Order of St. Thomas of Acre', *EHR* xcii (1977), 481–503.

[184] The comparative lack of interest in the Hospitallers, their great rivals, is striking. The kings supported the orders raising aid in England for the crusade or their own institutions. As early as 1207, for example, protection was granted to messengers of

We have already seen how both kings, at times, lent their support to promotional campaigns by subsidizing preachers and helping the executors of the Cross and their agents in their various tasks.[185] Only once, in 1245, it seems, was an attempt made to prevent the promotion of the crusade when Henry III discouraged Bishop Waleran of Beirut from preaching the Cross in England.[186] Waleran was not treated discourteously, however, for he was granted a silver chalice and a mitre, each worth around 100*s*., a further 100*s*. with which to buy a palfrey, 40*m*. (probably towards his expenses), and free passage back across the Channel for himself and his household.[187] Such treatment was typical of the honourable reception enjoyed by nuncios and messengers from the Latin East at the Plantagenet court, in part because etiquette dictated it but also because both kings seem to have been genuinely concerned to display their sympathy with the cause.[188] Their patronage extended to those refugees from the Latin East who sought and received asylum in England. In June 1260, for example, Henry III granted an annual fee of 60*m*. for the maintenance of Augustine of Nottingham, the English bishop of Laodicea (Latakia); the king expressed his particular compassion for the impoverished prelate, driven from his see by the Saracens.[189] The dwellings of the king's household chaplains and clerics at Windsor were requisitioned for Augustine's use, and extensive repairs, alterations, and decorations carried out at Henry's expense.[190] Augustine died in January 1261; Henry graciously paid off his debts and granted 10*m*. for the maintenance of Cecily, his sister.[191]

Finally, Henry and Edward took steps to provide aid for the

the Order of St Thomas as they collected alms for the redemption of captives in the Holy Land: *RLP*, p. 76. For similar grants to the Order of St Lazarus, and for grants to the house of St Robert of Knaresborough, of the Trinitarians, see e.g. *CPR 1266–72*, p. 526; *CPR 1281–92*, pp. 113, 137, 431; *CPR 1292–1301*, p. 253.

185 See above, esp. pp. 44–5, 59, n. 70.

186 Paris, *CM* iv. 488–9. Henry's recorded objections seem reasonable enough considering the military activity against David of Snowdonia at this time, the show of strength for the benefit of Alexander II of Scotland in 1244, and difficulties in England and Gascony.

187 On Waleran's visit, see above, pp. 29–30, and below, appendix 2.

188 See references cited below, appendix 2.

189 *CLR 1251–60*, pp. 510, 516–17. He was the brother of William of Nottingham, provincial minister of the English Franciscans, 1240–54. See *Monumenta Franciscana*, ed. J. S. Brewer and R. Howlett, 2 vols. (RS; 1858, 1882), i. 62, 551; further, B. Hamilton, *The Latin Church in the Crusader States: The Secular Church* (London, 1980), 233, 235 n.

190 *CLR 1251–60*, pp. 514, 525; *CLR 1260–7*, p. 14. Wine and firewood were also supplied: *CR 1259–61*, pp. 307, 313, 325.

191 *CLR 1260–7*, pp. 18, 39; *CR 1259–61*, p. 331. In gratitude, Augustine left Henry various personal possessions, including his relics: *CPR 1258–66*, p. 138. For William, titular archbishop of Edessa, in asylum in England, probably his homeland, *c.*1264/5–1282, see *CPR 1258–66*, pp. 405, 461, 463, 553, 571, 680; *CLR 1260–7*,

crusade posthumously, partly in the attempt to ensure the fulfilment of their unredeemed vows. As early as 1253 Henry instructed that upon his death all his gold, excepting his jewels, should be taken to the Holy Land, together with his Cross.[192] Shortly before his own death, Edward willed that his heart be buried in the Holy Land and that 100 knights perform posthumous service for one year in the East. Certain evidence that his wishes were fulfilled is lacking, but Otto de Grandson, his close friend and comrade-in-arms for so many years, may have left England in 1307 to carry out his master's will.[193] There is also evidence that Edward had maintained a standing force of knights at Acre between 1272 and 1291.[194]

However welcome this support, the inhabitants of the Latin East may nevertheless have recalled that famous statement attributed to Patriarch Eraclius, despondent after his failure to secure Henry II's personal support in 1185: 'Almost all the world will offer us money, but it is a prince we need; we would prefer a leader even without money, to money without a prince.'[195] Precisely because they were princes, and wealthy princes at that, all of the Plantagenets came under pressure to go in aid of the Latin East in person, and the rulers of Outremer understood well enough that where they led their subjects would follow. Equally, Henry II could not, or would not, go in person for broadly the same sort of reasons which prevented his grandson and great-grandson from fulfilling their vows. Henry II, too, accepted a duty towards the crusading movement and did what he could to aid the cause, but ultimately he would not sacrifice Plantagenet interests in the West to that goal. He also subsidized knights in the Holy Land, patronized the military orders, lent his support to promotional campaigns and taxation on behalf of the Holy Land, received nuncios with honour and dispatched them home disappointed yet with gifts, sent money to the East, and left considerable sums in his will for the support of the Holy Land and its institutions.[196] The failure of Henry III and Edward I to set out on crusade may, then, be located within a wider English royal pattern, to

p. 181; *CR 1264–8*, p. 292; *CCR 1272–9*, pp. 30, 370; *CCR 1279–88*, pp. 155, 180; PRO, C 62/49, m. 2; C 62/50, m. 7. Bishop Hugh of Gibelet stayed for two years, 1289–91, with Edward's licence. Probably English, certainly a Franciscan, Hugh seemingly left the East on the fall of Tripoli in 1289: *Chron. Lanercost*, p. 130; Hamilton, *Latin Church*, p. 240.

[192] *Foedera*, I. i. 496 (misdated).

[193] C. L. Kingsford, 'Sir Otho de Grandison (1238–1328)', *TRHS* 3rd ser. iii (1909). 138. 160.

[194] Rishanger, *Chron.*, p. 78.

[195] Gerald, *Opera*, viii. 208; and v. 362–3.

[196] See, now H. E. Mayer, 'Henry II of England and the Holy Land', *EHR* xcvii (1982), 721–39.

which Richard I was the exception because he alone, as king, took support to the extent of personal participation. The way in which society was structured rendered that failure critical to the overall level of participation in the crusades in thirteenth-century England.

CONCLUSION

Most historians of later medieval England have attached little importance to the place of the crusade in English society and have regarded the crusade as possessing no more than marginal and occasional significance for English history. This is understandable but it is not justifiable. It is true that the English contribution to the crusading movement throughout its history was modest—in so far as participation provides a rough-and-ready yardstick—although the considerable sums raised for the crusade should not be forgotten. Moreover, those who went on crusade achieved comparatively little. The only notable exception is Richard I, for his crusade established the kingdom of Cyprus and ensured the survival of the Latin kingdom of Jerusalem for another century: it is no coincidence that more attention has been paid to his crusade than any other venture. As far as the period covered by this book is concerned, when English crusading activity was in its heyday, the expeditions of such men as Ranulf of Chester, Richard of Cornwall, Simon de Montfort, William Longespee, Lords Edward and Edmund, or Otto de Grandson, can scarcely be considered glittering successes in the field. There are no great feats of English arms to record, though credit is due especially to Richard of Cornwall for his diplomatic successes on behalf of the Latin kingdom. It is further the case that English settlement in the crusader states was minimal. A few individuals made careers for themselves in Church or State, some rising high up the social order, but there never existed the mesh of ties, going back to the original conquest, which linked the crusader states closely to Italy and, above all, France. This is true also of the kingdom of Cyprus which, though conquered by Richard I, never saw significant English settlement or influence. And, for these reasons, if the crusader states were the first essay in European colonialism, as some contend, then it is scarcely surprising that English historians have not been drawn strongly to the subject.

Nor is it possible to argue that the crusading movement had any profound or decisive impact upon English historical development in other ways. The crusade played no part in the establishment of the English State, nor did it play a role in its territorial extension. So far as constitutional development is concerned, it is sometimes argued that the communal movement at Acre provided a model for the baronial movement in England in 1258, and that Simon de Montfort especially may have been influenced by what he experienced on crusade in 1240–1. There is, however, no definite proof that knowledge of conditions in Outremer, then or at any other time, directly affected developments in England.

Account should also be taken of the influence of that narrowly Anglocentric outlook of many nineteenth- and early twentieth-century historians for this too has tended to militate against consideration of the subject. Apart from the deeds of Richard I, incongruously a source of national pride since Richard was not English (nor Anglo-Norman), the English role in the crusading movement was scarcely conducive to extensive historical exploration. Indeed, this limited achievement led some, building upon the judgements of Hume, Gibbon, and others, to question the wisdom of English involvement at all, especially that of kings. According to this line of thought, the crusade was a regrettable distraction, deflecting the ruler from his proper concerns at home, and leading in the case of Richard I to disastrous consequences for both himself and his subjects. Logically, the crusade could also be seen as a deplorable squandering of resources which could have been more profitably employed in England or to England's advantage.

This Anglocentric perspective is to be rejected, not least because it fails to allow for the international pull of the crusade and England's place within the wider world of Christendom, and because Anglocentrism is simply inappropriate for approachig the period. It opbscures and distorts the place of the crusading movement in English society. It is also unwise to dismiss the crusade as being only marginally significant in England, and therefore unworthy of investigation, and it is fallacious to judge the importance of the crusading effort in England by its limited results in the East. First, that effort was, in fact, very considerable. The evidence shows that the scale of the English contribution was no consequence of a failure to promote the crusade to the Holy Land, at least, once Pope Alexander III, breaking with the attitude of his predecessors, came to regard England as a major source of aid. If Powicke was correct in saying that the notion of the recovery of the Holy Land was inseparable from the air men breathed, then the primary reason must lie in the persistent and extensive measures taken to propagate the crusading cause. As far as our period is concerned, every decade between 1181 and 1291 saw the launching of a new preaching campaign on a national scale. Scarcely a year went by without some promotional activity on the part of the papacy, the Latin East, or their Eastern allies. Few, then, can have remained ignorant of the fortunes of the Latin East or of their obligations to the crusading movement, which the agents of promotion sought to impress upon them.

Awareness is one thing, opinion another matter altogether. It lies beyond the scope of this book to investigate systematically the matter of the crusade in contemporary opinion, but had the crusade been of only marginal interest, limited significance, and viewed with general scepticism or cynicism in England, it would be difficult to explain why men sometimes dated their charters by reference to crusading activity and events in the East, why histories of the crusade continued to be copied and translated into the vernacular, why descriptions, guides, and maps of Jerusalem and the holy places were made, why poems in praise of contemporary crusading heroes were composed, why ancestral crusading was proudly cherished, and why many romances required some crusading experience for their subjects. It would also be extremely difficult to explain how crusading ideology and crusading rewards could have been applied in the political struggles of 1215–17 and 1263–5. Evidently, the crusade was far from being moribund or of no import in thirteenth-century England.

Nor does the limited numerical participation of Englishmen in the thirteenth-century crusades necessarily imply that the crusade commanded limited support. Much of this book has been concerned to explore how a papal crusading policy operated in tandem with the considerable controls and restraints immanent in English society itself to restrict the exercise of the free will of many—combatants as well as non-combatants— in the matter of the crusade. The preferences of crusade leaders, faced by the immense difficulties presented by crusading in practice, worked in the same direction. Limited numerical participation, then, reflected the successful implementation of policy and the potency of social controls, rather than a lack of contemporary commitment to the crusade. (Allowance must be made, however, for adverse reaction to certain aspects of that profound evolution which was occurring in the concept and application of the crusade.)

Investigation of these matters throws much light upon the nature of English society in the period, and upon the workings of papal policy in practice. It also shows how the crusade became increasingly institutionalized, and integrated with social structures in the thirteenth century. Study of the attempt to raise, organize, and finance English crusading forces points in the same direction. The inhabitants of the Latin East and their Eastern allies, no less than the papacy, appreciated that it was crucial to secure the commitment of the great to the crusading cause precisely because of the way in which society was organized and the influence which the social élite exerted within it. Accordingly, their vows were critical, for where they led, men of their connection would follow: in a sense recruitment of participants looked after itself once the services of the great were secured. Preaching campaigns in the field, then, came to be intended to secure money from the general populace in return for indulgence, the cash raised then going to subsidize that knightly body and their retainers judged fit to prosecute crusading warfare in person. The evidence suggests that grants from the crusade subsidy were normally made to the chief leaders and their commanders in accordance with the way in which forces were organized under contingent commanders, these contingents being largely a function of pre-existing social ties. Study of the organization of crusading forces also sheds light upon the way in which contract usage became steadily more common in the thirteenth century. Indeed, so far as England is concerned, the crusade of 1270–2 was perhaps the first English military force to be systematically organized by the use of written contracts, with standard terms available for service. Here, at least crusading experience may have encouraged important developments, though they would surely have emerged in any case.

Finally, study of the responses of Henry III and Edward I to the crusading call reveals a great deal regarding the complex interplay of interests, ideals, dynastic tradition, and a concern with prestige which governed their conduct of external relations. Neither king went on crusade, and the workings of social structure ensured that this would have a profound bearing upon the level of crusading activity of their subjects. The English contribution to the crusade may have been limited, judged in terms both of numbers and results, but that is no reason to ignore the relationship between England and the crusading movement. It has much to reveal concerning the nature and development of both.

APPENDIX 1

Calendar of Letters Dispatched to English Correspondents from the Latin East and its Allies, 1216–1307

Date	Correspondents	Contents	Source
1220	Master of the Temple to *locum tenens* of the English preceptor	Events at Damietta, battle of Mansourah; appeal for aid from the Temple	Wendover, *Flores*, iv. 77–9.
1229	Patriarch of Jerusalem to all the faithful	Events of Frederick II's crusade	Paris, *CM* iii. 179–84.
1231–6	Master of the Hospital to the bishop of Chichester	Protection of Hospital possessions in Chichester diocese; events in the Holy Land	*Dipl. Docs.* i. No. 248; *Anc. Corr.* 6. 63; *Cart. Gen. Hosp.* iv. No. 1982.
1240	Emperor Baldwin II of Constantinople to Henry III	Events in Latin Greece	Paris, *CM* iv. 54.
1240	Master of the Temple to the English preceptor	Treaty in the Holy Land	Paris, *CM* iv. 64–5.
1243–4	Master of the Temple to the English preceptor	Treaty in the Holy Land; reoccupation of the Temple in Jerusalem	Paris, *CM* iv. 288–91.
1244	Master of the Hospital to M. de Merlai	Fall of Jerusalem; battle of La Forbie	Paris, *CM* iv. 307–11; 'Waverley', pp. 334–5.
1244	Patriarch of Jerusalem to all the faithful	Fall of Jerusalem; battle of La Forbie; appeal for aid	Röhricht, *Regesta Regni Hieros.*, No. 1124.
1244	Patriarch of Jerusalem and other ecclesiastics (given) to the prelates of France and England	Fall of Jerusalem; battle of La Forbie; appeal for aid	Paris, *CM* iv. 337–44; BL Add. MS 46352, fos. 50b–52b.

1249	Master of the Temple to the English preceptor	Capture of Damietta by Louis IX	Paris, *CM* vi. No. 82.
1250	Anon. to Richard of Cornwall	Battle of Mansourah	Paris, *CM* v. 147–53.
1251	Master of the Hospital to Walter de St. Martin	Release of Louis IX; events in Holy Land	Paris, *CM* vi. No. 100.
1251	Master of the Hospital to Walter de St. Martin	Release of Hospitallers	Paris, *CM* vi. No. 101.
1252	Treasurer of the Hospital, Acre, to Walter de St. Martin	Events in Holy Land	Paris, *CM* vi. No. 102.
1254	Secular and religious leaders of the Latin kingdom of Jerusalem to Henry III	Events in Holy Land; Henry urged to accelerate his crusading plans	'Burton', pp. 368–9; *Foedera*, I. i. 308.
1255	Bohemund VI of Antioch to Henry III	Events in Outremer; appeal for aid to Bohemund	'Burton', pp. 369–71; *Foedera*, I. i. 321.
1257	Anon. to anon.	Events in Arabia; Moslem reversals	Paris, *CM* vi. No. 183.
1260	Bishop of Bethlehem (papal legate in the Holy Land) and others to princes of the West	Mongol threat; appeal for aid	Röhricht, *Regesta Regni Hieros.*, No. 1288.
1260	Master of the Temple to the English preceptor	Mongol threat; appeal for aid	*Flores*, ii. 451–2.
1260	Master of the Temple to Henry III	Mongol threat; appeal for aid	*Flores*, ii. 451–2.
1261	Bishop of Acre to Henry III	Battle of Aïn Jalud; affairs of Hospital of St. Thomas	*Dipl. Docs*. i. No. 343; *Anc. Corr.* 47. 27.
1261	Master of the Temple to the English preceptor	Mongol devastation; appeal for aid from Temple and Henry III	'Burton', pp. 491–5.
1263	Bishop of Bethlehem (papal legate in the Holy Land) and others to Henry III	State of the Holy Land; appeal for aid	*Dipl. Docs*. i. No. 385; *Anc. Corr.* 55. 2; *Foedera*, I. i. 395 (misdated).

Date	Correspondents	Contents	Source
1263	Master of the Temple to Henry III	Corroboration of the above; appeal for aid	*Dipl. Docs.* i. No. 386; *Anc. Corr.* 5. 56; *Foedera*, I. i. 396 (misdated).
Early Edward I	Provost and community of St. Edward, Acre, to Edward I	Affairs of the community	*Anc. Corr.* 14. 133.
Early Edward I	Provost and community of St. Edward, Acre, to Edward I	Affairs of the community	*Anc. Corr.* 14. 134.
1273–91	Master of the Temple to Edward I	Events in the East; commendation for Odin, *valettus*	*Anc. Corr.* 21. 1.
1273–91	Master of the Temple to Edward I	Financial affairs; news of events in the Holy Land	*Anc. Corr.* 21. 3.
1275	Mongol khan to Edward I	Prospect of a new crusade; appeal for aid	*CPR 1272–81*, p. 116; *Foedera*, I. ii. 520.
1275?	Master of the Temple to Edward I	Events in the East; appeal for aid for Temple and Holy Land	Kohler and Langlois, 'Lettres inédites', No. 2.
1275	Master of the Hospital to Edward I	Events in the East	*Anc. Corr.* 18. 136; Kohler and Langlois, 'Lettres inédites', No. 1.
1276	Mongol khan to Edward I	Events in the East; prospect of a new crusade	Kohler and Langlois, 'Lettres inédites', No. 3.
1276	Master of the Temple to Edward I	Situation at Acre; appeal for aid for Temple	*Anc. Corr.* 21. 2.
1276–7	Master of the Temple to Edward I	Activities of Mongols and Moslems; appeal for aid for Temple and Holy Land	*Anc. Corr.* 21. 100.
1278–85	Master of the Hospital to Edward I	Debts of Hospital	*Anc. Corr.* 18. 140; *Cart. Gen. Hosp.* iv. No. 3653.
1279	Brethren of St Thomas of Acre to Edward I	Events in Holy Land and the East; state of the hospital	*Anc. Corr.* 20. 99.

1279–80	Master of the Hospital to Edward I	Conditions in the Holy Land	*Anc. Corr.* 18. 138.
1280	Bishop of Hebron (vicar of the patriarch of Jerusalem) to Edward I	Events in the East; prospects of the Holy Land; recommendation of business of the Holy Land	*Anc. Corr.* 18. 98; *Foedera*, I. ii. 586–7.
1281	Master of the Hospital to Edward I	Activities of Moslems and Mongols	*Anc. Corr.* 18. 137; Kohler and Langlois, 'Lettres inédites', No. 4.
1281	Master of the Hospital to Edward I	Battle of Homs; appeal for aid	Kohler and Langlois, 'Lettres inédites', No. 5.
1282	Joseph de Chauncy to Edward I	Battle of Homs; appeal for aid	*Cart. Gen. Hosp.* iii. No. 3782.
1282	Joseph de Chauncy to Edward I	Events in the Holy Land	*Anc. Corr.* 55. 18.
1282	Master of the Hospital to Edward I	Events in the Holy Land; battle of La Chamelle	*Anc. Corr.* 18. 139; *Cart. Gen. Hosp.* iii. No. 3781.
1283	Joseph de Chauncy to Edward I	Events in the East; attacks on Armenia; appeal for aid for Hospital	*Anc. Corr.* 18. 134.
1283	Joseph de Chauncy to Edward I	Events in the Holy Land	*Anc. Corr.* 18. 135.
1285	Mongol khan to Edward I	Appeal for aid in projected crusade	J. B. Chabot, 'Relations du roi Argoun avec l'Occident', *Revue de l'Orient Latin*, ii (1894), 566–629.
1285–9	Castellan of Château Pelerin (Templar) to Edward I	Mongol plans	*Anc. Corr.* 17. 196.
1289	Mongol khan to Edward I	Prospect of a new crusade; appeal for aid	*Foedera*, I. ii. 713.
1290	Mongol khan to Edward I	Prospect of a new crusade; appeal for aid	*CCR 1288–96*, p. 145.
1291	Hethoum II of Armenia to Edward I	Fall of Acre; appeal for aid	Cotton, *Hist.*, pp. 219–23.
1291	Sultan al-Ashraf Khalil to Hethoum II of Armenia (forwarded to Edward I?)	Fall of Acre	Cotton, *Hist.*, pp. 215–17; *Reg. Pontissara*, pp. 481–2.

Date	Correspondents	Contents	Source
1291	Sultan al-Ashraf Khalil to Hethoum II of Armenia (forwarded to Edward I?)	Fall of Tyre	Cotton, *Hist.*, pp. 217–19.
*c.*1295–8	Master of the Temple to Edward I	Poverty of the Temple	*Anc. Corr.* 21. 4.
1296–1305	Master of the Hospital to Edward I	Events in Outremer; appeal for aid to Hospital	*Anc. Corr.* 14. 85; *Cart. Gen. Hosp.* iii. No. 4308.
1296–1305	Master of the Hospital to Edward I	Events in Outremer; appeal for aid to Hospital	*Anc. Corr.* 14. 84; *Cart. Gen. Hosp.* iii. No. 4309.
1298	Hethoum II of Armenia to Edward I	Prospect of a new crusade; appeal for aid	*CCR 1296–1302*, p. 305; *Foedera*, I. ii. 900.
1299	Master of the Temple to the English master	Events in Outremer; appeal for aid	Rishanger, *Chron.*, p. 400.
1299	Master of the Temple to Edward I	Events in Outremer; appeal for aid	Rishanger, *Chron.*, p. 400.
1300	Patriarch of Jerusalem to all	Events in the Holy Land; on behalf of Geoffrey de Semary, collecting alms	Rishanger, *Chron.*, pp. 442–4.
1300?	Master of the Temple to Edward I	Events in the Holy Land	*Anc. Corr.* 55. 22.
1301	Master of the Temple to Edward I	Events in the Holy Land	M. L. Bulst-Thiele, *Sacrae Domus Militiae Templi Hierosolymitana Magistri* (Göttingen, 1974), p. 366.
1303	Mongol khan to Edward I	Prospect of a new crusade; appeal for aid	*CCR 1302–7*, pp. 77–8.
1307	Leon IV of Armenia to Edward I	Threats to Armenia; appeal for aid	Kohler and Langlois, 'Lettres inédites', No. 6.

APPENDIX 2

Embassies Sent to Henry III and Edward I from the Latin East and its Allies, 1216–1307

GENERALLY the purpose of the visit in question is clear, but in some instances it has not been possible to determine if the individual concerned came in a private capacity or as the representative of an Eastern principal. I have sought to exclude from the list those who came from the East on matters clearly unconnected with the promotion of the cause of the Latin East. As the distinction between nuncios and envoys, proctors and ambassadors was not always clear, I have included all such mentioned in the sources. It should be stressed that in a few instances the records may be referring only to letter-bearers. It is impossible to be certain.

1221 Gerard, nuncio of the Latin emperor of Constantinople, was granted safe conduct and protection for his journey home from England. Nothing further is known. *RLC* i. 465.

1223 Visit of King John of Jerusalem to Henry III as part of a general fund-raising mission in the West. Paris, *CM* iii. 82, says that the master of the Hospital accompanied him. He received various gifts from Henry: *RLC* i. 563b. Chief sources for the visit: 'Continuation' of Gervase of Canterbury, ii. 112–13; Coventry, *Memoriale*, ii. 252; Coggeshall, *Chron.*, pp. 193–4; 'Dunstable', pp. 80, 85; *Chron. Mailros*, p. 140. On the taxation voted for John, see Mitchell, *Taxation*, esp. pp. 19–20, 138–9.

1238 Visit of Emperor Baldwin II of Constantinople to Henry III as part of a general promotional campaign in the West. He received 500*l*. from Henry as a gift. Richard of Cornwall also made an offering: *CLR 1226–40*, pp. 326–7; Paris, *CM* iii. 480–1, 486. According to the annals of Southwark he was sent by the pope to seek aid: BL Cotton Faustina A. viii, fo. 146.

1245 Bishop Waleran of Beirut and Arnulph, a Dominican, sent to the West to seek aid in Nov. 1244. After visiting Innocent IV they proceeded to Louis IX and Henry III. Paris, *CM* iv. 431, describes Waleran as 'totius Syriae nuntius generalis et sindicus omnium Christianorum Terrae Sanctae'. They brought letters directed to the prelates of France and England. A charter of the bishop and various Chancery enrolments reveal that they stayed in England for some time. They were discouraged by Henry III from preaching the crusade, says Paris, but the king granted them some valuable gifts and paid for their passage back across the Channel: *CLR 1245–51*, pp. 10, 11, 15, 37; *CR 1242–7*, p. 372; Paris, *CM* iv. 337–45, 433, 488–9; *Cartulary of Oseney Abbey*, ed. H. E. Salter (Oxford Hist. Soc., 1929–36), iii. 22.

1247 Second visit of Emperor Baldwin II of Constantinople as part of a general promotional campaign. He was granted 500*m.* by Henry III as a gift, 20*l.* for expenses, and his passage across the Channel: Paris, *CM* iv. 626; *CR 1242–7*, p. 510; *CLR 1245–51*, p. 119.

1248 John, canon of the Holy Sepulchre, came to Henry III on the business of the patriarch of Jerusalem. He took a cope, mitre, and chasuble back to the patriarch. His visit may have been connected with the sending of the Holy Blood, around Michaelmas 1247: *CR 1247–51*, p. 60.

1251 The prior of the Holy Sepulchre visited Henry III, probably on behalf of the patriarch of Jerusalem and perhaps other principals. He returned with a mitre or ring for the patriarch: *CR 1247–51*, p. 454.

1255 Robert de Attrabato and H., Dominicans, Ralph de Lyndes' and Hugh de With, Franciscans, and John Pelevyleyn, knight, were sent to Henry III on the common business of the Holy Land and brought letters with them. They received money towards their expenses and for shoes: 'Burton', pp. 368–9; *Föedera*, I. i. 308; *CLR 1251–60*, p. 244.

1255 Conrad de Duce, knight, and Guarennus, chaplain, sent by Bohemund VI of Antioch to seek aid from Henry III. They brought their master's letters. They received robes of the king's gift. 'Burton', pp. 369–71; *Foedera*, I. i. 321; *CLR 1251–60*, p. 261.

1256 Roland, nuncio of Queen Plaisance of Cyprus, visited Henry III regarding marriage alliance proposals involving Plaisance and the Lord Edmund, and Hugh II of Cyprus and Beatrice, Henry III's daughter. He brought the letters of the bishop of Bethlehem. *CR 1254–6*, pp. 354, 445–6; *CLR 1251–60*, p. 319.

1257 The master of the Order of St. Thomas came to England, his business unknown. He brought letters with him, but whether he came as a representative of the East is uncertain. Paris, *CM* vi. No. 183; v. 630.

1276 John and James Vassal sent as nuncios of the Mongol khan to Edward I on the business of the Holy Land. Kohler and Langlois, 'Lettres inédites', No. 3.

1278 Envoys of Leo III of Armenia came to Edward I, the precise purpose of their visit unknown, but probably connected with securing Edward's aid or crusading vow. *CPR 1272–81*, p. 265.

1286 William de Vaux, knight, and a Templar sent to Edward I from Acre as nuncios of an unknown principal, their business unknown. They received cups of the king's gift: *Records of the Wardrobe and Household 1285–1286*, ed. B. F. and C. R. Byerly (London, 1977), Nos. 1988, 2019.

1286 Julian of Genoa, John Skabozyn, and Robert de Furno, knight, sent as nuncios of the king of Cyprus to Edward I, their business unknown. They received cups of the king's gift: ibid., Nos. 1988, 1990–1, 2015.

1287 Rabban Sauma sent to the West by the khan to raise aid. He met Edward I at Bordeaux. See E. A. W. Budge, *The Monks of Ḳûblâi Khân* (London, 1928), 164–97.

1289 Hugh de Matisson' and John, Dominicans, Peter de Hezqam, Hospitaller, and Hertand, Templar, sent to the West by an unknown principal in the East, perhaps the khan. Nicholas IV sent them on to Edward I with letters of commendation: *Foedera*, I. ii. 712; *Reg. Nicholas IV*, No. 7509.

1289 Buscarellus de Gisolfi of Genoa sent to Edward I by the Mongol khan. He brought letters with him concerning the possibility of joint action against the Saracens: *Foedera*, I. ii. 713.

1291 Four anon. envoys came to Edward I from the Mongol khan on the business of the Holy Land. Nicholas IV sent them on to Edward with letters of commendation: *Foedera*, I. ii. 742–3; *Reg. Nicholas IV*, Nos. 7578, 7583.

1291 Bishop Bernard of Tripoli sent on the business of the Holy Land to the prelates and all religious of England, and probably Edward I. This may have been a papal initiative: Cotton, *Hist.*, pp. 223–6; *Reg. G. Giffard*, ii. 407–8; *Reg. Nicholas IV*, No. 7632.

1292 Marchus de Monte Lupone, Thomas de Tolentino, Franciscans, and a noble, Geoffrey Comitissae, sent to the West on the business of the Holy Land by Hethoum II of Armenia. Nicholas IV sent them on with letters of commendation to Edward I: *Reg. Nicholas IV*, No. 6853. They presumably brought the letters of Hethoum to Edward, in Cotton, *Hist.*, pp. 219–23.

1298 James de Arul' and anon., Dominicans, sent by Hethoum II of Armenia to the West. Boniface VIII provided them with letters of commendation to Edward I: *Reg. Boniface VIII*, No. 2654; *Foedera*, I. ii. 900; *CCR 1296–1302*, p. 305.

1300 William Prepositi, Franciscan, came to Edward I as the envoy of the king of Cyprus, his business unknown: *CCR 1296–1302*, p. 355.

1302 Buscarellus de Gisolfi of Genoa sent again by the Mongol khan to Edward I on the business of the Holy Land. He brought the khan's letters with him. *CR 1302–7*, pp. 77–8.

1305 The bishop of 'Thefelicen' sent to Edward I by Clement V with letters of commendation. His principal is unknown, but the visit was concerned with the affairs of the Holy Land. *Foedera*, I. ii. 977–8.

1307 Theodor, cantor of the abbey of Trazargne, and Baldwin de Negrino and Leon, knights, sent by Leon IV of Armenia to Edward I on Leon's affairs. Kohler and Langlois, 'Lettres inédites', No. 6.

APPENDIX 3

Newsletters Concerning Crusade Matters Sent to English Correspondents by Westerners, 1216–1307

Date	Correspondents	Contents	Source
	1. LETTERS SENT DIRECTLY TO ENGLISH CORRESPONDENTS BY CRUSADERS ON CAMPAIGN		
1219	William de Ferrers to Peter des Roches	Events at Damietta	*Royal Letters* i. 24–5; *Dipl. Docs.* i. No. 30.
1220	Richard de Argentein to Prior Richard of Bury St Edmunds	Events at Damietta	*Memorials of St. Edmund's Abbey*, ed. T. Arnold (RS; 1890–6), i. appendix E, No. 32.
1221	Legate Pelagius to Henry III	Prester John	'Dunstable', pp. 69–74.
1221	Philip Daubeny to Ranulf of Chester	Battle of Mansourah; loss of Damietta	Wendover, *Flores*, iv. 75–7.
1228	Frederick II to Henry III	The emperor's crusade	*CR 1227–31*, p. 93; *Foedera*, 1. i. 187.
1229	Anon. to anon.	Frederick's treaty with the sultan	'Waverley', pp. 305–7.
1240	Anon. to anon.	Battle of Gaza	Paris, *CM* iv. 25.
1241	Richard of Cornwall to Baldwin de Redvers, the abbot of Beaulieu, and Robert	Events of Richard's crusade	Paris, *CM* iv. 138–44.
1249	Anon. to Henry III	Capture of Damietta	Paris, *CM* v. 81.
1249	Anon. to anon.	Capture of Damietta	*De ant. leg.*, p. 15.
1250	Anon. to anon.	Disaster at Mansourah; ransom of Louis IX	Paris, *CM* vi. No. 95.

1250	Anon. to anon.	Disaster at Mansourah; ransom of Louis IX	*De ant. leg.*, p. 17.
1251	Louis IX to Henry III	Events in the Holy Land	*CPR 1247–58*, p. 157.
1253	Anon. to Richard of Cornwall	Moslem attacks in the Holy Land	Paris, *CM* v. 411.
1253	Louis IX to Henry III	Events in the Holy Land	'Burton', p. 293.
1266–9	Hugh de Neville to Hawisia de Neville	Hugh's crusade	*Archaeologia*, lvi, part 2 (1899) pp. 358–61.
1270	Anon. to anon.	Events at Tunis	*De ant. leg.*, p. 126.
1270	Anon. to anon.	Agreement of crusade leaders in Sicily	*De ant. leg.*, p. 131.
1270	Lord Edward to anon.	Edward's progress to Acre	*De ant. leg.*, p. 141.
1271	?Lord Edward to anon.	Crusade proposals of the Mongol khan	*De ant. leg.*, p. 143.
1271	Lord Edward to Henry III	Events of his crusade	*CR 1268–72*, pp. 397–8; *Foedera*, I. i. 487.

2. LETTERS SENT FROM OR FORWARDED BY THE PAPACY

1218	Honorius III to all prelates of France and England	Events at Damietta	*Reg. Honorius III*, No. 1716.
1219	Honorius III to ?all the faithful/all prelates	Capture of Damietta	*Chron. Lanercost*, p. 27; cf. Coventry, *Memoriale* ii. 240–3.
1219	Master of the Teutonic Knights to the cardinal of Holy Cross	Capture of Damietta	*Chron. Mailros*, pp. 135–7.
1220	Honorius III to ?all the faithful/all prelates	Arabic prophecies concerning the fate of Egypt and the Holy Land	'Dunstable', p. 62.
1221	Honorius III to prelates of England and elsewhere	Events of the crusade	*Reg. Honorius III*, No. 3637.

Date	Correspondents	Contents	Source
1224	Honorius III to Henry III	Events of the crusade; Frederick II's proposed crusade	*Foedera*, I. i. 172–3; *Reg. Honorius III*, No. 4262.
1227	Gregory IX to all the faithful	Events at Acre (incorporating letters of patriarch *et al.*)	Wendover, *Flores* iv. 145–8.
1228	Gregory IX to Henry III	Frederick II's crusade	*CR 1227–31*, p. 93; *Foedera*, I. i. 187.
1229	Gregory IX to the archbishops of Canterbury, York and their suffragans	Frederick II's crusade	*Reg. Gregory IX*, No. 324.
1229	Gregory IX to Henry III	Frederick II's crusade	*Reg. Gregory IX*, No. 324.
1231	Gregory IX to all prelates	Threats to the Holy Land	*Reg. Gregory IX*, No. 577.
1234	Gregory IX to all the faithful	State of the Holy Land	*Reg. Gregory IX*, No. 2200; Wendover, *Flores* iv. 327–30; Paris, *CM* iii. 280–7, 309–12.
1234	Gregory IX to all prelates	State of the Holy Land	*Reg. Gregory IX*, No. 2202.
1237	Godfrey, papal penitentiary, to the Dominican priors of France and England	Conversion of Nestorians (incorporating letters from Prior Philip in the Holy Land)	Paris, *CM* iii. 396–9.
1237	Gregory IX to the bishop of Winchester	Oppressions of the E. Empire	*Reg. Gregory IX*, No. 3944.
1244	Patriarch of Jerusalem *et al.* to Innocent IV	Fall of Jerusalem	*Chron. Mailros*, pp. 156–62.
1244	Patriarch of Jerusalem to Innocent IV	Fall of Jerusalem (Innocent requested to further news to Henry III and Louis IX with papal letters)	'Burton', pp. 257–63.
1245	Innocent IV to Henry III	Fall of Jerusalem	*Foedera*, I. i. 254–5.

1249	Bishop of Marseilles to Innocent IV	Supposed fall of Cairo	Paris, *CM* vi. No. 87; cf. v. 87, 118; BL Cotton Cleopatra A. vii, fos. 103v–104.
1250	Patriarch of Jerusalem to the cardinals of Rome	Disaster at Mansourah	'Burton', pp. 285–9.
1250	Innocent IV to the archbishops of Canterbury, York and other ecclesiastics (given)	Injuries to the Holy Land	*Foedera*, I. i. 272–3.
1251	Innocent IV to Henry III	Events in the Holy Land	'Burton', pp. 293–6.
1260	Alexander IV to Lord Edward	Attacks of the Mongols	*Foedera*, I. i. 403.
1260	Alexander IV to the archbishop and clergy of Canterbury	Attacks of the Mongols	'Burton', pp. 495–9.
1266	Clement IV to the legate Ottobuono	Losses in the Holy Land	*Reg. Clement IV*, No. 1146.
1280	Nicholas III to the archbishop of Canterbury	State of the Holy Land	*Reg. Nicholas III*, No. 1065; *Reg. G. Giffard*, p. 124.
1287	Honorius IV to the archbishop of Canterbury	State of the Holy Land	HMC, *Eighth Report* (1881), I. i. 345b.
1289	Nicholas IV to Edward I	Events in the Holy Land	*Reg. Nicholas IV*, No. 7509; *Foedera*, I. ii. 712.
1291	Nicholas IV to all the faithful	Fall of Tripoli	*Reg. Nicholas IV*, No. 6800; *Foedera*, I. ii. 749.
1291	Nicholas IV to all the faithful	Fall of Acre	*Reg. Nicholas IV*, No. 7625; Cotton, *Hist.*, pp. 199–203; Guisborough, *Chron.*, p. 231; *Reg. Pontissara*, pp. 474–7.
1292	Nicholas IV to all the faithful	Oppressions of Armenia	*Reg. Nicholas IV*, Nos. 6850–1.
1300	Boniface VIII to Edward I	Victory of Mongols and Armenians over the sultan of Egypt	*Foedera*, I. ii. 919–20; Rishanger, *Chron.*, pp. 465–70.

Date	Correspondents	Contents	Source
	3. LETTERS FROM OTHER WESTERN CORRESPONDENTS		
1229	Duke Henry of Lorraine to Henry III	Frederick II's crusade	*Royal Letters* i, 343.
1240	The countess of Montfort to Richard of Cornwall	Battle of Gaza	Paris, *CM* iv. 25.
1240	Frederick II to Henry III	Events in the Holy Land	*Hist. dipl. Fred. II*, v. 921–3.
1240	Frederick II to Henry III	Battle of Gaza; Frederick's crusading plans	Paris, *CM* iv. 26–9.
1241	Frederick II to Henry III	Threat of the Mongols	Paris, *CM* iv. 112–19.
1244	Frederick II to all princes	Fall of Jerusalem	*Hist. dipl. Fred. II*, vi. 236–40.
1244–5	'D. . . . arch' Cireñ' to John and Andree 'ultra mare'	Battle of La Forbie	*Chron. Mailros*, p. 163.
1245	Frederick II to Richard of Cornwall	Attacks of the Khwarismian Turks; fall of Jerusalem	Paris, *CM* iv. 300–5.
1249	Queen Blanche of France to Henry III	Events of Louis IX's crusade	Paris, *CM* vi. No. 85; BL Cotton Cleopatra A. vii, fos. 102v–103.
1251	Louis IX to the Cistercian general chapter	Louis IX's position in the Holy Land	Paris, *CM* v. 257.
1252	Bishop of Orleans to the bishop of Chichester	Louis IX's peace treaty	Paris, *CM* v. 308–9.
1252	Cardinal John Tolet to the Cistercian general chapter	Events in the Holy Land and Syria	Paris, *CM* v. 306.
The Following were Most Probably Forwarded by Westerners to English Recipients			
1221	Master of the Temple to the bishop of Elmne	Events at Damietta; developments in Egypt and the Holy Land	Wendover, *Flores* iv. 72–5.

1249	Robert of Artois to Queen Blanche of France	Louis IX's crusade	Paris, *CM* vi. No. 80.
1249	Guy, knight of the viscount of Melun, to Master B. of Chartres	Capture of Damietta	Paris, *CM* vi. No. 81.
1249	Mongol khan to Louis IX	Possibility of khan's conversion and support against Moslems	Paris, *CM* vi. No. 84.
1250	?Hospital brethren in Holy Land to ?Hospitallers in France	Disaster at Mansourah	Paris, *CM* vi. No. 95.
1251	Louis IX to Queen Blanche of France	Crusaders' needs	Paris, *CM* v. 260.
1251	Patriarch of Jerusalem to Queen Blanche of France	Moslem wars; events of the crusade	'Burton', pp. 296–7.
1300	James de Ferraria to Gilbert de Mainarda	Events in the Holy Land	BL Cotton Vespasian B. xi, fos. 47v–48v.
1300	Anon. to anon.	Events in the Holy Land	BL Cotton Vespasian B. xi, fo. 48v.

4. LETTERS FROM DIPLOMATIC REPRESENTATIVES AND INTELLIGENCE GATHERERS

1216	Anon., at papal curia, to King John	Siege of Acre; crusade plans	*Anc. Corr.* 1. 16; *Dipl. Docs.* i. No. 21.
1250	John, chancellor of Earl Richard of Cornwall, to the earl	Disaster at Mansourah	Paris, *CM* v. 165–9.
1261	Roger Lovel, procurator at papal curia, to Henry III	Relief of Holy Land	*Anc. Corr* 4. 40; *Dipl. Docs.* i. No. 335.
1298	Anon., proctors of Bishop Godfrey Giffard at papal curia, to the bishop	News concerning events connected with the East	*Reg. G. Giffard*, p. 500.

APPENDIX 4

The English Crusading Force of 1270–1272[1]

[The notes appear at the end of the table]

Crusader[2]	Sailing with Edward or Edmund[3]	Status[4]	Curial connections: Henry III[5]	Curial connections: Lord Edward[6]	Curial connections: Lord Edmund[6]	Curial connections: Edward I[7]	Other lordship connection[8]	Regional ties[9]	Rebel[10]	In possession of rebel properties[11]: A	In possession of rebel properties[11]: B	Family precedent	Participation of kinsmen
Adam de Gesemue (Jesmond)	Edward	K	X	X				Northumberland		X	?		
Adam de Monte Alto (Monthaut)	Edward	K	X			X		Lancashire, Yorkshire, Welsh March		X	?	Roger de Monthaut (1250)	John, Simon de Monthaut
Adam de Northampton	Edward	B	X	X		X		Hampshire					
Adam Skirelock of Aynstapelith (Ainstaple)	Edmund							Cumberland					
Alan de Castell	Edward	M				X		London					
Alan de Lascelles	Edmund	K			X	X (Edmund)		Cumberland, Northumberland				Geoffrey de Lascelles (1191)	
Alan de Neville	Edward	K	X					Cambridgeshire, Huntingdonshire				Hugh de Neville (1192), John de Neville (1240)	Hugh de Neville (1266)
Alexander de Balliol	Edward	K	X			X		Northumberland		X	X		Eustace de Balliol
Alexander Luterel (Luttrell)	Edward	K	X				Robert Tiptoft	Lincolnshire, Leicestershire, Somerset					
Alexander de Setun (Seaton)[12]		K					?Alexander Balliol, ? Robert Bruce	Northumberland, Scotland					
Alexander of Westiderleg (W. Tytherly)	Edward	C						Hampshire					

Antony Bek	Edward	C	X	X		X		Lincolnshire, Yorkshire	X	X	—	
Arnulf de Munteny	Edward	K	X			X		Essex, Hertfordshire, Suffolk				Robert de Munteny
Baldwin de Basingburn	Edmund	K	X					Cambridgeshire				
Bartholomew de Brianso (Brianzon)	Edward	K	X	X		X		Essex				
Benedict le Canun of Alfemeston (Alphamstowe)	Edward	K						Essex				
Berenger le Moyne	Edward	K	X					Huntingdonshire, Cambridgeshire	R			
Bertram de Draycot	Edward											
Brian de Brampton (Brompton)	Edward	K	X			X		Shropshire, Herefordshire, Oxfordshire	X	?		
Edmund of Almain	Edmund	K	X			X					Richard of Cornwall (1240)	Other Plantagenet kin; Henry of Almain
Ellis de Rabeyn	Edward	K	X	X		X	William de Valence	Dorset, Somerset	X	?		
Ellis de Rolleston (Helias of Rilleston)[13]	Edward	K						Yorkshire				
Elye de Eshwell (Ashwell)	Edward	S	X									
Eudo fitzWarin	Edward											
Eustace de Balliol	Edward	K	X					Cumberland, Westmorland				Alexander de Balliol
Fowin	Edward	G		X								
Geoffrey fitzGeoffrey de Langley	Edmund	K			X	X						
Geoffrey Gacelyn	Edward	K	X	X		X	William de Valence	Herefordshire, Wiltshire, Dorset	X	?		

Crusader[2]	Sailing with Edward or Edmund[3]	Status[4]	Curial connections				Other lordship connection[8]	Regional ties[9]	Rebel[10]	In possession of rebel properties[11]		Family precedent	Participation of kinsmen
			Henry III[5]	Lord Edward[6]	Lord Edmund[6]	Edward I[7]				A	B		
Geoffrey de Geneville (Joinville)	Edward	K	X	X		X		Herefordshire, Shropshire, Ireland		X		French Joinvilles	William de Geneville, John de Verdun
Geoffrey de la Hyde	Edward												
Geoffrey Payne	Edward							Norfolk					
Geoffrey de Scoftinton	Edward						James de Audley	Leicestershire	X				
Geoffrey de Toucestre (Towcester)	Edward	C							X				
Gerard de Fanacurt	Edward	K	X					Nottinghamshire, Lincolnshire		X	X		
Gerard de Grandson	Edmund	C	X		X	X							Otto de Grandson
Gerard de Saint Laurent	Edward	K		X		X							
Gilbert de Middleton	Edward	K	X			X		Northumberland					
Giles de Fenes (Fiennes)	Edward	K		X		X		Sussex				Ingelram de Fiennes (1190)	William de Fiennes; Eleanor of Castile
Godfrey de Waus (Vaux)	Edward			X									
Godin	Edward												
Guy Ferre	Edmund	K	X			X							John Ferre
Hamo Lestrange	Edmund	K	X	X				Shropshire, Staffordshire, Hampshire		X	?		Robert Lestrange
Hamundus de Gayton	Edward												John, Walter and William de Gayton
Henry of Almain	Edward	K	X	X						X	?	Richard of Cornwall (1240)	Edmund of Almain; other Plantagenet kin
Henry de Burghull (Burghill)	Edward	K	X				Roger de Clifford	Herefordshire, Gloucestershire					

Henry fitzGeoffrey de Horsede	Edward												
Henry fitzHenry de Stonebrok	Edward												
Henry Hay[14]	Edward								?				
Henry Jordan	Edward	B						Nottingham					
Henry de Langedon	Edward												
Henry de Peremor	Edward	?K						Worcestershire					
Henry le Waleys[15]	Edward	K	X	X		X		Worcestershire, Yorkshire					
Herbert de Boyville[16]	Edward	K						Essex					Robert de Boyville
Hervey de Chaworth	Edward	K	X					Hampshire, Welsh March					Patrick and Payn de Chaworth
Hubert de Rolly (Ruylly)	Edward	K	X	X				Essex, Suffolk, Ireland					
Hugh de Aungerville	Edmund	K	X		X			Suffolk	X				
Hugh de Berewic	Edward	?K						Oxfordshire					
Hugh fitz Otto	Edward	K	X	X		X		Essex, Hertfordshire, London		X	X		
Hugh de Plugenet (Plukenet)	Edward		X				Payn de Chaworth	Berkshire, Wiltshire					
Hugh Sauvage	Edward	Su	X										
Hugh de Spalding	Edmund												
Ingelram de Ivrvy	Edward												
James de Alditeleg (Audley)	Edward	K	X	X				Staffordshire, Shropshire, Ireland, Cheshire		X	?		
John de Ardern	Edward	K	X	X			Richard de la Rochelle	Yorkshire, Essex		X	?	Ralph de Ardern (1191), William de Ardern (1233)	Peter and Ranulf de Ardern
John de Badebury	Edward	C						Gloucestershire					
John de Balrewyk[17]		?S					John Hardel						

Crusader[2]	Sailing with Edward or Edmund[3]	Status[4]	Curial connections				Other lordship connection[8]	Regional ties[9]	Rebel[10]	In possession of rebel properties[11]		Family precedent	Participation of kinsmen
			Henry III[5]	Lord Edward[6]	Lord Edmund[6]	Edward I[7]				A	B		
John de Baskerville	Edward	K	X	X		X	James de Audley	Shropshire, Herefordshire, Ireland					
John de la Bere	Edward	?K				X	?Luke de Tany						
John de Berkham	Edward	S	X										
John de Blankeneye	Edward												
John de Briddeport (Bridport)	Edward	C				X		Dorset, Devonshire					
John de Chanceus		K	X			X		Essex, Northamptonshire					
John de Ernefeud	Edward	C											
John le Espeynol	Edward	V		X						X	X		
John de Everley	Edmund	V	X			X		Worcestershire, Hampshire		X			
John Fancellun (Faucyllun)	Edward	?K					Arnulf de Munteny	Essex					
John Ferre	Edward	K	X	X		X		Kent		X	X		Guy Ferre
John de Fifhide	Edward	C		X		X	Richard de la Rochelle	Ireland					
John fitzThomas of Wrastulingewrth	Edward	C						Bedfordshire					
John de Gayton	Edward	V		X		X		Northamptonshire, Buckinghamshire					Hamundus, Walter and William de Gayton
John de Goer[18]	Edward	?K					John de Ardern	Yorkshire					Juliana de Goer
John de la Grave	Edward												
John de Grely (Grailly)	Edward	K	X	X		X							
John de Gurnay[19]	Edmund	K				X		Norfolk, Suffolk	?				
John Hardel[20]		V	X	X		X		Essex					
John de Heynouz	Edmund	K						Isle of Wight					

John de Ingolthorpe	Edward	K			X		Norfolk					
John Lovel	Edward	K	X	X			Norfolk, Northamptonshire		X		William Lovel (1191)	
John de Monte Alto (Monthaut)	Edward	K	X	X	X		Cheshire, Yorkshire, Northamptonshire, Buckinghamshire		R		Roger de Monthaut (1250)	Adam and Simon de Monthaut
John de Niwenton	Edmund											
John de Osbeston (Ulbeston)	Edward	V		X	X		Suffolk		X	?		
John le Parker	Edward	K	X	X			Hampshire					
John de Peyton	Edward	K			X		Suffolk					
John de Portes	Edward	C	X									Roger and Walter de Portes
John Pute	Edward	C										
John Rok	Edward	K				?Roger de Leyburn						
John le Romeyn	Edward	S	X									
John de Romundeby (Romanby)	Edmund	K	X			Robert Bruce	Yorkshire					
John de S. John	Edmund	K	X	X	X		Hampshire, Sussex					
John de Scalariis of Babraham	Edmund	K	X		X		Cambridgeshire, Huntingdonshire	X				
John de Selleston (Selston)	Edward	C				John de Vescy	Yorkshire					
John de Tybetot (Tiptoft)	Edward	K	X				Cambridgeshire		X			Robert Tiptoft
John de Verdun	Edward	K	X	X			Shropshire, Staffordshire, Herefordshire, Leicestershire, Ireland		X	?		Geoffrey de Geneville
John de Vescy	Edward	K	X	X	X		Northumberland, Yorkshire	X			William de Vescy (1240)	
John de Warrewyk (Warwick)	Edmund	C										
John de Weston	Edward	K	X	X	X		Devonshire, Somerset, Staffordshire					
John de Wodestok (Woodstock)	Edward	S	X	X	X							

Crusader[2]	Sailing with Edward or Edmund[3]	Status[4]	Curial connections				Other lordship connection[8]	Regional ties[9]	Rebel[10]	In possession of rebel properties[11]		Family precedent	Participation of kinsmen
			Henry III[5]	Lord Edward[6]	Lord Edmund[6]	Edward I[7]				A	B		
John de Yaveneswyth (Yanwath)	Edward							Cumberland					
Jordan de Pyvelesdon (Pulesdon)[21]	Edward	?K		X				Staffordshire, Shropshire, Cheshire	X				
Jul' fitzWalter Hok	Edward												
Juliana de Goer	Edward												John de Goer
Laurence de Lovershale (Luversal)	Edward	C	X	X		X							
Laurence de S. Mauro (Seymour)	Edmund	K			X	X (Edmund)	John de Vescy	Northumberland, Wiltshire, Somerset		X	?		
Luke de Tany (Thany)	Edward	K	X	X		X	Henry of Almain	Yorkshire, Northumberland					
Matthew de Gelham (Yeldham)	Edmund	K						Essex					
Mauger de S. Albino	Edmund	K	X	X		X		Devonshire		R			
Nicholas[22]		?V					Alexander de Seaton						
Nicholas de Attrabato	Edward	C		X		X							
Nicholas Crok	Edward					X		Ireland					
Nicholas de Marton	Edward							Yorkshire					Robert de Marton
Nicholas Peshun (Pesson)	Edward	?K	X			X	Roger de Leyburn	Kent					
Nicholas de Segrave	Edmund	K	X		X	X		Leicestershire, Warwickshire, Huntingdonshire	X				
Nicholas de Shelton	Edmund							Norfolk					
Nicholas de Sifrewast	Edward	K	X			X	Thomas de Clare	Oxfordshire, Berkshire					
Odo de Polecote	Edward												

Oliver de Punchardun	Edward	K	X	X	X		Hampshire, Berkshire	R		Richard de Punchardun (1240)	
Osbert de Augo (Eu)	Edward		X								
Otto de Grandson	Edward	K	X	X	X			X	?		Gerard de Grandson
Patrick de Chaworth	Edward	K	X	X	X		Hampshire, Berkshire, Gloucestershire, Welsh March				Hervey and Payn de Chaworth
Payn de Chaworth	Edward	K	X	X	X		Hampshire, Wiltshire, Northamptonshire, Gloucestershire, Welsh March	X	?		Hervey and Patrick de Chaworth
Peter de Ardern	Edmund	K		X			Cheshire, Staffordshire, Lincolnshire	R		Ralph de Arden (1191), William de Ardern (1233)	John and Ranulf de Ardern
Peter de Castro Novo	Edward	K		X			?Gascony				
Peter des Chalons	Edward	K	X		X	Hamo Lestrange	Devonshire	X	X		
Peter de Chaumpayne (Campania)	Edward	K			X		Norfolk, Suffolk, Lincolnshire				
Peter fitzRobert	Edward	B					Lincoln				
Peter fitz Serlo of Arunbouch	Edmund										
Philip de Coleville[23]	Edward	?K			X		Cambridgeshire, Huntingdonshire ?				
Philip de Lacu	Edward		X								
Philip de Wilughby (Willoughby)	Edward	C		X	X		Lincolnshire, Yorkshire				William fitzRobert de Willoughby
Ralph Barry	Edward	K	X	X			Northamptonshire, Berkshire, Buckinghamshire				
Ralph de Cotun	Edward	K	X		X	Adam de Jesmond	Northumberland				
Ralph de Gorges	Edward	K	X				Wiltshire, Dorset, Isle of Wight, Devonshire				

Crusader[2]	Sailing with Edward or Edmund[3]	Status[4]	Curial connections				Other lordship connection[8]	Regional ties[9]	Rebel[10]	In possession of rebel properties[11]		Family precedent	Participation of kinsmen
			Henry III[5]	Lord Edward[6]	Lord Edmund[6]	Edward I[7]				A	B		
Ralph le Sauser	Edward	S	X	X		X		Winchester		R			
Ralph de Wodeburgo (Woodborough)	Edward	K	X	X		X	William de Huntercumbe	Nottinghamshire, Derbyshire		X	?		William de Woodborough
Ranulf de Ardern	Edward	K	X	X		X	Thomas de Clare	Essex, Suffolk, Lincolnshire				Ralph de Ardern (1191), William de Ardern (1233)	John and Peter de Ardern
Reginald Rossel	Edward	F		X									
Reynold de Pavely	Edward	K	X			X		Wiltshire					William de Pavely
Richard de Afton	Edward	K						Isle of Wight, Hampshire, Ireland	X				
Richard de Balescote	Edward												
Richard de Boys	Edward	K	X			X		Dorset, Wiltshire		X	?		
Richard de Brus (Bruce)	Edward	K	X			X		Essex, Suffolk				Peter Bruce (1240)	Robert Bruce, IV, V
Richard le Eyr[24]	Edward												
Richard fitzHenry de Malesours	Edward							Yorkshire					
Richard Fillyol	Edward	K	X			X		Essex, Suffolk					
Richard Foun	Edward	S		X		X		Hampshire, Derbyshire					
Richard de la Garderobe	Edward	T		X		X							
Richard de Glen[25]	Edmund												
Richard Maylard	Edmund	?S						Essex					
Richard de la More	Edward	K	X			X		Gloucestershire					
Richard Pochel	Edward												
Richard de Pouton	Edmund												
Richard de la	Edward	K	X	X				Ireland, Essex					

Rokele (Rochelle)												
Richard le Rus of Denham	Edmund	C	X				Norfolk, Suffolk					
Richard de Salesbyry (Salesbury)	Edward	C				X						
Richard de Saundon	Edward	S		X								
Richard le Sauvage	Edward											
Richard de Styveton[26]	Edward	K	X				Yorkshire					
Richard de Swafham	Edward						Norfolk					
Richard Turpin	Edmund						Yorkshire					
Richard de Wykes	Edmund	?K			X	X (Edmund)	Suffolk					
Robert Amaury	Edward	B					Lincoln					
Robert de Asshedon	Edmund											
Robert de Bodeham	Edward	K				X	Herefordshire, Gloucestershire					
Robert de Boyville	Edmund											Herbert de Boyville
Robert IV de Brus (Bruce)	Edmund	K	X			X	Cumberland, Scotland, Essex		X	?	Peter Bruce (1240)	Richard and Robert V Bruce
Robert V de Brus (Bruce)	Edward	K					Scotland, Essex		X	?	Peter Bruce (1240)	Richard and Robert IV Bruce
Robert Burnel	Edward	C	X	X		X			X	X		
Robert de Cadamo (Caen)	Edward		X				Cambridgeshire	X				
Robert Charles	Edward			X		X	Norfolk				Thomas Charles (1252)	
Robert le Clerk	Edward	V		X								
Robert Colier	Edward											
Robert de Crok	Edward											
Robert fitzSimon de Wy	Edward											
Robert de Haulton	Edward	V				X	Yorkshire	X				
Robert le Keu[27]	Edward							?				
Robert Lestrange	Edmund	K	X				Shropshire, Cheshire, Hampshire		X	X		Hamo Lestrange

Crusader[2]	Sailing with Edward or Edmund[3]	Status[4]	Curial connections				Other lordship connection[8]	Regional ties[9]	Rebel[10]	In possession of rebel properties[11]		Family precedent	Participation of kinsmen
			Henry III[5]	Lord Edward[6]	Lord Edmund[6]	Edward I[7]				A	B		
Robert de Marisco	Edward												
Robert de Marton	Edward	S				X		Yorkshire					Nicholas de Marton
Robert de Mitteford	Edward												
Robert de Munteny	Edward	K	X					Suffolk, Essex, Norfolk		R			Arnulf de Munteny
Robert de Murisien	Edward	C											
Robert de Neuton	Edward	K						Lincolnshire					
Robert Selisaule	Edmund												
Robert Spenchehose (Springhouse)	Edmund							Shropshire, Staffordshire					
Robert de Stanes	Edmund					X							
Robert de Staundon	Edmund	K				X	Urian de S. Petro	Staffordshire, Oxfordshire	X				
Robert de Turberville	Edmund	K	X		X			Herefordshire, Gloucestershire, Shropshire		X	?		
Robert de Tybetot (Tiptoft)	Edward	K	X	X		X		Lincolnshire, Cambridgeshire, Suffolk, Welsh March		X	X		John Tiptoft
Robert de Ufford (Offord)	Edward	K	X	X		X	Henry of Almain	Norfolk, Suffolk, Ireland					
Robert la Warre	Edward	S	X	X?		X		Wiltshire					
Roger de Clifford	Edward	K	X	X		X		Gloucestershire, Worcestershire, Herefordshire		X	?	Giles de Clifford (1239)	
Roger Atte Clyve	Edward							Isle of Wight					
Roger de Conyers	Edmund	V			X	X		Northumberland					
Roger Gulafre[28]	Edward	C		X?		X							
Roger de Leyburn	Edward	K	X	X				Kent, Essex, Welsh March		X	X		

Roger de Portes	Edward	C			X						
Roger de Reymes	Edward	K	X	X		Suffolk, Essex	X			William de Reymes (1191)	
Roger de Trompyton (Trumpington)	Edward	K			X	Cambridgeshire, Huntingdonshire					
Rowland Malet	Edmund	C				Buckinghamshire					
Russel	Edward	Sum		X							
Simon de Andrewyk (Anderwick)	Edward	S	X		X						
Simon de Henesale						Yorkshire					
Simon de Kelworth	Edward										
Simon de Monte Alto (Monthaut)	Edward	K	X		X	Yorkshire, Somerset, Dorset			Roger de Monthaut (1250)	Adam and John de Monthaut	
Simon Peche	Edward	K	X			Norfolk, Essex				Hamo Peche (1240)	William Peche
Siward de Mapeldorham	Edward										
Stephen de Fulburn[29]	Edward	H	X	X	X						
Stephen de Houton (Hoitton)	Edward		X			Huntingdonshire, Cambridgeshire		R			
Stephen de London	Edward	C	X	X		Shropshire					
Stephen de Sele	Edward										
Tassardus de Cluse	Edward	S	X								
Thomas le Arcedeakne	Edmund	K			X	Cornwall					
Thomas Boter	Edward				X						
Thomas de Clare	Edward	K	X	X	X	Welsh March, Ireland		X	?		
Thomas de Fenwick	Edmund	K	X			Northumberland					
Thomas de Gunneys (Gouneis)	Edward	C		X	X						
Thomas Maudut	Edward	K	X			Wiltshire, Hampshire, Shropshire		X	?		

Crusader[2]	Sailing with Edward or Edmund[3]	Status[4]	Curial connections				Other lordship connection[8]	Regional ties[9]	Rebel[10]	In possession of rebel properties[11]		Family precedent	Participation of kinsmen
			Henry III[5]	Lord Edward[6]	Lord Edmund[6]	Edward I[7]				A	B		
Thomas le Norreys	Edmund							Huntingdonshire					
Thomas de Pyn	Edward	K				X		Devonshire, Somerset					
Thomas de Sandwyco (Sandwich)	Edward	K	X	X		X	Roger de Leyburn	Kent					
Thomas Tredegold	Edward							Sussex					
Urian de S. Petro	Edmund	K	X	X		X	Hamo Lestrange	Shropshire, Staffordshire, Cheshire					William Patrick
W. de Latun	Edward												
Walter Basset	Edmund											Philip Basset (1240)	
Walter de Batonia (Bath)	Edmund	K	X			X (Edmund)		Somerset, Devonshire, Wiltshire					
Walter de Bibleswrth (Bibbesworth)	Edward	K	X			X		Hertfordshire, Essex		X	?		
Walter de Cambhou (Cambo)	Edward	K	X			X		Northumberland					
Walter fitzHildebrand	Edward												
Walter de Gayton	Edward							Buckinghamshire					Hamundus, John and William de Gayton
Walter de Morton	Edmund	K						Buckinghamshire					
Walter de Percy	Edward	K	X		X			Yorkshire					
Walter de Portes	Edward							Hertfordshire					
Walter de Wygeton (Wigton)	Edward	?K				X		Cumberland, Essex					
William de Aure	Edward	C		?X									

William de Belcheford	Edmund										
William Belet	Edward	K	X	X	X		Norfolk, Suffolk, Essex	X	X		
William de Bevill	Edmund	K	X		X		Northamptonshire, Leicestershire				
William le Blont (Blund)[30]	Edward		X	X	X						
William de Blyburgh	Edmund	C		X	X						
William le Brun	Edward	K	X		X	John de S. John	Hampshire, Dorset, Oxfordshire				
William de Columbariis	Edmund	V	X				Somerset	X	?		
William de Detling	Edward	K	X		X		Kent	R			
William de Eversle	Edward	B	X				Scarborough				
William de Fenes (Fiennes)	Edward	?K		X	X		Buckinghamshire, Essex, Hertfordshire			Ingelram de Fiennes (1190)	Giles de Fiennes, Eleanor of Castile
William fitzLaurence de Naffreton (Nafferton)	Edward										
William fitzRalph[31]	Edmund	?K					Yorkshire			William fitzRalph (1218)	
William fitzRobert de Wilgheby (Willoughby)	Edward				X		Lincolnshire				Philip de Willoughby
William fitzWarin[32]	Edmund	K	X	X	X		Ireland, Herefordshire				
William fitzWilliam de Coleston	Edward										
William de Gayton	Edward										Hamundus, John and Walter de Gayton
William de Geneville (Joinville)[33]	Edward	C					Ireland			French Joinvilles	Geoffrey de Geneville
William Gifford[34]	Edward	?K	X	X	X		Norfolk, Suffolk, Essex	X	?		

Crusader[2]	Sailing with Edward or Edmund[3]	Status[4]	Curial connections				Other lordship connection[8]	Regional ties[9]	Rebel[10]	In possession of rebel properties[11]		Family precedent	Participation of kinsmen
			Henry III[5]	Lord Edward[6]	Lord Edmund[6]	Edward I[7]				A	B		
William de Gleseby	Edward	C						Lincolnshire					
William Graundyn	Edward	K		X		X	Roger de Leyburn	Sussex		R			
William le Graunt (Grant)	Edward	K	X			X		Nottinghamshire					
William de Hedley	Edward	F											
William de Holm	Edmund	S				X		Yorkshire					
William de Huntercumbe	Edward	K	X	X				Oxfordshire, Essex					
William le Latimer	Edward	K				X		Yorkshire					
William Leoyn of Brampton	Edward												
William de Maketayn	Edward	S	X										
William le Maréchal[35]	Edward	S	X			X							
William de Mazun (Masson)	Edward	C				X							
William de Moleford	Edmund	V	X	X									
William de Monte Canisio (Munchensi)		K				X		Norfolk, Essex, Kent	X				William de Valence
William Mowyn[36]	Edward	K	X					Sussex, Huntingdonshire					
William de Northdye (Northie)	Edmund	K						Sussex					
William de Norton	Edward												
William de Pageham	Edward	K	X			X		Sussex, Hampshire					
William Patrick	Edward	K						Cheshire					Urian de Sancto Petro

William Pavely	Edward						Somerset, Welsh March					Reynold de Pavely
William de Pecco (Peche)	Edward	S	X	X			Suffolk		X	?		Simon Peche
William de Saundon	Edward	C/Co	X	X			Essex					
William de Tackley	Edward	C		X								
William Thurebert	Edward						Essex					
William de Valence	Edward	K	X	X	X		Welsh March, Ireland				Lusignan ancestors; Geoffrey and Guy de Lusignan (1248)	Other Plantagenet and Lusignan kin; William de Munchensi
William Wether	Edward					William de Tackley						
William de Wistenston (Wiston)	Edward	K	X				Sussex					
William de Wodeburg (Woodborough)	Edward	K			X		Nottinghamshire, Derbyshire					Ralph de Woodborough
William Wodekock	Edmund					Robert de Staundon?						
William de Yattinden (Yattendon)	Edward	C	X	X								
William de Ylleye (Ely)	Edward						Norfolk	X				
Abbot (Anon.) of St. Edward, Netley	Edward	C					Hampshire					

The following crusaders of Scotland, recorded in English royal records as making preparations, have been excluded because they appear to have sailed independently of the English forces: David of Strathbogie, earl of Atholl; John, Ralph, and William de Mowbray. Earl David joined Louis IX's force, dying at Tunis in Aug. 1270. John and Ralph de Mowbray seem to have been of the Scottish branch of the family; William was perhaps of the Yorkshire branch. Adam of Kilconquhar, earl of Carrick, died at Acre in 1271 or 1272. He may have joined Edward's force following Louis IX's death.

The following may have sailed with the English force, or later joined it, but definite evidence to this effect is lacking: Walter, *crucesignatus*, younger son of William de Beauchamp of Elmley, was left 200*m*. by his father in Jan. 1268 to perform a vicarious crusade for his parents. Ralph, son of Thomas fitzPeter of Aldeburgh was left 10*m*. in his father's will, in Feb. 1272, to go to the Holy Land. Henry de Amaury, presented at Michaelmas 1271 for taking venison in Cannock forest, was said to have become a Hospitaller, presently in the Holy Land. The following were sentenced to go to the Holy Land as king's pardon for homicide between 1268 and 1272: Alexander de Ramese, Peter de Basceles, Stephen de Hegham (who *is* recorded as being in the Holy Land with Edward), William Artur, and William de Berkeley. In May 1265 Robert fitzRalph de Seynt Marbright was sentenced to go to Jerusalem at the end of a five-year term of remission of the king's suit for homicide, viz. 1270. A number of individuals are known from PRO, E 101/350/5 and C 62/49–52 to have been with Edward in Gascony upon his return, but definite evidence that they were also with him on crusade is lacking.

A contingent of Hospitallers probably sailed with Edward. In July 1270 they received royal safe conduct in going to the Holy Land, sent there by Prior Roger de Vere. The master of the English Temple was granted letters of attorney and protection in June 1271 for three years since he was going to the Holy Land, apparently on crusade.

Tout, *Chapters*, ii. 15 n. 2, considered, tentatively, that Walter de Langdon, one of Edward's most trusty servants and future bishop of Lichfield, may have gone with Edward in 1270. There seems to be no conclusive evidence to this effect.

Notes

1. Edward, Edmund, and Eleanor of Castile are excluded. Those known to have sailed with Louis IX independently, such as John I and John II of Brittany, are omitted, even if they later joined the English force following Louis's death at Tunis. Those, like Earls Gilbert de Clare and John de Warenne, who took the Cross but did not make final preparations to depart have also been excluded. The previous listings of R. Röhricht, 'Études sur les derniers temps du royaume de Jérusalem: A. La croisade du Prince Édouard d'Angleterre (1270–1274)', *Archives de l'Orient Latin*, i (1881), 617–32; and Beebe, 'The English Baronage', pp. 143–8, are unsatisfactory on various grounds. Neither can this list, of course, be regarded as definitive; other crusaders will doubtless come to light.

   The table condenses the details of each crusader's career and connections so far as they are known. For each, the full range of printed central government records have been consulted, and, where appropriate, papal and episcopal registers, *DNB*, *Complete Peerage*, W. Farrer, *Honors and Knights' Fees* (London, Manchester, 1932–5), and publications of local record societies.
2. Most are known from references to them as *crucesignati* in the published Patent, Close, Liberate, Fine, and Charter Rolls. Others appear from the records of local and central courts; from Exchequer materials, especially E 101/350/5, E 368/44–7, E 159/44–7; and from the Liberate Rolls of early Edward I, especially C 62/49–52. It should be emphasized that firm evidence that the individual duly departed is generally lacking, but the preparations known to us suggest firm intent in 1270–1. Some can be shown to have remained at home or to have returned soon after departure, but the fact that they responded to the crusade call is the significant thing.
3. This can be deduced from the dating of protections and other documentary references in most cases.
4. Status where known is indicated by the following letters:

B	Burgess
C	Clerics, and others in ecclesiastical orders, excepting friars
Co	Cook
F	Friar

G Groom
H Hospitaller
K Knight, or qualified for knighthood, though not necessarily belted by 1270–1
M Merchant
N Sergeant
Su Surgeon
Sum Sumpter
T Tailor
V *Valettus*; some were later knights; this is their recorded status in or before 1270–1

5. The column designates all those with demonstrably close ties to Henry III and Eleanor of Provence before the crusade. It includes those in close household service, those in receipt of wages, fees, or robes, those who served in administrative and military positions in the Plantagenet lands, and those whose enjoyment of royal gifts and patronage on a number of occasions argues for a significant curial tie.
6. The column designates those with demonstrable ties to Edward (or Eleanor of Castile) and Edmund before 1270–1. Many, of course, enjoyed ties with the king or queen as well.
7. The column designates those with demonstrably close ties to Edward I and Eleanor of Castile after their return to England in 1274, using the same criteria in n. 5 above. Those closely tied to Edmund are indicated.
8. The column indicates other crusaders with whom the individual enjoyed a close and direct lordship connection in or before 1270–1.
9. Identification of an individual's regional association is often difficult, esp. for those whose material interests and career postings were widely spread. The following indicators have been used in this categorization: land holdings, with an attempt to pinpoint an individual's major interests if he held lands in more than one county; demonstrably close associations with men of a particular county or region; appointments to administrative or military positions which led to identification of the individual with a particular county or region; and clear indicators of an individual's field of action. These together allow reasonably clear definition. If the evidence is insufficient, in quality or quantity, no attempt to categorize has been made. Only data relating to the period in or before 1270–1 has been used; many, after the crusade, came to be identified with additional or different regions.
10. Only those who lost their lands and stood to the Dictum of Kenilworth are identified. See above, pp. 128–9.
11. Column A identifies those granted rebel properties by the king. R indicates that the individual was in possession of Michaelmas 1265 rents alone, or had seized properties in the disturbances and was later obliged to surrender them. Column B identifies those still definitely in possession of rebel properties in 1270–1. A ? indicates that seisin in 1270–1 is unknown, or that the process of restitution had definitely begun by 1270–1, generally the latter.
12. *Chron. Mailros*, p. 218, refers to him as a knight of Scotland, with Edward in the Holy Land. His exact identification is unclear, and it is not certain that he enlisted in the English force in 1270–1. Seatons are found with ties to the Balliol and Bruce families in Northumbs. and Scotland.
13. *CPR 1266–72*, p. 479: Ellis de Rolleston. He could be a kinsman of Benedict de Rolleston or Ralph de Rolleston, knights of Leics. and Derbys., but I am inclined to think, considering the career of Elias or Helias de Rilston (Rilleston), that Rolleston is clerical error for Rilleston.
14. Two or three men of this name appear in the records. This may have been the parson of Halton (Yorks.), who appears as a rebel in 1266.
15. This could be the London vintner, sheriff in 1270–1 and mayor 1273–4 and later, but considering these posts it is more likely that it was the knight who was the crusader, referred to as *miles* in the letters of attorney granted for the crusade in July 1270.
16. He received a protection, going to the Holy Land, in May 1267, but it seems that he remained in England, and in May 1270, as a crusader, received licence to alienate Terling manor (Essex).
17. Recorded as going to the Holy Land with supplies for Edward in Aug. 1272. He may not have been a crusader.

18. Identification difficult, but his connection with John de Ardern in 1270, linked with other evidence, suggests he was the Yorkshire knight.
19. Identification unclear. He may have been the rebel of this name, or perhaps the Somerset knight who later served Edward I.
20. Recorded as going to the Holy Land with supplies for Edward in Aug. and Sept. 1272. He then apparently travelled back with Edward. See above, ch. 4, n. 127.
21. A Jordan de Pyvelesdon (Staffs.), is recorded as a rebel in 1268, but it is much more likely that the crusader is that Jordan who was sheriff of Cheshire for Lord Edward in 1267.
22. Recorded as the *armiger* of Alexander de Seaton. See n. 12, above.
23. A number of men of this name appear in the records, but he was probably the rebel. If so, it seems that he was pardoned and did not stand to the Dictum.
24. A number of men of this name appear in the records. Identification unclear.
25. He may have been a vassal of the king of Scotland, but more likely the servant of Archbishop Walter Giffard of York.
26. Recorded in 1270 as going on a vicarious crusade for Peter de Percy.
27. A number of men of this name appear in the records. He was possibly the rebel.
28. Probably on crusade with Edward, but it is only recorded that a horse was taken from him in Gascony during Edward's sojourn there, 1273–4.
29. Treasurer of the Hospital, Clerkenwell, in 1270. Recorded as going to the Holy Land with Edward in Aug. 1270, but if he set out he returned almost immediately.
30. A number of men of this name appear in the records. However, he cannot possibly have been the rebel, since that man, recorded as being against the king at Lewes, was dead by Hilary 1270. See PRO, E 159/44, m. 6.
31. A number of men of this name appear in the records, but he was most likely the Northern royalist, from a family of royal servants.
32. A number of men of this name appear in the records, but he was almost certainly the loyal servant of Henry III and Edward who became seneschal of Ulster in 1271, and not the rebel of that name.
33. *CPR 1266–72*, p. 480: Gessevill; but PRO, C 66/88, m. 15 d. reveals a misreading for Genevill.
34. Unlikely that he was the rebel of this name. More probably he was the royalist who indeed was granted rebel properties and had close ties with Henry III and Edward.
35. Probably Henry III's sergeant, but many men of this name appear in the records, including one who was a rebel.
36. Identification difficult, but it is likely that he was the former *valettus* of Henry III's daughter, Beatrice.

APPENDIX 5

Notification of Agreement between John de Neville and Philip Basset

(PRO, Duchy of Lancaster, Deeds, DL 25/1, L 175)

Domino reverendo et amico karissimo domino J. de Nevill, suus Johannes de Hulecote salutem. Noveritis conventiones prime [*sic*] inter vos et dominum Philipum Basset apud Norhamton coram me, Alexandro Giffard et Thomam de la Hose[1] tunc ibi presentibus perlocutis[2] [*sic*] tale fuisse, videlicet quod dictus Philipus iter ariperet [*sic*] vobiscum ad custum suum proprium ultra mare grecie usque in terram sanctam adducentes secum quattuor equos de precio, quos habuit ut dixit, pro quindecim liberatis [*sic*] terre quas obtuleristis, in villa de Witum.[3] Et cum ultra mare grecie usque in terram sanctam insimul perveniretis dictus Philipus vobiscum remaneret ad omnes custris [*sic*] vestros se tertio milite, et de familia vestra, vos ibidem bene et fideliter servientes, et non omiteres vos nec amoveres se a servicio vestro in dictam terram pro ditiori neque pro pauperiorum [*sic*], nec similiter in Anglia si forte rediretis, qui de familia vestra moraret se tertio milite. Preterea dictus Philipus concessit quod si opus habueritis apponeret in servicio vestro septies centum marcarum et amplius prout opus fuerit. Et ita se in servicio vestro haberet; quod servitium suum merito commendatum habere deberetis, set de predictas [*sic*] quindecim liberatis [*sic*] terre tunc temporis insimul convenire non potuistis, antequam dictus Philipus cum domino G. Basset fratre suo habuisset colloquium; nichil inde facere voluit. In cuius rei testimonium has litteras meas testimoniales vobis transmitto. Valete.

1. John de Hulecote, Alexander Giffard, and Thomas de la Hose appear elsewhere in association with John de Neville. e.g. the three witnessed Neville's grant to the monks of Stogursey, 1236–46, and his demise of part of his forest bailiwick to Ralph de Neville in 1240. *Stogursey Charters*, eds. T. D. Tremlett and N. Blakiston (Somerset Rec. Soc. 61; 1949), 43; PRO, DL 25/1, L 1280. John de Hulecote was a man with some considerable experience of the law, frequently a justice in the 1220s and 1230s, which might explain his role in drawing up the terms of the agreement. See Farrer, *Honors and Knights' Fees*, i. 30–1, for him.
2. Presumably meaning they had negotiated long and hard. See R. E. Latham, *Revised Medieval Latin Word-List* (London, 1965), q.v. 'perloquor'.
3. Probably Witham, Essex, not far from Philip's manor of Tolleshunt and other lands at Legre and Kersey, Suffolk. See *VCH Essex*, i. 344; *CIPM* i. 272–3.

APPENDIX 6

Some Dynastic Connections (simplified) of Henry III, Edward I and the Rulers of the Latin East

Tree 1

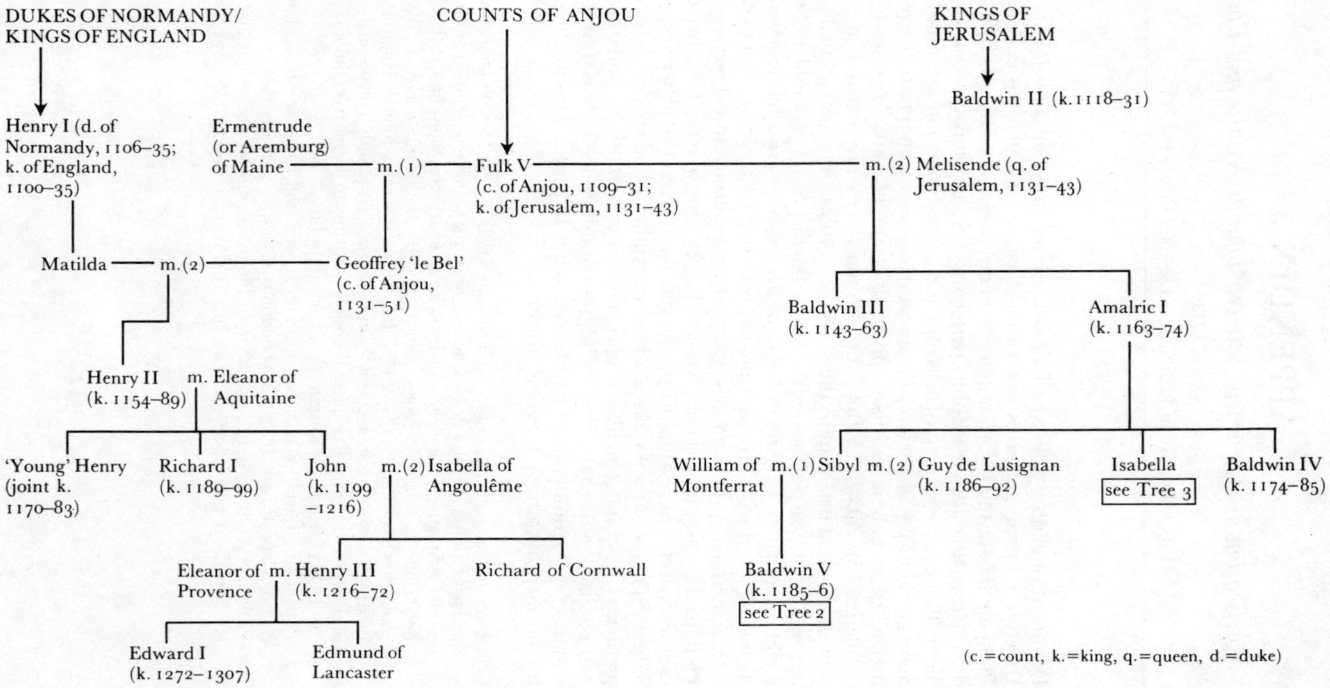

(c. = count, k. = king, q. = queen, d. = duke)

Tree 2

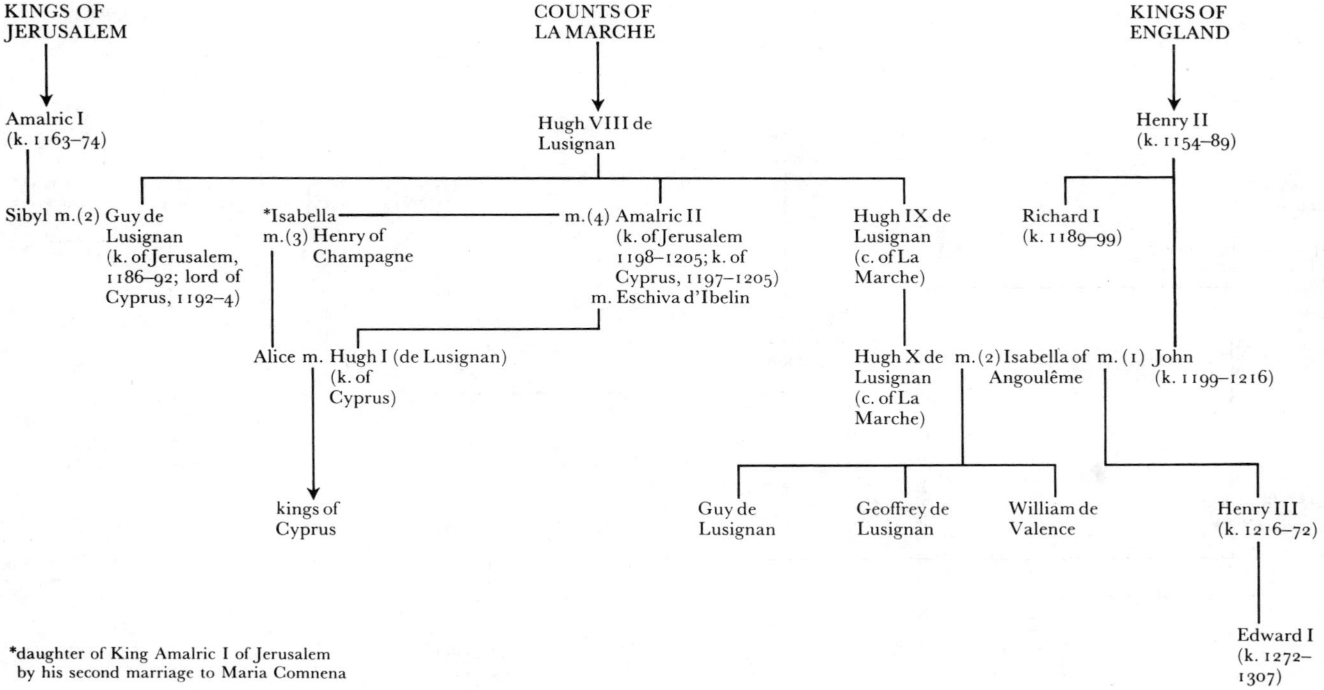

*daughter of King Amalric I of Jerusalem by his second marriage to Maria Comnena

Tree 3

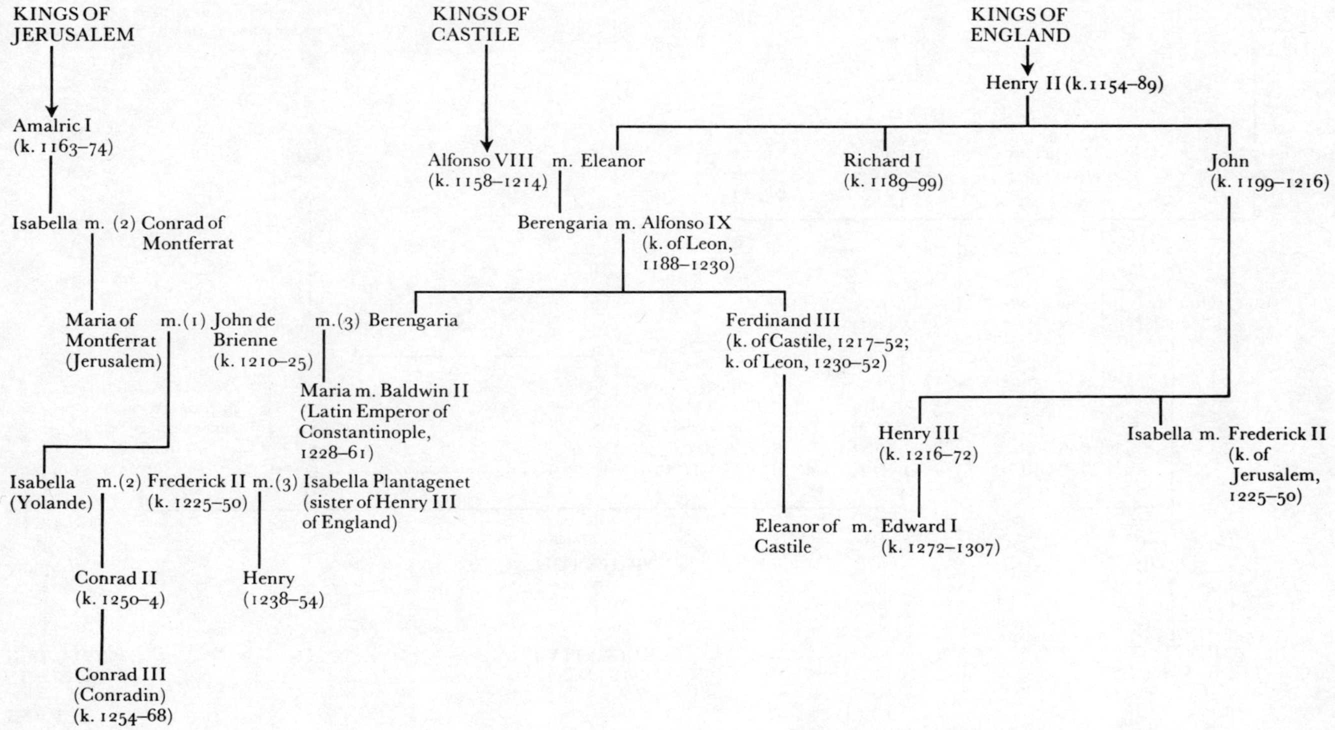
KINGS OF JERUSALEM
Amalric I (k. 1163–74)
Isabella m. (2) Conrad of Montferrat
Maria of Montferrat (Jerusalem)
m. (1) John de Brienne (k. 1210–25)
m. (3) Berengaria
Maria m. Baldwin II (Latin Emperor of Constantinople, 1228–61)
Isabella (Yolande)
m. (2) Frederick II (k. 1225–50)
m. (3) Isabella Plantagenet (sister of Henry III of England)
Conrad II (k. 1250–4)
Henry (1238–54)
Conrad III (Conradin) (k. 1254–68)
KINGS OF CASTILE
Alfonso VIII (k. 1158–1214)
m. Eleanor
Berengaria m. Alfonso IX (k. of Leon, 1188–1230)
Berengaria
Ferdinand III (k. of Castile, 1217–52; k. of Leon, 1230–52)
Eleanor of Castile
m. Edward I (k. 1272–1307)
KINGS OF ENGLAND
Henry II (k.1154–89)
Richard I (k. 1189–99)
John (k. 1199–1216)
Henry III (k. 1216–72)
Isabella m. Frederick II (k. of Jerusalem, 1225–50)

BIBLIOGRAPHY

A. Manuscript Sources

1. Balliol College, Oxford MS 167

2. British Library, London

Additional Charters 1351, 19828, 19829
Additional MSS 15351, 38821, 46352
Cotton Charters viii. 7, xii. 27, xxix. 65
Cotton MSS Cleopatra A. vii, Faustina A. viii, Julius A. ix, Vespasian B. xi
Harleian MS 4333

3. Hereford and Worcester County Record Office, Worcester

Register of Godfrey Giffard, BA 2648/1 (i)

4. Public Record Office, London

Chancery, Diplomatic Documents, C 47
Chancery, Fine Rolls, C 60
Chancery, Liberate Rolls, C 62
Chancery, Patent Rolls, C 66
Court of Common Pleas, Feet of Fines, CP 25 (1)
Duchy of Lancaster, Deeds, DL 25/1
Exchequer, King's Remembrancer, Accounts Various, E 101
Exchequer, King's Remembrancer, Memoranda Rolls, E 159
Exchequer, Lord Treasurer's Remembrancer, Memoranda Rolls, E 368
Exchequer, Lord Treasurer's Remembrancer, Originalia Rolls, E 371
Exchequer, Lord Treasurer's Remembrancer, Pipe Rolls, E 372
Exchequer of Receipt, Issue Rolls, E 403
Exchequer of Receipt, Miscellaneous Books, E 36
Justices Itinerant, JUST. 1
King's Bench, Curia Regis Rolls, KB 26
Special Collections, Ancient Correspondence, SC 1

B. Printed Sources

Not all works consulted in the writing of this book are included. In particular, the many publications of local record societies have been excluded unless they have been cited in footnotes.

1. Documents and Collections of Materials

Abstracts of the Charters and Other Documents Contained in the Chartulary of the Priory of Bridlington in the East Riding of the County of York, ed. W. T. Lancaster (Leeds, 1912).

Acta Stephani Langton Cantuariensis Archiepiscopi, 1207–1228, ed. K. Major (Canterbury and York Soc. 50; 1950).

ADAM MARSH, 'Epistolae Adae de Marisco', in *Monumenta Franciscana*, i. 77–489.

'Anglo-Norman Bidding Prayers from Ramsey Abbey', ed. K. V. Sinclair, *Medieval Studies*, xlii (1980), 454–62.

The Antient Kalendars and Inventories of the Treasury of His Majesty's Exchequer, ed. F. Palgrave, 3 vols. (London, 1836).

The Beauchamp Cartulary Charters, 1100–1268, ed. E. Mason (Pipe Roll Soc., NS 43; 1980).

'Bulle d'Innocent IV pour la Croisade (6 février 1245)', ed. F. M. Delorme, *Archivium Franciscanum Historium*, vi (1913), 386–9.

Calendar of the Charter Rolls Preserved in the Public Record Office, 1226–1516, 6 vols. (London, 1903–27).

Calendar of the Close Rolls Preserved in the Public Record Office, 1272–1307, 5 vols. (London, 1900–8).

Calendar of Documents Relating to Ireland Preserved in Her Majesty's Record Office, 1171–1307, ed. H. S. Sweetman and G. F. Handcock, 5 vols. (London, 1877–86).

Calendar of Documents Relating to Scotland Preserved in the Public Record Office, ed. J. Bain, 4 vols. (Edinburgh, 1881–8).

Calendar of Entries in the Papal Registers Relating to Great Britain and Ireland: Papal Letters I (1198–1304), ed. W. H. Bliss (London, 1893).

Calendar of the Fine Rolls Preserved in the Public Record Office, 1272–1307 (London, 1911).

Calendar of Inquisitions Miscellaneous (Chancery) Preserved in the PRO, 1219–1349, 2 vols. (London, 1916).

Calendar of Inquisitions Post Mortem in the Public Record Office (Henry III–Edward II), 6 vols. (London, 1904–10).

Calendar of Liberate Rolls Preserved in the Public Record Office, 1226–72, 6 vols. (London, 1917–64).

Calendar of the Patent Rolls Preserved in the Public Record Office, 1232–1307, 8 vols. (London, 1898–1908).

Cartulaire des Comtes de la Marche et d'Angoulême, ed. G. Thomas (Angoulême, 1934).

Cartulaire général de l'Ordre des Hospitaliers de S. Jean de Jérusalem, 1100–1310, ed. J. M. A. Delaville Le Roulx, 4 vols. (Paris, 1894–1906).

Cartularium prioratus de Gyseburne, ed. W. Brown, 2 vols. (Surtees Soc., 76, 89; 1889, 1894).

Cartulary of Oseney Abbey, ed. H. E. Salter, 6 vols. (Oxford Hist. Soc. 89, 90, 91, 97, 98, 101; 1929–36).

Chartulary of the Cistercian Abbey of Fountains, ed. W. T. Lancaster, 2 vols. (Leeds, 1915).

The Chartulary of the Cistercian Abbey of St. Mary of Sallay (Sawley) in Craven, ed. J. McNulty, 2 vols. (Yorkshire Archaeological Soc., Rec. Ser. 87, 90; 1933, 1934).

The Chartulary of the Priory of St. Pancras of Lewes (Sussex portion), ed. L. F. Salzman, 2 vols. (Sussex Rec. Soc. 38, 40; 1933, 1935).

Chartulary of St. John of Pontefract (c. 1090–1258), ed. R. Holmes, 2 vols. (Yorkshire Archaeological Soc., Rec. Ser. 25, 30; 1899, 1902).

Civil Pleas of the Wiltshire Eyre, 1249, ed. M. T. Clanchy (Wiltshire Rec. Soc. 26; 1971).

Close Rolls of the Reign of Henry III Preserved in the Public Record Office, 1227–72, 14 vols. (London, 1902–38).

Close Rolls (Supplementary) of the Reign of Henry III, 1244–1266, ed. A. Morton (London, 1975).

'Compte d'une mission de prédication pour secours à la Terre Sainte (1265)', ed. Borrelli de Serres, *Mémoires de la Société de l'Histoire de Paris et de l'Ile de France*, xxx (1903), 243–80.

'Copy of a Roll of Purchases Made for the Tournament of Windsor Park, in the Sixth Year of Edward the First', ed. S. Lysons, *Archaeologia*, xvii (1814), 297–310.

Correspondance administrative d'Alfonse de Poitiers, ed. A. Molinier, 3 vols. Documents inédits. (Paris, 1894–1900).

The Coucher Book of Furness Abbey, ed. J. C. Atkinson and J. Brownbill, 5 vols. (Chetham Soc., NS 9, 11, 14, 76, 78; 1886–1919).

Councils and Synods, with Other Documents Relating to the English Church, II: 1205–1313, ed. F. M. Powicke and C. R. Cheney, 2 parts. (Oxford, 1964).

Curia Regis Rolls Preserved in the Public Record Office, Richard I–1242, 16 vols. (London, 1922–).

Deputy Keeper of the Public Records, *Third Report* (London, 1842).

A Descriptive Catalogue of Ancient Deeds in the Public Record Office, 6 vols. (London, 1890–1915).

Diplomatarium Norvegicum, ed. C. R. Unger and C. C. A. Lange, 5 vols. (Christiania, 1849–60).

Diplomatic Documents (Chancery and Exchequer), I (1101–1272), ed. P. Chaplais (London, 1964).

'Diplomatique des actes de Robert II, comte d'Artois (1266–1302)', ed. Comte de Loisne, *Bulletin Philologique et Historique* (1916).

'Documents divers relatifs à la croisade de saint Louis contre Tunis (1270)', ed. P. G. G., *Les Cahiers de Tunisie*, xxv (1977).

Documents historiques inédits, ed. M. Champollion-Figeac, 2 vols. (Paris, 1841–3).

Documents of the Baronial Movement of Reform and Rebellion, 1258–1267, selected R. F. Treharne, ed. I. J. Sanders (Oxford, 1973).

Durham Annals and Documents of the Thirteenth Century, ed. F. Barlow (Surtees Soc. 155, for 1940, 1945).

'Early Manumissions at Staunton, Nottinghamshire', ed. F. M. Stenton, *EHR* xxvi (1911), 93–7.

English Gilds: The Original Ordinances of more than One Hundred English Gilds, ed. L. T. and T. Smith (Early English Text Soc., OS 91; 1870).

'Estate Records of the Hotot Family', ed. E. King in *A Northamptonshire Miscellany*, ed. E. King (Northamptonshire Rec. Soc. 32; 1983), 1–58.
Excerpta e Rotulis Finium in Turri Londinensi asservatis, 1216–72, ed. C. Roberts, 2 vols. (London, 1835–6).
'Exchequer and Wardrobe in 1270', ed. L. Ehrlich, *EHR* xxxvi (1921), 553–4.
'Extracts from Plea Rolls', trans. G. Wrottesley (William Salt Archaeological Soc., *Collections*, 6, part 1; 1885), 37–300.
Feet of Fines for the County of York, 1272–1300, ed. F. H. Slingsby (Yorkshire Archaeological Soc., Rec. Ser. 121; 1956).
Feet of Fines for Oxfordshire, 1195–1291, ed. H. E. Salter (Oxfordshire Rec. Soc. 12; 1930).
Feudal Aids: Inquisitions and Assessments Relating to Feudal Aids, with Other Analogous Documents Preserved in the PRO, 1284–1431, 6 vols. (London, 1899–1920).
Final Concords of the County of Lincoln, 1244–1722, ed. C. W. Foster (Lincoln Rec. Soc. 17; 1920).
Foedera, conventiones, litterae, et cuiuscunque generis acta publica inter reges Angliae et alios quosvis imperatores, reges, pontifices, principes vel communitates, 1101–1654, ed. T. Rymer; new edn., ed. A. Clarke *et al.* 4 vols. in 7 parts. (London, 1816–69).
Gascon Register A (Series of 1318–19), ed. G. P. Cuttino and J-P. Trabut-Cussac, 3 vols. (London, 1975–6).
General and Provincial Chapters of the English Black Monks (1215–1540), ed. W. A. Pantin (Camden Soc., 3rd ser. 45; 1931).
Historia diplomatica Friderici secundi, ed. J. L. A. Huillard-Bréholles, 6 vols. (Paris, 1852–61).
HMC, *Eighth Report* (London, 1881).
HMC, *Fifth Report* (London, 1876).
HMC, *Lisle and Dudley MSS, I* (London, 1925).
HMC, *Middleton MSS* (London, 1911).
HMC, *Reports: Various Collections, I* (London, 1901).
Historical Papers and Letters from the Northern Registers, ed. J. Raine (RS; 1873).
'An Indenture between Robert, Lord Mohaut, and Sir John de Bracebridge for Life Service in Peace and War, 1310', ed. M. Jones, *Journ. of the Soc. of Archivists*, iv (1972), 384–94.
'Innocentii III Romani pontificis regestorum sive epistolarum', in *Patrologiae cursus completus: Series Latina*, ccxiv–ccxvii.
Issues of the Exchequer (Extracts, Hen. III–39 Hen. VI), trans. F. Devon (London, 1837).
'A propos de Jacques de Vitry: Une lettre d'Olivier de Cologne', ed. D. U. Berlière, *Revue Bénédictine*, xxvii (1910), 521–4.
Kirkby's Inquest. The Survey of the County of York taken by John de Kirkby, called Kirkby's Inquest, ed. R. H. Skaife (Surtees Soc. 49; 1867).
Lancashire Lay Subsidies: An Examination of the Lay Subsidy Rolls, Henry III–Charles II: I (1216–1307), ed. J. A. C. Vincent (Lancashire and Cheshire Rec. Soc. 27; 1893).
Layettes du Trésor des Chartes: Inventaire et documents publiés par la Direction des Archives, ed. A. Teulet *et al.* 5 vols. (Paris, 1863–1909).

Letter Book of William of Hoo, Sacrist of Bury St. Edmunds, ed. A. Gransden (Suffolk Rec. Soc. 5; 1963).

'Letters of Cardinal Ottoboni', ed. R. Graham, *EHR* xv (1900), 87–120.

The Letters of Pope Innocent III (1198–1216) Concerning England and Wales: A Calendar, ed. C. R. and M. G. Cheney (Oxford, 1976).

'Letters of Ralph de Neville, Bishop of Chichester and Chancellor to Henry III', ed. W. H. Blaauw, *Sussex Archaeological Collections*, iii (1850), 35–76.

'Lettre addressée en Égypte à Alphonse, Comte de Poitiers, frère de Saint Louis', ed. T. Saint-Bris, *Bibliothèque de l'École des Chartes*, i (1839–40), 394–403.

'Lettres inédites concernants les croisades (1275–1307)', ed. C. Kohler and C. V. Langlois, *Bibliothèque de l'École des Chartes*, lii (1891), 46–63.

Liber Feudorum: The Book of Fees Commonly Called Testa de Nevill, 1198–1293, 2 vols. in 3. (London, 1920–31).

List of the Ancient Correspondence of the Chancery and Exchequer Preserved in the Public Record Office (PRO, Lists and Indexes, 15; repr. London 1968).

'Liste des chevaliers croisés avec Saint Louis', *RHGF* xx. 305–8.

Mémoires pour servir de preuves à l'histoire ecclesiastique et civile de Bretagne, ed. H. Morice (Paris, 1742).

Memorials of St. Edmund's Abbey. ed. T. Arnold, 3 vols. (RS; 1890–6).

Monasticon Anglicanum, ed. W. Dugdale; new edn., ed. J. Caley, H. Ellis, and B. Bandinel, 6 vols. (London, 1817–30, repr. 1846).

Monumenta Franciscana, ed. J. S. Brewer and R. Howlett, 2 vols. (RS; 1858–82).

Monumenta Germaniae Historica, Scriptores, ed. G. H. Pertz *et al.* 32 vols. (Hanover, Weimar, Stuttgart, Cologne, 1826–1934).

Northumbrian Pleas from De Banco Rolls 1–19, ed. A. H. Thompson (Surtees Soc. 158; 1950).

Parliamentary Writs and Writs of Military Summons, Edw. I–Edw. II, ed. F. Palgrave, 2 vols. in 4. (London, 1827–34).

Patent Rolls of the Reign of Henry III Preserved in the Public Record Office, 1216–32, 2 vols. (London, 1901–3).

Patrologiae cursus completus: Series Latina, comp. J. P. Migne, 221 vols. (Paris, 1844–64).

PETER OF BLOIS, 'Epistolae', in *Patrologiae Latina*, ccvii.

Pipe Roll 14 Henry III: The Great Roll of the Pipe for the Fourteenth Year of the Reign of Henry III, Michaelmas 1230, ed. C. Robinson (Pipe Roll Soc., NS 4; 1927).

Pipe Roll 2 Richard I: The Great Roll of the Pipe for the Second Year of the Reign of Richard the First, ed. D. M. Stenton (Pipe Roll Soc., NS 2; 1925).

Placita de Quo Warranto, Edward I–Edward III, in curia receptae scaccarii Westm. asservata, ed. W. Illingworth (London, 1818).

'Pleas of the Forest, Staffordshire, *temp.* Henry III–Edward I', trans. G. Wrottesley (William Salt Archaeological Soc., *Collections*, 5, part 1; 1884), 123–80.

'Une prédication de la croisade à Marseille en 1224', ed. E. Baratier, in *Économies et Sociétés au Moyen Âge: Mélanges offerts à E. Perroy* (Paris, 1973), 690–9.

Records of Antony Bek, Bishop and Patriarch, 1283–1311, ed. C. M. Fraser (Surtees Soc. 162; 1953).

Records of the Borough of Leicester 1103–1603, ed. M. Bateson, 3 vols. (Cambridge, 1899–1905).
Records of the General Eyre, ed. D. Crook (PRO Handbook, No. 20; London, 1982).
Records of the Wardrobe and Household 1285–1286, ed. B. F. and C. R. Byerly (London, 1977).
Recueil des historiens des croisades: Historiens occidentaux, ed. Académie des Inscriptions et Belles-Lettres, 5 vols. (Paris, 1844–95).
Recueil des historiens des Gaules et de la France, ed. M. Bouquet *et al.* 24 vols. (Paris, 1737–1904).
The Red Book of the Exchequer, ed. H. Hall, 3 vols. (RS; 1896).
Regesta Honorii Papae III, ed. P. Pressutti, 2 vols. (Rome, 1888, 1895).
Regesta Pontificum Romanorum inde ab anno post Christum natum 1198 ad annum 1304, ed. A. Potthast, 2 vols. (Berlin, 1874, 1875).
Regesta Regni Hierosolymitani, 1097–1291, ed. R. Röhricht (Innsbruck, 1893); *Additamentum* (1904).
Register and Records of Holm Cultram, ed. F. Grainger and W. G. Collingwood (Cumberland and Westmorland Antiquarian and Archaeological Soc., Rec. Ser. 7; 1929).
Register of Bishop Godfrey Giffard, 1268–1301, ed. J. W. Willis-Bund, 2 vols. (Worcestershire Hist. Soc.; 1898, 1902).
Register of Bishop William Ginsborough, 1303–7, ed. J. W. Willis-Bund (Worcestershire Hist. Soc.; 1907).
The Register of John le Romeyn, Lord Archbishop of York, 1288–96, ed. W. Brown, 2 vols. (Surtees Soc. 123, 128; 1913, 1916).
The Register of Thomas of Corbridge, Lord Archbishop of York, 1300–4, ed. W. Brown, 2 vols. (Surtees Soc. 138, 141; 1925, 1928).
The Register of Walter Giffard, Lord Archbishop of York, 1266–79, ed. W. Brown (Surtees Soc. 109; 1904).
The Register of William Wickwane, Lord Archbishop of York, 1279–85, ed. W. Brown (Surtees Soc. 114; 1907).
The Register or Rolls of Walter Gray, Archbishop of York, ed. J. Raine (Surtees Soc. 56; 1872).
The Registers of Walter Bronescombe and Peter Quivil, Bishops of Exeter, ed. F. C. Hingeston-Randolph (London, 1889).
Les Registres d'Alexandre IV, ed. C. Bourel de la Roncière *et al.* 3 vols. (Bibliothèque des Écoles françaises d'Athènes et de Rome, 1895–1953).
Les Registres de Benoît XI, ed. C. Grandjean (Bibliothèque des Écoles françaises d'Athènes et de Rome, 1883–1905).
Les Registres de Boniface VIII, ed. G. Digard *et al.* 4 vols. (Bibliothèque des Écoles françaises d'Athènes et de Rome, 1884–1935).
Les Registres de Clément IV, ed. E. Jordan (Bibliothèque des Écoles françaises d'Athènes et de Rome, 1893–1945).
Les Registres de Grégoire IX, ed. L. Auvray, 3 vols. (Bibliothèque des Écoles françaises d'Athènes et de Rome, 1899–1955).
Les Registres de Grégoire X, ed. J. Guiraud (Bibliothèque des Écoles françaises d'Athènes et de Rome, 1892–1906).

Les Registres d'Honorius IV, ed. M. Prou (Bibliothèque des Écoles françaises d'Athènes et de Rome, 1886–8).

Les Registres d'Innocent IV, ed. E. Berger, 3 vols. (Bibliothèque des Écoles françaises d'Athènes et de Rome, 1884–1921).

Les Registres de Martin IV, ed. F. Olivier-Martin *et al.* (Bibliothèque des Écoles françaises d'Athènes et de Rome, 1901–35).

Les Registres de Nicholas III, ed. J. Gay (Bibliothèque des Écoles françaises d'Athènes et de Rome, 1898–1938).

Les Registres de Nicholas IV, ed. E. Langlois, 2 vols. (Bibliothèque des Écoles françaises d'Athènes et de Rome, 1886–93).

Les Registres d'Urbain IV, ed. L. Dorez and J. Guiraud, 4 vols. (Bibliothèque des Écoles françaises d'Athènes et de Rome, 1899–1958).

I Registri della cancelleria angioina ricostruiti, ed. R. Filangieri di Candida *et al.* Testi e documenti di storia napoletana pubblicati dall'Accademia pontaniana, 28 vols. (Naples, 1950–).

Registrum Antiquissimum of the Cathedral Church of Lincoln, ed. C. W. Foster and K. Major (Lincoln Rec. Soc.; 1931–).

Registrum Epistolarum Johannis Peckham Archiepiscopi Cantuariensis (1279–92) , ed. C. T. Martin, 3 vols. (RS; 1882–5).

Registrum Johannis de Pontissara, Episcopi Wyntoniensis, 1282–1304, ed. C. Deedes, 2 vols. (Canterbury and York Soc. 19, 30; 1915, 1924).

Registrum Ricardi de Swinfield, Episcopi Herefordensis, ed. W. W. Capes (Canterbury and York Soc. 6; 1909).

Registrum Roberti de Winchelsey, Archiepiscopi Cantuariensis, 1294–1313, ed. R. Graham, 2 vols. (Canterbury and York Soc. 51, 52; 1952–6).

Registrum Thome de Cantilupo, Episcopi Herefordensis, 1275–1282, ed. R. G. Griffiths (Canterbury and York Soc. 2; 1907).

Regula (or *Consuetudines*) of Hereford Cathedral (extract), ed. J. Merewether, *Archaeologia*, xxxi (1845), 251 n.

ROBERT GROSSETESTE, *Epistolae Roberti Grosseteste Episcopi Lincolniensis*, ed. H. R. Luard (RS; 1861).

Rôles Gascons, ed. C. Bémont, 3 vols. Documents inédits. (Paris, 1896–1906).

Rôles Gascons, 26–38 Henry III (1242–54), ed. F. Michel. Documents inédits. (Paris, 1885).

The Rolls and Registers of Bishop Oliver Sutton, ed. R. M. T. Hill, 8 vols. (Lincoln Rec. Soc.; 1948–86).

Rotuli Chartarum in Turri Londinensi asservati, 1199–1216, ed. T. D. Hardy (London, 1837).

Rotuli de oblatis et finibus in Turri Londinensi asservati, ed. T. D. Hardy (London, 1835).

Rotuli Hugonis de Welles, Episcopi Lincolniensis, ed. W. P. W. Phillimore and F. N. Davis, 3 vols. (Canterbury and York Soc. 1, 3, 4; 1908–9).

Rotuli Hundredorum temp. Hen. III et Edw. I. in turr. Lond. et in curia receptae scaccarii West. asservati, 2 vols. (Record Commission, 1812, 1818).

Rotuli Litterarum Clausarum in Turri Londinensi asservati, 1204–27, ed. T. D. Hardy, 2 vols. (London, 1833–44).

Rotuli Litterarum Patentium in Turri Londinensi asservati, 1201–16, ed. T. D. Hardy. (London, 1835).

Rotuli Ricardi Gravesend, Diocesis Lincolniensis, 1258–79, ed. F. N. Davis *et al.* (Lincoln Rec. Soc. 20; 1925).

Royal and Other Historical Letters Illustrative of the Reign of Henry III, ed. W. W. Shirley, 2 vols. (RS; 1862, 1866).

Sacrorum Conciliorum nova, et amplissima collectio, ed. G. D. Mansi *et al.* 31 vols. (Florence, Venice, 1759–98).

The Sandford Cartulary, ed. A. M. Leys, 2 vols. (Oxfordshire Rec. Soc. 19, 22; 1938, 1941).

Select Cases in the Court of King's Bench, 1272–1422, ed. G. O. Sayles, 7 vols. (Selden Soc. 45, 47, 48, 74, 76, 82, 88; 1936–71).

Select Cases in the Exchequer of Pleas (1236–1304), ed. H. Jenkinson and B. Formoy (Selden Soc. 48; 1931).

Selected Letters of Pope Innocent III Concerning England (1198–1216), ed. C. R. Cheney, trans. W. H. Semple (London, 1953).

Somersetshire Pleas, Civil and Criminal, from the Rolls of the Itinerant Justices, ed. C. E. H. C. Healey and L. C. Landon, 4 vols. (Somerset Rec. Soc. 11, 36, 41, 44; 1897–1929).

Statutes and Constitutions of the Cathedral Church of Chichester (1198–1832) , ed. F. G. Bennett *et al.* (Chichester, 1904).

Statutes of Lincoln Cathedral, ed. H. Bradshaw and C. Wordsworth, 3 vols. (Cambridge, 1892–7).

Stogursey Charters: Charters and Other Documents Relating to the Property of the Alien Priory of Stogursey, ed. T. D. Tremlett and N. Blakiston (Somerset Rec. Soc. 61; 1949).

The Stoneleigh Leger Book, ed. R. H. Hilton (Dugdale Soc. Publicns. 24; 1960).

Swinburne (Capheaton MSS), 2 parts (National Register of Archives; 1962, 1963).

'On the Testament of Sir Hugh de Nevill, Written at Acre, 1267', ed. M. S. Giuseppi, *Archaeologia*, lvi, part 2 (1899), 351–70.

Thesaurus novus anecdotorum, ed. E. Martène and U. Durand, 5 vols. (Paris, 1717).

'Three Early Assize Rolls for Northumberland', ed. W. Page (Surtees Soc. 88; 1891).

'Voici les chevaliers de l'ostel le roi croisiés', *RHGF* xxii. 732–4.

Warwickshire Feet of Fines, ed. E. Stokes *et al.* (Dugdale Soc. 11, ,15, 18; 1932–43).

Yorkshire Deeds, I, ed. W. Brown (Yorkshire Archaeological Soc., Rec. Ser. 39; 1909).

Yorkshire Deeds, III, ed. W. Brown (Yorkshire Archaeological Soc., Rec. Ser. 63; 1922).

Yorkshire Deeds, VII, ed. C. T. Clay (Yorkshire Archaeological Soc., Rec. Ser. 83; 1932).

Yorkshire Inquisitions (1241–1316), ed. W. Brown (Yorkshire Archaeological and Topographical Assoc., Rec. Ser. 12, 23, 31, 37; 1892–1906).

2. Narrative and Literary Sources, Treatises, etc.

AMBROISE, *The Crusade of Richard Lion-Heart*, ed. and trans. M. J. Hubert and J. L. La Monte (Columbia Univ. Records of Civilization; New York, 1941).
Analecta Novissima Spicilegii Solesmensis, ed. J. B. Pitra (repr. Farnborough, 1967).
Annales Cestrienses or Chronicle of the Abbey of S. Werburg, Chester, ed. R. C. Christie (Lancashire and Cheshire Rec. Soc. 14; 1887).
'Annales Herbipolenses', *MGH SS* xvi. 1–12.
'Annales Londonienses', in *Chronicles of the Reigns of Edward I and Edward II*, ed. W. Stubbs, 2 vols. (RS; 1882–3), i. 1–251.
'Annales de Margan (*recte* Margam) sive chronica abbreviata', in *Annales monastici*, i. 1–40.
'Annales monasterii de Burton', in *Annales monastici*, i. 181–510.
'Annales monasterii de Osneia', in *Annales monastici*, iv. 1–352.
'Annales monasterii de Theokesberia', in *Annales monastici*, i. 41–180.
'Annales monasterii de Waverleia', in *Annales monastici*, ii. 127–411.
'Annales monasterii de Wintonia', in *Annales monastici*, ii. 1–125.
Annales monastici, ed. H. R. Luard, 5 vols. (RS; 1864–9).
'Annales prioratus de Dunstaplia', in *Annales monastici*, iii. 1–420.
'Annales prioratus de Wigornia', in *Annales monastici*, iv. 353–564.
Annals of Southwark and Merton, ed. M. Tyson (Surrey Archaeological Collections, 36; 1925), 24–44.
ARNOLD FITZTHEDMAR, *De antiquis legibus liber: Cronica majorum et vicecomitum Londoniarum*, ed. T. Stapleton (Camden Soc., os 34; 1846).
BARTHOLOMEW COTTON, *Historia Anglicana, necnon ejusdem Liber de archiepiscopis et episcopis Angliae*, ed. H. R. Luard (RS; 1859).
BENEDICT OF PETERBOROUGH (attrib.), *Gesta Regis Henrici Secundi Benedicti Abbatis*, ed. W. Stubbs, 2 vols. (RS; 1867).
BERTRAND OF PONTIGNY (attrib.), 'Vita B. Edmundi, auctore Bertrando Priore Pontiniacensis monasterii', in *Thesaurus novus anecdotorum*, ed. E. Martène and U. Durand (Paris, 1717), iii. cols. 1775–1826.
'Chronica Albrici monachi Trium Fontium', *MGH SS* xxiii. 631–950.
Chronica de Mailros, ed. J. Stevenson (Bannatyne Club, 50; 1835).
Chronica monasterii de Melsa, ed. E. A. Bond, 3 vols. (RS; 1866–8).
'Chronicle of Barlings' (extracts), in *Chronicles of the Reigns of Edward I and Edward II*, ed. W. Stubbs, 2 vols. (RS; 1882–3), ii. cxiv-cxviii.
Chronicle of Bury St. Edmunds, 1212–1301, ed. A. Gransden (London, 1964).
Chronicle of the Monastery of Abingdon, 1218–1304, ed. J. O. Halliwell (Berkshire Ashmolean Soc.; 1844).
'A Chronicle Roll of the Abbots of Abingdon', ed. H. E. Salter, *EHR* xxvi (1911), 727–38.
Chronicon de Lanercost, 1201–1346, ed. J. Stevenson (Bannatyne Club, 1839).
The Crusade and Death of Richard I, ed. R. C. Johnston (Anglo-Norman Text Soc. 17; 1961).
'L'Estoire de Eracles empereur et la conqueste de la Terre d'Outremer', *RHC Occ.* ii. 1–481.

'Extrait d'une chronique anonyme', *RHGF* xxi. 124–30.
'Extraits de la chronique attribuée à Baudouin d'Avesnes', *RHGF* xxi. 161–81.
Exuviae sacrae constantinopolitanae, ed. P. Riant, 2 vols. (Geneva, 1877, 1878).
FLORENCE OF WORCESTER, *Chronicon ex Chronicis, with two continuations*, ed. B. Thorpe, 2 vols. (English Historical Soc.; 1848, 1849).
Flores Historiarum, ed. H. R. Luard, 3 vols. (RS; 1890).
GAUTIER CORNUT, 'Opusculum Galteri Cornuti archiepiscopi Senonensis: De Susceptione Coronae Spinae Jesu Christi', *RHGF* xxii. 26–32.
GEOFFROY DE VILLEHARDOUIN, *La Conquête de Constantinople*, ed. E. Faral, 2 vols. (2nd edn., Paris, 1961).
GERALD OF WALES (Giraldus Cambrensis), *Opera*, ed. J. S. Brewer *et al.* 8 vols. (RS; 1861–91).
GERVASE OF CANTERBURY, *The Historical Works of Gervase of Canterbury*, ed. W. Stubbs, 2 vols. (RS; 1879, 1880).
GUIBERT OF NOGENT, 'Gesta Dei per Francos', *RHC Occ.* iv.
GUIBERT OF TOURNAI, *Gilbertus Tornacensis: Sermones ad status diversos pertinentes*, ed. Joannes de Westfalia (Louvain, 1475–83).
HENRY DE BRACTON, *Bracton's Note Book*, ed. F. W. Maitland, 3 vols. (London, 1887).
—— (attrib.) *De Legibus et Consuetudinibus regni Angliae*, ed. G. E. Woodbine, 3 vols. (New Haven, 1915–40).
Histoire de Guillaume le Maréchal, comte de Striguil et de Pembroke, régent d'Angleterre (c. 1140–1219), ed. P. Meyer, 3 vols. (Société de l'histoire de France; 1891–1901).
Histoire des Ducs de Normandie et des Rois d'Angleterre, ed. F. Michel (Société de l'histoire de France; 1840).
'Historia Albigensium, auct. Guillelmo de Podio Laurentii', *RHGF* xx. 764–76.
Historia Karoli Magni et Rotholandi ou Chronique du Pseudo-Turpin, ed. C. Meredith Jones (Paris, 1936).
'Historia Peregrinorum', in *Quellen zur Geschichte des Kreuzzuges Kaiser Friedrichs I*, ed. A. Chroust, *MGH SS* NS 5.
Historiae Dunelmensis Scriptores Tres, Gaufridus de Coldingham, Robertus de Graystones, et Willelmus de Chambre, ed. J. Raine (Surtees Soc. 9; 1839).
HUMBERT OF ROMANS, *Sermones Beati Umberti Burgundi*, ed. Venantius Honorius, 2 vols. (Venice, 1603).
—— *Tractatus Solemnis Fr. H. de Praedicatione Sanctae Crucis*, ed. P. Wagner (Nuremberg, *c.* 1495).
'Itinerarium Peregrinorum et Gesta Regis Ricardi', in *Chronicles and Memorials of the Reign of Richard I*, ed. W. Stubbs, 2 vols. (RS; 1864, 1865), i.
JEAN DE JOINVILLE, *Histoire de Saint Louis*, ed. J. Natalis de Wailly (Paris, 1872).
—— *The Life of St. Louis by John of Joinville*, trans. R. Hague (London, 1955).
JOCELIN OF BRAKELOND, *Cronica Jocelini de Brakelonda de rebus gestis Samsonis abbatis monasterii Sancti Edmundi*, ed. and trans. H. E. Butler (London, 1949).

JOHN CAPGRAVE, 'Vita S. Richardi Episcopi Cicestrensis', in *Acta Sanctorum quotquot toto urbe coluntur vel a catholicis scriptoribus celebrantur* (Antwerp, Brussels, 1643–), *April*, i. 278–82.

JOHN OF HOWDEN, *Rossignol*, ed. (in part) L. Stone, 'Jean de Howden poète anglo-Normand du XIIIe siècle', *Romania*, lxix (1946–7), 496–519.

Leges Henrici Primi, ed. and trans. L. J. Downer (Oxford, 1972).

Liber Exemplorum ad Usum Praedicantium, ed. A. G. Little (British Soc. of Franciscan Studies, 1; 1908).

MATTHEW PARIS, *Chronica majora*, ed. H. R. Luard, 7 vols. (RS; 1872–83).

—— *Historia Anglorum sive historia minor*, ed. F. Madden, 3 vols. (RS; 1866–9).

MENKO, 'Menkonis Chronicon', *MGH SS* xxiii. 523–61.

NICHOLAS TREVET (Trivet), *Annales sex Regum Angliae, 1135–1307*, ed. T. Hog (English Historical Soc.; 1845).

'Notes on an English Cluniac Chronicle', ed. H. M. Cam and E. F. Jacob, *EHR* xliv (1929), 94–104 (Chronicle of St Andrews, Northampton).

'Oberti Stanconi, Iacobi Aurie, Marchisini de Cassino et Bertolini Bonifatii Annales', *MGH SS* xviii. 267–78.

ODO OF DEUIL, *De Profectione Ludovici VII in Orientem*, ed. and trans. V. G. Berry (Columbia Univ. Records of Civilization; New York, 1948).

The Old French Johannes Translation of the Pseudo-Turpin Chronicle, ed. R. N. Walpole, 2 vols. (Berkeley, 1976).

ORDERIC VITALIS, *Historia Ecclesiastica*, ed. M. Chibnall, 6 vols. (Oxford, 1969–80).

'Ordinacio de Predicatione Sanctae Crucis in Anglia', in *Quinti Belli Sacri Scriptores Minores*, ed. R. Röhricht (Société de l'Orient Latin, 2; 1879), 3–26.

PETER OF BLOIS, 'De Hierosolymitana Peregrinatione Acceleranda', in *Patrologiae Latina*, ccvii, cols. 1057–70.

—— 'Passio Reginaldi Principis olim Antiocheni', in *Patrologiae Latina*, ccvii, cols. 957–76.

PETER LANGTOFT, *The Chronicle of Pierre de Langtoft in French Verse*, ed. T. Wright, 2 vols. (RS; 1866, 1868).

PETER OF PECKHAM, 'La Vie Seint Richard', ed. A. T. Barker, in 'Vie de Saint Richard évêque de Chichester', *Revue des langues romanes*, liii (1910), 245–396.

The Political Songs of England, from the Reign of John to that of Edward II, ed. T. Wright (Camden Soc. os 6; 1839).

RALPH BOCKING, 'Vita S. Richardi Episcopi Cicestrensis', in *Acta Sanctorum quotquot toto urbe coluntur vel a catholicis scriptoribus celebrantur* (Antwerp, Brussels, 1643–), *April*, i. 282–318.

RALPH OF COGGESHALL, *Chronicon Anglicanum*, ed. J. Stevenson (RS; 1875).

RALPH DE DICETO (Diss), *Opera historica*, ed. W. Stubbs, 2 vols. (RS; 1876).

RALPH NIGER, *De re militari et triplici via peregrinationis Ierosolimitanae*, ed. L. Schmugge (Berlin, 1977).

RANULF DE GLANVILL, *Tractatus de legibus et consuetudinibus regni Angliae qui Glanvill vocatur*, ed. G. D. G. Hall (London, Edinburgh, 1965).

RAYMOND D'AGUILERS, 'Historia Francorum qui ceperunt Iherusalem', *RHC Occ.* iii. 230–309.

'Récit du XIIIe siècle sur les translations faites en 1239 et en 1241 des saintes reliques de la Passion', ed. N. de Wailly, *Bibliothèque de l'École des Chartes*, xxxix (1878), 401–15.

RICHARD OF DEVIZES, *Chronicon Richardi Divisensis De tempore regis Richardi primi*, ed. and trans. J. T. Appleby (London, 1963).

RICHARD FITZNEAL (Nigel), *De necessariis observantibus scaccarii dialogus commonly called Dialogus de Scaccario*, ed. and trans. C. Johnson (London, 1950).

ROGER OF HOWDEN (Hoveden), *Chronica Rogeri de Houedene*, ed. W. Stubbs, 4 vols. (RS; 1868–71).

—— (attrib. Benedict of Peterborough), *Gesta Regis Henrici Secundi Benedicti Abbatis*, ed. W. Stubbs, 2 vols. (RS; 1867).

ROGER OF WENDOVER, *Flores historiarum*, ed. H. O. Coxe, 4 vols. (English Historical Soc.; 1841–4).

Speculum Laicorum, ed. J. Welter (Paris, 1914).

STEPHEN OF BOURBON, *Ancedotes Historiques, Légendes et Apologues d'Étienne de Bourbon*, ed. A. Lecoy de la Marche (Société de l'histoire de France; 1877).

THOMAS WYKES, 'Chronicon vulgo dictum Thomae Wykes', in *Annales monastici*, iv. 6–319.

WACE, *Le Roman de Rou et des Ducs de Normandie*, ed. F. Pluquet, 2 vols. (Rouen, 1827, 1829).

WALTER OF COVENTRY, *Memoriale fratris Walteri de Coventria: The Historical Collections of Walter of Coventry*, ed. W. Stubbs, 2 vols. (RS; 1872, 1873).

WALTER OF GUISBOROUGH, *The Chronicle of Walter of Guisborough, Previously Edited as the Chronicle of Walter of Hemingford or Hemingburgh*, ed. H. Rothwell (Camden Soc., 3rd ser. 89; 1957).

WILLIAM DE BRIANE, *The Anglo-Norman 'Pseudo-Turpin Chronicle' of William de Briane*, ed. I. Short (Anglo-Norman Text Soc. 25; 1973).

WILLIAM OF NEWBURGH, 'Historia rerum Anglicarum', in *Chronicles of the Reigns of Stephen, Henry II, and Richard I*, ed. R. Howlett, 2 vols. (RS; 1884, 1885).

WILLIAM RISHANGER, *Chronica et annales, regnantibus Henrico tertio et Edwardo primo*, ed. H. T. Riley (RS; 1865).

—— *De duobus bellis apud Lewes et Evesham commissis* (*The Chronicle of William de Rishanger of the Barons' War*), ed. J. O. Halliwell (Camden Soc., OS 15; 1840).

3. Secondary

ALEXANDER, J. W., *Ranulf of Chester: A Relic of the Conquest* (Athens, Ga; 1983).

ALTSCHUL, M., *A Baronial Family in Medieval England: The Clares, 1217–1314* (Johns Hopkins Univ. Studies, 83; Baltimore, 1965).

BALDWIN, J. W., *Masters, Princes, and Merchants: The Social Views of Peter the Chanter and His Circle*, 2 vols. (Princeton, 1970).

BAYLEN, J. O., 'John Maunsell and the Castilian Treaty of 1254: A Study of the Clerical Diplomat', *Traditio*, xvii (1961), 482–91.

BEAN, J. M. W., *The Decline of English Feudalism, 1215–1540* (Manchester, 1967).
BEEBE, B., 'The English Baronage and the Crusade of 1270', *BIHR* xlviii (1975), 127–48.
BÉMONT, C., *Simon de Montfort, Comte de Leicester* (Paris, 1884).
—— *Simon de Montfort, Earl of Leicester, 1208–1265*, trans. E. F. Jacob (Oxford, 1930).
BERGER, E., *Histoire de Blanche de Castille, reine de France* (Paris, 1895).
—— *Saint Louis et Innocent IV: Étude sur les rapports de la France et du Saint-Siège* (Paris, 1893).
BLAESS, M., 'L'Abbaye de Bordesley et les livres de Guy de Beauchamp', *Romania*, lxxviii (1957), 511–18.
BORENIUS, T., 'The Cycle of Images in the Palaces and Castles of Henry III', *Journ. of the Warburg and Courtauld Institutes*, vi (1943), 40–50.
BOUSSARD, J., 'Les mercenaires au XIIe siècle: Henri II Plantagenêt et les origines de l'armée de métier', *Bibliothèque de l'École des Chartes*, cvi (1945–6), 189–224.
BOUTARIC, E. P., *Saint Louis et Alphonse de Poitiers* (Paris, 1870).
BRAND, P. A., 'The Control of Mortmain Alienation in England, 1200–1300', in J. H. Baker (ed.), *Legal Records and the Historian* (London, 1978), 29–40.
BRANNER, R., 'Westminster Abbey and the French Court Style', *Journ. of the Soc. of Architectural Historians*, xxiii (1964), 3–18.
BRETT, E. T., *Humbert of Romans: His Life and Views of Thirteenth-Century Society* (Pontifical Institute of Mediaeval Studies, Studies and Texts, 67; Toronto, 1984).
BRIDREY, E., *La Condition juridique des croisés et le privilège de Croix: Étude d'histoire de droit français* (Paris, 1900).
BRIEGER, P., *English Art, 1216–1307*. Oxford Hist. of English Art, 4 (Oxford, 1957).
BROWN, R. A., COLVIN, H. M. and TAYLOR, A. J. (eds.) *The History of the King's Works, I: The Middle Ages* (London, 1963).
BRUNDAGE, J. A., 'The Crusader's Wife: A Canonistic Quandary', *Studia Gratiana*, xii (1967), 425–41.
—— 'The Crusader's Wife Revisited', *Studia Gratiana*, xiv (1967), 241–52.
—— *Medieval Canon Law and the Crusader* (Madison, Milwaukee, London, 1969).
—— 'A Transformed Angel (X 3. 31. 18): The Problem of the Crusading Monk', in *Studies in Medieval Cistercian History Presented to J. F. O'Sullivan* (Cistercian Studies Ser. 13; Spencer, Mass., 1971), 55–62.
BUDGE, E. A. W., *The Monks of Kûblâi Khân, Emperor of China* (London, 1928).
BULST-THIELE, M. L., *Sacrae Domus Militiae Templi Hierosolymitana Magistri* (Göttingen, 1974).
CAM, H. M., *The Hundred and the Hundred Rolls* (London, 1930).
—— *Liberties and Communities in Medieval England* (London, 1963).
CARPENTER, D. A., 'The Gold Treasure of King Henry III', in Coss and Lloyd, *Thirteenth Century England I*, 61–88.

CARTELLIERI, A., *Philipp August: König von Frankreich*, 4 vols. (Leipzig, Paris, 1899–1922).
CHABOT, J. B., 'Relations du roi Argoun avec l'Occident', *Revue de l'Orient Latin*, ii (1894), 566–629.
CHAYTOR, H. J., *The Troubadours and England* (Cambridge, 1923).
CHENEY, C. R., *Hubert Walter* (London, 1967).
—— *Innocent III and England* (Päpste und Papsttum, 9; Stuttgart, 1976).
CHRISTIE, A. G. I., *English Medieval Embroidery* (Oxford, 1938).
CLANCHY, M. T., 'Did Henry III Have a Policy?', *History*, liii (1968), 203–16.
—— *England and Its Rulers 1066–1272* (Glasgow, 1983).
The Complete Peerage by G. E. C., ed. V. Gibbs *et al.* 12 vols. (2nd edn., London, 1910–59).
CONSTABLE, G., 'The Second Crusade as Seen by Contemporaries', *Traditio*, ix (1953), 213–79.
CONTAMINE, P., *War in the Middle Ages*, trans. M. Jones (Oxford, 1984).
COSS, P. R., and LLOYD, S. D. (eds.), *Thirteenth Century England I: Proc. of the Newcastle upon Tyne Conference 1985* (Woodbridge, 1986).
COWDREY, H. E. J., 'Pope Urban II's Preaching of the First Crusade', *History*, lv (1970), 177–88.
COX, E. L., *The Eagles of Savoy: The House of Savoy in Thirteenth-Century Europe* (Princeton, 1974).
CRITCHLEY, J. S., 'The Early History of the Writ of Judicial Protection', *BIHR* xlv (1972), 196–213.
DAVID, C. W., *Robert Curthose, Duke of Normandy* (Harvard Hist. Studies, 25; Cambridge, Mass., 1920).
D'AVRAY, D. L., *The Preaching of the Friars: Sermons Diffused from Paris before 1300* (Oxford, 1985).
DEHIO, L., *Innozenz IV und England: Ein Beitrag zur Kirchengeschichte des 13 Jahrhunderts* (Berlin, 1914).
DELABORDE, H-F., *Jean de Joinville et les Seigneurs de Joinville* (Paris, 1894).
DENHOLM-YOUNG, N., *Richard of Cornwall* (Oxford, 1947).
—— *Seignorial Administration in England* (Oxford Hist. Ser.; Oxford, 1937).
—— 'The Tournament in the Thirteenth Century', in R. W. Hunt *et al.* (eds.), *Studies in Medieval History Presented to Frederick Maurice Powicke* (Oxford, 1948), 240–68.
DENTON, J. H., *Robert Winchelsey and the Crown, 1294–1313: A Study in the Defence of Ecclesiastical Liberty.* (Cambridge Studies in Medieval Life and Thought, 3rd ser. 14; Cambridge, 1980).
Dictionary of National Biography, ed. L. Stephen and S. Lee, 63 vols., with supplements. (London, 1885–1900); repr. 24 vols. (London, 1921–7).
DOSSAT, Y., 'Alfonse de Poitiers et la préparation financière de la croisade de Tunis: Les ventes de forêts (1268–70)', in *Septième Centenaire de la mort de saint Louis* (Paris, 1976), 121–32.
DUBY, G., *La Société aux XIe et XIIe siècles dans la région mâconnaise* (2nd edn., Paris, 1971).
EAMES, E. S., *Catalogue of Medieval Lead-Glazed Earthenware Tiles in the Department of Medieval and Later Antiquities, British Museum*, 2 vols. (London, 1980).

Edbury, P. W. (ed.), *Crusade and Settlement: Papers Read at the First Conference of the Society for the Study of the Crusades and the Latin East and Presented to R. C. Smail* (Cardiff, 1985).

Edbury, P. W., 'John of Ibelin's Title to the County of Jaffa and Ascalon', *EHR* xcviii (1983), 115–33.

Emden, A. B., *A Biographical Register of the University of Oxford to A.D. 1500*, 3 vols. (Oxford, 1957–9).

Erdmann, C., *Die Entstehung des Kreuzzugsgedankens* (Stuttgart, 1935).

Eyton, R. W., *Antiquities of Shropshire*, 12 vols. (London, 1853–60).

Farrer, W., *Honors and Knights' Fees*, 3 vols. (London, Manchester, 1923–5).

Finke, H., *Konzilienstudien zur Geschichte des 13 Jahrhunderts* (Münster, 1891).

Forey, A. J., 'The Crusading Vows of the English King Henry III', *Durham University Journ.* lxv (1973), 229–47.

—— 'The Military Order of St. Thomas of Acre', *EHR* xcii (1977), 481–503.

Fraser, C. M., *A History of Antony Bek, Bishop of Durham, 1283–1311* (Oxford, 1957).

Gould, K., 'The Sequences *De Sanctis Reliquiis* as Sainte-Chapelle Inventories', *Medieval Studies*, xliii (1981), 315–41.

Grabois, A., 'Christian Pilgrims in the Thirteenth Century and the Latin Kingdom of Jerusalem: Burchard of Mount Sion', in Kedar, *Outremer*, 285–96.

Hamilton, B., *The Latin Church in the Crusader States: The Secular Church* (London, 1980).

Harriss, G. L., *King, Parliament and Public Finance to 1369* (Oxford, 1975).

Harvey, B., *Westminster Abbey and Its Estates in the Middle Ages* (Oxford, 1977).

Heyd, W., *Histoire du Commerce du Levant*, trans. F. Raynaud, 2 vols. (Leipzig, 1936).

Hill, G. F., *A History of Cyprus*, 3 vols. (Cambridge, 1940–52).

Hill, R., *Ecclesiastical Letter-Books of the Thirteenth Century* (privately printed, no date).

Hilpert, H-E., 'Richard of Cornwall's Candidature for the German throne and the Christmas 1256 Parliament', *Journ. of Medieval History*, vi (1980), 185–98.

Hodgson, J., *A History of Northumberland*, 7 vols. (Newcastle, 1820–58).

Holmes, G. A., *The Estates of the Higher Nobility in Fourteenth Century England* (Cambridge, 1957).

Holt, J. C., 'Feudal Society and the Family in Early Medieval England: III. Patronage and Politics', *TRHS* 5th ser. xxxiv (1984), 1–25.

—— 'Feudal Society and the Family in Early Medieval England: IV. The Heiress and the Alien', *TRHS* 5th ser. xxxv (1985), 1–28.

—— *Magna Carta* (Cambridge, 1965).

—— *The Northerners: A Study in the Reign of King John* (Oxford, 1961).

Housley, N., 'Crusades against Christians: Their Origins and Early Development, *c.* 1000–1216', in Edbury, *Crusade and Settlement*, 17–36.

—— *The Italian Crusades: The Papal–Angevin Alliance and the Crusades against Christian Lay Powers, 1254–1343* (Oxford, 1982).

Hurnard, N. D., *The King's Pardon for Homicide* (Oxford, 1969).

JACOB, E. F., *Studies in the Period of Baronial Reform and Rebellion, 1258–1267* (Oxford Studies in Social and Legal Hist. 8; Oxford, 1925).
JACKSON, P., 'The End of Hohenstaufen Rule in Syria', *BIHR* lix (1986), 20–36.
JOHNSTONE, H., 'The County of Ponthieu, 1279–1307', *EHR* xxix (1914), 435–52.
—— *Edward of Carnarvon, 1284–1307* (Univ. Manchester Hist. Ser.; Manchester, 1947).
JORDAN, E., *Les Origines de la Domination angevine en Italie* (Paris, 1909).
JORDAN, W. C., *Louis IX and the Challenge of the Crusade: A Study in Rulership* (Princeton, 1979).
KAEPPELI, T., *Scriptores Ordinis Praedicatorum Medii Aevi* (Rome, 1970–).
KAEUPER, R. W., *Bankers to the Crown: The Riccardi of Lucca and Edward I* (Princeton, 1973).
KANTOROWICZ, E., *Frederick the Second 1194–1250*, trans. E. O. Lorimer (London, 1931).
KEDAR, B. Z., 'The Passenger List of a Crusader Ship, 1250: Towards the History of the Popular Element on the Seventh Crusade', *Studi medievali*, 3rd ser. xiii (1972), 267–79.
—— 'The Patriarch Eraclius', in Kedar, *Outremer*, 177–204.
KEDAR, B. Z., *et al.* (eds.), *Outremer: Studies in the History of the Crusading Kingdom of Jerusalem Presented to Joshua Prawer* (Jerusalem, 1982).
KEEN, M. H., *Chivalry* (New Haven, London, 1984).
KENNAN, E., 'Innocent III and the First Political Crusade: A Comment on the Limitations of Papal Power', *Traditio*, xxvii (1971), 231–49.
—— 'Innocent III, Gregory IX, and Political Crusades: A Study in the Disintegration of Papal Power', in G. F. Lytle (ed.), *Reform and Authority in the Medieval and Renaissance Church* (Washington, 1981), 15–35.
KING, E., *Peterborough Abbey, 1086–1310: A Study in the Land Market* (Cambridge, 1973).
KINGSFORD, C. L., 'Sir Otho de Grandison (1238–1328)', *TRHS* 3rd ser. iii (1909), 125–95.
KITTELL, E. E., 'Was Thibaut of Champagne the leader of the Fourth Crusade?', *Byzantion*, li (1981), 557–65.
KNOWLES, C. H., 'The Resettlement of England after the Barons' War, 1264–67', *TRHS* 5th ser. xxxii (1982), 25–41.
KNOWLES, D., and HADCOCK, R. N., *Medieval Religious Houses: England and Wales* (2nd edn., London, 1971).
LAMBRICK, G., 'Abingdon Abbey Administration', *Journ. of Ecclesiastical Hist.* xvii (1966), 159–83.
LANGLOIS, C. V., *Le Règne de Philippe III le Hardi* (Paris, 1887).
LARKING, L. B., 'On the Heart-shrine in Leybourne Church: A letter', *Archaeologia Cantiana*, v (1863), 133–92.
LAWRENCE, C. H., *St. Edmund of Abingdon: A Study in Hagiography and History* (London, 1960).
LECOY DE LA MARCHE, A., *La Chaire française au Moyen Âge, spécialement au XIIIe siècle* (2nd edn., Paris, 1886).

—— 'La Prédication de la Croisade au XIIIe siècle', *Revue des questions historiques*, xlviii (1890), 5–28.

LEGGE, M. D., *Anglo-Norman Literature and its Background* (Oxford, 1963).

LLOYD, J. E., *A History of Wales from the Earliest Times to the Edwardian Conquest*, 2 vols. (2nd edn., London, 1912).

LLOYD, S. D., 'Gilbert de Clare, Richard of Cornwall and the Lord Edward's Crusade', *Nottingham Medieval Studies*, xxx (1986), 46–66.

—— 'The Lord Edward's Crusade, 1270–2: Its Setting and Significance', in J. B. Gillingham and J. C. Holt (eds.), *War and Government in the Middle Ages: Essays in Honour of J. O. Prestwich* (Woodbridge, 1984), 120–33.

—— ' "Political Crusades" in England, *c.*1215–17 and *c.*1263–5', in Edbury, *Crusade and Settlement*, 113–20.

LONGNON, J., *Les Compagnons de Villehardouin: Recherches sur les croisés de la quatrième croisade* (Geneva, 1978).

—— *Recherches sur la vie de Geoffroy de Villehardouin* (Paris, 1939).

LOT, F., and FAWTIER, R., *Histoire des institutions françaises au moyen âge, II* (Paris, 1958).

LUCAS, H. S., 'John of Avesnes and Richard of Cornwall', *Speculum*, xxiii (1948), 81–101.

LUNT, W. E., 'The Consent of the English Lower Clergy to Taxation during the Reign of Henry III', in *Persecution and Liberty: Essays in Honor of George Lincoln Burr* (New York, 1931), 117–71.

—— *Financial Relations of the Papacy with England to 1327* (Studies in Anglo-Papal Relations during the Middle Ages, 1; Cambridge, Mass., 1939).

—— *Papal Revenues in the Middle Ages*, 2 vols. (Columbia Univ. Records of Civilization, 19; New York, 1934).

—— 'Papal Taxation in England in the Reign of Edward I', *EHR* xxx (1915), 398–417.

—— 'A Papal Tenth Levied in the British Isles from 1274 to 1280', *EHR* xxxi (1916), 49–89.

—— *The Valuation of Norwich* (Oxford, 1926).

MADDICOTT, J. R., 'Thomas of Lancaster and Sir Robert Holland: A Study in Noble Patronage', *EHR* lxxxvi (1971), 449–72.

MASON, E., 'Timeo barones et donas ferentes', in D. Baker (ed.), *Studies in Church History*, xv (1978), 61–75.

MAYER, H. E., *The Crusades*, trans. J. B. Gillingham (Oxford, 1972).

—— 'Henry II of England and the Holy Land', *EHR* xcvii (1982), 721–39.

—— 'Ibelin *versus* Ibelin: The Struggle for the Regency of Jerusalem 1253–1258', *Proc. of the American Philosophical Soc.* cxxii (1978), 25–57.

—— 'John of Jaffa, his Opponents, and his Fiefs', *Proc. of the American Philosophical Soc.* cxxviii (1984), 134–63.

MEHL, D., *The Middle English Romances of the Thirteenth and Fourteenth Centuries* (London, 1969).

MITCHELL, S. K., *Studies in Taxation under John and Henry III* (New Haven, 1914).

—— *Taxation in Medieval England*, ed. S. Painter (New Haven, 1951).

MOOR, C., *Knights of Edward I*, 5 vols. (Harleian Soc. Publications, 80–84; 1929–32).

MORRIS, J. E., *The Welsh Wars of Edward I: A Contribution to Mediaeval Military History* (Oxford, 1901).

MULLER, K., *Die ältesten Weltkarten*, 3 vols. (Stuttgart, 1895).

PAINTER, S., 'The Crusade of Theobald of Champagne and Richard of Cornwall, 1239–1241', in R. L. Wolff and H. W. Hazard (eds.), *A History of the Crusades, II* (Philadephia, 1962), 463–85.

—— *The Scourge of the Clergy: Peter of Dreux, Duke of Brittany* (Johns Hopkins Hist. Publications; Baltimore, 1937).

—— *Studies in the History of the English Feudal Barony* (Johns Hopkins Univ. Studies, 56; Baltimore, 1943).

—— *William Marshal, Knight-Errant, Baron, and Regent of England* (Johns Hopkins Hist. Publications; Baltimore, 1933).

PARIS, G., 'Robert Court-Heuse à la première croisade', *Comptes Rendus des Séances de l'Académie des Inscriptions et Belles-Lettres*, xviii (1890), 190–215.

—— 'Le Roman de Richard Coeur de Lion', *Romania*, xxvi (1897), 353–93.

PARSONS, J. C., *The Court and Household of Eleanor of Castile* (Pontifical Institute, Texts and Studies, 37; Toronto, 1977).

PHILLIPS, J. R. S., *Aymer de Valence, Earl of Pembroke 1307–24* (Oxford, 1972).

PIXTON, P. B., 'Die Anwerbung des Heeres Christi: Prediger des Fünften Kreuzzuges in Deutschland', *Deutsches Archiv*, xxxiv (1978), 166–91.

PLATT, C., *The Monastic Grange in Medieval England: A Reassessment* (London, 1969).

POWICKE, F. M., *King Henry III and the Lord Edward: The Community of the Realm in the Thirteenth Century*, 2 vols. (Oxford, 1947).

—— *The Loss of Normandy, 1189–1204: Studies in the History of the Angevin Empire* (2nd edn., Manchester, 1961).

—— *Stephen Langton* (Oxford, 1928).

—— *The Thirteenth Century, 1216–1307* (Oxford Hist. of England, 4; 2nd edn., Oxford, 1962).

POWICKE, M. R., *Military Obligation in Medieval England: A study in Liberty and Duty* (Oxford, 1962).

PRESTWICH, J. O., 'The Military Household of the Norman Kings', *EHR* xcvi (1981), 1–35.

PRESTWICH, M. C., 'Royal Patronage under Edward I', in Coss and Lloyd, *Thirteenth Century England I*, 41–52.

—— *War, Politics and Finance under Edward I* (London, 1972).

PRÉVOST, A., 'Les Champenois aux Croisades', *Mémoires de la Société academique d'agriculture, des sciences, arts et belles-lettres du département de l'Aube*, lviii (1921), 109–85.

PRUTZ, H., *Kulturgeschichte der Kreuzzüge* (Berlin, 1883).

PURCELL, M., *Papal Crusading Policy: The Chief Instruments of Papal Crusading Policy and Crusade to the Holy Land from the Final Loss of Jerusalem to the Fall of Acre, 1244–1291* (Studies in the Hist. of Christian Thought, 11; Leiden, 1975).

QUELLER, D. E., 'L'évolution du rôle de l'Ambassadeur: Les Pleins pouvoirs et le traité de 1201 entre les croisés et les Vénitiens', *Le Moyen Age*, lxvii (1961), 479–501.

RABAN, S., *The Estates of Thorney and Crowland: A Study in Medieval Monastic Land Tenure* (Cambridge, 1977).
—— 'The Land Market and the Aristocracy in the Thirteenth Century', in D. Greenaway *et al.* (eds.), *Tradition and Change: Essays in Honour of Marjorie Chibnall* (Cambridge, 1985), 239–61.
—— *Mortmain Legislation and the English Church, 1279–1500* (Cambridge, 1982).
RAFTIS, J. A., *The Estates of Ramsey Abbey: A Study of Economic Grbwth and Organization* (Toronto, 1957).
RAIMES, A. L., 'The Family of Reymes of Wherstead in Suffolk', *Suffolk Institute of Archaeology and Natural History*, xxiii (1939), 89–115.
RHODES, W. E., 'Edmund, Earl of Lancaster', *EHR* x (1895), 19–40, 209–37.
RIANT, P., 'Privilèges octroyés à l'Ordre Teutonique', *Archives de l'Orient Latin*, i (1881), 416–22.
RICHARD, J., 'La politique orientale de saint Louis. La croisade de 1248', in *Septième centenaire de la mort de saint Louis: Actes des colloques de Royaumont et de Paris* (Paris, 1976), 197–207.
RICHARDSON, H. G., *The English Jewry under Angevin Kings* (London, 1960).
RICHARDSON, H. G., and SAYLES, G. O., *The Governance of Mediaeval England from the Conquest to Magna Carta* (Edinburgh, 1963).
RILEY-SMITH, J. S. C., *The Feudal Nobility and the Kingdom of Jerusalem, 1174–1277* (London, 1973).
—— *The First Crusade and the Idea of Crusading* (London, 1986).
—— 'A Note on Confraternities in the Latin Kingdom of Jerusalem', *BIHR* xliv (1971), 301–8.
—— *What were the Crusades?* (London, 1977).
RÖHRICHT, R., 'Études sur les derniers temps du royaume de Jérusalem: A. La croisade du Prince Édouard d'Angleterre (1270–1274)', *Archives de l'Orient Latin*, i (1881), 617–32.
RUNCIMAN, S., *A History of the Crusades*, 3 vols. (Cambridge, 1951–4).
SANFORD, E. M., 'Honorius, *presbyter* and *scholasticus*', *Speculum*, xxiii (1948), 397–425.
SCHMANDT, R. H., 'The Fourth Crusade and the Just-War Theory', *Catholic History Review*, lxi (1975), 191–221.
SCHNEYER, J. B., *Repertorium der Lateinischen Sermones des Mittelalters für die Zeit von 1150–1350*, 9 vols. (Münster, 1969–79).
SCHWERIN, U., *Die Aufrufe der Päpste zur Befreiung des Heiligen Landes von den Anfängen bis zum Ausgang Innozenz IV* (Historische Studien, 301; Berlin, 1937).
SIBERRY, E., *Criticism of Crusading 1095–1274* (Oxford, 1985).
SIEDSCHLAG, B., *English Participation in the Crusades, 1150–1220* (Bryn Mawr, 1939).
SMAIL, R. C., 'Latin Syria and the West, 1149–1187', *TRHS* 5th ser. xix (1969), 1–20.
SMALLEY, B., 'John Russel, O.F.M.', *Recherches de Théologie Ancienne et Médiévale*, xxiii (1956), 277–320.
SNELLGROVE, H. S., *The Lusignans in England, 1247–1258* (Albuquerque, 1950).

SOMERVILLE, R., 'The Council of Clermont and the First Crusade', *Studia Gratiana*, xx (1976), 323–38.

STEPHENSON, C., 'The Seignorial Tallage in England', in *Mélanges d'histoire offerts à Henri Pirenne par ses anciens élèves et ses amis a l'occasion de sa quarantième année d'enseignement à l'Université de Gand*, 2 vols. (Brussels, 1926), 465–74.

STERNFELD, R., *Karl von Anjou als Graf der Provence, 1245–1265* (Berlin, 1888).

—— *Ludwigs des Heiligen Kreuzzug nach Tunis 1270 und die Politik Karls I von Sizilien* (Historische Studien, 4; Berlin, 1896).

STRAYER, J. R., 'The Crusades of Louis IX', in R. L. Wolff and H. W. Hazard (eds.), *A History of the Crusades, II* (Philadelphia, 1962), 487–518.

—— 'France: The Holy Land, the Chosen People, and the Most Christian King', in T. K. Rabb and E. Seigel (eds.), *Action and Conviction in Early Modern Europe* (Princeton, 1969), 3–16.

STUBBS, W., *The Constitutional History of England*, 3 vols. (4th edn., Oxford, 1906).

STUDD, J. R., 'The Lord Edward and King Henry III', *BIHR* l (1977), 4–19.

—— 'The Lord Edward's Lordship of Chester, 1254–72', *Transactions of the Historic Soc. of Lancashire and Cheshire*, cxxviii (1979), 1–25.

—— 'The Seals of the Lord Edward', *Antiquaries Journ.* lviii (1979), 310–19.

SYDENHAM, J., *The History of the Town and County of Poole* (Poole, London, 1839).

THOMPSON, A. H., 'Diocesan Organization in the Middle Ages: Archdeacons and Rural Deans', *Proc. of the British Academy*, xxix (1943), 153–94.

THOMSON, W. R., 'The Image of the Mendicants in the Chronicles of Matthew Paris', *Archivium Franciscanum Historium*, lxx (1977), 3–34.

THROOP, P. A., *Criticism of the Crusade: A Study of Public Opinion and Crusade Propaganda* (Amsterdam, 1940).

TOUBERT, P., 'Les déviations de la Croisade au milieu du XIIIe siècle: Alexandre IV contre Manfred', *Le Moyen Age*, lxix (1963), 391–9.

TOUT, T. F., *Chapters in the Administrative History of Mediaeval England*, 6 vols. (Manchester, 1937).

—— *Edward the First* (London, 1893).

—— 'Wales and the March during the Barons' Wars', in *The Collected Papers of Thomas Frederick Tout with a Memoir and Bibliography*, 3 vols. (Manchester, 1932–4), ii. 47–100.

TRABUT-CUSSAC, J-P., *L'Administration anglaise en Gascogne, 1254–1307* (Paris, Geneva, 1972).

—— 'Le financement de la croisade anglaise de 1270', *Bibliothèque de l'École des Chartes*, cxix (1961), 113–40.

TREHARNE, R. F., *The Baronial Plan of Reform, 1258–1263* (Univ. Manchester Hist. Ser., 62; 2nd edn., Manchester, 1971).

TRISTRAM, E. W., *English Medieval Wall Painting*, 3 vols. (London, Oxford, 1944–50).

TURNER, R. V., 'William de Forz, Count of Aumale: An Early Thirteenth-Century English Baron', *Proc. of the American Philosophical Soc.* cxv (1971), 221–49.

TURNER, T. H., 'Unpublished Notices of the Time of Edward I', *Archaeological Journ.* viii (1851), 45–51.

TYERMAN, C. J., 'Some English Evidence of Attitudes to Crusading in the Thirteenth Century', in Coss and Lloyd, *Thirteenth Century England I*, 168–74.

VALE, J., *Edward III and Chivalry: Chivalric Society and its Context* (Woodbridge, 1982).
VAN CLEVE, T. C., *The Emperor Frederick II of Hohenstaufen, Immutator Mundi* (Oxford, 1972).
VAN WERVEKE, H., 'La Contribution de la Flandre et du Hainaut à la Troisième Croisade', *Le Moyen Age*, lxxviii (1972), 55–90.
VAUGHAN, R., *Matthew Paris* (Cambridge Studies in Medieval Life and Thought, 2nd ser., 6; Cambridge, 1958).
Victoria History of the Counties of England, ed. H. A. Doubleday *et al.* (London, 1900–).
VILLEY, M., *La Croisade: Essai sur la formation d'une théorie juridique* (L'Église et l'État au Moyen Age, 6; Paris, 1942).
WALPOLE, R. N., 'Charlemagne and Roland: A Study of the Source of Two Middle English Metrical Romances, *Roland and Vernagu* and *Otuel and Roland*', *Univ. of California Publications in Modern Philology*, 21 (1944).
WARREN, W. L., *Henry II* (London, 1973).
WAUGH, S. L., 'Reluctant Knights and Jurors: Respites, Exemptions, and Public Obligations in the Reign of Henry III', *Speculum*, lviii (1983), 937–86.
WIGHTMAN, W. E., *The Lacy Family in England and Normandy, 1066–1194* (Oxford, 1966).
WILLIAMS, G. A., *Medieval London: From Commune to Capital* (Univ. London Hist. Studies, 11; London, 1963).
WORMALD, F., 'The Rood of Bromholm', *Journ. of the Warburg Institute*, i (1937–8), 31–45.
YOUNG, C. R., *The Royal Forests of Medieval England* (Philadelphia, 1979).

C. Unpublished dissertations

BEEBE, B., 'Edward I and the Crusades', Ph.D. thesis (St Andrews, 1970).
COSS, P. R., 'The Langley Cartulary', Ph.D. thesis (Birmingham, 1971).
D'AVRAY, D. L., 'The Transformation of the Medieval Sermon', D. Phil. thesis (Oxford, 1976).
ELLIS, J., 'Gaston de Béarn: A Study in Anglo-Gascon Relations (1229–90)', D. Phil. thesis (Oxford, 1952).
KNOWLES, C. H., 'The Disinherited, 1265–80', Ph.D. thesis (Wales, 1959).
LEWIS, A., 'The English Activities of Cardinal Ottobuono, Legate of the Holy See', MA thesis (Manchester, 1938).
LLOYD, S. D., 'English Society and the Crusade, 1216–1307', D. Phil. thesis (Oxford, 1983).
MUMFORD, W. F., 'England and the Crusades During the Reign of Henry III', MA thesis (Manchester, 1924).
STUDD, J. R., 'A Catalogue of the Acts of the Lord Edward, 1254–72', Ph.D. thesis (Leeds, 1971).
WALKER, R. F., 'The Anglo-Welsh Wars, 1217–67', D. Phil. thesis (Oxford, 1954).
WILLIAMSON, D., 'The Legation of Cardinal Otto, 1237–41', MA thesis (Manchester, 1947).

Index

ABBREVIATIONS

ab. abbot of
abp. archbishop of
b. bishop of
c. count of
d. duke of
e. earl of
emp. emperor
k. king of
q. queen of
St saint

* indicates crusader or *crucesignatus*.
Appendices 4 and 6 are not indexed.
Those comprising the crusading force of 1270–2 are listed alphabetically under personal names in app. 4.